CANINE
COLORADO

— SECOND EDITION —

D0188461

CANINE
COLORADO

SECOND EDITION

WHERE TO GO
AND WHAT TO DO
WITH YOUR DOG

Cindy Hirschfeld

FULCRUM PUBLISHING
Golden, Colorado

To Clover:
May you always bark softly
and carry a big stick.

Library of Congress Cataloging-in-Publication Data

Hirschfeld, Cindy.
  Canine Colorado : where to go and what to do with your dog / Cindy Hirschfeld.— 2nd ed.
     p. cm.
  ISBN 1-55591-239-7
  1. Travel with dogs—Colorado—Guidebooks. 2. Colorado—Guidebooks.
I. Title.
  SF427.4574.C6 H56 2001
  917.8804'34—dc21
                          2001001235

Printed in the United States of America
0 9 8 7 6 5 4 3 2

Editorial: Daniel Forrest-Bank, Michelle Asakawa
Design: Rudy Ramos
Cartography: Marge Mueller, Gray Mouse Graphics
Interior Illustrations: Shawn Shea
Front cover photographs (clockwise from top right): Golden retriever and fallen skier buried in snow, copyright © DenverBryan.com; Joel Bradley and Clover atop Castle Peak, copyright © Cindy Hirschfeld; woman running with golden retriever in the Rocky Mountains, copyright © DenverBryan.com; hiker with leashed dog in Boulder's Flatirons, copyright © Phil Mislinski.
Back cover photographs: top—the author and Clover on the Rio Grande Trail in Aspen, copyright © Bob Hirschfeld; bottom—Clover on Mount Princeton, copyright © Cindy Hirschfeld.

CATHY (p. xii) © Cathy Guisewite. Reprinted with permission of UNIVERSAL PRESS SYNDICATE. All rights reserved.

FULCRUM PUBLISHING
16100 Table Mountain Parkway, Suite 300
Golden, Colorado 80403
(800) 992-2908 • (303) 277-1623
www.fulcrum-books.com

Contents

Acknowledgments

This book was made a reality with the support and encouragement of many people. A special thank-you for research assistance for the first edition goes to Jamie Kim. Thanks also to Daniel Forrest-Bank at Fulcrum Publishing for his patient oversight of the production process for both editions and to Michelle Asakawa for her conscientious copyediting of both manuscripts. The scores of hotel owners, Forest Service rangers, National Park representatives, Bureau of Land Management staffers, state parks personnel, animal control officers, and others with whom I spoke during the course of my research provided essential information.

Dr. Steve Peterson, formerly of Alameda East Veterinary Hospital in Denver, deserves special credit for repairing Clover's two torn ACLs that occurred right in the middle of our research efforts for the first edition. Rick Kahl and Lindsey Diforio at *Skiing* magazine graciously allowed me to take the time I needed from my previous job there to finish the first edition of this book. Thanks to Patrick Kruse and the gang at Ruffwear for letting Clover try out their cool dog gear.

I'm also extremely grateful to the following friends, who accompanied Clover and me on outings, provided valuable tips on dog-friendly places, hosted us as houseguests during our travels, helped with research, or supplied photos: Joel Bradley; Carolyn Carstens; Meg and Bailey Chamblin; Jennifer and Dakota Cook; Teri Craig; Tammy, Greg, and Woods Deranlau; Amy Ditsler; Terry DuBeau; Arlan and Nancy Flax; Stacy Gardner; Tim and Bismarck Hancock; Lowell Hart; Alex and Major Heller; Tamra Hoppes; Diane Kane and John Eakin; Carol and Spro Kauder; Beth Litz; Jim Margolis; Sean, Frostbite, and Rodney McCullough; Peggy McGuinness; Patrick Meiering of A Guy and His Dog; Judy Nishimoto; Connie and Bess Oehring; Sven Osolin; Karen Pauly; Tim and Abby Reid; Jonathan Satz; Dan and Buck Shore; Pam and Bart Simich; Erik and Sundog Skarvan; Helmut and Jasmine Tingstad; Greg Trainor; Bevin and Lewis Wallace; Claire Walter; Anne, Don, Cara, and DeChelly Webster; Mary and Tundra Winquest; and Sarah and Burley Woodberry.

A special acknowledgment to all the readers who gave me feedback on the first edition, whether by letter or e-mail, or at one of the many book signings Clover and I did. If you have comments you'd like to share on this new edition, please e-mail Clover or me at Caninecolorado@aol.com.

Of course, thanks go to my family, most especially my mother, who kept Clover's energy level up during research with home-baked dog biscuits. And finally, thanks to my cat, Blue, who is getting really tired of all this dog stuff and for accepting the fact that there will still be no *Feline Colorado*.

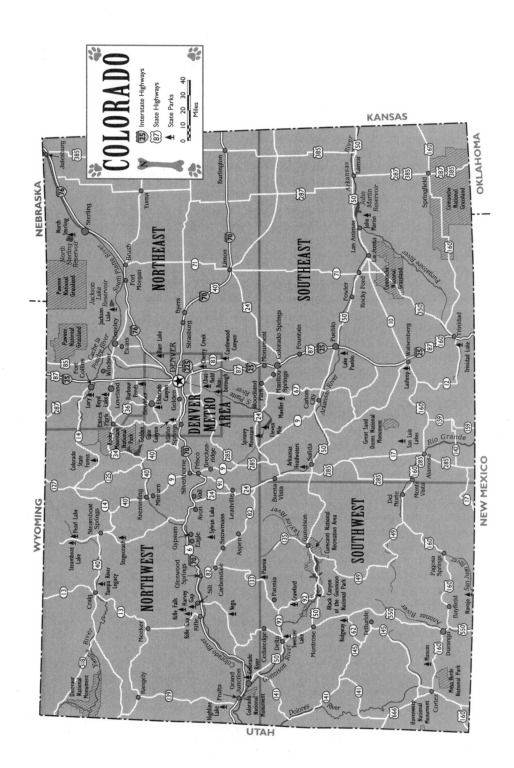

Introduction

A survey by the American Animal Hospital Association (AAHA) shows that 77 percent of dog owners in the United States bring along their pets when they travel. This proves something that you and I have known for a long time: Dogs are part of the family—if not your primary family—and vacations can be a lot more fun when shared with a furry, four-legged companion. Traveling with Rover in tow, however, requires a bit of prep work because, believe it or not, not everyone loves our dogs as much as we do! To this end, my faithful research assistant, Clover (herself a native Coloradan), and I have scoured the state searching out dog-friendly activities and accommodations. We hope the results of our research will help you and your dog discover that Colorado is a great place for canines!

In this introduction, you'll find some of the headings that are used throughout the book, with explanations of what each section contains, the criteria for selection, and other tips that will help you and your dog make informed travel decisions.

The information in this book is accurate as of spring 2001. *Please keep in mind that policies, prices, or regulations are always subject to change. Just because you read it here doesn't mean a detail is set in stone. It's best to call ahead, especially for lodging, to confirm that Rover is indeed still welcome.* Traveling with a dog can be like traveling with kids: The keys to success are to be flexible and have some alternate plans to fall back on, if necessary.

The maps in this book are for general reference purposes only. You'll need to consult a topographic map for specifics on the trails described herein.

THE MUCH-MALIGNED DOG

Allow me to mount my soapbox for a minute in defense of dogs. During the course of researching this book, I encountered many people who visibly flinched at the mere mention of the word "dog." People like these don't want dogs to be

Don't let your dog do the driving. (photo by Cindy Hirschfeld)

able to hike on trails, stay at hotels, or participate in a whole range of day-to-day activities with their owners. As a result of such attitudes, dogs have acquired a strange status: not quite human, not quite animal. They're not allowed in most public places because they're, well, dogs, yet many people believe dogs should be restricted in the natural world as well. One woman at a Forest Service office, who will remain unidentified, patiently explained to me that dogs must be kept leashed in designated wilderness areas so that they won't harass wildlife. As she spoke, my eyes were drawn to a hunting guide prominently displayed on the counter. I mentioned that it seemed ironic that hunting is allowed in these areas yet dogs are required to be restrained; the woman responded with a blank look. "Well," she finally said, "all those animals would just starve to death otherwise." Oh.

I firmly believe that dogs—and humans, too—are a part of nature, not apart from it. We should all do our best to reasonably minimize our impact. Yet dogs have the same right to be outside, to run in the grass, to follow a scent, to play in the snow as any other animal. Those who would scowl at a dog are missing out on one of life's greatest opportunities to share and to bond with another living creature.

Okay, it's time to dismount and get on with the nitty-gritty.

TAIL-RATED TRAILS

Clover and I have "sacrificed" many hours to hike most of the trails described in this book and determine their dog suitability. We considered several factors that seem to make a trail particularly enjoyable for dogs: whether or not they can be off leash, if water is readily available for a drink or for swimming, and if other dogs (and their owners) frequent the trail. For your sake I've also taken the scenic component into account.

Four tail wags

Trails are rated on a scale of one to four tail wags, with four signifying the hikes that were our favorites. Also included are trails or areas where dogs

Drooping tail

are not allowed—indicated by a drooping tail symbol— so you'll know ahead of time to leave your dog at home. Naturally there are many more dog-suitable trails than I've been able to describe in this book. When making the final selection, I deferred to my faithful companion. (Of course, because golden retrievers are always happy, I couldn't go wrong no matter what I chose!) Consider our recommendations either a jumping-off point or a foolproof list if you have limited time to spend in an area.

Land-Use Policies

Following are general guidelines for the different types of land you may encounter on your excursions. For more specifics, refer to the descriptions of the individual trails and parks in each chapter.

National Parks and Monuments

First, the bad news: In general, dogs are not allowed on any of the trails in Colorado's national parks and monuments. And you cannot leave your dog unattended anywhere, be it at a campsite, at a trailhead, or in your car. The good news is that they're not banned entirely. As long as you keep your dog on a leash no longer than six feet, you can bring him (or her) to the campgrounds and picnic areas. And you can take a walk with your leashed dog on closed roads (i.e., during the winter, when they're not plowed), though your dog must not venture more than 100 feet from the roadside or parking area. So if you're planning to center your trip on hiking or backpacking in a national park or monument, Rover will need to stay home.

As with most rules, however, a few exceptions exist. Leashed dogs are allowed to hike at the Great Sand Dunes National Monument (in the process of being designated a national park) near Alamosa, and they're permitted on a few short trails in the Black Canyon of the Gunnison National Park. You can also bring your dog to visit Bent's Old Fort in eastern Colorado and Hovenweep National Monument, which straddles the Colorado–Utah border. And, finally, dogs are allowed on the trails at Curecanti National Recreation Area, which is managed by the National Park Service, outside Gunnison.

An entry fee is required at all national parks and monuments.

National Forest and National Forest Wilderness Areas

Here's a "secret": Dogs are not required to be leashed on national forest land unless it is a designated wilderness area (though the Forest Service often advises that they be on a leash). I call this a secret

TRAVEL TIPS

In March 2000, Congress approved regulations that require airlines to disclose how many animals were killed or injured on flights. In response, many airlines changed their pet-travel policies. Continental and United, for example, no longer allow dogs to travel as checked baggage. Small dogs can still travel in the cabin; otherwise, you'll have to send Fido separately through the airlines' cargo service. Other airlines will allow dogs to travel in plane cargo holds only within certain outside temperature ranges.

If Fido does get the go-ahead to travel in the baggage compartment, he'll have to ride in an airline–approved cage, labeled "Live Animal." Feed and water him within four hours of the flight's departure. Provide a dish of fresh water in his cage; consider freezing the water first so it won't spill during transport but will melt in time for a midflight drink. Ten days or less before your flight, bring Rover to his vet to undergo an exam and get a current health certificate and proof of rabies vaccination, which you'll often need to present at the airport. Tranquilizing your dog before travel is controversial. Many animal experts advise against it—dogs who have a bad reaction to sedatives or who receive too large a dose can die. If you have a particularly hyperactive dog, talk to your vet about alternatives to sedation. Your airline may have additional requirements, which you should inquire about when making your reservation.

When traveling by car, avoid feeding your dog for at least three hours before you leave to help prevent carsickness.

Make sure your dog's vaccinations are up-to-date. Bring along copies of his rabies certificate and proof of other vaccinations in case you need to day-board him while traveling.

Consider having a tag made up with a friend or neighbor's phone number that you can attach to your dog's collar when traveling. If you and your dog become separated while on the road, the person who (hopefully) finds him will be able to actually get in touch with someone rather than just your answering machine. PetsMart stores offer a nifty option for ID'ing your pet: in-store machines that produce customized tags in just a few minutes. If you'll be in one location for most of your stay, stop by PetsMart and make up a tag with your temporary phone number on it.

because, unfortunately, many of the Forest Service employees with whom I spoke are not familiar with their own agency's policy. If you ask about dogs on trails at a ranger district office, chances are the person behind the desk will insist that dogs have to be leashed everywhere. In actuality, leash laws apply only in the following situations: (1) You are in what's considered a "developed recreation site," such as a campground or picnic area; or (2) the Forest Service supervisor in a particular district has issued an "order" specifying that dogs be leashed on a particular trail (some of the more heavily used trails have leash regulations and should be signed as such at the trailhead).

Dogs are required to be leashed, however, within most designated wilderness areas. You and your dog will know you're entering a wilderness area from signs either at the trailhead or on the trail if a wilderness boundary lies along your route. (Note that mountain bikes are not allowed in designated wilderness areas.) Wilderness boundaries are also clearly indicated on topographic maps. And a handful of wilderness areas in Colorado actually don't have a leash requirement (another little-known fact). Refer to individual chapters for more information.

State Parks

In general, you must keep your dog on a leash no longer than six feet in all state parks. The exceptions are the couple of state parks that have off-leash dog areas: Cherry Creek and Chatfield. And some parks don't allow any dogs whatsoever: Roxborough, Harvey Gap, and Mueller (dogs can stay at Mueller's campgrounds). Keep in mind that dogs are not permitted in any swim or water-ski beach areas in any of the state parks.

An entry fee is required at all state parks. If you're a frequent visitor, you'll save a bundle by getting a season pass, which is good at all the parks.

Bureau of Land Management (BLM) Land

The BLM, more than any land overseer in Colorado, has the most liberal policies regarding dogs. Dogs are not required to be leashed anywhere on BLM land, even in wilderness study areas. Of course, much BLM land is undeveloped, meaning there aren't nearly as many trails as on national forest land. The flipside is, because these areas can be remote, you're less likely to encounter other people who may be bothered by your dog.

Hunting Season

When fall comes, so comes hunting season in Colorado. And that means that from about mid-September to the beginning of November you should take extra care when hiking with your dog in national forest (including wilderness) areas. This is definitely not the time to let your dog run around wearing those fake antlers you bought him last Christmas. One of my friends went to her local WalMart and bought a bright orange hunting vest—for her dog to wear. Ruffwear offers the Lab Coat, a reflective safety vest made of fluorescent orange urethane-coated cloth (see the "Gearhound" appendix for contact information). You can take a precaution as simple as tying bright orange tape to your dog's collar. The point is to avoid having your dog wind up like Tripod, a dog we met near Aspen who had been shot in the leg by a hunter's errant bullet. For information about specific hunting seasons, contact the Colorado Division of Wildlife office in Denver at 303-297-1192 (www.dnr.state.co.us/wildlife).

TRAIL ETIQUETTE
The Leash

I'm lucky in that Clover is well behaved on trails: She doesn't stray, she doesn't chase deer or elk, she waits for me to catch up if she gets too far ahead, and she goes off the trail to poop. Nevertheless, I always carry her leash, just in case. If your dog can be an unruly hiker, keep him leashed on heavily used trails; your outing will be more pleasant without the glares of other hikers. And if your dog is a wildlife chaser, definitely keep his leash at the ready. According to Colorado state law, dogs can be shot for harassing live-stock or wildlife. Some people claim that you can never control a dog in time to keep him from taking off after a deer. I disagree, simply because I've seen other-wise. If you pay attention to your dog and your surroundings, you can nab him and put him on his leash before he dash-es. But you know your dog the best. If you feel you can't control him or don't want to stay on the alert during a hike, keep him leashed.

Ask Before He Sniffs

You and your dog will win many friends if you train him not to approach other people or dogs uninvited. When your off-leash dog encounters an on-leash dog, communication is especially important. That dog may be leashed for reasons other than simple owner control: He may be sick, skittish around other dogs, or even downright unfriendly.

The Clean-up Routine

Those plastic bags that your newspaper comes in serve double duty as handy pooper scoopers. Many forward-thinking towns also provide dispensers of plastic pet-pick-up baggies at popular parks and trailheads.

If you're on a trail in a national forest or other more remote location, I think it's perfectly acceptable to train your dog to poop off trail; or you can fling the poop off the trail into the woods with a stick. After all, no one's cleaning up after all those other animals that use the outdoors as their restroom!

CYCLING FOR CANINES

As an added activity bonus, Clover and I have scoped out places where your dog and your mountain bike can travel in tandem. For the fit dog, nothing beats a run beside one's pedaling owner for exercise efficiency. But—and this is an important but—you must approach biking with your dog differently than a solo ride. This should be a shared activity; if you're a hardcore rider, for example, don't expect your dog to keep up while you try to ride faster than your friends—the results could be fatal! And cycling with your dog is not the time to engage in screaming descents; in fact, you should stop often, allowing your dog plenty of time to catch up with you and to rest. The bottom line is that your dog, not you, should dictate the pace of the ride. If your primary purpose in riding is to get an intense cardiovascular workout, leave Fido at home.

Your dog should be in good condi-tion before you ask him to keep up with you when you're biking. (Though if you're

on a very technical trail, he may well out-run you!) You are the best judge of your dog's physical fitness; if he gets regular exercise and is generally healthy, he's probably able to accompany you on a short bike ride. The fact that you're reading this book is a good sign that you keep your dog fairly active. Just remember that your dog can't tell you that he's too tired to keep running. Make sure that he will have access to water and bring extra for rides in dry areas. And save those 30-mile cycles for a time when your dog is at home resting.

The rides listed range from easy to moderately technical in terms of terrain and are generally under 10 round-trip miles in length (keep the distance under 10 miles for the few rides described that have slightly higher mileage). I've only included areas where dogs can safely be off leash. Unfortunately, this leaves out a lot of good biking terrain. If you've figured out how to ride on singletrack or otherwise technical trails with your dog on a leash, more power to you! None of the rides involves traveling on paved roads, even for a short segment. Traffic and dogs just don't mix. And, as a final caveat, I've steered away from some of the more heavily trafficked biking trails, popular as they may be, because I know you'd hate to have your pooch mowed down by one too many kamikaze cyclists.

POWDERHOUNDS

Most dogs I know love the snow, so what better way to enjoy the winter together than to take your dog along skiing or snowshoeing? Most chapters include a few suggestions on where you can do this. Plowing through snow when you have four legs and are only a foot or so off the ground takes a lot of effort and can even result in injury. Trails or roads that have been packed down by other skiers or snowshoers are the most canine friendly. If Rover is lagging behind or is otherwise obviously tired, shorten your outing so he'll still be able to accompany you on the

next one. It's also a good idea to invest in some booties to protect your dog's paws from painful snow and ice buildup; dogs with webbed feet are especially prone to this. See the "Gearhound" appendix for more information.

As this book is by no means intended to be a backcountry ski guide, I've only included trails that have minimal avalanche danger and are fairly straightforward. In addition, you'll see that several Nordic ski areas have some trails set aside for dogs and their owners, ideal for the type of short ski outings that will keep your dog healthy and happy.

CREATURE COMFORTS

Before I began researching accommodations that accept dogs, I envisioned quaint bed and breakfasts (B&Bs) that would welcome canine guests with open arms, presenting them with freshly baked dog biscuits and perhaps even a resident play companion. Clover and I would spend the day frolicking in a beautiful mountainside setting and then return to a charmingly furnished room. Well, I quickly discovered that such was not the case. Many hotels, motels, and, alas, B&Bs in Colorado want nothing to do with four-legged visitors. (Some proprietors, however, admitted regret at not being able to put out the canine welcome mat; said one innkeeper, "If it makes you feel any better, we don't accept children, either!") Diligent research, however, turned up many places that do accept pets, with a broad range of prices and lodging styles from rustic to ultraluxurious. You may be pleasantly surprised at how many accommodations will welcome you and your dog.

Unfortunately, since the first edition of this book came out, an appreciable number of accommodations have changed their pet policy, and dogs are no longer welcome. Even more unfortunately, this is due in large part to inconsiderate owners who allowed their canines to wreak havoc. *I cannot emphasize enough how important it is to ensure that your dog is well mannered before you allow him to be a travel companion.*

The good news is that many places that used to restrict dogs and their owners to smoking rooms have broadened their policy to include a choice of nonsmoking rooms too. I certainly appreciate their recognition that smokers and dog owners are hardly one and the same.

I've included any and every place I could track down that accepts pets. (By the way, tourism brochures, while helpful, were by no means always accurate or comprehensive.) This means not every accommodation listed is a place you, let alone your dog, would choose to spend the night. But sometimes the need to find somewhere to stay (especially one that's within your budget) outranks preference. A few places will accept pets on a case-by-case basis, depending on who else is staying there, the dog's temperament, and so on, but they didn't want to be listed in this book. If you have your heart set on a particular hotel, it doesn't hurt to ask if they'll take your dog too.

Here's a brief rundown of what you can expect to find in the lodging listings:

Price symbols: Because rates are often in flux, I've devised a simple scale to guide your expectations rather than give specific prices. Rates are based on a standard room for two people per night unless otherwise indicated:

$ = up to $49
$$ = $50–$99
$$$ = $100–$149
$$$$ = $150 and up

You'll notice that many lodgings straddle price categories.

Name, address, phone number, website: Many of the toll-free phone numbers listed for chain hotels and motels go to a national reservations center. Although you can find out rates and room availability through these centers, contact the individual lodging directly to notify the management that you'll be bringing your dog and to confirm the pet policy.

Brief description: For places other than chain accommodations or standard motels, I've provided a summary of the lodging set-up and amenities. If an owner or manager seemed particularly friendly toward dogs, I mentioned it.

Dog policy: A frequent response to the question "Do you allow dogs?" was "Yes, if they're well behaved and housebroken." Because it should almost go without saying that you should not impose your dog on any hotel, motel, or other accommodation if he doesn't match that description, I didn't mention it repeatedly in every lodging write-up. But I'll say it here: *Please, for the sake of the rest of our dogs, leave your dog at home until you've trained him to be a courteous guest. I have heard earfuls of stories from disillusioned lodging owners who used to allow pets but stopped doing so because they had too many bad experiences.*

When inquiring about dog policy, I asked if a fee or deposit is required; about any guidelines that dictate the size, type, or number of dogs in a room; and whether a dog can be left unattended in the room. As you'll note, the answers varied among lodging providers. I've noted which places request a fee or deposit, and how much; if a listing doesn't include either, you can assume your pet is gratis, though it's always a good idea to double-check. As for deposits, the most common way to put one down is with a credit-card imprint; you won't actually be charged unless Fido does damage. Some places will put up you and your dog in a smoking room only—good news if your dog is a smoker (though personally I don't think that dog breath is anywhere near as foul-smelling as stale smoke!). Some managers

I spoke with were adamant that guests not leave their dogs unattended in the rooms, while others didn't have a problem with it as long as the housekeeping staff is notified—presumably so that a housekeeper won't be licked to death while trying to change your sheets! If a listing has no specific information on dog policy, it means that no fee or deposit is charged, you and your dog can stay in any room, and you cannot leave your dog unattended inside.

Some experts advise against leaving a dog unattended in a hotel room. If your lodging choice allows this, I feel it's a useful option to have as long as you're confident that your dog can stay on his best behavior. Although I don't recommend leaving Fido for more than a couple of hours, it's a far better alternative than leaving him in a car in warm weather if you're headed into "absolutely no dogs" territory (e.g., a restaurant). Of the lodging operators who permit this, many rationalized that a dog's owner is the one who will best know if the dog can be left alone. All emphasized that dogs on their own must be quiet and nondestructive. Some places will allow you to leave Rover unattended as long as he's in a travel kennel—an item you might consider bringing along just for that purpose. If you're staying at a place where your dog cannot be left unattended, please don't jeopardize the pet policy for the rest of us by ignoring the rules.

Following each chapter's listing of accommodations is a selection of nearby campgrounds, in case your dog decides he'd rather "ruff" it for the night.

WORTH A PAWS

This is a catch-all category. I've included out-of-the-ordinary dog activities, ranging from benefit events in which you can participate with your four-legged friend to Frisbee competitions and self-service dog washes. Not only are these diversions fun for the pooch (well, except for the dog washes, maybe), they allow you

My "research assistants" hard at work— Blue, this one's for you! (photo by Cindy Hirschfeld)

to mingle with other dog owners who may be just as nuts about their canines as you are about yours.

DOGGIE DAYCARE

Despite your best intentions, you may want to do or attend something while traveling that your dog just can't join in on (e.g., a day at a national park, a hike up a challenging "fourteener," or that fancy-dress family reunion party). Although I don't think road-tripping with your canine friend should entail stashing him in a kennel on a regular basis (after all, you could have just left the dog at home), it's handy to know there are places that will welcome your dog for a day or even for just a few hours. Most "daycare providers" require reservations a few days in advance, as well as proof that your dog is up-to-date with his vaccinations, including rabies, distemper, and bordatella (kennel cough). Moreover, if your dog is not a Colorado resident, he's technically supposed to have a health certificate from his hometown veterinarian in order to cross state lines. While only a few of the kennels included here actually require this, it wouldn't hurt to procure a certificate before leaving home if you think you might need to board Rover.

PET PROVISIONS

You've run out of IAMS halfway through your trip, and your dog only turns up his nose at supermarket dog food. I've included selected lists of where to restock. Note that for ethical reasons, I've tried to avoid listing pet stores that market puppies and kittens along with supplies. If you're far from the nearest pet emporium, remember that most vets carry specialty dog foods and other supplies. Look under "Canine ER" for locations of the nearest veterinarians in each region.

CANINE ER

One of the worst potential travel scenarios for your dog would be to get sick or injured while on the road, far from the friendly scalpel of the hometown vet. The veterinarians and clinics listed throughout the book offer either 24-hour or on-call emergency service. I used a few methods to narrow down the listing of veterinarians within each area. If a region has veterinary clinics that are open 24 hours a day—generally in cities such as Boulder, Denver, Colorado Springs, and Fort Collins—I've listed only these clinics, since they'll be able to serve all your dog's needs at any time. In areas that have no 24-hour clinics but still offer a wide range of veterinary services, I honed the list to include just those veterinary hospitals that are certified by the American Animal Hospital Association; you'll see "AAHA certified" in parentheses after the hospital's name. The AAHA has stringent standards that a hospital must meet in order to be certified, including complete diagnostic and pharmacy facilities, sanitary conditions, proper anesthetic procedures, modern surgical facilities, nursing care, dental service, medical records for each patient, and emergency service. Although my method of selection undoubtedly omits many caring and qualified veterinarians, relying on the AAHA certification allowed me to point your pet in the right direction without actually evaluating each vet. And, finally, in areas that have neither 24-hour clinics nor AAHA-certified hospitals, I've listed all the veterinarians that provide on-call emergency service. Hopefully you and your dog will never need to use any of this information.

RESOURCES

Here you'll find addresses and phone numbers of tourist information centers, chambers of commerce, and land-use agencies that can provide additional information for your travels.

WHY YOU WON'T FIND PLACES TO EAT WITH YOUR DOG IN THIS BOOK

It's often nicer to have your best friend at your feet during mealtime than stashed in a room or a car (assuming, of course, that Rover is not up for membership in "Beggers Anonymous"). Unfortunately, Colorado law prohibits dogs from being in any area where food is served, even if it's an outdoor patio. Of course, this doesn't mean that you won't see dogs and their owners enjoying a bite to eat together at outside dining venues. But I didn't want to get any of these accommodating restaurants in trouble by letting the dog out of the bag, so to speak. Your best bet is to scope out places that offer dining al fresco and then ask if Rover can join you.

CLOVER'S PACKING LIST	
portable food/ water bowl	fluffy toy
leash	*Optional:*
dog food/biscuits	dog bed or
doggie backpack	blanket
booties (in winter)	medication
towel	travel kennel or
brush	crate

FIRST AID FOR FIDO

Can my dog be affected by the altitude?

Dogs who already have some sort of heart or respiratory illness at sea level may have trouble at higher altitude. But, in general, healthy, active dogs should have no problems. Chances are good that if you're doing okay at a higher altitude, your dog definitely is.

Will my dog get giardia from drinking out of streams?

Just like humans, dogs can get giardia, a single-cell parasite that often causes cramps and diarrhea, from drinking untreated water. Many dogs who have been exposed to it, however, never show any symptoms. Or your dog might get the runs for just a few days. Bottom line: When you're out hiking with your dog, it's going to be difficult to prevent him from slurping out of streams. And he'll probably be fine. If you prefer to take precautions, ask your vet about a new giardia vaccine. Of course, if your dog has persistent diarrhea or other gastrointestinal problems, bring him to a vet to be treated with antibiotics.

Can my dog get dehydrated?

Yes! Remember that your dog is probably working harder than you during most physical activities. Dogs seem to cover about twice the mileage of their owners, running back and forth on the trail. And they have those fur coats to deal with. Sticky gums are a sign of dehydration. Make sure that your dog always has an ample water supply, whether you're carrying it (along with something he can drink out of) or from streams or ponds in the area you'll be hiking, running, or biking through.

What should I do if my dog gets heatstroke?

Difficulty breathing or rapid breathing, vomiting, high body temperature, or out-and-out collapse are all signs of heatstroke. Submerge your dog briefly in cool (not ice) water. Keep him wet and cool—wrap him in a wet towel if you have one—and encourage but don't force him to drink water. Follow up immediately with a visit to the vet.

What should I do if my dog gets hypothermia?

Low body temperature, a decreased breathing rate, and shivering are all signs of excessive chilling or hypothermia. Move your dog to a sheltered area or, ideally, inside, and wrap him up in a sleeping bag or multiple blankets. Gently rub him to help rewarming. Never put an electric heating pad against your dog—it can easily burn him.

What should I do if my dog is bitten by a snake?

Restrain and calm him so that the venom won't spread further. Apply a flat tourniquet if he's been bitten on the leg. Encourage the wound to bleed and wash the bite area with soap and water. Apply a cold compress, if possible. Take Fido to the vet ASAP.

For more information on helping your dog if he's injured, refer to *First Aid for Dogs: What to Do When Emergencies Happen,* by Bruce Fogle, D.V.M., or *Emergency First Aid for Your Dog,* by Tamara S. Shearer, D.V.M.

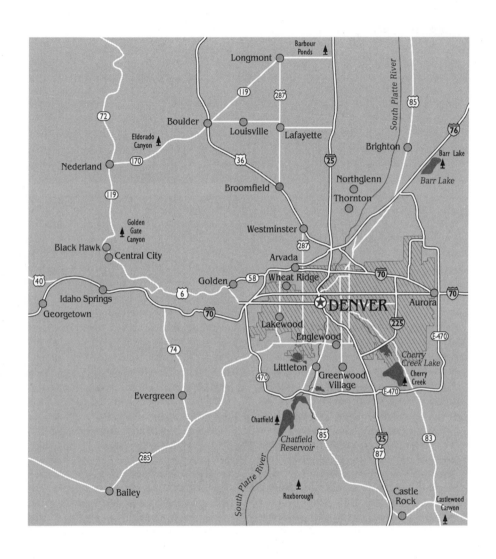

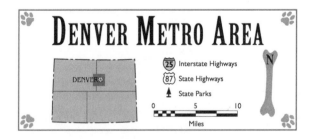

DENVER METRO AREA

🐾 Interstate Highways
🐾 State Highways
🐾 State Parks

0   5   10
Miles

N

Denver and Vicinity

THE BIG SCOOP

For a city, Denver's not a bad place in which to be a dog. Lots of hotels and motels welcome four-legged travelers, and there's plenty to do out of doors. The mile-long 16th St. pedestrian mall in the heart of Denver's downtown is the perfect place for the urban dog to catch up on his people watching. Chic dogs will want to stroll with their owners through Cherry Creek, the city's toniest shopping district. Or they might opt to visit trendy LoDo, which includes Coors Field; though not allowed inside the baseball stadium, dogs can gaze longingly at the exterior and imagine all the balls that could be chased down inside.

Within the City and County of Denver, as well as in surrounding towns in the Denver metro area, dogs must be leashed when not on private property. Resident dogs must be vaccinated annually against rabies once they're six months and older, and dogs are required to wear a city license tag within thirty days of moving to the city.

Both Jefferson and Adams Counties (west of Denver and northeast of Denver, respectively) have leash laws as well. Dogs may be walked under voice command, however, in the unincorporated parts of Arapahoe and Douglas Counties (east of Denver and south of Denver, respectively).

TAIL-RATED TRAILS

As might be expected in a city that is home to an active population, it's not difficult to find a great selection of easily accessible hiking trails near Denver. You and your dog will have to travel to the outskirts of the city and beyond to reach many of the trails that will allow you to enjoy a "less-developed" hiking experience. Denver and its surrounding communities, however, have an extensive network of paved bike paths and trails, often known as greenways, that your dog will enjoy exploring. Some extend for several miles, others for just a few blocks. An excellent resource that maps out many of these trails is "Your Guide to Colorado Trails: Denver Metro Area," a free brochure put out by Colorado State Parks and the Colorado Lottery (once you've read the brochure, you'll understand the connection). Look for it at visitor centers and Forest Service offices.

You'll find some of the best hiking opportunities in the Jefferson County Open Space parks, many of which are described in this section. Not all of these parks, however, are necessarily suitable for dog hikes, due to heavy mountain-bike use. If you don't want to worry about Fido and his leash having a too-close encounter with spokes (or don't want to put up with the exasperated looks of riders who think you didn't get out of their way quickly enough), bring your dog somewhere other than White Ranch (north of Golden), Apex (on Golden's western side), and Matthews Winters (next to Red Rocks) parks. Mount Falcon Park is also popular with mountain bikers, though most seem to start out on the front side, so I've described access via the "back way" here. Of course, when the trails are snowy or especially muddy, you and your dog will encounter relative solitude in these latter parks—just make sure to bring a large towel for after-hiking paw and leg cleanup.

A more recent addition to the Denver dog scene are dog parks. Two have been set up in Highlands Ranch, just southwest of Denver, with four more in the works, and another one has been established in Denver proper, with an additional park planned at the former Stapleton Airport site. In addition, a canine-advocacy group, DenFidos, has been formed by Denver resident and dog owner Oneida Meranto in the hopes of creating at least five dog parks within the city (see "Resources").

For more information on specific trails west of Denver, refer to *Foothills to Mount Evans: West-of-Denver Trail Guide*, by Linda McComb Rathbun and Linda Wells Ringrose. For information on other trails in the Denver area, look at the *12 Short Hikes* series, by Tracy Salcedo (three volumes cover the Denver foothills). The Pike National Forest southwest of Denver, including the Lost Creek Wilderness area, has an extensive trail system. The South Platte Ranger District (see "Resources") provides informative, detailed written descriptions of a wide range of hikes in this area.

Denver

There are more than 300 city-maintained parks throughout Denver. Three of the most popular are described here, but there are plenty more for your dog to explore. For a "Parks and Recreation Facility Map" that details all of them, contact the Denver Parks office at 303-964-2500.

 Washington Park. Denver dogs in the know come to "Wash Park" to participate in one of the city's best canine social scenes. Bordered by Virginia Ave., Franklin St., Louisiana Ave., and Downing St., the 154-acre

park is also one of Denver's largest, with two small lakes, colorful flower gardens (one a duplicate of George Washington's gardens at Mount Vernon), an indoor recreation center, playground, lawn bowling court, soccer field, and lighted tennis courts. You and your dog have several strolling options: a 2.6-mile crushed-gravel trail goes around the park's outer edges, while a paved inner trail makes two loops within the park, each about a mile in length. *Dogs must be leashed.*

 Cheesman Park. Close to Capitol Hill, 82-acre Cheesman Park is between 13th and 8th Aves., Humboldt St., and Race St. The park is a pleasant oasis, with gardens, a pavilion, and a view west to the mountains. Make sure your dog takes time to sniff the flowers here, as he's not permitted in the adjoining Denver Botanic Gardens. Two main walkways wind around the park: a gravel-surfaced one that's 1.6 miles long, and a paved one at 1.4 miles. *Dogs must be leashed.*

 City Park. Denver's largest park at 314 acres, City Park is also the site of the Denver Museum of Natural History, the Denver Zoo, and a public golf course. Dogs will have to content themselves with a saunter around the park's two lakes and its gardens. A 1.6-mile paved trail encircles Ferril Lake, while a 3-mile natural surface trail tours the park's perimeter. You'll also find playing fields, a band shell, playgrounds, picnicking spots, and lighted tennis courts on park grounds. The park is located north of 17th Ave. between York St. and Colorado Blvd. *Dogs must be leashed.*

 Denver Animal Shelter Dog Park. The park, the first officially designated off-leash area within Denver, is located behind the Denver Municipal Animal Shelter at 666 S. Jason St. (three blocks west of Santa Fe; three blocks south of Alameda).

If your dog wants to come here, it'll be to run and socialize, not for the scenery. The park consists of a half-acre grassy, fenced-in field in an industrial section of the city. No water was available as of spring 2001, but thirsty hounds may be able to get a drink in the future. If your dog is looking for others to play with, tell him that summer is the most popular time to visit the park. Dogs must have a valid rabies tag, and the provided poop pick-up bags should be used by owners.

Clover's cardio workout—the bigger the stick, the better. (photo by Cindy Hirschfeld)

North of Denver

Golden Gate Canyon State Park. Located 16 miles northwest of Golden, this 14,000-acre mountainous park offers almost 35 miles of trails, all with animal names, that you and your dog can enjoy together. The main access from the eastern side, which will bring you by the park's visitor center, is via Golden Gate Canyon Rd., a signed turnoff from Highway 93 just north of Golden. The drive to the park is 13 miles from the turnoff. *Dogs must be leashed.*

One particularly nice hike follows the **Horseshoe Trail**, a 3.6-mile round-trip route from the Frazer Meadow trailhead to Frazer Meadow and back. To reach the trailhead, turn right at the T-intersection just after the visitor center, pass the Ralston Roost trailhead on the left, then pull into the next trailhead parking area on the left. You'll ascend a moderate uphill alongside a creek for most of the hike, then will reach a large meadow flanked by stands of aspen. Head right for a few minutes on the intersecting **Mule Deer Trail** to view the old homestead in the meadow. Other park trails that follow streams for a good portion of their length include the 2.5-mile **Raccoon Trail**, which makes a loop from the

Reverend's Ridge Campground in the park's northwestern corner; the **Mountain Lion Trail**, which forms a 6.7-mile loop that begins and ends at the Nott Creek trailhead in the northeastern corner of the park; the 2.4-mile round-trip **Buffalo Trail**, which goes from the Rifleman Phillips Group Campground in the northern part of the park to Forgotten Valley; and the 2.5-mile **Beaver Trail**, which follows a loop beginning and ending at the visitor center and includes a short detour to Slough Pond.

Barr Lake State Park. Take I-76 northeast from Denver for about 20 miles to the Bromley Ln. exit. Turn right on Bromley, then right on Picadilly Rd. Look for the well-signed park entrance on your right. *Dogs must be leashed.*

Barr Lake, a day-use park, provides an easily accessible refuge for the dog who wants to get out of the city. He'll get a panoramic view of the Front Range foothills and the snow-capped peaks beyond. The lake itself is ringed by shady cottonwood trees, a habitat that attracts more than 300 bird species. A 9-mile gravel and natural-surface trail loops around the lake—the canine caveat is that dogs are not allowed on the southern part of the trail, about a 4-mile section, because it is in the park's wildlife refuge. Dogs are usually permitted, however, to accompany their owners in viewing the exhibits at the indoor nature center at park headquarters. A nice semi-loop hike of several miles heads north from the parking area on the lakeside trail; walk on top of the dam at the lake's northeast end, then return via the trail below the dam.

 Crown Hill Park. From Lakewood, take Kipling Ave. north to W. 26th Ave. and make a right. Two parking areas for the park are on the left-hand side of the block. *Dogs must be leashed.*

This 177-acre Jefferson County Open Space park is a perfect spot for an after-work stroll with Rover. The most obvious route to take is the 1.2-mile **Lake Loop Trail**, a paved path that encircles Crown Hill Lake and its resident ducks; just keep your dog on a short leash so that he doesn't have any entangling encounters with a bicyclist or in-line skater. The **Outer Loop Trail** takes you around the park's perimeter, but you won't be near the water. A number of unnamed horse trails, on which dogs are allowed, too, wind through the park. There's also a 1-mile **fitness course** near the lake that includes access for disabled exercisers. Note that dogs are not allowed on the nature trail that loops around Kestral Pond in the northwest part of the park—the area is designated as a wildlife sanctuary.

 Van Bibber Park. Located in Arvada, the park has two main access areas with parking lots: off Indiana St. and off Ward Rd., both just south of W. 58th Ave. *Dogs must be leashed.*

From either side of the park, start out on the paved **Van Bibber Creek Trail**, which is 1.5 miles from end to end. You'll soon reach a small network of natural-surface trails that meander through the 130-acre Jefferson County Open Space park. Van Bibber Creek, which runs through the park's northern section, is often dry midsummer but has water at other times of the year. As you and your dog walk (or jog—this is a good venue for a run), you'll see the somewhat odd combination of farmland and suburban palaces that's becoming common to the metro area. If you're starting out at the eastern side of the park, you'll reach the middle before leaving behind the rush of traffic on busy Ward Rd. No dogs are allowed on the Jimmy Go Trail, which leads to an observation deck in the wetlands section of the park; if your dog wants to walk a large loop, you and he will need to briefly exit, then reenter the park.

West of Denver

 Maxwell Falls Trail. 3.5 miles round-trip. From the stoplight on Highway 74 in downtown Evergreen, head south on Highway 73 for about a mile. Make a right on Brook Forest Rd. Drive for 3.6 miles to the lower trailhead parking in a small fenced area on the left side of the road. *Dogs can be off leash.*

One of the closest national forest trails to Denver, the Maxwell Falls Trail has recently been rerouted (including a new trailhead) because of some private property issues along the old trail. This hike features plenty of access to water, lots of trees to sniff, and a brief scenic vista. Begin by heading up the path marked by the brown carsonite post in the southwest corner of the parking area. You'll make a moderate ascent through a forest of fir, pine, and aspen, contouring southwest across a hillside and following the route of an unnamed creek. The trail eventually fords the creek and switchbacks up to a clearing on a small saddle (this is where you'll get the view). Cross an old dirt road and follow the trail down

Sean McCullough and Clover on the Maxwell Falls Trail. (photo by Cindy Hirschfeld)

the other side of the saddle. From here the trail stays fairly level as it goes into the Maxwell Creek drainage. After crossing the creek, head left (upstream); you've now joined up with the original portion of the Maxwell Falls Trail. The falls themselves are about a quarter mile ahead.

After viewing the falls, you can either return the way you came or, if your dog is up for a longer hike, follow a loop that adds about 1.25 miles to the total distance. To access the loop, backtrack from the falls a few hundred yards to an intersection. Follow the intersecting trail as it switchbacks uphill and then runs above the creek. In about a third of a mile, this trail ends at the upper trailhead for Maxwell Falls, at an unmarked parking pullout off of Brook Forest Rd. Before reaching trail's end, however, ford the creek and head left on a wide dirt path that doubles back along the creek. This path, which is actually the old dirt road that you crossed earlier in the hike, starts to head away from the creek. After about a mile, you'll come out on the same saddle that you traversed earlier. Look for the intersection with the Maxwell Falls Trail (unmarked) and go right to return to the lower trailhead parking area.

Elk Meadow Park. From Denver, take I-70 west to Exit 252, then head toward Evergreen on Highway 74 east. At 5.3 miles from the first traffic light after crossing over I-70, turn right (west) on Stagecoach Blvd. Drive 1.25 miles to the parking area on the right. *Dogs must be leashed, except in the dog training area.*

This Jefferson County Open Space park, on 1,280 acres, has 11.5 miles of trails, including a 4.7-mile (one-way) ascent of 9,600-foot Bergen Peak, which will give you a panoramic view of the Continental Divide. Your dog might be most interested, however, in sniffing out the off-leash area. To access it, cross Stagecoach Blvd. from the parking area and go through the gate. A quarter-mile trail leads off to the right, with signs for the dog training area (you're supposed to keep your dog leashed on this trail). The training area itself is a large field, bordered by aspen along one side. Although a couple of footpaths lead into the field, it's not really a hiking area. But it's a fine place to let your dog go through his paces, retrieve a stick or ball, or play with another four-legged friend. And if he needs to pause for a drink, there's a running spigot alongside the access trail for easy refreshment.

Pine Valley Ranch Park. Head south on U.S. Highway 285, going through Morrison, Aspen Park, and Conifer. In Pine Junction, make a left at the traffic light onto Pine Valley Rd. Head southeast on Pine Valley Rd. for about 6 miles, until you come to a hairpin turn in the road. Go right on Crystal Lake Rd. and follow the signs to Pine Valley Ranch. *Dogs must be leashed.*

Pine Valley Ranch Park, on 820 acres, has a beautiful, wide-open feel. And though somewhat removed from the madding crowd, it's still a Jefferson

County Open Space property. In the middle lies small, scenic Pine Lake, and the North Fork of the South Platte River runs across the park. As a bonus, the park's southern boundary abuts Pike National Forest, where your dog can hike leash free. To hike along the rushing waters of the South Platte, take the 2-mile **Narrow Gauge Trail** in either direction from the parking area; the trail follows the route used by the Colorado and Southern Railroad in the early part of the century. A very short trail loops around Pine Lake. To head into the national forest, follow the **Buck Gulch Trail** for 1 mile to the park boundary; the trail then continues for 2.2 miles as a Forest Service trail. It's possible to do a long loop (5.3 miles) by combining the **Buck Gulch, Skipper, and Strawberry Jack Trails**; note that these are also popular mountain-biking trails.

Lair o' the Bear Park. From Morrison, take Highway 74 west toward Evergreen. After going through Idledale (don't blink), look for the signed park entrance on the left. *Dogs must be leashed.*

Tucked into the side of Bear Creek Canyon, this 319-acre Jefferson County Open Space park offers a healthy-sized stream with easy access for dog dips as well as 4 miles of trails. And because the park is relatively small, you're not likely to encounter the mountain bikers who frequent many of the other Jeffco Open Space areas. The **Creekside Trail** parallels Bear Creek for nearly 1.5 miles; head toward the creek from the parking area and pick up the trail going in either direction. If you go left (east), you'll eventually cross the Ouzel Bridge— keep an eye out for these small gray birds plunging into the water—and meet up with the **Bruin Bluff Trail**. Keep heading east to connect with Little Park, primarily a picnic spot, in

about a quarter mile. Another portion of the Bruin Bluff Trail forms a 1.3-mile loop through the forest above the creek's south side.

Lookout Mountain and Beaver Brook Trails. Up to 16.5 miles round-trip. This hike starts across from the Lookout Mountain Nature Center, which you can reach in one of two ways: From U.S. Highway 6, coming from Golden or Lakewood, turn west on 19th St., which becomes Lookout Mountain Rd., and follow the switchbacks up, past Buffalo Bill's grave, to Boettcher Mansion and the nature center. From I-70 west from Denver, take Exit 256, make a right at the stop sign, and follow the brown signs along Paradise and Charros Rds. to Lookout Mountain Rd., where you'll turn right to head up to the nature center. Either way, look for the parking pull-out on the other side of the road from the nature center main entrance. *Dogs must be leashed.*

The Lookout Mountain Trail drops down a hillside in the cool shade of lodge-pole pine for a mile before intersecting with the Beaver Brook Trail. Take a left at the trail intersection; the right ends at a busy trailhead on Lookout Mountain Rd. known as Windy Saddle. As you hike, you and your dog can take in a bird's-eye view of Clear Creek Canyon below and the Front Range's northern foothills—as well as of the gamblers speeding toward Black Hawk and Central City on curvy Highway 6. Shortly after joining up with the Beaver Brook Trail (there's no brook along this part), you'll encounter two short talus fields, which may test your pooch's rock-hopping skills. The next section of trail includes a few places where you'll have to scramble up and over some rocks; the trail then mellows out again as it continues to wind along the south side of the canyon. If you and your dog are particularly ambitious, or if you've arranged a car shuttle, you can hike for a total of about 8.25 miles from the Lookout Mountain trailhead to the Beaver Brook Trail's western terminus in Genesee Mountain Park (Exit 253 off I-70).

Meyer Ranch Park. Head south on Highway 285 from Denver. Before you reach the town of Aspen Park, you'll see a turnoff for South Turkey Creek Rd. and a sign for the park on the left. From South Turkey Creek Rd., the parking area is almost immediately on the right. *Dogs must be leashed.*

This 397-acre Jefferson County Open Space park has about 4 miles of trails that wind through the forested hillside to the south. This is a particularly nice place to hike in September when the aspen change color. The trails are wide and well graded, with benches conveniently placed along them if you or your dog needs to stop for a breather. In the early 1940s, a small ski area was located on the southern end of the property, now overgrown with aspen. The **Old Ski Run Trail** takes you to this spot, though you probably won't be able to recognize the formerly skiable terrain. There's no water along any of the trails, just a small creek near the parking lot.

Mount Falcon Park. Head south on Highway 285 from Denver, which can be accessed from C-470 just past Morrison, to the Parmalee Gulch Rd. exit. Drive north on this road for 2.5 miles; you'll see a sign for the park indicating a right turn. From here, follow the signs through a residential area to the parking lot. *Dogs must be leashed.*

This park, another Jefferson County Open Space property, features 11.2 miles of trails spread over 1,415 acres. It's located on land formerly owned by John Brisben Walker, a wealthy gent who lived here at the turn of the century until his house burned down in 1918 (you can visit the remains). The directions I've given take you and your dog to the west parking lot, which receives a little less mountain-bike use than the east parking lot, off Highway 8 outside of Morrison. However, if you are in the eastern part of the park, your dog might want to sniff out the 3.4-mile out-and-back **Turkey Trot Trail,** which is for hikers only. From the western side, a nice 3-mile loop involves taking the **Castle Trail,** passing by the castlelike Walker Home Ruins, to the aptly named **2-Dog Trail,** which ends at a lookout with a view of Denver and Lakewood, Red Rocks Amphitheater, and the plains to the east. Return via the **Meadow Trail,** which hooks up with the Castle Trail not too far from the parking area. There's no water along this route.

Clear Creek and Tucker Gulch Trails. Located in the town of Golden, the trails can be accessed from Vanover Park, one block east of Washington St. (the main downtown thoroughfare) at Ford and 10th Sts. Parking is available. *Dogs must be leashed.*

Admittedly not the most scenic hike, this is nonetheless a fine option if your dog wants to stretch his legs while you're visiting the former territorial capital of Colorado. To reach the 0.9-mile-long Clear Creek Trail, cross the larger bridge from the parking area and then pick up the red dirt trail across the street. When you come to Washington St. one block later, you'll need to pick up the trail on the north side of the creek. Your walk will take you along Clear Creek to Lions Park and the Golden Community Center. The trail continues for about a quarter mile past the park before crossing under Highway 6 and becoming a gravel road; it is decidedly less scenic from this point on. The paved Tucker Gulch Trail begins at the east end of the parking lot at Vanover Park and runs for 1.1 miles along a stream through a peaceful suburban landscape before ending at Ford Rd. across from Normandy Park.

 O'Fallon Park. Part of Denver's Mountain Parks system, O'Fallon is located just east of Kittredge off Highway 74. If you're coming from Denver, look for a large, three-sided chimney/fireplace structure after passing Corwina Park—this is your cue that the entrance to O'Fallon is coming up on the left. Follow the road from the entrance as it goes left, until it ends in a parking area. *Dogs must be leashed.*

Although there are some picnic sites near the park entrance, O'Fallon, like most other Denver mountain parks, doesn't have a developed trail system. Yet there are certainly hiking opportunities within the park, and because they're not mapped out, you and your dog may be less likely to encounter the hiking masses here. From the parking area, cross the bridge over Bear Creek and walk up a dirt service road (closed to regular vehicle traffic). The road ascends amid stands of caramel-scented ponderosa pine. As there's no particular destination for this hike, let your dog determine the length of your outing.

Dog Training Area at the Jefferson County Government Center. From Denver, take Highway 6 west to Golden. Make a right on Jefferson County Pkwy., which is just past the Taj Mahal-like government building. Turn left on Illinois. Drive to the parking lot on the right, near the end of the road. *Dogs can be off leash.*

The dog training area is a small field at the north end of the parking lot (look for the sign). There's not much to recommend the site except that dogs can be off leash (Clover seemed to like it well enough). If you really need to find a place where your dog can run, and

you're on the west side of Denver, check it out.

South of Denver

 Chatfield State Park. You can easily access the park, which is southwest of Denver, via C-470 east or Wadsworth Blvd. south. If you're coming from C-470, take the Wadsworth Blvd. exit and drive south for 1 mile to the park entrance on the left. *Dogs must be leashed except in the dog training area.*

Like Cherry Creek State Park (see next entry), Chatfield is best known for its reservoir and the water recreation it provides, but dogs will be much more interested in the off-leash area set aside for them. Located in the northeast corner of the park, the **dog training and exercise area,** as it's officially known, encompasses about 25 acres. There's even a pond, where several dogs were practicing their stick-in-the-water retrieval skills when we visited.

To reach the site, turn left (north) at the T-intersection after going through the park entrance station. Follow the road up and around the top of the dam to the Stevens Grove picnic area, where parking is available. From there, a trail leads around the pond. You and your dog can also head east on the trail (away from the pond), but Fido will have to leash up when crossing the marked dog area boundary; you'll connect with the paved **Centennial Trail,** which runs along C-470.

The dog training area also extends on the other side of the road from Stevens Grove as well as from the next picnic area, Cottonwood Grove; your dog can either follow some small social trails here or explore among the trees—just keep an eye out for the boundary markers. For the best meet-and-greet opportunities, however, the pond's the place.

The park has some paved trails that run along the west and south sides of the reservoir. And the **Highline Canal Trail** is just outside the park's south and east boundaries.

Cherry Creek State Park.

The park, located in Aurora, has two main entrance gates: The east entrance station is off of Parker Rd., 1.5 miles south of I-225; the west entrance station is reached via Yosemite St., south of I-225, and Union Ave. Currently, if you walk (or bike) into the park from one of the numerous trail accesses (pick up a park map for locations), you don't need to pay an entrance fee. *Dogs must be leashed except in the dog training area.*

Although known primarily for its reservoir, Cherry Creek State Park rates high among the canine set because of the **off-leash dog area** at the southern end of the park. To reach this area, which covers about 60 acres, drive south on the main park road from the east entrance station and park in the lower parking lot for the 12 Mile House group picnic site. You'll need to keep your dog leashed for about the first 500 yards, until you pass the dog area boundary sign. You can also access the off-leash area by heading west on Orchard Ave., off Parker Rd., for about a half block to a small parking area (there's a self-service fee station). The dog area consists mainly of open grassland traversed by a wide gravel trail; water-loving hounds will seek out the small creek. There's plenty of room for your dog to get a good workout, play with a friend, or chase down a ball.

If he tires of the scenery, put him back on his leash and bring him to explore the rest of the park, which has about 12 miles of trails. The paved **Cherry Creek Trail** runs through the park from north to south; north of the dam, outside the park boundary, a portion connects to the **Highline Canal Trail**. A network of trails lies west of the Shop Creek trailhead, which is off the main park road south of the east entrance station—note that these trails can get very muddy in late winter and spring. Another trail goes along the southern end of the reservoir, from the marina area east to the Shop Creek area. The park is still in the process of mapping out and improving the signage on its trails, so you and your dog should expect to do some exploring rather than following a set route. Dogs are not allowed at the reservoir's swim beach.

Hound Hill.

This 3-acre off-leash dog area opened in the fall of 2000. To reach it, take C-470 south to the Quebec St. exit. Turn right (south) onto Quebec and pass the intersection with University Blvd. Just after the entrance to Highland Heritage Park, make a right on Dutch Creek St. and go left into the large parking area.

Don't be deterred by the signs stating that no dogs are allowed in Highland Heritage Park; Hound Hill takes exactly the opposite approach. Dogs have ample room to romp in the dog park's fenced area, which is adjacent to Quebec St. The small hill provides a venue for canine uphill sprints. A water pump provides necessary refreshment in the summer (it's shut down in winter). Park rules are that dogs must be vaccinated, no puppies younger than four months are allowed, and owners must have a leash at the ready and pick up after their canines (bags and trash cans are provided).

Rover's Run.

Opened in June 2000, this off-leash dog area at the east end of Redstone Park provides dogs with some much-needed roaming space in hyper-developed Highlands Ranch. To reach it, take the Lucent Blvd. exit off C-470 south and make a right on Town Center Dr. Look for Foothills Canyon Blvd. on the left after about a mile. Parking is available in a lot on the right; the park itself is on the left.

Once your dog enters the park's three

acres, he'll probably want to make a bee-line for the fire hydrant in the middle to make his mark (the hydrant is purely for "aesthetic" purposes). Then you can relax at one of the picnic tables while Rover runs. Water is available during the summer. Park rules are the same as for Hound Hill.

Castlewood Canyon State Park. This day-use park is in Franktown, south of Denver and east of Castle Rock. From Denver, take either Highway 83 (S. Parker Rd.) south or I-25 south to Castle Rock, then Highway 86 east 6 miles to the intersection with Highway 83. The main park entrance (and visitor center) is 5 miles south of this intersection, on the right. There's also a west entrance, reached via Castlewood Canyon Rd. off Highway 86 from Castle Rock. *Dogs must be leashed.*

Castlewood Canyon seems something of an anomaly, a small canyon set near the edge of the eastern plains. The park provides a nice alternative to a mountain hike; you and your dog will be surrounded by farmland yet can still view the peaks of the Front Range in the distance, including Pikes Peak. A pleasant short hike (about 2 miles) combines the Lake Gulch and Inner Canyon Trails. From the parking area, the **Lake Gulch Trail** (there is no lake) begins as a paved path before changing to gravel surface. You'll hike among ponderosa pine and juniper before descending to Cherry Creek and its riparian habitat. After crossing the creek, go right to pick up the **Inner Canyon Trail.** You may want to make a short detour to the left, however, to view the ruins of the dam, which collapsed in 1933. The Inner Canyon Trail follows the course of the creek before crossing it and switchbacking up to the parking area. If your dog is interested in a much longer hike, you can add on a loop of the **Creek Bottom** and **Rim Rock Trails**

(about 3.6 miles), which cover the park's western section. Castlewood Canyon is also popular with rock climbers, so your dog shouldn't be alarmed if he spots a gear-laden human spider.

Roxborough State Park. Dogs are not permitted in this day-use state park southwest of Denver.

Waterton Canyon. You'll have to leave your dog at home if you want to hike or bike the 6.2-mile trail that winds through this scenic canyon along the South Platte River. The northern terminus of the **Colorado Trail,** which traverses the state for 469 miles, is at the end of the canyon. You will need to bypass the first part of the trail and pick it up at County Rd. 96 (S. Platte River Rd.) if you're planning a cross-state hike with Rover.

CYCLING FOR CANINES

One of the nearest places to Denver for singletrack mountain biking with Rover in tow is the **Buffalo Creek** area, about 45 miles southwest of the city. All trails are in the Pike National Forest. To access the area, take Highway 285 south, then either Highway 126 south from Pine Junction or County Rd. 68 southeast from Bailey. Both routes lead to Forest Rd. 550 and the trailheads. Ten short trails can be ridden in a variety of combinations. The **Miller Gulch and Homestead Trails** form a 6.1-mile loop on easy to moderate terrain. For a shorter loop (about 4.7 miles), ride Miller Gulch to Homestead but take **Charlie's Cut Off,** which goes off to the left about 0.4 mile up the Homestead Trail. Reach these trails from the Miller Gulch trailhead off Forest Rd. 553. Farther up the road is the Buck Gulch trailhead, from which you can ride the **Buck Gulch, Strawberry Jack,** and **Skipper Trails,** a 5.3-mile loop of moderate to difficult terrain. (Note that you won't be able to ride with your dog in adjoining Pine Valley Ranch Park, as dogs must be leashed.) Both the Miller Gulch and Buck Gulch Trails have water nearby. The **Colorado Trail** also runs through the Buffalo Creek area and can be accessed from the trailhead at the intersection of Highway 126 and Forest Rd. 550.

Other recommended biking options are the **Maxwell Falls Trail**, especially if you do the loop option (see "Tail-Rated Trails"), and trails in **Clear Creek County** (see Chapter 3).

POWDERHOUNDS

See Chapters 2 (Boulder and Vicinity) and 3 (Central City, et al.) for some of the nearest canine-suitable skiing and snowshoeing trails.

CREATURE COMFORTS

Unless otherwise stated, dogs should not be left unattended in the room or cabin.

Arvada

$$$ On Golden Pond Bed and Breakfast, 7831 Eldridge St., 303-424-2296 (www.bbonline.com/co/ongoldenpond). The B&B has one room where dogs may stay, and it comes complete with a fireplace and private patio. There's a $10 one-time fee for a small dog, and $20 for a large dog. The house is situated on 10 acres of land with a private pond. You must keep your dog leashed on the property.

Aurora

$–$$ Blue Spruce Motel, 12500 E. Colfax, 303-343-3303. Dogs are allowed with—get this—a $300 one-time fee. If it really comes down to that, sharing the back seat of your car with Fido is probably the more sane choice.

$–$$ Ranger Motel, 11220 E. Colfax, 303-364-3386. Dogs are permitted with a $50 deposit, of which $40 is refunded if there's no damage. You can leave your

dog unattended in the room at your own discretion.

$$ Hampton Inn Aurora, 1500 S. Abilene St., 303-369-8400 (800-HAMPTON [national number]). Dogs under 40 pounds are permitted and can be left unattended in the room.

$$ La Quinta, 1011 S. Abilene St., 303-337-0206 (800-531-5900 [national number]). You can leave your dog unattended in the room if necessary.

$$ Sleep Inn–DIA, 15900 E. 40th Ave., 303-373-1616 (800-SLEEP-INN [national number]). Dogs are charged a $25 one-time fee.

Castle Rock

$–$$ Castle Rock Motel, 125 S. Wilcox, 303-688-9728. Dogs are welcome in some of the motel's rooms for stays of one or two nights.

$–$$ Super 8 Motel, 1020 Park St., 303-688-0880 (800-800-8000 [national number]). Dogs are permitted in smoking rooms only.

$$ Quality Inn, 200 Wolfensberger Rd., 303-660-2222 (800-228-5151 [national number]). Dogs are allowed in smoking rooms only for $10 extra per night. Rates include continental breakfast.

$$–$$$ Best Western Inn and Suites Castle Rock, 595 Genoa Way, 303-814-8800 (800-528-1234 [national number]). It's smoking rooms only for dogs, with a $10 nightly fee per pet.

Denver—Downtown

$–$$ Motel 6 Central, 3050 W. 49th Ave., 303-455-8888 (800-466-8356 [national number]). Dogs under 30 pounds make the guest grade here, with a limit of one dog per room.

11

$$ Continental Hotel, 2601 Zuni St., 303-433-6677. Dogs under 25 pounds are welcome at this former Super 8, with a $25 deposit.

$$ La Quinta Inn Denver Downtown, 3500 Park Ave. West (Fox St.), 303-458-1222 (800-531-5900 [national number]). Dogs under 20 pounds are allowed.

$$–$$$ Executive Tower Hotel, 1405 Curtis St., 303-571-0300 (800-525-6651). You'll need to put down a $50 deposit to bring your dog along, and you can leave him unattended in the room. The hotel features an athletic club on premises.

$$–$$$ The Holiday Chalet, A Victorian Hotel, 1820 E. Colfax Ave. (18 blocks east of downtown), 303-321-9975 (800-626-4497). "We're puppy-dog friendly," says the owner of this small, homey B&B in a restored 1896 former private residence, "but they have to be well mannered." For $5 extra per night, your dog can stay with you in one of the ten rooms, each with Victorian-style or wicker furnishings and fully equipped kitchen with cool vintage appliances. Cheesman Park is only two blocks away.

$$–$$$ Red Lion Denver Downtown, 1975 Bryant, 303-433-8331. Dogs who love the Broncos will want to stay at this hotel within barking distance of the new football stadium. There's a $25 deposit, and you can leave your dog unattended in the room.

$$–$$$$ The Burnsley Hotel, 1000 Grant St., 303-830-1000 (800-231-3915; www.burnsley.com). This apartment-style suite hotel near Capitol Hill accepts dogs under 20 pounds with a $100 one-time fee. All of the recently renovated suites include one bedroom with king-size bed and full kitchen.

$$–$$$$ Marriott–City Center, 1701 California St., 303-297-1300 (888-238-1439 [national number]). You can leave your dog unattended in the room here. There's a fitness center with pool, sauna, Jacuzzi, and massage service at the hotel.

$$–$$$$ Warwick Hotel–Denver, 1776 Grant St., 303-861-2000 (800-525-2888). The Warwick was completely remodeled in 2000; the large rooms have fairly plush, traditional-style furnishings. Dogs are welcome with a $100 deposit, and you can leave your dog unattended in the room. The hotel is a few blocks from downtown; some grassy areas for dog walks are nearby.

$$$–$$$$ Hotel Monaco, 1717 Champa St., 303-296-1717 (800-397-5380; www.monaco-denver.com). Part of a group of hip city hotels, the Monaco takes pride in its pet friendliness. Not only can you bring your dog, but if you want extra company, a "companion" goldfish can be brought to your room for the length of your stay. And resident canine Lily Sopris, a confident Jack Russell terrier, keeps a close eye on the front desk. The hotel is housed in two renovated historic buildings near the 16th St. Mall; rooms are large with vividly colored yet traditional furnishings and decor. Complimentary wine is served each evening in the fancifully ceilinged lobby, and your pooch is welcome to accompany you. During our stay a therapist from the Aveda Renaissance Spa off the lobby was giving free chair massages during the happy hour, and Clover was delighted to find that the woman had just completed a course in canine massage. The pet agreement you'll sign at check-in states that dogs are not to be left unattended in the room, but you may find the hotel flexible on this policy.

$$$–$$$$ Residence Inn by Marriott, 2777 Zuni St., 303-458-5318 (800-331-3131 [national number]). The Residence

Inn offers studio or penthouse suites, both with fully equipped kitchens. There's a $10 fee per night per dog, for up to fifteen nights, and you can leave your dog unattended in the suite.

$$$–$$$$ The Westin Hotel Tabor Center Denver, 1672 Lawrence St., 303-572-9100 (800-228-3000 [national number]). The nicely appointed Westin has dog-loving management that accepts canines 50 pounds and under, with some exceptions to the size limit occasionally made (one Aspen golden retriever—and no, it's not Clover—is such a frequent visitor he's known by name). You can leave your dog unattended in the room while you peruse the shops downstairs in the Tabor Center. And if it's not too busy, the concierge may be able to provide dog-walking outings.

$$$$ Hotel Teatro, 1100 14th St., 303-228-1100 (800-223-5652; www.hotel teatro.com). The Teatro scores extra high on the dog welcome meter; Clover rates it as one of her favorite hotels in Colorado. The hotel resides in what was once the home of the Denver Tramway Company, built in 1911. Afterward the building housed the University of Colorado at Denver before sitting empty for almost a decade. It's now been beautifully restored into the Teatro, which pampers its human guests with sleek furnishings, luxurious marble baths, Frette linens, and impeccable service. As for canine amenities, dogs receive a special gift bag on check-in, with a welcome note from the director of guest services and an assortment of chew toys, leash, and "poochie sushi" from the pet store Pooch! And waiting for them in the room are food and water bowls on bone-shaped placemats. You can leave your dog unattended in the room, perhaps while you catch a performance at the Denver Center for the Performing Arts across the street, and the concierge will walk him on request.

Denver—East

$–$$ Motel 6 Denver East, 12020 E. 39th Ave., 303-371-1980 (800-466-8356 [national number]). Small dogs (30 pounds or under) get the nod here.

$–$$ Rodeway Inn, 12033 E. 38th Ave., 303-371-0740 (800-228-5160 [national number]). Dogs are allowed for a $5 fee per night, per pet.

$$ Drury Inn Denver, 4400 Peoria St., 303-373-1983 (800-325-8300 [national number])

$$ Holiday Inn Denver International Airport, 15500 40th Ave. (10 miles from DIA), 303-371-9494 (800-HOLIDAY [national number]). The hotel allows small dogs (though no one I spoke to was able to define exactly what "small" means) for a $20 one-time fee.

$$ La Quinta Inn–Denver Airport South, 3975 Peoria Way (15 miles from DIA), 303-371-5640 (800-531-5900 [national number]). Dogs less than 20 pounds are permitted. You can leave your dog unattended so long as you let the front desk staff know.

$$ Ramada Inn Stapleton, 3737 Quebec St., 303-388-6161 (800-999-8338). The hotel is across the street from the old Stapleton Airport, hence the name. Dogs are allowed in designated pet rooms with a $50 deposit. You can leave your dog unattended in the room.

$$ Red Lion Denver Central, 4040 Quebec, 303-321-6666 (800-733-5466 [national number]). Dogs are permitted in first-floor smoking rooms only, partly so that they have easy access to going outdoors. Call to check on a possible pet fee or deposit.

$$–$$$ Amerisuites, 16250 E. 40th Ave. (11 miles from DIA), 303-371-0700 (800-833-1516 [national number]). Dogs 25

pounds and under are allowed for a $25 one-time fee. Rooms come equipped with microwave and refrigerator.

$$–$$$ Best Western Executive Hotel, 4411 Peoria St., 303-373-5730 (800-848-4060). Dogs under 25 pounds are permitted with a $15 one-time charge. "Good-natured dogs"—that is, those who won't bark the day away—can stay unattended in the room as long as they are in a travel kennel.

$$–$$$ Doubletree Denver Hotel, 3203 Quebec St., 303-321-3333 (800-222-TREE). Located across from the former Stapleton Airport, the hotel permits dogs with a $50 deposit.

$$–$$$ La Quinta Inn & Suites DIA, 6801 Tower Rd. (6 miles from DIA), 303-371-0888 (800-531-5900 [national number]). Most dogs are allowed (ill-behaved large ones will likely be turned away), and they can be left unattended in the room if they have a travel crate to stay in.

$$–$$$ Red Roof Inn and Suites, 6890 Tower Rd. (8 miles from DIA), 303-371-5300 (800-THE-ROOF [national number])

$$$ Embassy Suites Denver International Airport, 4444 N. Havana St. (15 miles from DIA), 303-375-0400 (800-345-0087). The two-room units are equipped with refrigerator, microwave, and coffee maker. There's a $50 deposit for a dog, and you can leave yours unattended in the room but housekeeping won't come in.

Denver—North

$ Valli Hi Motor Hotel, 7320 Pecos Ave., 303-429-3551. There's a $3 fee per night.

$ Western Motor Inn, 4757 Vasquez Blvd., 303-296-6000. Dogs are welcome for $5 extra per night.

$$ Best Western–Central, 200 W. 48th Ave., 303-296-4000 (800-528-1234 [national number])

$$ Super 8, 5888 N. Broadway, 303-296-3100 (800-800-8000 [national number]). Dogs under 20 pounds are permitted with a $25 deposit, and they can be left unattended in the room, though the housekeepers probably won't come in during that time.

Denver—South

$–$$ Cameron Motel, 4500 E. Evans, 303-757-2100. Lap-sized dogs are allowed in five of the smoking rooms for $5 extra per night.

$$ Best Western Landmark Hotel, 455 S. Colorado Blvd., 303-388-5561 (800-528-1234 [national number]). A $25 deposit is required, and you can leave your dog in the room unattended (perhaps while you dash to the upscale Cherry Creek Mall, nearby). The Cherry Creek bike path runs right behind the hotel, convenient for walks with Rover.

$$ La Quinta Inn Denver Cherry Creek, 1975 S. Colorado Blvd., 303-758-8886 (800-531-5900 [national number]). Dogs under 35 pounds are welcome. You can leave your dog unattended in the room if he has a travel kennel in which to stay.

$$ Quality Inn–Denver South, 6300 E. Hampden Ave., 303-758-2211 (800-647-1986). There's a $6 nightly fee for a dog.

$$ TownePlace Suites Denver Southeast, 3699 S. Monaco, 303-759-9393 (800-257-3000 [national number]). If your dog is set on this extended-stay hotel, he'd be better off checking out the one in Lakewood, due to the $200 one-time fee he'd have to pay here. Dogs can be left unattended inside the suites, which range from studio to two bedrooms, with full kitchens.

$$–$$$ **Denver Marriott Southeast, 6363 E. Hampden Ave., 303-758-7000 (800-228-9290 [national number]).** Dogs are permitted in ground-floor rooms only, which have direct access outside. You can leave your dog unattended inside the room at your discretion.

$$–$$$ **Drury Inn and Suites Tech Center, 9445 E. Dry Creek Rd., 303-694-3400 (800-325-8300 [national number]).** The suites have separate bedroom and living areas.

$$–$$$ **Holtze Executive Village DTC, 6380 S. Boston, 303-290-1100 (800-422-2092).** The hotel offers standard guest rooms as well as one- and two-bedroom apartment-style suites with fully outfitted kitchens. There's a pricey $100 one-time fee to stay with your dog, which won't seem so bad if your stay is long term. You can leave your dog unattended inside as long as you let the front desk know so that arrangements can be made for housekeeping.

$$–$$$$ **Loews Giorgio Hotel, 4150 E. Mississippi Ave., 303-782-9300 (800-345-9172; www.loewshotels.com).** Thanks to its enlightened general manager, Matthew Kryjak, and his dog, Blondie, this particular hotel spearheaded the now-nationwide Loews Loves Pets program. It's been so successful that even *People* magazine has covered it. Dogs are welcomed in rooms on the second and third floors of the posh Giorgio. On check-in, Fido receives his own paw-print bag full of complimentary treats and toys as well as a personal welcome note from the GM that includes a list of nearby walking routes to sniff out (such as the Cherry Creek bike path, two blocks away), veterinary info, locations of pet shops and groomers, pet sitters, and pet-friendly restaurants. The hotel also offers a special room-service menu for pets, which includes grilled lamb or chicken with rice (and grilled liver or salmon with rice for visiting cats). The recipes were developed with a veterinarian's assistance and are designed to help your dog deal with travel stress, including jet lag or altitude adjustment. If you don't want your dog to get too used to specially cooked meals, you can also order him up some regular old dry or canned dog food. Regardless of choice, he can nosh in style with hotel-provided food and water bowls on a special pet placemat. And for canines who turn up their noses at mere tap water, bottled water is available. Once he's happily sated, Fido can take a long snooze on the dog bed that awaits him in the room, and you can even put out a special "do not disturb" sign when you head out for your own gourmet meal. Pet videos are available if he wants something to be entertained by while you're gone. And when Fido is ready to explore the city, the Giorgio will loan him a leash or collar if he forgot to pack his. If you're visiting in June, be sure to check out the annual Loews Loves Pets Bark Breakfast (see "Worth a Paws").

$$–$$$$ **Marriott Denver Tech Center, 4900 S. Syracuse St., 303-779-1100 (800-228-9290 [national number]).** Dogs 40 pounds and under are permitted. You can leave your dog unattended in the room as long as he's in a travel kennel and you inform the front desk.

Denver—West
$$ **Days Inn Central, 620 Federal Blvd., 303-571-1715 (800-DAYS-INN [national number]).** Your dog, who must weigh in at under 20 pounds, needs to provide a $50 deposit to stay here.

Englewood
$$ **Super 8, 5150 S. Quebec, 303-771-8000 (800-800-8000 [national number]).** Dogs are allowed in most of the motel's rooms with a $25 one-time fee.

$$–$$$ AmeriSuites–Denver Tech Center, 8300 E. Crescent Pkwy., 303-804-0700 (800-833-1516 [national number]). Technically dog guests must be 50 pounds and under, but this AmeriSuites is flexible on the policy. And you can leave your dog unattended in the room provided you let the front desk know. The one-bedroom suites have microwaves and refrigerators. Rates include a large continental breakfast.

$$–$$$ Holiday Inn Hotel and Suites–Denver South, 7770 S. Peoria St., 303-790-7770 (800-HOLIDAY national number]). Dogs are permitted in ground-floor rooms only, most of which are smoking, with a $50 deposit.

$$–$$$ La Quinta Inn and Suites Denver Tech Center, 7077 S. Clinton St., 303-649-9969 (800-531-5900 [national number]). Dogs 20 pounds and under (with exceptions occasionally made) are permitted. You can leave your dog unattended inside but housekeeping won't clean the room during that time.

$$–$$$ Quality Suites, 7374 S. Clinton St., 303-858-0700 (800-228-5151 [national number]). Dogs 25 pounds and under are welcome with a $50 one-time fee. Queen suites consist of one large room; king suites have doors that can partition off the bedroom. All suites are equipped with a microwave and refrigerator; some also have Jacuzzis. You can leave your dog unattended inside.

$$$ Residence Inn by Marriott Denver South, 6565 S. Yosemite, 303-740-7177 (800-331-3131 [national number]). You and your dog can stay in either studio or penthouse suites, both with fully equipped kitchens, but it won't be cheap for a short-term stay. There's a $100 one-time pet fee, as well as an additional charge of $5 per night. You can leave Rover unattended inside as long as you put out the "pet in room" sign.

$$$–$$$$ Summerfield Suites Hotel by Wyndham, 9280 E. Costilla Ave., 303-706-1945 (800-833-4353 [national number]). You'll find one- and two-bedroom suites here with lots of amenities as well as fully equipped kitchens. But there's a $150 one-time fee for a dog as well as a $10 nightly charge. You can leave your dog unattended inside, but housekeeping won't enter during that time.

Golden
$–$$ Golden Motel, 510 24th St., 303-279-5581. There's a $6 fee per night, per dog.

$$ La Quinta, 3301 Youngfield Service Rd., 303-279-5565 (800-531-5900 [national number]). You can leave your dog unattended in the room.

$$–$$$ Holiday Inn, 14707 W. Colfax Ave., 303-279-7611 (800-HOLIDAY [national number]). Dogs are permitted in outside-facing, ground-level rooms only with a $50 deposit. You can leave your dog unattended inside the room, but housekeeping won't enter during that time.

$$–$$$ Marriott West, 1717 Denver West, 303-279-9100 (800-228-9290 [national number]). For $10 extra per night, dogs can stay in first-floor rooms at the hotel. And you can leave your dog unattended inside.

$$–$$$ A Touch of Heaven/Talmar Bed and Breakfast, 16720 W. 63rd Pl., 303-279-4133 (www.talmar.com). This B&B offers several elaborately decorated rooms, including the Royal Suite, which features a sunken bathroom with waterfall, Jacuzzi, and sauna as well as a sitting room with marble fireplace and a white baby-grand piano. Small dogs are welcome on a case-by-case basis, and an outside run is available for times when you may need to leave your pooch behind. There's a $5 pet fee per night.

Horseback riding lessons are also available, as the B&B is home to several Arabian stallions.

Greenwood Village
$–$$ Motel 6, 9201 E. Arapahoe Rd., 303-790-8220 (800-466-8356 [national number]). The motel allows one dog per room.

$$–$$$ Wellesley Inn and Suites, 5200 S. Quebec St., 303-220-8448 (800-444-8888 [national number]). Dogs up to 30 pounds are allowed at this all-suite hotel (studios with full kitchens). You can leave your dog unattended in the room as long as you notify the housekeeping staff.

$$–$$$ Woodfield Suites, 9009 E. Arapahoe Rd., 303-799-4555 (800-338-0008 [national number]). The suites range from studios to one bedrooms, some with kitchens that include a stove but no oven, some with minirefrigerator and microwave only. Cooking utensils are supplied on request. Dogs 50 pounds and under are allowed in twenty of the suites, all of them smoking units.

Highlands Ranch
$$–$$$ Residence Inn by Marriott–Highlands Ranch, 93 W. Centennial Blvd. 303-683-5500 (800-331-3131 [national number]). The apartment-style suites range from studios to one and two bedrooms. All have fully equipped kitchens, and the two-bedroom units have gas fireplaces, too. There's a $100 one-time fee for a dog, and he can be left unattended inside. You'll want to let the front desk know if your dog's alone so housekeeping can be alerted.

Lakewood
$ Motel 6, 480 Wadsworth Blvd., 303-232-4924 (800-466-8356 [national number]). Dogs up to 30 pounds get the nod here.

$$ Ramada Inn Denver West, 7150 W. Colfax Ave., 303-238-1251 (800-321-7187). There's a limit of one dog per room, with a $50 deposit. You can leave your dog unattended in the room.

$$ TownePlace Suites, 800 Tabor St., 303-232-7790 (800-257-3000 [national number]). It's $10 per night extra for dogs to stay at these studios to two-bedroom suites, with kitchens, run by Marriott. You can leave your dog unattended inside. Studios can be rented on a nightly basis, though other units have a 30-day minimum stay.

$$–$$$ Comfort Inn and Suites–Southwest Denver, 3440 S. Vance St., 303-989-5500 (800-228-5150 [national number]). Dogs are allowed in smoking rooms and suites with a $50 deposit. You can leave Fido unattended inside, but housekeeping won't enter during that time. (Note that the Comfort Suites on W. 6th Ave. does not accept pets.)

$$–$$$ La Quinta Inn and Suites Denver Southwest/Lakewood, 7190 W. Hampden Ave., 303-969-9700 (800-531-5900 [national number]). Dogs under 20 pounds only are allowed, and they can be left unattended in the room.

Littleton
$$–$$$ AmeriSuites–Denver/Park Meadows, 9030 E. Westview Rd., 303-662-8500 (800-833-1516 [national number]). The hotel, across the street from the massive Park Meadows Mall, allows dogs 50 pounds and under. All one-bedroom suites are equipped with microwave and small refrigerator. Dogs can be left unattended inside. A large continental breakfast is included.

Northglenn
$$ Days Inn Denver North, 36 E. 120th Ave., 303-457-0688 (800-874-4513). Dogs under 15 pounds are always welcome;

those larger must be approved by a manager. There's a $6 fee per night for a dog, with a limit of two dogs per room. You can leave your dog unattended in the room as long as he's in a travel kennel and you put up the "do not disturb" sign to alert housekeeping.

$$ La Quinta Inn Denver Northglenn, 345 W. 120th Ave., 303-252-9800 (800-531-5900 [national number])

$$ Ramada Inn Limited Denver North, 110 W. 104th Ave., 303-451-1234 (800-2-RAMADA [national number]). Dogs are allowed in smoking rooms only for a $10 one-time fee. You can leave your dog unattended in the room, but housekeeping won't come in to clean during that time.

$$–$$$ Holiday Inn Northglenn, 10 E. 120th Ave., 303-452-4100 (800-HOLIDAY [national number]). You and your dog can stay in a first- or second-floor room with a $50 deposit.

Thornton
$$ Sleep Inn, 12101 N. Grant St., 303-280-9818 (800-SLEEP-INN [national number]). There's an additional $5 nightly fee for a dog.

$$$ Motel 6, 6 W. 83rd Pl., 303-429-1550 (800-466-8356 [national number]). Although the motel prefers small dogs, you probably won't be turned away if your pooch weighs in on the larger side.

Westminster
$ Turnpike Motel, 7151 Federal Blvd., 303-429-2569. The hotel has weekly as well as nightly rates.

$$ Hawthorne Inn, 10179 Church Ranch Way, 303-438-5800 (800-527-1133 [national number]). Small to medium-sized dogs are allowed in smoking rooms with a $50 deposit.

$$ La Quinta Inn Westminster, 8701 Turnpike Dr., 303-425-9099 (800-531-5900 [national number]). You can leave your dog unattended in the room if you let the front desk staff know.

$$ Super 8, 12055 Melody Dr., 303-451-7200 (800-800-8000 [national number]). The motel permits dogs in pet-designated rooms with a $20 deposit.

$$$ Residence Inn Westminster, 5010 W. 88th Pl., 303-427-9500. There's a $100 one-time fee for dogs to stay in any of the suites, which range from studios to two bedrooms. Unlike at many apartment-style hotels, you're not supposed to leave your dog unattended in the room here.

$$$–$$$$ Westin Hotel Westminster, 10600 Westminster Blvd., 303-410-5000. Only dogs 30 pounds and under are permitted, with a $100 deposit. This new Westin (it opened in 2000) has two restaurants, an indoor pool, workout room, and sauna as well as a large conference center. Grassy areas for dog walking are nearby.

Wheat Ridge
$–$$ Motel 6, 9920 W. 49th Ave., 303-424-0658 (800-466-8356 [national number])

$–$$ Motel 6 Wheat Ridge South, 10300 S. I-70 Frontage Rd., 303-467-3172 (800-466-8356 [national number]). One dog per room is allowed.

$$ Holiday Inn Express, 4700 Kipling, 303-423-4000 (800-HOLIDAY [national number]). Dogs are welcome with a $10 one-time fee per pet, and you can leave yours unattended in the room.

$$ Quality Inn–Denver West, 12100 W. 44th Ave. (Exit 266 off I-70), 303-467-2400 (800-449-0003). The motel has

only two rooms (one smoking, one non-smoking) where dogs 25 pounds and under can stay. A $50 deposit is required. You can leave your dog unattended inside, but housekeeping won't enter during that time.

Mountain Communities Southwest of Denver

Bailey

$$ Glen Isle Resort, 573 Old Stage Coach Rd., 303-838-5461. This longtime family-owned resort is situated on the South Platte River. The lodge building, which dates from 1900, is on the National Register of Historic Places. Dogs are permitted only in the resort's nineteen cabins, most with fireplaces and kitchens, for $5 extra per night. The resort is in full operation from June through mid-September. During the winter, only five of the cabins remain open.

$$ Mooredale Ranch Resort, U.S. Highway 285 (2.5 miles south of Bailey), 303-816-9433 (888-334-9433). The resort offers lodge rooms that consist of one bedroom plus living area. Dogs are welcome for $10 extra per night, per dog. You'll need to keep your dog leashed while on the property, which borders the South Platte River.

Evergreen

$$–$$$ Bauer's Spruce Island Chalets, 5937 S. Brook Forest Rd., 303-674-4757 (www.bsichalets.com). Located on nineteen acres, these nine units range in size from studios to three bedrooms. The studios come with kitchenettes; the multiroom units have full kitchens, and some have fireplaces. There's a $15 fee per night for dogs, and you can leave Rover unattended inside as long as he's in a travel kennel.

$$$ Abundant Way Chalet Lodge, 4980 Highway 73, 303-674-7467 (www.abundantwaychalet.com). The lodge allows small shorthaired dogs in one of its units, a fully equipped two-bedroom cabin, with a $100 deposit. You can leave your

dog unattended inside, if absolutely necessary, only if he has a travel kennel in which to stay. And you'll be able to exercise Fido, on his leash, on the surrounding acre of mountain property.

Pine

$$–$$$ Crystal Lake Resort/B&B, 29200 Crystal Lake Rd., 303-838-5253 (www.crystallakeresort.com). This resort's namesake lake is a well-known fly-fishing spot. From 1919 to 1943 the main lodge building was an ice house, supplying Denverites with ice cut in blocks from the lake during the winter. Dogs are permitted in the seven bed-and-breakfast rooms as well as in twelve new cabins on a case-by-case basis (the owners are a bit wary due to some irresponsible dog owners who have visited). If your dog gets the okay, you may be asked to put down a damage deposit. The B&B rooms feature rustic log furniture and feather beds; all have fireplaces. The cabins, which sleep from four to six people, are slated to open in late summer 2001. Each will have a kitchenette and fireplace or woodstove; some will have private hot tubs. You can leave your dog unattended inside and should keep him leashed when outside. Massage is offered at the resort, and plans call for additional spa services. Dinner is available at the on-site Trout River Grill by reservation. There's a two-night minimum stay. Open Memorial Day to Labor Day.

Campgrounds

Bear Creek Lake Park. Off Morrison Rd., 0.25 mile east of C-470, in Lakewood (52 sites).

Chatfield State Park. 1 mile from the intersection of C-470 and Wadsworth Blvd., southwest of Denver (153 sites).

Cherry Creek State Park. 1.5 miles south of I-225, off Parker Rd. in Aurora (102 sites).

WORTH A PAWS

Furry Scurry. The first weekend in May, dogs from all over the metro area and their owners convene in Denver's Washington Park to participate in this walk/run, which raises money for the Denver Dumb Friends League. The 2-mile course circles one of the park's lakes. After the "race," dogs can check out the booths purveying pet products and information, enjoy a variety of treat samples, or enter competitions such as best trick or closest owner/dog look-alike. Owners can fuel up on bagels and other snacks and model their Furry Scurry T-shirts. It's the canine social event of the year! You can register in advance or on race day; in addition to the registration fee, funds are raised through pledge donations collected by participants. For more information, contact the Dumb Friends League at 303-696-4941 (www.ddfl.org).

Bark in the Park. Billed as a canine carnival, Bark in the Park takes place the third weekend in May at City Park in Denver. Dogs can partake in activities offered at various "fun stations," which include things like an agility course, musical hoops (a variant on musical chairs), a swimming pool, bobbing for biscuits, and paw print art. Or they can have their future foretold via an astrology or paw reading ("you will get lots of treats in your lifetime . . ."). There are also demonstrations by especially skilled canines and a mutt mall with dog-product vendors. All the fun benefits Harrison Memorial Animal Hospital (the only nonprofit veterinary hospital in the state), the Diana Price Fish Foundation (which assists cancer patients), and Lesbian Cancer Support Services. Call 303-639-9110 for specifics.

Loews Loves Pets Bark Breakfast. This annual June morning event, held at the exceedingly pet-friendly Loews Giorgio Hotel at 4150 E. Mississippi Ave. in south Denver, features educational information on traveling with your pet, human and canine food, and goodie bags for one and all. Proceeds raised from the breakfast benefit the Tendercare Emergency Fund for needy pets. Call the hotel at 303-782-9300 (800-345-9172) for additional information.

Maxfund Lucky Mutt Strut. Since 1988, the Maxfund Animal Adoption Center, a nonprofit no-kill shelter, has helped injured animals who are ownerless. The 2-mile Lucky Mutt Strut (a run/walk) for dogs and people is held in May or June at Denver's Washington Park, and registration fees and pledges raised benefit the Maxfund. Dogs should be at least six months old to participate, and one dog per

The Furry Scurry is the canine social event of the year in Denver. (photo by Sean McCullough)

runner or walker is allowed. Each human participant gets a Mutt Strut T-shirt. Register in advance or on race day, either as an individual or as a team of people and dogs. Call 303-595-4917 for details.

ESA's Walkin' the Dog. This event is part of an annual nationwide campaign of Walkin' the Dogs that raises funds for the St. Jude's Children's Research Hospital in Memphis, Tennessee, which treats children with catastrophic illnesses, especially cancer, from around the world. Epsilon Sigma Alpha International sorority is the sponsor, and a black lab named Chuck serves as the national mascot. The Denver walk is held the third weekend in September at Washington Park and follows a 3-kilometer course. Money is raised through the entry fee and pledges. Call the sorority offices at 970-223-2858 or 800-704-7336 (or log on to www.esaintl.com/ chuck) for more information.

Remington and Friends Neighborhood Bakery, 278 S. Downing, Denver, 303-282-8188. The healthy canine will want to make this bakery—a purveyor of all-natural treats for dogs, cats, and even horses—a must-sniff. Biscuits such as doggone danish, tail-wagging veggie, and F. liver pâté (named after Frank, the golden retriever customer who deemed it his favorite) are baked daily on the premises. And for that special day, bone-shaped, chicken-flavored birthday cakes can be made to order. Remington, the Irish setter who is the bakery's namesake, as well as Clancy and Riley, both border collies, are usually present to help dogs whose taste buds are overwhelmed with their selection. Meanwhile, you can browse through the assortment of canine paraphernalia—collars, leashes, beds, bowls, and the like—that's also on hand.

Colorado Petfitters, 2075 S. University, Denver, 303-282-0020 and 3390 W. 32nd Ave., Denver, 720-854-0120. The Denver area has long had a multitude of mountaineering stores to supply the gear needs of outdoor recreationists. Now dogs have a specialty gear store (with two locations) to call their own. Colorado Petfitters carries everything for the outdoor dog. Before heading to the mountains, bring Fido here to choose from a fine assortment of packs, booties, bowls, leashes, and treats. The store also sells pet-related books, premium dog food, doggie health foods, and maps. Your dog is welcome to accompany you inside; store policy is, "if he pees on it, he buys it." The University Blvd. location also has a self-service dog wash; $9 covers washing-bay rental, shampoo, and use of towels, dryers, and grooming tools.

Pooch!, 3000 E. 3rd Ave., Denver, 303-333-4677 (www.poochemporium.com). Located in high-end shopping mecca Cherry Creek, Pooch! is more than your average pet store. In addition to toys, leashes, bowls, and dog-themed accessories, this is where Rover can come for "poochie sushi," a soft biscuit that bears a resemblance to a California roll. The store also hosts a multitude of events for dogs and their people, including an annual spring celebrity dog wash to benefit Harrison Memorial Veterinary Hospital, a Valentine's Day party, summertime patio parties, and the Halloween Pooch! Parade, for four-legged ghouls on the Sunday before the holiday. From December 1 through Christmas, Pooch! sponsors Drop and Shop, which means you can bring your dog by for anywhere from a half hour to a full day of day care (for a fee) while you stock up on his holiday presents at the shops nearby. The store even had an informal dating service for single dog owners before it became too popular for its own good. Full-service grooming is also available in case your dog needs to spruce up his look before cruising the streets of Cherry Creek.

Colorado Disc Dogs Frisbee Competitions. These two events are part of an annual series of canine Frisbee contests put on by the Colorado Disc Dogs. The first is held in Thornton during the third weekend of May, at the Thornton Rec Center (108th St. and Colorado Blvd.). Dogs compete in two categories: the minidistance, in which they receive points for catching distance and style in sixty-second rounds (with bonus points for midair catches); and the free flight, in which they demonstrate their best freestyle tricks. A two-day event, the Colorado Canine Challenge, takes place the second weekend of August at Arapahoe Community College in Littleton (Santa Fe and Church). In addition to the minidistance and free flight, dogs can compete in the Quadruped, in which the winner is the owner who can throw the Frisbee the farthest and the dog who can then catch it. Bring your dog to participate or just to watch; no previous competitive experience is necessary. For more information, contact Rick Brydum at 303-759-8785 (frflyers@ aol.com) or look at the Colorado Disc Dog website, www.varinet.com/~eyebum/noco dido.html.

When at the wheel, dogs will sometimes pick up canine hitchhikers. (photo by Cindy Hirschfeld)

Red Rocks Park and Amphitheater. Red Rocks is a spectacular outdoor concert venue nestled among a natural amphitheater of—as the name implies—striking red sandstone. Though your dog is unable to come howl and cheer with the crowd during the annual summer concert series, he can pay a visit with you during nonevent times. You can even bring him onstage to play air guitar and imagine an appreciative audience of thousands before him—as long as he stays on a leash. Some hiking trails run through the park, including a 1.5-mile loop trail at the Trading Post gift shop. To reach Red Rocks, take I-70 west from Denver to the Morrison exit (259); head south on Highway 26 for about a mile to the park entrance on the right.

Buffalo Bill's Grave. Okay, so it's not quite Graceland, but your dog may be interested in sniffing out a bit of the Wild West with a visit to the final resting place of William F. Cody, a.k.a. Buffalo Bill. Rover won't be able to enter the Memorial Museum or gift shop, but he can walk with you (on leash) to the gravesite as well as enjoy the view from Lookout Mountain. From Highway 6, coming from Golden or Lakewood, turn west on 19th St. and follow the switchbacks up to the signed turnoff for the grave. From I-70 west coming from Denver, take Exit 256, make a right at the stop sign, and follow along Paradise and Charros Rds. to Lookout Mountain Rd. Go right at the T-intersection and follow Lookout Mountain Rd. to the signed turnoff for the grave. The museum is open 9 a.m.–5 p.m., every day, from May 1–October 31; 9 a.m.–4 p.m., Tuesday through Sunday, from November 1 to April 30. Call 303-526-0747 for additional information.

The Museum of Outdoor Arts. Does your dog complain that he never gets to go to museums? Bring him to the Museum of Outdoor Arts, a "museum without walls," located in Englewood's Greenwood Village area, just west of I-25 on Orchard Rd. The forty-plus pieces of artwork—90 percent of which is outdoor sculpture—are spread out among seven locations in this office-park complex. You'll need to stop in at the museum offices at 1000 Englewood Pkwy., Suite 2-230 (second floor of the Englewood civic center building), about 25 minutes north of the museum, to pick up a map. Guided tours can also be arranged for $3 per person ($1 for 17 and under). Call 303-806-0444.

Bathing Beauty. Fido's been tromping through the mud all afternoon, and you don't want him to leave paw prints all over your hotel room. Lucky for you (he may have a different opinion), the Denver area has several self-service dog washes.

Stinky Dog No More at 1222 E. 6th Ave. (near Cherry Creek; 303-282-1894) lives up to its promise by providing washing bays, shampoo and conditioner, and use of towels, dryers, and grooming tools for $10–$15 per dog, depending on size. Cosmo's Bakery dog biscuits and canine accessories are also available.

Mutt Puddles, with two locations, offers rental of a small washing bay (for dogs under 25 pounds) for $8 per hour, a large one for $12 per hour. Prices include shampoo and cream rinse as well as use of a towel, blow dryer, and grooming tools: 8700 Wadsworth Blvd. in Arvada (303-403-9901) and 120th St. and Colorado Blvd. in Thornton (303-255-7611). Also in Thornton is **Pawz 'n' Clawz Dog and Cat Grooming**, at 951 E. 88th St.(303-286-7297). Washing-bay rental is $15 ($5 per additional dog) and includes shampoo, towels, and use of brushes and a blow dryer.

Denver Dog-o-Mat, at 1842 S. Parker Rd. in Denver (303-695-1213), charges $7–$10, depending on the size of dog, and includes shampoo and the use of towels, brushes, and a dryer. **Laund-Ur-Mutt**, 7475 E. Arapahoe Rd., Suite 18, in Englewood (303-850-7266),

provides washing-bay rental and use of a dryer and brushes for $8 for the first half hour, $6 per additional half hour, and $2 per additional dog. Towel rental is available for 75 cents, and you can buy shampoo, including one-wash-size bottles, at the store. Or bring your own towel and shampoo. **Chow Down Self-Service Doggie Wash**, 28608 Buffalo Park Rd. in Evergreen (303-674-8711), provides washing-bay rental, shampoo, and the use of towels, grooming tools, and blow dryer—as well as treats—for $15 per dog. Also, see entry for **Colorado Petfitters**.

DOGGIE DAYCARE

Because there are so many boarding kennels in the Denver area, veterinarians that also offer boarding haven't been listed here. But if you're having difficulty finding a place for your loyal companion to spend the day, you might try the vet option.

Arvada

Action Kennel, 12975 W. 80th Ave., 303-423-2243. $5/day. Open 8 a.m.–5 p.m., Monday to Thursday and Saturday; 8 a.m.–6 p.m., Friday; 9–9:30 a.m. and 7–7:30 p.m., Sunday.

Alpine Pet Center, 9530 W. 80th Ave., 303-421-3758. $10/day. Open 7:30 a.m.–6 p.m., Monday to Friday.

Aurora

Academy Acres Kennels, 16501 E. Arapahoe Rd., 303-690-1188. $8–$14/day, depending on the size of dog. Open 7 a.m.–6 p.m., Monday to Friday; 7 a.m.–noon, Saturday.

B&B for Dog LLC–Large Breeds, 10 S. Potomac St., 303-361-0061. $15/day. Monday to Friday, dropoff is between 6:30 a.m. and 6 p.m., and pickup is any time until 10 p.m.; Saturday and Sunday, dropoff is between 7 a.m. and 6 p.m., and pickup is until 10 p.m.

Broadview Kennels, 2155 S. Havana St., 303-755-0471. $7–$10/day, depending on the size of dog. Open 7 a.m.–5:30 p.m., Monday to Friday; 7:30 a.m.–noon, Saturday.

Pets Control/Rocwind Canine Center, 16255 E. 4th Ave., 303-364-8586. $12/day. Open 7 a.m.–7 p.m., Monday to Saturday; 8 a.m.–5 p.m., Sunday. The kennel may have since moved, so call to check on location.

Tenaker Pet Care Center, 895 Laredo St., 303-366-2376. $12–$17/day, depending on the size of dog. Veterinarians are on staff, and there's even a recreational swimming pool on the premises that's open during the summer. Open 7:30 a.m.–6 p.m., Monday to Friday; 7:30 a.m.–1 p.m., Saturday.

Broomfield
Colorado Dog Academy, 12180 N. Sheridan Blvd., 303-465-1703. $7/day. Open 8 a.m.–5:30 p.m., Monday to Friday; 8 a.m.–3 p.m., Saturday.

Castle Rock
Beau Monde Kennels, 660 E. Happy Canyon Rd., 303-688-9578. $14/day. The kennel features a 1-acre fenced-in exercise and play area for its guests. Open 7:30 a.m.–6 p.m., Monday, Tuesday, Thursday, Friday; 7:30 a.m.–noon, Wednesday and Saturday.

Denver
Allbrick Boarding Kennels, 8700 Zuni St., 303-429-2433. $6/day. Open 7 a.m.– 6 p.m., Monday to Friday; 7 a.m.–5 p.m., Saturday.

B&B for Dog LLC–Small Breeds, 1842 S. Parker Rd., 303-745-8538. $12/day for dogs 35 pounds and under (larger dogs go to the B&B for Dog in Aurora). Monday to Friday, dropoff is between 6:30 a.m. and 6 p.m., and pickup is any time until 10 p.m.; Saturday and Sunday, dropoff is between 7 a.m. and 5 p.m., pickup until 10 p.m.

The Dog House, 659 Santa Fe Dr., 720-904-2180. $20/day (package prices available). Open 7 a.m.–7 p.m., Monday

A visit to Denver wouldn't be complete without a treat. Surprise Fido with one of these:

• A Barker's Dozen, thirteen Milkbones dipped in white chocolate. The bones come in two sizes and can also be purchased individually. Rocky Mountain Chocolate Factory, 1512 Larimer St. in downtown Denver; also two locations at Denver International Airport.

• Cosmo's Dog Biscuit Bakery no longer has a retail outlet, but dogs hankering for a natural treat—such as a good dog star, barbecued mail carrier, or fresh breath frisbee—should check out the selection of Cosmo's biscuits at Pet Outfitters, Cigi's Natural Pet Supplies,

and Stinky Dog No More (see "Pet Provisions" and "Worth a Paws").

• Ice-cream sandwiches for dogs—two biscuits with vanilla ice cream in between. Bonnie Brae Ice Cream, 799 S. University Blvd., Denver.

• A "sundae"—a scoop of vanilla ice cream topped with a large dog biscuit. Soda Rock Fountain, 2217 E. Mississippi Ave. (near Washington Park), Denver.

• Einstein's Bagels recognizes that dogs need something to nosh on too. Pick up a couple of special doggie bagels at any of the store's numerous outlets in the Denver metro area.

to Friday; 8 a.m.–6 p.m., Saturday. "Dogs must be friendly, nonaggressive, and ready to have a good time," notes owner Betsy Kelso, who is also a professional dog trainer. As long as your pup is older than four months and fully vaccinated, he can join the other daycare guests here. Dogs older than six months must be spayed or neutered.

Englewood
Doggy Day Camp, 15350 E. Hinsdale Dr., 303-680-4001. $13/day. Open 7 a.m.–6:30 p.m., Monday to Friday.

Golden
Sage Valley Pet Center, 16400 W. 54th Ave., 303-279-6969. $14–$17/day, depending on the size of dog. Open 8 a.m.–6 p.m., Monday to Saturday. Daycare can also be arranged on Sundays.

Waggin' Tails, 17731 W. Colfax Ave., 303-215-0413. $13/day on weekdays; $10/day on weekends. Open 7 a.m.–6:30 p.m., Monday to Friday; 7–10 a.m. for dropoff and 4–7 p.m. for pickup, Saturday, Sunday, and holidays.

Highlands Ranch
Tenaker Pet Care Center, 5790 E. County Line Rd., 303-694-5738. $18.50–$23.50/day, depending on the size of dog. Dogs play outside for most of the day, unless it's really cold out. Veterinarians are on staff. Open 7:30 a.m.–6:00 p.m., Monday to Friday; 7:30 a.m.–1 p.m., Saturday; 5–6 p.m. for pickups only, Sunday.

Lakewood
Mantayo Kennels and Dog School, 1220 S. Wadsworth Blvd., 303-985-4011. $10–$14/day, depending on the size of dog. Open 8 a.m.–5 p.m., Monday to Friday; 8 a.m.–noon, Saturday. Sundays by appointment.

Pinehurst Animal Center, 6500 W. Hampden Ave., 303-985-1845. $6/day. Open 8 a.m.–noon and 1:30–5:30 p.m., Monday to Friday; 8 a.m.–noon, Saturday.

Littleton
High Country Kennels, 8290 W. Coal Mine Ave., 303-979-3353. $5/day. Open 7:30 a.m.–5:30 p.m., Monday to Friday.

Pampered Pets, 13906 Kuehster, 303-697-6824. $18/day. This home-based boarding service is run by a certified vet technician. Dogs have 4 fenced-in acres on which to romp with no cages or kennels. Arrangements made by appointment only. Note that though the address is officially Littleton, the house is located in the mountains near Conifer.

Pet Ranch Kennel, 12725 W. Belleview Ave., 303-973-0542. $10/day. Open 8 a.m.–6 p.m., Monday to Friday; 8 a.m.–noon, Saturday.

Parker
Club Pet, 10719 E. Parker Rd., 303-841-3227. $12–$16/day, depending on the size of dog. Open 8 a.m.–6 p.m., Monday to Saturday.

Wheat Ridge
American School of Dog Training, 4219 Xenon St., 303-940-9188. $7/day. Open 8 a.m.–7 p.m., Monday to Thursday; 8 a.m.–6 p.m., Friday; 9 a.m.–5 p.m., Saturday.

Pet Village, 11440 W. 44th Ave., 303-422-2055 (888-FOR-PETS). $10/day. The kennel is part of a national chain. Open 8 a.m.–6 p.m., Monday to Friday; 8 a.m.–5 p.m., Saturday; 3–6 p.m. for pickups only, Sunday.

PET PROVISIONS
Arvada
Dakotah Feed and Supply, Inc., 5870 Olde Wadsworth Blvd., 303-431-5285

PetsMart, 5285 Olde Wadsworth Blvd., 303-456-1114

Aurora
Petco, 16960 E. Quincy Ave., 303-699-5061; 13750 E. Mississippi Ave., 303-695-1223

PetsMart, I-225 (Abilene) and Mississippi Ave., 303-695-4532

Brighton
Brighton Feed and Farm Supply, 370 N. Main, 303-659-0721

Broomfield
Clarkston Feed and Supply, 11177 Dillon Rd., 303-469-1951

Front Range Pet & Supply, 11177 Dillon Rd., 303-464-0956

Willow Run Marketplace, 5700 W. 120th Ave., 303-466-5971

Castle Rock
Castle Rock Feed and Western Wear, 210 Perry, 303-688-3016

Rampart Feed and Pet, Inc., 1233 N. Park, 303-688-7360

Denver
Cashway Pet Supply, 1325 S. Cherokee, 303-777-1556

Cigi's Natural Pet Supplies, 2260 Kearney, 303-322-8000

Colorado Petfitters, 2075 S. University Blvd., 303-282-0020; 3390 W. 32nd Ave., 720-854-6120 (see "Worth a Paws")

Curve Feed and Supply, 6750 W. Mississippi Ave., 303-934-1249

Jersey John's Pet Supply, 5900 E. Colfax, 303-377-1943

Ooh la Poochez, 2625 E. 2nd Ave., Denver, 303-355-4444

PetsMart, 7440 Pecos Ave. (off Highway 36), 303-428-4231

Pooch! 3000 E. 3rd Ave., 303-333-4677 (see "Worth a Paws")

6th Ave. Pet Supplies, 810 E. 6th Ave., 303-733-6410

Englewood
Petco, 9425 E. County Line Rd., 303-708-0616

South Side Feed and Supplies, 4332 S. Broadway, 303-761-1075

Evergreen
Chow Down, 28608 Buffalo Park Rd., 303-674-8711

Glendale
PetsMart, Colorado Blvd. and Alameda Ave., 303-394-4406

Greenwood Village
Pet Outfitters, 5942 S. Holly St., 303-290-0430

Lakewood
Petco, 475 S. Wadsworth Blvd., 303-985-0050

PetsMart, W. 1st Ave. and Wadsworth Blvd., 303-232-0858

Pets-n-Stuff, 7777 W. Jewell Ave., 303-989-5380

Littleton
Animal Crackers Pets and Supplies, 10121 W. Bowles Ave., 303-948-2713; 6657 Ottawa Ave., 303-972-2213

Central Bark, 1621 W. Canal Cir., 303-730-1001

Mutt Hutt, 4181 E. County Line Rd., Suite A, 303-779-1046; 395 N. Littleton Blvd., 303-797-0304

Petco, 8100 W. Crestline Ave., 303-973-7057

PetsMart, northwest corner of C-470 and I-25 (Park Meadows location), 303-799-3575; South University Blvd. and County Line Rd., 303-220-0215; Wadsworth Blvd. and Quincy Ave., 303-971-0016

Pets-n-Stuff, 5150 E. Arapahoe Rd., 303-771-5109

Northglenn
Petco, 450 E. 120th Ave., 303-255-4528

Parker
Parker Feed and Garden Supplies, 11703 N. Highway 83, 303-841-3955

Westminster
Petco, 6735 W. 88th Ave., 303-432-9230

Pets Express, 9100 W. 100th Ave., 303-421-1225

PetsMart, 92nd Ave. and Sheridan Blvd. (Westlake Shopping Center), 303-426-4999

Wheat Ridge
PetsMart, 32nd Ave. and Youngfield St., 303-424-0123

Walkers Quality Cage and Feed Supply, 9900 W. 44th Ave., 303-424-0305

Wardle Feed and Pet Supply, W. 42nd Ave. and Wadsworth Blvd., 303-424-6455

CANINE ER
Denver
Alameda East Veterinary Hospital (AAHA certified), 9870 E. Alameda Ave.

(2 blocks west of Havana), 303-366-2639. Open 24 hours.

Greenwood Village
Tendercare Veterinary Medical Center (AAHA certified), 5930 S. Holly St., 303-689-9500. Open 24 hours.

Highlands Ranch
Highlands Ranch Animal Hospital Center (AAHA certified), 5640 County Line Pl., 303-740-9595. Open 24 hours.

Littleton
Littleton Animal ER, 221 W. County Line Rd., 720-283-9348. Open 6 p.m.–8 a.m. the following morning, Monday to Friday; 24 hours on weekends and holidays.

Thornton
Northside Emergency Pet Clinic, 123rd and Washington Sts., 303-252-7722. Open 6 p.m.–8 a.m. the following morning, Monday to Friday; from noon Saturday until 8 a.m. the following Monday; 24 hours on holidays.

Wheat Ridge
Wheat Ridge Animal Hospital (AAHA certified), 3695 Kipling St., 303-424-3325. Open 24 hours.

RESOURCES
DenFidos, 303-433-0034; www.denfidos.org

Denver Metro Convention and Visitors Bureau, 1668 Larimer St., Denver, 303-892-1112 (800-645-3446); www.denver.org

South Platte Ranger District, Pike National Forest, 19316 Goddard Ranch Ct. (past the N. Turkey Creek Rd. turnoff from Highway 285 South), Morrison, 303-275-5610

Boulder and Vicinity

THE BIG SCOOP

The communities of Boulder County, including Boulder, Louisville, Lafayette, Longmont, and the mountain town of Nederland, provide lots of great outdoor opportunities for dogs, even though development in the area increases at a rate faster than a wagging tail.

Boulder is in general a dog-friendly town, though environmental and shared-use concerns have recently made dogs on trails the subject of occasionally heated debate. A local group known as FIDOS (Friends Interested in Dogs and Open Space) has become an advocate of canine rights, working to keep the majority of trails accessible to dogs (it even sponsors monthly "poop pick-ups"). Given the occasionally lukewarm reception that some Boulder residents may give you and your dog, therefore, be sure to help your own Fido brush up on etiquette before hitting the trails.

Dogs are not allowed on Boulder's downtown, pedestrian-only Pearl Street Mall, which limits their sightseeing and shopping options somewhat. A leash law is enforced within the city limits of all towns in Boulder County, though not in unincorporated Boulder County. And though there's no direct ordinance against public tethering, the City of Boulder leash law can be interpreted as prohibiting it. So you're better off leaving your dog in the car with the windows wide open when running that quick errand than tying him up outside the store.

TAIL-RATED TRAILS

Boulder dogs are extremely lucky.

Current regulations allow dogs to be off leash on much of City of Boulder Open Space and Mountain Parks trails (but not on Boulder County Open Space), though they must always be within their owner's sight and under voice control. (Voice control means a dog must come immediately when called, no matter what distractions of other dogs, wildlife, or people may tempt him to do otherwise.) You should also have a leash handy at all times, and no more than two dogs per person can be off leash. Rangers will test your dog's obedience level on occasion (a pocketful of treats can be helpful in such situations—for your dog, not the ranger!). Plastic "pet pickup" baggies are considerately provided at many trailheads to encourage you to clean up after your dog's pit stops—use them!

The trail map put out by the Colorado Mountain Club (Boulder Group) includes many hiking options in addition to the

So you consider yourself your dog's owner? Not anymore in Boulder, where in the summer of 2000 a proposal was approved to change the designation "owner" to "guardian" in animal ordinances. The change was made in the hopes of enlightening people that dogs are not things that can be owned and then, perhaps, neglected or abused. To err on the safe side in typically forward-thinking Boulder, you could always just refer to yourself as Fido's "mom" or "dad."

ones suggested here. Look for it at the Chautauqua Park ranger's cottage as well as at local mountaineering stores. *Boulder Hiking Trails,* by Ruth and Glenn Cushman, is another good resource.

Boulder

Boulder Dog Parks. Thanks to a cooperative effort between dog owners and the Parks and Recreation Department, Boulder is now home to three off-leash dog parks, all of which have proven to be immensely popular. So popular, in fact, that additional parks have been proposed for other areas in Boulder. The parks are usually busiest after work and on weekends, and they're great places for owners to socialize. The rules for each park state that dogs must be vaccinated and have a current license, a guardian (owner) must be present at all times, and you must clean up after your dog (poop pickup bags and trash cans are on hand) and have a leash at the ready for each dog, if needed.

The **Valmont Dog Park,** on the north side of Valmont Rd. between Foothills Pkwy. and 55th St., is on about 3.5 acres adjacent to a former chicken farm. Parking is available directly off Valmont. Although dogs may rue the fact that the farm no longer generates the pungent odoriferousness that used to permeate the neighborhood on warm summer days, their humans will appreciate its absence. The park is currently fenced on three sides, with one of the old farm buildings forming the fourth barrier. There's also a smaller fenced area within which the Humane Society holds dog agility classes. If you have a smaller pooch who doesn't like to run with the big dogs, he may be more comfortable staying in this area. A permanent agility course—including tunnels, stairs, and other fun obstacles—for all visiting dogs is slated to be in place by summer 2001. There's no water available at the park.

The 1.5-acre **East Boulder Dog Park** is located on the west side of the East Boulder Community Center (north on 55th St. off S. Boulder Rd.), between the lake and the playing fields. When Clover and I visited one fall evening, dogs of all shapes and sizes were frolicking together. A couple of picnic tables provide a place for owners to gather. Best of all, part of the lake and a small swimming beach are within the park, allowing your dog to try out a new stroke or play water polo with the other canines.

The **Howard Heuston Dog Park,** the first off-leash dog area to be established in the city, consists of two acres within the larger community park (take 34th St. south from the Diagonal Hwy. for several blocks to its end). The dog park is outlined with markers rather than a fence, so you'll want to make sure that Fido's up for responding to voice commands before bringing him here. No water is available.

Marshall Mesa. 2.1 miles round-trip. Take Highway 93 (S. Broadway) south out of Boulder to the intersection with Highway 170 (Eldorado Springs Dr.) and the turnoff for Eldorado Springs. Turn left; the trailhead is 0.9 mile ahead on the right. *Dogs can be off leash.*

Although less than a mile from a major thoroughfare, the trails on Marshall Mesa convey the flavor of Boulder County's less-developed past, allowing you and your dog to experience some vestiges of a rural landscape among the ponderosa pines. In fact, cows sometimes roam on the mesa; if your pooch is prone to chase them, it's wise to keep him leashed. This was Clover's favorite evening hike when we lived in Boulder, as the views west to the foothills (and Longs Peak) provide good sunset watching.

Begin on the **Community Ditch Trail,** which heads left shortly after the trailhead. After a short climb this wide gravel service road parallels an irrigation ditch,

Abby snags a stick in Boulder Creek.
(photo by Chris Doelling)

And you'll enjoy the panoramic vistas of Boulder and the eastern plains offered at a couple of vantage points as well as the sense of being miles away from population density when you're really just a few minutes from downtown.

Clover's favorite route—best for the aerobically fit dog and owner—involves climbing on the **Mount Sanitas Trail**, which branches off to the left after the bridge. You'll reach the summit after 1.2 miles of steady climbing (a gain of 1,280 feet). Descend 0.8 mile by the steep **East Ridge Trail** (shoes with good tread or hiking boots come in handy) and walk along the ridge past the trophy homes until you reach the top of the **Sanitas Valley Trail**. This wide gravel path descends gradually for 1.1 miles back to your launching point. (If you're into practicing your rock-climbing moves, there are some good bouldering sites along the hike up Sanitas—just look for the signs and chalk marks.)

A less strenuous alternative would be to forgo the vertical and hike along the **Valley Trail**, which affords views of rolling green hills capped by the famous Flatirons. Or your dog may prefer to hike up the Valley Trail and return on the 1-mile **Dakota Ridge Trail**, which begins to the right of the Valley Trail's "summit" and eventually rejoins this trail about three-quarters of the way down.

usually filled during the spring and summer, where your dog can have lots of fun frolicking in the water. After 1.3 miles the trail meets up with the **Marshall Mesa Trail** to the right, on which wet dogs get a little under a mile to dry off before arriving back at the trailhead (and the car). As an added bonus for the literate canine, signs along the loop describe the history and geology of the mesa.

Mount Sanitas. Either 3.1 or 2.2 miles round-trip. Drive on Mapleton Ave. west from Broadway in downtown Boulder; after the Mapleton Center for Rehabilitation on the corner of 4th St., you'll see several parking turnouts on the right that provide access to the trailhead. Recommended starting point is the picnic shelter right before the small bridge. *Dogs can be off leash.*

The Sanitas trails are "doggie central" in Boulder (some would say too much so). Your dog will love you for bringing him here if he's the social type, as there are always plenty of opportunities to do the "doggie handshake" (i.e., butt sniffing).

A small brook by the picnic shelter provides a cooling rest for your dog after hiking and socializing. A "swimming hole" about halfway up the Sanitas Valley Trail on the left is usually full of water in the summer, and a trickling rivulet on the trail's right provides the opportunity for some slurps. As there are no water sources on the Mount Sanitas Trail, you may want to bring extra water to share with your dog.

 Chautauqua Park. Drive west on Baseline Rd.; the park entrance is on the left after 9th St. *Dogs can be off leash except in the large lawn area that fronts the Chautauqua Auditorium and restaurant.*

This is perhaps Boulder's best-known spot for hiking and playing, with a stunning location at the base of the town's signature Flatirons. It's wise to avoid this area midday on warm, sunny weekends (summer or winter), when everyone and their dog seem to come here (pardon the play on words). Several trails originate from here, including the popular **Mesa Trail**, which runs almost 7 miles south to Eldorado Springs. For great views of Boulder, hike to Saddle Rock or Royal Arch (both are slightly more than 2 miles round-trip and involve some climbing).

Doudy Draw (from the Flatirons Vista trailhead). About 5 miles round-trip. Take Highway 93 (S. Broadway) south from Boulder. About 2 miles south of the stoplight at the Eldorado Springs turnoff, you'll see a fenced-in parking area on the right. The trailhead is here. *Dogs can be off leash* (though from August 15 to October 15 there is a leash requirement on about a mile of trail that leads into the Community Ditch Trail).

This is a popular trail with horses as well as hikers. If your dog has an aversion to equine creatures, note the number of horse trailers in the parking lot before setting out. Begin by hiking west on a service road, taking in, as the trailhead name implies, a beautiful vista of the Flatirons, the vertical rock slabs that front the foothills. After the second livestock gate, the trail narrows, winding along a ridge through fragrant ponderosa pine. It then follows a couple of switchbacks down to a small gully, where you'll come to a dog rest stop (i.e., stream). After crossing, follow the trail sign to the right (note that dogs are prohibited on the other side of the interior fence you'll pass). A good turnaround point for your hike is a bridge you'll come to just before

the Community Ditch Trail, which allows your dog another respite near water. Hiking farther would bring you to a final paved portion of the trail that ends at a trailhead on Eldorado Springs Dr. (Highway 170), a total of 3.4 miles from the Flatirons Vista trailhead.

 Boulder Creek Path. Runs 9 miles from the mouth of Boulder Canyon to east of 55th St. *Dogs must be leashed.*

If possible, avoid bringing your dog on the downtown section of this often crowded paved path—in the wink of an eye he could easily become tangled up with the multitude of bicyclists, in-line skaters, runners, and amblers who use this popular route. The stretch of path that runs east of Foothills Highway and initially parallels Pearl St., however, offers more breathing space, especially on weekdays. See if your clever canine spots the "paw prints" embedded in the concrete just east of the office park on Pearl—they lead to a small, refreshing pool where dogs can partake of the waters while you relax on a nearby bench.

Despite the many places in and around Boulder where you can hike with your dog, certain areas lie at the other end of the spectrum—that is, dogs are banned. Fido is not welcome on the following trails on City of Boulder and Boulder County Open Space as well as on Mountain Parks land:

- a portion of the **Lindsey property**, via County Rd. 67 off Eldorado Springs Dr. You must keep your dog on the road and trail in this hiking area— when the trail forks, dogs are permitted on the right branch; there's a no-dog policy on the left branch;

- the **Eldorado Mountain** area south of the quarry road;

- the **Tall Grass Prairie Natural Area** near the Big Bluestem Trail (part of the Shanahan Ridge trail network);

- the 1.5-mile section of the **South Boulder Creek Trail** that runs south of South Boulder Rd. (also known as the Van Vlete property);

- the **White Rocks section of the East Boulder Trail,** bounded to the south by Valmont Rd. and to the north by a trail through the Gunbarrel Farm open space area;

- the **Prairie Dog Habitat Conservation Area** east of the Greenbelt Plateau Trail;

- the **Hogback Trail,** which branches off the Foothills Trail north of Wonderland Lake, and all the land north and west of the **Foothills Trail** on the west side of Highway 36 (several "social trails" criss-cross this area);

- the **Prairie Dog Habitat Conservation Area** north of the Boulder Valley Ranch Trail;

The outskirts of Boulder have some canine-friendly biking trails. (photo by Arlan Flax)

- various city open space properties that have no established trails—check fence lines for "no dogs" postings;

- the relatively new **Hall Ranch** area north of Boulder, off Highway 36—in May 2000, the county commissioners voted to extend the ban that was already in place for at least five more years, though they may consider a "time-share" plan that would allow on-leash dogs limited trail access on certain days;

- the new **Heil Ranch** area, near the mouth of Lefthand Canyon;

- the **McClintock Trail,** a self-guided nature walk between the Enchanted Mesa and Mesa Trails in Chautauqua Park.

 South shore of Boulder Reservoir. During the summer, dogs are prohibited from this area.

Eldorado Springs

 Eldorado Canyon State Park. From Highway 93 just south of Boulder, turn right on Highway 170 at the Eldorado Springs turnoff. The park is about 3 miles ahead. *Dogs must be leashed.*

When your dog has had his fill of watching climbers attempt the numerous technical routes for which "Eldo" is renowned, he'll probably be interested in doing a bit of hiking. At 2.8 miles round-trip, the **Rattlesnake Gulch Trail** begins off the one road through the park. It climbs gradually but steadily to a flat overlook, former site of the Crags Hotel, which burned in 1912. The only remains of this once-luxurious retreat are a couple of fireplaces, sections of the foundation, and scattered pieces of charred dinnerware—as well as a spectacular view of the canyon and the plains beyond on one side and the rugged

Indian Peaks on the other. The trail continues to an upper loop near the railroad tracks (you might spot an Amtrak train traveling high above during your hike), but the overlook makes a good turnaround point. The **Eldorado Canyon Trail** takes off from the end of the park road, climbing, at times steeply, through ponderosa pine and intersecting after a couple of miles with the **Walker Ranch Loop Trail**, a popular mountain-biking area on Boulder County Open Space. Taking a left at the intersection puts you on the **Crescent Meadows Trail,** which leads to another parcel of state park land (known as Crescent Meadows). The trail eventually ends at the Gross Dam Rd.; the round-trip distance from the trailhead is 11 miles.

Lafayette

Waneka Lake. A 1.2-mile loop. From South Boulder Rd. in Lafayette, head west and turn right (north) onto Centaur Village Rd. Turn left onto Caria at the stop sign, then drive up the hill and turn right into Waneka Park; park in the lot. Alternatively, you can access a second parking lot on the east side of the lake: turn right onto Caria at the stop sign, then left at the intersection with Emma St. *Dogs must be leashed.*

A gravel foot and bike path extends along the periphery of this small reservoir, which was dug out by the pioneering Waneka family on the site of a spring more than 100 years ago. The trail is best for sociable dogs and people who won't mind sharing the path with bicycles and families. About half is shaded by trees and brush; the rest is open to sunshine, occasional blustery winds, and a knockout view of the Front Range. The surrounding park has a playground and picnic gazebos in addition to a small boathouse and pier with bathrooms and canoe and paddle-boat rentals (the boathouse is open from Memorial Day through Labor Day).

Longmont

Longmont Dog Park. The 2.5-acre fenced park, situated at 21st St. and Francis, opened in the summer of 2000 and is the first of several proposed off-leash dog areas in Longmont. The park is "open" from dawn to dusk; dogs must be vaccinated, obey voice control commands, and be supervised by an adult. You'll need to pick up after Fido—bags and trash cans are available. Several benches around the park allow owners to take a breather while their dogs run themselves silly. Bring water, as there's no source handy. The one caveat is parking: You'll have to leave your car at either Garden Acres Park or Carr Park, both about a block and a half away on 21st St. (the neighbors will raise a howl if you park on the residential streets near the dog run). And do keep your dog on leash while walking to and from the off-leash venue.

Louisville

Davidson Mesa Dog Run Area. This Louisville open space area on the west side of McCaslin Blvd., a half mile south of South Boulder Rd., has a fenced-in area of about four acres where dogs can play off leash, in addition to surrounding trails that you and your leashed dog can enjoy. You may want to bring water for your dog, since none is on site; also, try to avoid the heat of the day in summer, as the yucca-filled terrain lacks shade. It can also be notoriously windy, but the sunset views are spectacular. No specific rules regarding dogs apply to the area. Do note, however, that canines are not allowed at Harper Lake, across the road. Parking is available.

Coal Creek Trail. 7 miles one way. There are numerous access points for this trail. The western terminus is on Dillon Rd. in Louisville at the Coal Creek golf course; the eastern end is at 120th St., a few blocks south of South Boulder Rd., in Lafayette. One easily accessible place to reach the trail is at the Aquarius trailhead in Louisville, on Highway 82 (a.k.a. 96th St.), where parking is available. *Dogs must be leashed.*

This primarily flat pedestrian and bike trail follows Coal Creek for most of its length, winding through neighborhoods in Louisville and Lafayette. With its semi-rural character in parts, you and your dog may even forget you are still in town. There's water galore if Rover wants to splash in the creek. Parts of the trail have been paved for bicycles, though a dirt trail leading to the river often parallels the paved one.

 Rock Creek Farm. 5 miles of trails. Take Dillon Rd. east from McCaslin Blvd. Look for a trailhead and parking area on the right, shortly after the intersection with 104th St. An alternate entrance on 104th St. brings you directly to Stearns Lake: From Dillon Rd., go south on 104th St. The trailhead is 0.7 mile ahead on the left. *Dogs must be leashed.*

Don't confuse this Boulder County Open Space area with the monolithic Rock Creek subdivision visible from Highway 36. In fact, with the wide openness of this area, you and your dog might think you're in Nebraska, except for the stunning view of Longs Peak to the west. This would be a great place for a sunset walk. The most scenic hiking section begins at the Dillon Rd. trailhead; a wide, flat trail leads through fields, then goes almost all the way around Stearns Lake (keep an eye out for the wildlife area closure signs). From Stearns Lake, you can also continue hiking south from the dam; after going through a horse pasture, stay to the right, where a dirt service road will eventually bring you out on an unpaved section of 104th St. that's closed to traffic.

 Harper Lake. Because this small lake is home to a wildlife sanctuary as well as being part of the city's water supply, canines are verboten.

Nederland

Lost Lake. 4 miles round-trip. From Nederland, take Highway 72 east. Make a right on County Rd. 130 (toward Eldora Mountain Ski Resort). Stay on this road, going past the ski area turnoff and through the small hamlet of Eldora, after which the road turns to dirt. At the signed fork, stay left, to Hessie. In the spring, when the road past this point becomes streamlike, you may want to park near the fork. But if your vehicle has good clearance, the most available parking is at Hessie townsite, less than a quarter of a mile farther along. The trailhead is just up the road from here, at the North Fork of Boulder Creek. *Dogs can be off leash on this particular trail because it doesn't enter the Indian Peaks Wilderness Area.* If you continue hiking on one of the other trails accessed from here, be ready to leash your dog as soon as you cross the wilderness boundary.

This area is extremely popular on weekends year-round; midweek would be the best time to explore it. The first part of this trail follows an old mining road up a gradual ascent. Midsummer, you'll be greeted by a colorful profusion of wildflowers on the slopes alongside the trail. After about half a mile, cross a bridge over the South Fork of Boulder Creek and hike up parallel to it. A sign for Lost Lake soon indicates a turnoff to the left. From there, it's a short way to the lake itself, where your dog can frolic in the water while you pick out the mining ruins on the hillside across the lake.

CYCLING FOR CANINES

Of the handful of trails near Boulder

where you can bike, only a few allow free-running dogs: the **Community Ditch and Greenbelt Plateau Trails on Marshall Mesa** (see "Tail-Rated Trails"); the part of the **Community Ditch Trail** that also runs for 1.8 miles on the west side of Highway 93 (access this portion either by parking alongside Highway 93 or from the Doudy Draw trailhead off Eldorado Springs Dr. in order to avoid a dangerous crossing of the road with bike and dog in tow); the **Boulder Valley Ranch and Foothills Trails** off Highway 36 just north of Boulder (dogs are required to be leashed on the section of the Foothills Trail south of Lee Hill Rd., however); and the Teller Farm section of the **East Boulder Trail,** which runs by two lakes between Valmont Dr. and Arapahoe Ave. east of Boulder. Note that the popular Walker Ranch and Betasso Preserve loop trails both have a leash law.

You'll have more biking options outside of Nederland. The "Mountain Bike Map of Boulder County," published by Latitude 40° and available at area bike and mountaineering shops, is a good resource. Try the **Sourdough Trail,** a great moderate ride that runs about 7 miles (one way) from Rainbow Lakes Rd. to Brainard Lake Dr.; access it by driving 7 miles north of Nederland on Highway 72 and turning left at the University of Colorado Mountain Research sign. The **Switzerland Trail** follows a former narrow-gauge railroad track and has great views. There are several access points; one is reached via Sugarloaf Mountain Rd. out of Boulder Canyon, and another is about 3.5 miles past the town of Gold Hill, via Mapleton Ave./Sunshine Canyon Rd. out of Boulder. The trail runs about 4 miles down to Fourmile Creek from both of these starts. The **Bunce School Rd.** (now a jeep road) goes for about 6 miles from just past Peaceful Valley Campground, off Highway 72 north, to Highway 7; you'll have to do an out-and-back to avoid riding on the highway. Water is available near or along all of these trails.

POWDERHOUNDS

You and your dog will need to venture into the mountains around Nederland to find reliable snow for skiing or snowshoeing. Note, however, that certain trails are completely closed to dogs from December 1 through April 30: the Little Raven, Waldrop, and CMC Trails at the popular Brainard Lake area; the Jenny Creek and Guinn Mountain Trails by the Eldora Nordic Center; and the Buchanan Pass Trail in the northern Indian Peaks Wilderness area.

Some good routes to consider include the **Sourdough Trail** (see "Cycling for Canines"); the **Coney Flats Trail,** a jeep road that begins at Beaver Reservoir, off Highway 72 north of Ward; and the **Mammoth Gulch Rd.,** just past Tolland on the Rollins Pass Rd. outside Rollinsville. For more detailed descriptions of these routes as well as other options, refer to *Skiing Colorado's Backcountry,* by Brian Litz and Kurt Lankford, or *Snowshoeing Colorado,* by Claire Walter.

CREATURE COMFORTS

Unless otherwise stated, dogs should not be left unattended in the room or cabin.

Boulder

$$ Foot of the Mountain Motel, 200 Arapahoe Ave., 303-442-5688. The small, simply furnished wood-paneled rooms are contained in rustic-looking cabins. There's a $5 fee per night for a dog. A big plus is the motel's location across the street from Boulder Creek and Eben G. Fine Park; though dogs must be leashed, the park and adjacent Creek Path provide great sniffing opportunities. You may leave your dog unattended in the room as long as you notify the front office.

$$ Lazy L Motel, 1000 28th St., 303-442-7525. Not for the discriminating dog. There's a $10 nightly pet fee.

$$ Super 8 Motel, 970 28th St., 303-443-7800 (800-525-2149). Dogs are allowed in smoking rooms only. A $50 deposit is required as well as $5 extra per dog, per night.

$$–$$$ Best Western Boulder Inn, 770 28th St., 303-449-3800 (800-233-8469). Dogs are allowed in smoking rooms only, and a $100 deposit is required. Don't confuse this motel with the other Best Western in Boulder, the Golden Buff, which doesn't allow pets.

$$–$$$ Boulder Mountain Lodge, 91 Four Mile Canyon Rd., 303-444-0882 (800-458-0882; www.bouldermountain lodge.com). This motel complex, located streamside several miles from town, has a casual, summer-camp feel. In fact, campsites are available in addition to rooms. There's a $50 deposit for a dog, $25 if you're camping. Dogs can be left in rooms, if necessary, with approval of the front office, but housekeeping will not come in. Keep your dog leashed when outside.

$$–$$$ The Broker Inn, 30th St. and Baseline, 303-444-3330 (800-338-5407; www.boulderbrokerinn.com). Dogs can stay in any of the first-floor rooms at this comfortably appointed hotel, and they can be left unattended in the room—which will allow you ample time to sample one of the restaurant's decadent lunch or brunch buffets.

$$–$$$ Days Inn, 5397 S. Boulder Rd. (at Foothills Pkwy.), 303-499-4422 (800-329-7466 [national number]). Dogs are allowed in smoking rooms only.

$$–$$$ Ramada Inn, 800 28th St., 303-443-3322 (800-542-0304). Dogs are allowed in outside-facing rooms only but can be left unattended if housekeeping is notified. There's a $10 per night pet fee.

$$–$$$$ Colorado Chautauqua Association, 900 Baseline Rd., 303-442-3282 (www.chautauqua.com). Let your dog experience a bit of Boulder's intellectual past with a stay in one of these character-filled cottages in a stunning location at the base of the Flatirons. The adajcent Chautauqua Auditorium, built in 1898, was for many years the hub of summer retreats for associates of the University of Texas, who came to attend lectures and concerts. Most of the cottages were constructed in the early 1900s as summer homes; today some are privately owned while the others are rented out both nightly and long-term by the Chautauqua Association. Though most have been winterized, they definitely retain that "summer cabin at the lake" feel. Rentals range from studio/efficiencies to three bedrooms, and all have kitchens and necessary supplies. You can leave your dog unattended for a short time as long as he remains relatively quiet, perhaps while you enjoy a meal at the nearby dining hall. The catch is that there's a $100 one-time fee for a dog, but when Rover catches wind of the miles of trails starting right outside the door in Chautauqua Park, where he can hike off leash, he may give you that guilty "Aren't I worth it?" look. Among other events, the auditorium hosts concerts by local and national acts during the summer, and you can picnic on the lawn outside for free with your dog and still catch the music.

$$–$$$$ Homewood Suites, 4950 Baseline Rd. (behind the Meadows Shopping Center), 303-499-9922 (800-225-5466 [national number]). There's a $50 one-time fee for dogs to stay in the apartment-style suites. You can leave your dog unattended as long as housekeeping is notified.

$$$–$$$$ Pearl Street Inn, 1820 Pearl St., 303-444-5584 (888-810-1302; www.pearlstreetinn.com). One of the

nicest places in Boulder to which you can bring your dog is this Victorian bed and breakfast, voted the best B&B in Boulder in 2000 by the local newspaper. Three of the inn's eight Victorian-style rooms are dog-friendly, and all have a private bath, fireplace, and antique furnishings. There's a limit of one dog per room, with a $10 per-night fee. The dog-designated rooms all open onto the inn's gated courtyard, where on warm days you can enjoy a full breakfast, afternoon snack, or complimentary evening wine with your furry traveling friend.

$$$–$$$$ Residence Inn by Marriott, 3030 Center Green Dr., 303-449-5545 (800-331-3131 [national number]). There's a $50 one-time fee for dogs who stay up to ten nights at this all-suite hotel; it's $5 per night thereafter. You can leave your dog unattended in the room.

Longmont

$–$$ Travelodge, 3815 Highway 119, 303-776-8700 (800-578-7878 [national number]). The motel has designated pet rooms on the ground floor (both smoking and nonsmoking available) and charges $10 extra per night, per dog. You can leave your dog unattended in the room as long as you let the front desk know; housekeeping won't come in during that time.

$–$$ Twin Peaks Super 8, 2446 N. Main, 303-772-8106 (800-800-8000 [national number]). Dogs can stay in upstairs rooms only.

$$ Del Camino Super 8, 10805 Turner Ave. (intersection of Highways 25 and 119), 303-772-0888 (800-800-8000 [national number]).

$$ Ellen's Bed and Breakfast, 700 Kimbark St., 303-776-1676. Your dog may well appreciate this alternative to Longmont's chain motels. Set in a 1910 Victorian house, Ellen's offers two rooms, one with a queen-size bed and private bath, the other with bunk beds and a shared bath. An outdoor hot tub is available. You are able to leave your dog unattended inside the room at the discretion of the owners, though Fido may prefer to stay in the B&B's fenced yard. Two schnauzers serve as host dogs.

$$–$$$$ Raintree Plaza, 1900 Ken Pratt Blvd., 303-776-2000 (800-843-8240). The hotel has both standard rooms and suites with living room, kitchenette, fireplace, and separate bedroom. Dogs are permitted in either with a $50 deposit and your signature on the pet release form. You can leave your dog unattended in the room if you notify the front desk staff, so they can alert housekeeping.

Louisville

$$–$$$ Comfort Inn, 1196 Dyer Rd., 303-604-0181 (800-228-5150 [national number]). Dogs are allowed only in smoking rooms with a $100 deposit.

$$–$$$ La Quinta Inn and Suites, 902 Dillon Rd., 303-664-0100 (800-687-6667 [national number]). Dogs under 40 pounds are permitted.

Nederland

$ American Youth Hostel, 8 W. Boulder, 303-258-7788. If you're young, not picky, and are on a low budget, go for it. Otherwise, by-pass this bare-bones set-up. Dogs can be left unattended in the rooms. (By the way, you don't have to be a member of a hostel association to stay here.)

$$ Arapaho Ranch, 1250 Eldora Rd., 303-258-3405 (www.coloradodirectory.com/arapahoranch). This guest ranch near the Indian Peaks Wilderness area offers ten rustic cabins, all fully equipped, ranging in size from two to four bedrooms. Before the first of June and after Labor Day, the cabins are available for

nightly rentals, with a $5 fee per night for a dog. Otherwise, stays at the ranch are on a weekly basis, with a $25 one-time fee for your dog. Families will find a variety of recreational opportunities close at hand (though horseback riding is no longer offered), and dogs will appreciate Middle Boulder Creek, which runs through the property. Open mid-May to October 1.

$$ Inn at Nederland, 686 Highway 119, 303-258-3585 (800-422-4629). Formerly the Nederhaus Motel.

Campgrounds

National forest campgrounds: **Kelly-Dahl Campground,** 3 miles south of Nederland off Highway 119 (46 sites); **Rainbow Lakes Campground,** off Highway 72, 7 miles north of Nederland (16 sites); **Pawnee Campground,** at Brainard Lake Recreation Area, 14 miles north of Nederland off Highway 72 (55 sites).

Private campgrounds: **Boulder Mountain Lodge** (see "Creature Comforts").

WORTH A PAWS

Colorado Canines, 1738 Pearl St., Boulder, 303-449-5069 (www.colorado canines.com). You don't have to be from Colorado, or even be a canine, to find something at this fun boutique for cats and dogs. Major, the resident German shepherd, will help your dog sniff among the selection of all-natural treats and dog food, gear for the active outdoor dog, and toys and bowls. You, in the meantime, can browse among dog- and cat-related "people items." And if your dog's really lucky, he'll be at the store when there's a canine massage demonstration taking place. Closed Sunday.

P.C.'s Pantry for Dogs and Cats, 9th St. at Walnut, Boulder, 303-245-9909. Your dog's nose will start to quiver as soon as he enters this canine (and feline) bakery and smells some of the treats that are being baked. And then he'll be salivating in front of the display case as he tries to decide among the various-shaped biscuits flavored with ingredients such as yam, pumpkin, cheese, carob, peanut butter, and liver. Take-out deli items include lamb quiche, liver or turkey loaf, chicken, and goulash (and, yes, those are also for dogs, not people). A small selection of bowls, leashes, and gift items is also on hand. P.C., in case you're wondering, is the CEO (Cat Executive Officer).

Blue Hills Dog and Cat Shoppe, 2255 Main St. (in the Horizon Park Shopping Center), Longmont, 303-651-2955. Blue Hills is sort of like a Whole Foods Market for dogs, with a wide selection of natural foods and health-care items, an on-site "cafe," and a self-service dog wash. At Bubba and Ebonee's Cafe in the back of the store, dogs can choose from an array of organic items, such as biscuits made from peanut butter and applesauce or ones out of rice spelt and amaranth, flavored with mint or ginger, for canines who may be allergic to wheat. The eat-in Saturday buffet and the take-home box lunch include such delicacies as potato buffalo pie, liver brownies, salmon wrap, and doggie pizza (maybe your dog will share some with you if you don't feel like cooking that night!). The dog wash provides everything—a selection of shampoos and conditioners, grooming tools, towels, and dryers—for $10. Oh, and the cafe does sell home-baked cat treats, in case you have a jealous kitty waiting at home. Closed Sunday.

A Cause for Paws. Your dog (and his leash) can accompany you on this late-summer 4-mile walkathon along the Boulder Creek Path with lots of other dogs and their owners. Ideally you would register in advance, at the Humane Society of Boulder Valley, 2323 55th St., and collect pledges from fellow dog-lovers. However, if you're just in town for the weekend (the date of the walk changes but is always between mid-August and mid-September), you can register on the morning of the event. A pet fair, with various exhibitors, takes place before and after the walk. Call the Humane Society at 303-442-4030 for more details.

Dog Walk. This 3-mile pledge walk is held on the second weekend of May, to coincide with Be Kind to Animals week. The course follows the bike path along Rogers Grove in Longmont, and proceeds benefit the Longmont Humane Society. You'll need to collect a minimum of $20 in pledges (or you can register for $20 the morning of the event), and you'll receive a T-shirt and snacks for you and your dog. Call the Humane Society at 303-772-1232 for more information.

Canine Classic. The annual mid-April Spring Runoff at the Boulder Reservoir has morphed into a 10K and 5K race for people and their leashed dogs. Less fit canines may choose to walk the course. Prizes are awarded to the top three human finishers in a range of age groups, as well as the first three dogs overall in each race. All human and dog participants receive T-shirts and bandannas, respectively. All of the money raised through entry fees and pledges goes to the Boulder County Rape Crisis Team. Call 303-939-9661 for information.

Laund-Ur-Mutt, Table Mesa Shopping Center (near King Soopers), Boulder, 303-543-9592. Okay, this probably won't be as much fun for your dog as for you, but if he's starting to smell like a Deadhead-type who's been on the road too long, this self-service dog wash may be just the ticket. Washing bays rent for $9 for a half hour, which includes dog-friendly hoses, a scrubbing mitt, and use of a dryer. (Towels, at $1.25, and shampoo are extra. Or you can bring your own.)

Humane Society of Boulder Dog Washes. Annual summer dog washes have recently been held at Whole Foods Market (30th and Pearl Sts.) and the Lazy Dog Sports Grill (2880 Diagonal Highway). Proceeds benefit the Humane Society of Boulder Valley (303-442-4030).

Dog Wash. Consider this a "spa day" for your dog. The wash usually is held during May at the Lefthand Brewery, 1265 Boston Ave. in Longmont (it's at the actual brewery, not the restaurant). In addition to washers, groomers are on hand to coif drying fur and clip too-long nails, and massage therapists are available to give therapeutic treatments. Every dog gets a bandanna to top off the look. Proceeds benefit the Longmont Humane Society (303-772-1232).

DOGGIE DAYCARE
Boulder
Allpets Clinic, 5290 Manhattan Cir. (at Highway 36 and S. Boulder Rd.), 303-499-5335. $19.75/day. A vet will do a short health exam on your dog if he or she has not been to the clinic before. Open 24 hours. (Note that the Allpets Clinic in Lafayette no longer offers day boarding.)

Arapahoe Animal Hospital, 5585 Arapahoe Ave. (behind the Boulder Dinner Theatre), 303-442-7033. $15/day for puppies (under a year old); $18/day for adult dogs. Open 7:30 a.m.–6:30 p.m., Monday to Friday; 8 a.m.–3 p.m., Saturday.

Is your dog inspired by the beauty of the foothills to go on a long day hike or perhaps an overnight backpack outside of Nederland? Laund-Ur-Mutt (see "Worth a Paws") rents dog packs for $10 per day, with less expensive multiday rates.

Broadway Animal Medical, 1405 S. Broadway (1 mile south of Table Mesa Dr.), 303-499-5505. $9.50/day. Your dog will go outside and play with the other dogs every couple of hours. Open 7 a.m.–7:30 p.m., Monday to Friday; 7 a.m.–12 p.m., Saturday.

Dog City, 2907 55th St., 303-473-9963. $23/day. At this "interactive" daycare and boarding facility, dogs hang out and play with each other all day, both indoors and out. They also get two walks a day, which may include a visit to the nearby Valmont Dog Park. To top it off, there's a dog web cam so you can check up on your pampered pooch over the Internet. Open 7 a.m.–7 p.m., Monday to Friday; 7:30 a.m–noon and 2–7 p.m., Saturday and Sunday.

Gunbarrel Veterinary Clinic, 55th St. and Diagonal Highway, 303-530-2500. $15/day. If you don't have your dog's vaccination records along, the clinic can phone your vet or provide the vaccinations. Open 7:45 a.m.–5:45 p.m., Monday to Friday.

Erie
A Lov-in-Touch Pet Chalet and Spa, 7019 Weld County Rd. 5, 303-651-3999. $15/day. Dropoffs are from 7:30–9:30 a.m.; pickups from 4:30–6:30 p.m., Monday to Friday. The facility is located on 2 acres, where dogs can wear themselves out playing. A new addition for especially deserving pets is the "spa package": Drop your dog off for the day, and he'll be treated to a massage and grooming, then have the rest of the day to be admired and play.

Lafayette
Akasha's Doggy Daycare, 307 W. Oak, 303-666-0905. $15/day. Out-of-state dogs will need to present a health certificate in addition to the required proof of vaccination. You and your dog will be

asked to participate in an interview to make sure everyone's comfortable. Once in daycare, your dog will be let out of his kennel and allowed outside as much as possible; a wide selection of toys is available for his chewing and carrying pleasure. Open 6:30 a.m.–7 p.m., Monday to Friday; weekend boarding available by appointment only.

Nederland
Peak to Peak Animal Hospital, 75 E. 2nd St., 303-258-7004. $14/day. Open 8 a.m.–6 p.m., Monday, Wednesday, and Friday; 7 a.m.–6 p.m., Tuesday and Thursday; 8 a.m.–noon, Saturday.

PET PROVISIONS
Boulder
Animal Crackers Pets and Supplies, 2877 28th St., 303-402-0626

Aqua Imports, 2690 28th St., 303-444-6971

Colorado Canines, 1738 Pearl St., 303-449-5069 (see "Worth a Paws")

Exotic Aquatics, 1750 30th St., 303-442-5363

Humane Society of Boulder Valley Supply and Training Center, 5320 Arapahoe Ave., 303-442-5995

McGuckin Hardware, 2525 Arapahoe Ave. (in the Village Shopping Center), 303-443-1822. You and your leashed dog are welcome to browse among the cornucopia of pet items and just about anything else you can think of.

PetsMart, 2982 Iris (in the Albertson's shopping center), 303-939-9033

RAD Table Mesa Hardware, Table Mesa Shopping Center (next to World Gym), 303-499-7211

Whiskers, 1750 30th St. (Crossroads East Plaza), 303-442-3371

Lafayette
Bark Avenue, 101 E. Chester St., 303-664-9663. The shop bills itself as a "pet department store."

Lafayette Feed and Grain, 816 E. Baseline Rd., 303-665-5055

Longmont
Blue Hills Dog and Cat Shoppe, 2255 Main St. (in the Horizon Park Shopping Center), 303-651-2955 (see "Worth a Paws")

Diagonal Feed and Pet Supply, 1240 Ken Pratt Blvd., 303-776-9397

Rocky Mountain Feed and Pet, 208 S. Main, 303-651-6226

Louisville
Catfish Charlie's, 1140 Pine, 303-665-3322

Critters Corner, 1140 S. Boulder Rd., 303-665-8872

Nederland
Nederland Feed and Supply, 45 E. 2nd St., 303-258-7729

Superior
PetsMart, 402 Center Dr., Superior, 303-543-6060

CANINE ER
Boulder
Allpets Clinic (AAHA certified), 5290 Manhattan Cir. (at Highway 36 and S. Boulder Rd.), 303-499-5335. The clinic is staffed 24 hours, and walk-ins are welcome, though you should refrain from bringing in your pet for a routine checkup in the wee hours.

Boulder Emergency Pet Clinic, 1658 30th St. (in the Sunrise Shopping Center), 303-440-7722. Open 5:30 p.m.–8 a.m. the following morning, Monday through Friday; 24 hours on weekends and holidays.

North Boulder Companion Animal Hospital (AAHA certified), 2750 Glenwood, 303-443-9003. Open 7 a.m.–midnight daily.

Longmont
Animal Emergency Center, 230 S. Main, 303-678-8844. Open 6 p.m.–8 a.m. the following morning, Monday through Friday; 24 hours on weekends and holidays.

RESOURCES
Boulder Convention and Visitors Bureau, 2440 Pearl St., Boulder, 303-442-2911 (800-444-0447; www.bouldercolorado usa.com)

Boulder Ranger District, Arapaho and Roosevelt National Forests, 2140 Yarmouth Ave. (off Highway 36 on the north end of town) Boulder, 303-444-6600

FIDOS (Friends Interested in Dogs and Open Space), 303-447-FIDO (the Yap Line; www.fidos.org)

Nederland Visitor Center, 1st and Bridge St., Nederland, 303-258-3936

THREE

Central City, Clear Creek County, and Vicinity

THE BIG SCOOP

Traveling dogs will find it all here: scenic trails, 14,000-foot mountains, welcoming lodging, and mountain air—everything within a short drive of Denver. One thing your dog won't be able to do, however, is frequent the casinos in Black Hawk and Central City; to the best of our knowledge, paw-friendly slot machines have yet to be invented.

All the towns in this area have leash laws, as do Clear Creek and Gilpin Counties, though the county leash ordinance is not enforced on Forest Service trails that allow dogs that are under voice control.

TAIL-RATED TRAILS

The area surrounding Mount Evans, south of Idaho Springs, has the most concentrated selection of trails in the vicinity. Because of their proximity to Denver, many of these trails receive heavy use, especially on summer weekends, something to keep in mind if you're into more solitary hiking with your dog. And most of the trails are in the Mount Evans Wilderness Area or the Mount Evans Elk Management Area— where dogs must be kept leashed—for all or part of their length. A great resource for the Mount Evans trails is *Foothills to Mount Evans: West-of-Denver Trail Guide*, by Linda McComb Rathbun and Linda Wells Ringrose.

If you and your dog are staying near Idaho Springs, refer to the "West of Denver" section in Chapter 1, "Tail-Rated Trails," for more nearby options. And it's only a short drive to trails near Nederland (see Chapter 2) from the Central City area.

Herman Gulch. 5 miles round-trip. Take Exit 218 off I-70 (past Silver Plume). If you're coming from the east, turn right at the stop sign at the end of the exit ramp and double back on the dirt road that leads to the trailhead parking area; from the west, cross over the highway and turn right on the dirt road to the parking area. *Dogs can be off leash.* According to the Forest Service, the posted "dogs must be on leash" sign applies to the parking lot and trailhead area. *There's no regulation that dogs must be kept leashed on the trail. However, because this is a popular hike on summer weekends, you might want to keep Fido leashed if you visit during that time.*

This hike has become increasingly popular, especially with dogs and their owners, as the secret's out that a beautiful route hides behind the unmarked highway exit. The well-maintained trail first leads through a section of forest before popping out into a series of meadows, studded with colorful wildflowers in July and August. You'll then reenter the woods as you ascend the gulch, following closely along a stream. There are several nice areas along this stretch where you can sit on a downed log and enjoy a snack while Rover tests out the water. In the final half mile or so of trail, you'll hike above timberline, following a few steep switchbacks before reaching Herman Lake, nestled right at the base of the Continental Divide below the rocky slopes of 13,553-foot Pettingell Peak. Before heading back down valley, take a breather on one of the boulders along the shoreline and soak in the rugged surroundings; your dog will probably want to brave the frigid water for a quick dip. If he's lucky, he may even find a snowfield or two in which to play.

Silver Dollar Lake. 3 miles round-trip. From the Georgetown exit (228) off I-70, follow the signs to Guanella Pass at the western end of town. From the beginning of Guanella Pass Rd. (at the mileage signs), drive 8.6 miles, past the Guanella Pass Campground, to a T in the road and a sign for the Silver Dollar Lake Trail. Turn right and drive a mile to the parking area at the side of the road and the trailhead. *Dogs can be off leash.*

This short, scenic hike brings you and your dog to a lake, popular for fishing, near the base of the Continental Divide. The trail heads southwest from the parking area, winding through a stately forest of Douglas fir on a moderate ascent. Shortly after passing timberline, you'll reach the lake. To the southwest lies Square Top Mountain. After your dog enjoys splashing in the lake, you and he may want to do some exploring to the northwest to visit nearby Murray Lake, which is also above timberline, before hiking the return route.

Golden Gate Canyon State Park. The park has several access points, a couple of which are near Central City and Black Hawk. From Black Hawk, take Highway 119 north for about 5 miles to Highway 46; the park visitor center is 11 miles east on Highway 46. Or continue on Highway 119 about 3 miles past the Highway 46 turnoff, then turn right on Gap Rd., which leads into the park. For more details, see "Tail-Rated Trails" in Chapter 1.

Hells Hole. 7 miles round-trip. From Idaho Springs, drive southwest on Highway 103 for 5.5 miles. Make a

A new breed of mountain goat in the high country. (photo by Cindy Hirschfeld)

right onto West Chicago Creek Rd. (Forest Rd. 188) and drive for 3 miles. The trailhead is past the West Chicago Creek Campground at the end of the road. *Dogs can be off leash until the wilderness boundary, about a mile in.*

Despite the ominous name, this is a beautiful hike, especially during the autumn when the aspens change color. It is also one of the less-crowded hikes in the Mount Evans area. Because the very first part of the trail passes by some quasi-picnic areas popular with families, you might have to keep a close eye on Fido or leash him up so he doesn't make a nuisance of himself. The trail begins in forested terrain and follows West Chicago Creek, crossing various tributaries as well. After about a mile, you'll start to climb away from the creek, gradually at first, then more steeply as the trail switchbacks up amid a high wooded canopy of pine, fir, and aspen. Gray Wolf Mountain and Sugarloaf Peak come into view to the south and east, respectively. Eventually you'll break out of the trees into a spectacular high-alpine, marshy meadow bounded by a rocky cirque that includes the 13,602-foot Gray Wolf. The trail ends among the scree in a basin at the bottom of the cirque—the Hells Hole.

CYCLING FOR CANINES

Most of the biking routes in this area follow four-wheel-drive roads rather than singletrack trails. One recommended option is the **Old Squaw Pass Rd.**, which parallels Highway 103 east of Mount Evans for 3.25 miles. The trail has four access points from the south side of Highway 103: 4.5 miles east of Echo Lake, 5.8 miles east, 7.4 miles east, and 8.4 miles east.

The **Devil's Canyon jeep road** runs for 2.5 miles one way, ending on a ridge with views of the Mount Evans area. There are also some loop options in this area, on the small network of jeep roads. Drive on Highway 103 from Idaho Springs for 10 miles, then make a left just after the big curve beyond the Ponder Point Picnic Area onto Forest Rd. 246. The ride begins here. Bring extra water for Rover on Old Squaw Pass Rd. and Devil's Canyon.

The road up **Bard Creek** provides several miles of riding on an old mining roadbed that follows the path of the creek; access it via Bard Creek Dr. off U.S. Highway 40 through Empire.

For more specifics on rides, pick up the "Four-Wheel Driving" information sheet from the Clear Creek Ranger District (see "Resources") and the Trails Illustrated biking map for Idaho Springs/Clear Creek County.

POWDERHOUNDS

The Clear Creek County area has several fine trails for ski touring or snowshoeing with your dog.

The 4-mile round-trip **Butler Gulch Trail** is a personal favorite because it holds snow well and has fun telemarking terrain in the bowls at trail's end (rife with avalanche danger, however). It can

Major, a Colorado canine, basks on Grays Peak. (photo by Alex Heller)

get quite busy on weekends, so a mid-week tour, if possible, would be your dog's best bet. To reach the trailhead, take the Empire exit off I-70 and follow U.S. Highway 40 west to the sharp switchback at Henderson Mine (about 8 miles past Empire). The ski begins across from a small parking area, on a road. Watch out for snowmobilers on this first part; soon the Butler Gulch Trail splits off to the left and you'll leave motorized traffic behind.

The **Old Fall River Rd.** to Fall River Reservoir is a 6-mile round-trip easy ski on gentle terrain. From Exit 238 off I-70, turn north on Fall River Rd. Drive 6.5 miles to a right-hand switchback. The trail, which follows a jeep road, travels west-northwest from here.

The **Waldorf Rd.**, which follows a very gradual, wide ascent off the Guanella Pass Rd. outside of Georgetown, also makes a good dog ski. With Sidney Mine as the turnaround point, it's a 7-mile round-trip. To access the trail, head up the Guanella Pass Rd. for 2.5 miles to a pair of switchbacks; at the second switchback, you'll see a small parking area on the right. The Waldorf Rd. begins near the parking area.

For more information on these and other routes, refer to *Skiing Colorado's Backcountry,* by Brian Litz and Kurt Lankford, and *Snowshoeing Colorado,* by Claire Walter.

CREATURE COMFORTS
Unless otherwise stated, dogs should not be left unattended in the room or cabin.

Black Hawk
$–$$ Chase Mansion, 201 Chase Gulch, 303-582-0112. "I like pets," says the owner of this "B" (bed without the breakfast), housed in a 120-year-old Victorian. She allows dogs ("no barkers or biters") in four of the inn's six rooms, which are furnished in a "casual Victorian" style. You can leave your dog unattended in the room while you gamble away his dog-food allowance. Or the owner is happy to dog sit, if your pooch would prefer some company.

$$ The Shamrock Inn, 351 Gregory St., 303-582-5513. This B&B welcomes "responsible pets with responsible owners" in any of its three rooms. The house was built in 1870, and the rooms are furnished "grandma style," as the owner calls it. You can leave your dog unattended in the room upon consultation with the owner.

Central City
$$ Chateau L'Acadienne, 325 Spring, 303-582-5209 (800-834-5209; www.jamesvco.cs.com). The Chateau, which bills itself as a Cajun B&B, accepts dogs in any of its three rooms. The rooms are individually decorated, one with Victorian furnishings, one in a Mardi Gras theme, and one in a mountain scenery mode. You can leave your dog unattended in the room only if you have a travel kennel in which to keep him.

Georgetown
$ Alpine Inn, 1414 Argentine St., 303-569-2931. With a Swiss-chalet style and eight rooms, the motel welcomes people-friendly canines. Dogs can be left unattended in the room as long as they're quiet. There's a small yard around the inn where a leashed dog can stretch his legs.

$–$$ Georgetown Motor Inn, 1100 Rose, 303-569-3201 (800-884-3201). The motel allows dogs for a $10 one-time fee if you stay in a nonsmoking room; $5 in a smoking room.

Idaho Springs
$ 6 & 40 Motel, 2920 Colorado Blvd., 303-567-2691. There's a limit of one dog per room and a $5 nightly fee. The motel is situated along Clear Creek, where you can walk your dog on leash along the banks.

$ Peoriana Motel, 2901 Colorado Blvd., 303-567-2021

$–$$ H & H Motor Lodge, 2445 Colorado Blvd., 303-567-2838 (800-445-2893). Dogs are allowed for $5 extra per night. Clear Creek runs behind the lodge, and you can walk your dog here on leash.

$$$ St. Mary's Glacier Bed and Breakfast, 336 Crest Dr., 303-567-4084 (www.coloradovacation.com/bed/stmary/index.html). If your dog is into skiing virtually year-round, he'll want to pay a visit here, as St. Mary's Glacier is a popular backcountry ski spot in spring and early summer. The B&B, in a newer log house, is located about a mile above the glacier, northwest of Idaho Springs. A new owner changed the previous pet policy and now welcomes dogs, with a $50 deposit and a $10 nightly fee. The seven rooms all have private bath and country decor.

Campgrounds

Golden Gate State Park. The easiest way to access the campgrounds is via Gap Rd., a right turn off Highway 119, about 8 miles north of Black Hawk. The Reverend's Ridge Campground (106 sites) and Aspen Meadow Campground (35 sites) are both in the northwest part of the park. There are also four back-country shelters and twenty-three back-country tent sites throughout the park.

National forest campgrounds: **Columbine Campground**, 2.1 miles northwest of Central City on County Rd. 279 (47 sites); **Cold Springs Campground**, 4 miles north of Black Hawk on Highway 119 (38 sites); **West Chicago Creek Campground**, Forest Rd. 188, off Highway 103, south of Idaho Springs (16 sites); **Guanella Pass Campground**, about 8 miles out of Georgetown on Guanella Pass Rd. (18 sites).

WORTH A PAWS

Mount Evans Rd. For the quickest way to take your dog to the top of a fourteener (that's a 14,000-foot mountain, or, in this case, 14,264 feet), drive him up the paved road to the top of Mount Evans. Take Highway 103 south of Idaho Springs to Echo Lake; the road to the summit begins here. Fourteen miles later, your dog will feel like he's standing on top of the world. And he'll probably get excited at seeing the mountain goats that usually hang around roadside—viewing them from behind a car window, of course. The road is open to the summit from Memorial Day to the day after Labor Day; a fee per car is collected just beyond Echo Lake.

Argo Gold Mill. Does your dog harbor a secret desire to don a helmet, grab a pickax, and burrow into a hillside? If so, he might be interested in accompanying you on a forty-five-minute tour of this former gold mill, which dates from 1913 and once supplied much of the gold for the Denver Mint. The mill is now on the National Register of Historic Places. The tour includes a van ride up to the Double Eagle Gold Mine, which you'll be able to walk 300 feet into. Look for the big red building on the hillside in Idaho Springs—it's hard to miss. Call 303-567-2421 (or look at www.historicargo tours.com) for more information. Open May 1 to September 30.

 Georgetown Loop Railroad. Unfortunately, dogs are no longer allowed on this scenic narrow-gauge train trip between Georgetown and neighboring Silver Plume. But the operators will try to help you find doggie daycare while you ride the train. One option is the Complete Canine, a grooming salon at 1020 Griffith in Georgetown (303-569-2257). Owner Nancy Ego may be able to watch your dog. The railroad operates daily from Memorial Day through the first weekend of October, with a limited midweek schedule after Labor Day. Call 800-691-4386 (or 303-

Yuki stands proud atop Mount Evans. (photo by Holly Pumphrey)

569-2403 in Denver) for more information and current ticket prices.

DOGGIE DAYCARE
Genesee
Lookout Mountain Pet Lodge, 24059 Highway 40, Lookout Mountain, 303-526-0436. $9.50–$13.50/day, depending on the size of your dog. Dropoffs from 8–10 a.m. and pickups from 4–6 p.m., Monday to Saturday.

CANINE ER
Genesee
Canyon Animal Hospital (AAHA certified), 24059 Highway 40, 303-526-2652. Open 8 a.m.–6 p.m., Monday, Tuesday, Thursday, Friday; 8 a.m.–noon, Wednesday and Saturday.

RESOURCES
Clear Creek County Tourism Board, 303-567-4660 (800-882-5278)

Clear Creek Ranger District, Arapaho and Roosevelt National Forests, 101 Chicago Creek Rd., Idaho Springs, 303-567-2901

Georgetown Information Center, 612 6th St., 303-569-2405 (800-472-8230)

Idaho Springs Visitor Information Center, 2200 Miner St., Idaho Springs, 303-567-4382 (800-685-7785)

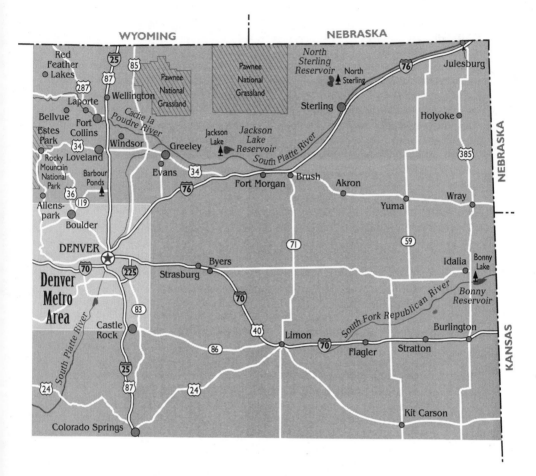

WYOMING NEBRASKA

Red Feather Lakes

(25) (85)

(287)

(87)

Laporte

Wellington

Bellvue

Fort Collins

Estes Park

(34)

Rocky Mountain National Park

Windsor

Loveland

Barbour Ponds

(36)

(119)

Allenspark

Boulder

DENVER

Pawnee National Grassland

Cache la Poudre River

Greeley

Evans

(34)

(76)

Fort Morgan

Brush

Akron

Pawnee National Grassland

North Sterling Reservoir

North Sterling

Julesburg

(76)

Sterling

Holyoke

(385)

Wray

Yuma

Jackson Lake

Jackson Lake Reservoir

South Platte River

(70) (225)

Denver Metro Area

Byers

Strasburg

South Platte River

Castle Rock

(83)

(70)

(40)

(25)

(86)

(87)

(24)

(24)

Colorado Springs

Limon

(70)

Flagler

Stratton

Burlington

(71)

(59)

Idalia

Bonny Lake

South Fork Republican River

Bonny Reservoir

Kit Carson

NEBRASKA

KANSAS

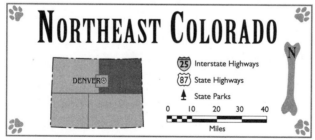

NORTHEAST COLORADO

DENVER⊙

(25) Interstate Highways

(87) State Highways

🔺 State Parks

N

0 10 20 30 40

Miles

Fort Collins and Vicinity

THE BIG SCOOP

Close to the foothills of the northern Front Range, Fort Collins and neighboring Loveland offer a variety of opportunities for canine recreation. If you're looking for a more rustic getaway, the Poudre River Canyon (which begins about 10 miles northwest of Fort Collins) and the village of Red Feather Lakes (about 50 miles northwest of Fort Collins) have cabin resorts, many of which allow canine guests. And your dog can rest easy about his health during a visit to Fort Collins: Colorado State University is home to one of the best veterinary schools in the country, and the Veterinary Teaching Hospital operates a 24-hour critical care clinic.

You'll have to keep your dog leashed within Fort Collins and Loveland city limits; in unincorporated Larimer County areas, dogs may be under voice command.

Fort Collins opened one of the first dog parks in the Front Range in September 1998 (see "Tail-Rated Trails"), and it's proven extremely popular. More are planned, with the next one officially slated for 2003, in the yet-to-be-built Fossil Creek Community Park in the southeast part of the city.

FortFIDOS, an offshoot of the original FIDOS (Friends Interested in Dogs and Open Space) in Boulder, represents the interests of local dogs and their owners.

TAIL-RATED TRAILS

Dogs in Fort Collins can enjoy several open space areas, three major recreational trails within or close to town, and two parks with hiking trails just west of Horsetooth Reservoir. Except for the new dog park, however, none include any off-leash dog areas. To find trails where Fido can hike leash-free, head up scenic Poudre Canyon (though note that the popular Greyrock National Recreation Trail has a leash policy) or to the Red Feather Lakes area. One close-by option in the canyon—Young Gulch—is described here. The Forest Service office in Fort Collins (see "Resources") has a good range of maps and trail descriptions for other hikes.

 Young Gulch. Up to 8 miles round-trip. Head north from Fort Collins on U.S. Highway 287 to the turnoff for Highway 14 and the Poudre Canyon (about 9 miles). Turn left onto a dirt road 12.8 miles up the canyon, just past the Ansel Watrous Campground on the right. Follow the dirt road to the parking area and trailhead. *Dogs can be off leash.*

This is a perfect trail for the dog who likes to get his paws muddy. Water-loving hounds will appreciate the numerous creek crossings (none on bridges), which apparently run into the forties (we lost count after about twenty). There's really no set destination for this hike, and the scenic factor remains about the same throughout, so don't feel that you must cover all 4 miles (one-way). You and your dog will have an enjoyable trip no matter how far you decide to go.

The easy-to-follow trail makes a very gradual ascent up a forested gulch, winding through sweet-smelling ponderosa and lodgepole pine, Rocky Mountain juniper, Douglas fir, and aspen. The last mile or so travels across an open meadow, where the trail narrows to a small footpath. A final climb up an old road brings you to a cattle fence signed for private property, and to the end of the trail; just beyond, you'll see Stove Prairie Rd.

Dog Park at Southwest Community Park.

Take Horsetooth Rd. west until just before it ends. There's a dirt parking area on the right. The future Southwest Community Park is planned for this location, but it won't be completed for another five years or so. Walk to the end of the road and follow the signs for the dog park, which is just off to the right. *Dogs can be off leash.*

This 3-acre fenced area provides plenty of room for dogs to romp, chase a ball, and socialize. There's no water, so you'll want to bring some along for rest breaks. Dispensers of poop-pickup bags and trash cans are thoughtfully staggered around the park's perimeter. Dogs must be licensed and vaccinated, and puppies under four months old are not allowed. You must have a leash on hand in case your pup gets unruly, and no more than three dogs per owner are allowed at one time. Dogs cannot be left unattended, and if your pooch is in heat, leave her at home.

The dog park is adjacent to the Pineridge Natural Area, 618 acres of short-grass prairie crossed by approximately 3 miles of wide dirt trails that are perfect for a pre- or post-park walk. You'll have to keep your dog on a leash in the natural area and pick up after him. The area abuts 40-acre Dixon Reservoir, where the Foothills Trail (see later description) begins.

Foothills Trail.

Runs 5.8 miles from Dixon Reservoir, near the south end of Horsetooth Reservoir, to the Campeau/Reservoir Ridge Open Space Area, near the north end of the reservoir. To access the trail at Dixon Reservoir, head west from downtown Fort Collins on one of the major cross streets (e.g., Prospect) to Overland Trail (a road). Go south on Overland Trail to County Rd. 42C and turn right. Just before the hairpin turn, an unsigned gravel road leads down to a parking area next to the water and the trail. *Dogs must be leashed.*

This is a great trail for water-loving dogs, as you start out near a small reservoir and eventually gain access to large, scenic Horsetooth Reservoir. Begin hiking at the northwest corner of the parking lot. After descending a short hill, stay left at the next two forks. Cross County Rd. 42C and pick up the trail again at the white "City of Fort Collins" sign that lists park regulations. The trail parallels a service road through the Maxwell Open Space Area west of Colorado State University's Hughes Stadium, then switchbacks up a dry hillside of grassland, yucca plants, and sagebrush. Shortly after reaching the hilltop, cross Centennial Rd., the north–south artery for Horsetooth Reservoir, and look for the continuation of the trail at the northeast corner of the paved parking area. Stay left at the first fork. The trail goes along the bluffs above the reservoir before descending toward shoreline. Several spur trails lead down to the water, so your dog can take a dip, well deserved on a hot day. If you continue hiking, follow the trail along the shore; it eventually ascends and crosses Centennial Rd. again to reach the parking area at Campeau/Reservoir Ridge Open Space Area.

If you want a shorter hike, or if your dog wants quicker access to water, you can access portions of the Foothills Trail from several parking areas off Centennial Rd. between Dixon Dam and Soldier Canyon Dam. You can also hike south from Dixon Reservoir; a trail follows the western shoreline before heading east to end at Taft Hill Rd.

Horsetooth Mountain Park. From College Ave. in Fort Collins, head west on Horsetooth Rd. (south of downtown). Drive 2 miles to Taft Hill Rd.; turn left, then take a right at the next traffic light (County Rd. 38E). Follow the road around the southern end of Horsetooth Reservoir (you'll see signs for the park). The parking area will be on the right. There's a $6 entry fee. *Dogs must be leashed.*

The park offers 28 miles of trails, including an ascent to the distinctive Horsetooth Rock, from which you get an encompassing view of the peaks on the eastern side of Rocky Mountain National Park. (Note that with the exception of part of the **Horsetooth Rock Trail**, the trails are multiuse, so you'll be sharing them with bikes and horses.) Most people stick to the first couple miles of trails, hiking to Horsetooth and Culver Falls, and to Horsetooth Rock. So if you're looking for more solitude with your pooch, venture a little farther. You'll find water along the 2-mile-long **Spring Creek Trail** (which requires about 1.5 miles of hiking to reach) and the nearly 3-mile **Mill Creek Trail** (which begins at the end of the Spring Creek Trail). If you're really ambitious, you can even hike into neighboring Lory State Park via two of the trails. Backcountry camping is allowed in Horsetooth Mountain Park, so you can do longer hikes broken up by an overnight stay. Remember to keep your dog leashed at all times; rangers do patrol, and they have a no-tolerance policy, which means you're pretty much guaranteed a fine if Fido's romping freely.

 Lory State Park. From Fort Collins, take Highway 287 north. After passing through Laporte, go left on County Rd. 52E to Bellvue. Drive about

Tundra and Spencer engage in a bit of step-sibling rivalry. (photo by John Sabol)

1 mile to County Rd. 23N; head south for about 1.5 miles to County Rd. 25G, on the right, and the park entrance. *Dogs must be leashed.*

The park offers 30 miles of well-marked trails for you and your dog to enjoy together. A few options that your dog may prefer: The 2-mile round-trip **Well Gulch Trail** heads west from the park road, up a drainage with a stream at the bottom. The trail up to **Arthur's Rock**, which provides a panoramic view of Horsetooth Reservoir and Fort Collins, is now for hikers only (there used to be a separate trail for horses and riders, but it's been flooded out); the route is 3.4 miles round-trip, and an intermittent stream alongside is a potential water source. If your dog wants to visit the water's edge, bring him on the Shoreline Trail, a 2-mile round-trip to the reservoir and back from the park road. There are also six backcountry campsites within the park, all of them along the 3.5-mile Timber Trail, where you can overnight with your dog.

Poudre River Trail. Runs 8.35 miles from North Taft Hill Rd. west of downtown Fort Collins, to East Drake Rd., near the Prospect Ponds open space area. *Dogs must be leashed.*

This paved bike and hike path parallels the Cache La Poudre River, passing several open space areas and city parks along its route (Lee Martinez Park is especially popular with dogs and their owners). It's a great place to take your dog for a stroll that's close to town, and it's usually less traveled than the Spring Creek Trail. As you head east from downtown, the trail passes through less-developed surroundings.

 Spring Creek Trail. Runs 6.6 miles from West Drake Rd. to East Prospect Rd., where it ends in the Poudre River Trail. *Dogs must be leashed.*

This paved trail follows Spring Creek and passes through several park and open space areas. As it runs close to the Colorado State University campus, it's more of a transportation corridor than a hiking trail, but it nonetheless provides your dog with some off-street walking space.

CYCLING FOR CANINES

You'll have to head up Poudre Canyon to find the closest areas to town where you can ride with a dog. The 8-mile round-trip **Young Gulch Trail** (see "Tail-Rated Trails") has the advantage of lots of water for dogs to run through; the first mile or so will have you walking up some rocky sections, but if you stick with it you'll reach some nice rolling singletrack. The 7-mile round-trip **Hewlett Gulch Trail**, out of the town of Poudre Park, follows Gordon Creek up a moderate ascent; your dog will have a chance to sniff among the remains of early homesteads. The **Mt. Margaret Trail**, just outside Red

Feather Lakes, is a scenic, rolling 8-mile round-trip to the top of Mt. Margaret and down.

POWDERHOUNDS

To find consistent snow for skiing or snowshoeing, you and your dog will need to drive to Cameron Pass at the top of Poudre Canyon, about 65 miles west of Fort Collins on Highway 14. A great short tour follows an old jeep road to **Zimmerman Lake**, a 2.2-mile round-trip from the Zimmerman Lake parking area off Highway 14, past Joe Wright Reservoir and about 2 miles below the pass. Another tour begins at the pass summit and follows the **Michigan Ditch Rd.** south into the upper part of the Michigan River drainage; a 2.6-mile round-trip brings you to some old cabins and back, though you can easily ski farther along the ditch. See *Skiing Colorado's Backcountry*, by Brian Litz and Kurt Lankford, and *Snowshoeing Colorado,* by Claire Walter, for more details on these and other routes.

CREATURE COMFORTS

Unless otherwise stated, dogs should not be left unattended in the room or cabin.

Bellvue

$$ **Tip Top Guest Ranch, 1300 County Rd. 41 (about 30 miles from Fort Collins, in Rist Canyon), 970-484-1215.** This 7,400-acre ranch, with views of Rocky Mountain National Park, offers horseback rides as well as three rustic cabins where you and your dog can overnight. There's a $5 per night fee for pets, with a limit of two dogs per cabin. The cabins have separate living and bedroom areas, cookstoves, and wood-burning stoves for heat, though no indoor plumbing. You can leave your dog unattended inside for short periods of time. Although you'll need to supply your own food for the most part, the ranch offers dinner rides on horseback.

Fort Collins

$ El Palomino, 1220 N. College, 970-482-4555. There are six pet rooms, and the charge is $5.50 per night, per dog.

$ Motel 6 Fort Collins, 3900 E. Mulberry, 970-482-6466 (800-4-MOTEL 6 [national number]). Dogs less than 30 pounds are permitted, with a limit of one pet per room.

$-$$ Days Inn, 3625 E. Mulberry, 970-221-5490 (800-DAYS-INN [national number]). The motel has some designated pet rooms, where dogs can stay for a $5 fee per night.

$-$$ Fort Collins Plaza Inn, 3709 E. Mulberry, 970-493-7800 (800-434-5548; www.plaza-inn.com). Dog guests are usually placed in ground-floor rooms at this full-service motel, for quicker outdoor access, with a $5 fee per night. You can leave your dog unattended in the room, but housekeeping won't enter unless he's safely contained in a travel kennel.

$-$$ Inn at Fort Collins, 2612 S. College, 970-226-2600. The motel has large, comfortable rooms and is a few blocks from the Colorado State Univer-sity Veterinary Teaching Hospital. There's a $5 fee per night, per dog; if your dog is visiting Fort Collins to receive treatment at the Vet Center, you'll get a $5 per night discount (so, in effect, no extra charge).

$-$$ Lamplighter Motel, 1809 N. College, 970-484-2764

$-$$ Mulberry Inn, 4333 E. Mulberry, 970-493-9000 (800-234-5548; www.mulberry-inn.com). Some of this motel's rooms have hot tubs in them (for humans only, of course). There's a $5 fee per night, per dog.

$-$$ Super 8 Motel, 409 Centro Way, 970-493-7701 (800-800-8000 [national

Hewlett Gulch, near Fort Collins, is a dog-friendly mountain biking route. (photo by Amy Ditsler)

number]). The motel requires a $20 pet deposit if you're paying with cash.

$$ Best Western University Inn, 914 S. College, 970-484-1984 (800-528-1234 [national number]). The motel has pet-specific rooms for $10 per night extra.

$$ Comfort Suites, 1415 Oakridge, 970-206-4597 (800-228-5150 [national number]). There's a $15 nightly fee for a dog, and you can leave yours unattended in the room for a short time.

$$ Holiday Inn I-25, 3836 E. Mulberry, 970-484-4660 (800-HOLIDAY [national number]). Dogs are put in outside-facing rooms. If you're paying with cash, you'll have to put down a $50 pet deposit.

$$ Sleep Inn, 3808 E. Mulberry, 970-484-5515 (800-627-5337 [national number]). There's a $10 one-time fee per dog. You can leave your dog unattended in the room only if he's secure in a travel cage.

$$-$$$ Quality Inn and Suites, 4001 S. Mason, 970-282-9047 (800-228-5151

[national number]). Dogs are allowed in smoking rooms only. You'll be asked for a $25 deposit if you're paying with cash.

$$–$$$ **Residence Inn by Marriott,** 1127 Oakridge, 970-223-5700 (800-331-3131 [national number]). Dogs are allowed on two of the three floors of this all-suite hotel, with a limit of two dogs per unit and a preference for those under 80 pounds. For a stay of up to four nights, there's a $50 one-time pet fee; that goes up to $100 for stays of five nights or longer, with a $10 per day cleaning fee usually added. You can leave your dog unattended in your unit. The hotel also provides pet pickup bags for your walks.

$$–$$$ **University Park Holiday Inn,** 425 W. Prospect, 970-482-2626 (800-HOLIDAY [national number]). The hotel has minisuites in addition to regular rooms. You can leave a well-behaved dog unattended inside.

Laporte
$ **Mile Hi KOA,** Highway 287 at the entrance to Poudre Canyon, 970-493-9758 (800-KOA-2648). Dogs are allowed in the camping cabins; you'll have to supply your own bedding and cooking gear. Open May 1 to October 15.

Loveland
$–$$ **Hiway Motel,** 1027 E. Eisenhower Blvd., 970-667-5224. Dogs are allowed in most rooms, for $5 extra per night. You can leave your dog unattended in the room only if he's in a travel kennel.

$–$$ **Kings Court Motel,** 928 N. Lincoln Ave., 970-667-4035. Dogs can stay in smoking rooms only, with a $50 deposit and a $10 one-time fee.

$–$$ **Loveland Motel,** 617 E. Eisenhower Blvd., 970-667-2748. Dogs are permitted with a $25 deposit, and they can be left unattended in the room.

$–$$ **Rose Bud Motel,** 660 E. Eisenhower Blvd., 970-669-9430. There's a $5 fee per night for Citizen Canines.

$$ **Best Western Coach House,** 5542 Highway 34, 970-667-7810 (888-818-6223; www.lovelandhotel.com). Dogs are permitted for $15 extra per stay. You can leave your dog unattended in the room, but the housekeepers won't come in to clean during that time.

Poudre Canyon
$ **Sportsman's Lodge,** 44174 Poudre Canyon Rd. (54 miles from Fort Collins), 970-881-2272 (800-270-2272; www.coloradodirectory.com/sportsmanslodge). Sportdogs are permitted in the eleven rustic one-room cabins (with shared baths and wood-burning cookstoves) or the one "modern" cabin, with kitchenette and private bath, for $8 extra per night. Open from the end of April to November 1.

$–$$ **Glen Echo Resort,** 31503 Poudre Canyon Rd. (41 miles from Fort Collins), 970-881-2208 (800-348-2208). Of the fifteen cabins at this riverside family resort, some are modern, with fireplaces; some are rustic, with no running water and shared bath facilities; and one is a large apartment that sleeps up to twelve guests. All have cooking supplies, however, and a restaurant and general store are located at the resort. There's a $5 fee per night, per dog. You are required to keep your dog leashed on the property. The full resort is open from mid-May to November 15.

$–$$ **Trading Post,** 44414 Poudre Canyon Rd. (55 miles from Fort Collins), 970-881-2215 (www.tradingpost resort.com). This small complex across the road from the river has a general store and twelve cabins: Rustic ones come with running water and wood-burning cookstoves; modern ones have kitchens and private baths.

Dogs are $2.50 per night extra, and you must keep yours leashed on the property.

$$–$$$ Poudre River Resort, 33021 Poudre Canyon Rd. (45 miles from Fort Collins), 970-881-2139 (888-822-0588; www.poudreriverresort.com). There are nine one- and two-bedroom, fully equipped cabins at the resort, and dogs are allowed for $10 per night per dog. The owners ask that you keep your dog leashed on the 7.5-acre riverside property. A general store is on-site.

Red Feather Lakes

$ Alpine Lodge, 157 Prairie Divide Rd., 970-881-2933. Located about half a mile from the village of Red Feather Lakes, the lodge has three fully furnished cabins and two mobile homes that you and your dog can stay in.

$$ Red Feather Ranch, 3613 County Rd. 68C, 970-881-3715 (877-881-5215; www.redfeatherranch.com). This bed and breakfast is set on 40 acres adjacent to the Roosevelt National Forest, and if your dog enjoys playing with others (there are a few resident dogs) and romping outdoors, he'll have a great time here. Potential guest dogs are screened over the phone, and "if the pet vouches for the owner, the owner can come too," quips owner Steve Horsman. Dogs are allowed in one of the main lodge's six guest rooms, done up in casual mountain-style decor, or in the rustic miner's cabin dating from 1895 (both options include a shared bath). There's a $100 pet deposit. Facilities are also available for visiting horses. Nearby hiking, mountain biking, and skiing trails all start from the ranch.

$$ Trout Lodge, 1078 Ramona Dr., 970-881-2964. You and your dog have your choice of nine fully equipped cabins, ranging from studio to two bedrooms, in the village of Red Feather Lakes. There's a $10 nightly fee per pet, and you'll need to keep your dog leashed when outside.

$$–$$$ Beaver Meadows Resort, 100 Marmot Dr., 970-881-2450 (800-462-5870; www.beavermeadows.com). Dogs are not permitted in the lodge or condos at the resort, but they can have their pick of five cabins to stay in for a $20 one-time fee. Four of the five cabins are equipped with kitchens, and some have wood-burning stoves or fireplaces and decks. You can leave your dog unattended inside. The resort borders national forest land and maintains 22 miles of hiking trails that you can bring your dog on. During the winter, however, the trails are groomed for skiing, and dogs are not permitted on them. There's also a restaurant on the premises.

$$$ Mountain Rose, 160 Comanche Cir., 970-881-2503 (800-477-7673; www.mountain-rose.com). This upscale, amenity-filled cabin in Crystal Lake, about 4 miles from the town of Red Feather Lakes, offers you and your dog a stellar weekend getaway. The three-bedroom, two-bath cabin, on five wooded acres, can sleep up to eight (the rates are higher than the category here for more than four visitors). You can leave your dog unattended inside so long as you're sure he won't jump on the furniture or chew any of the decor. And you'll need to clean up after him outdoors. A hot tub is available for guests for a $25 fee. Owner Maggie Mora emphasizes that you and your dog should book early, as the cabin has become popular with guests. The website has an availability calendar.

$$$ Sundance Trail Guest Ranch, 17931 Red Feather Lakes Rd., 970-224-1222 (800-357-4930; www.sundancetrail. com). This 140-acre ranch, offers horseback riding, fishing, jeep rides, and easy access to trails in the adjacent Roosevelt National Forest. If your dog is one of the lucky ones (only one set of guests at a time can bring pets), he can stay with you in one of the seven cabins or lodge suites, nicely done up in a mountain/western decor. And he can stay inside even when you're not there. Meals are served family-style in the lodge's dining room. From mid-May to the beginning of October, the ranch accepts guests on a weekly basis only, for an all-inclusive price from Sunday to Saturday. The rest of the year it operates as a bed-and-breakfast, with the option of additional meals.

Wellington

$ KOA Fort Collins North, Exit 281 off I-25, 970-568-7486 (800-KOA-8142). Dogs are allowed in the camping cabins; you'll have to supply your own bedding and cooking gear.

Campgrounds

Boyd Lake State Park. East of Loveland off U.S. Highway 34 (148 sites).

Larimer County Parks: Carter Lake, on County Rd. 31, about 5 miles west of Loveland (7 campgrounds); Horsetooth Reservoir, east of Fort Collins via County Rd. 38E (7 campgrounds); Flatiron Reservoir, off County Rd. 18E, about 7 miles west of Loveland (1 campground); Pinewood Reservoir, at the end of County Rd. 18E, about 10 miles from Loveland (1 campground).

National forest campgrounds: Several campsites are right off Highway 14 in Poudre Canyon, including Ansel Watrous Campground (19 sites); Stove Prairie Campground (9 sites); Narrows Campground (9 sites); Mountain Park Campground (55 sites); and Kelly Flats Campground (23 sites). Campgrounds near Red Feather Lakes include the Ballaire Lake Campground, Red Feather Lakes Rd. to Forest Rd. 162 (26 sites); Dowdy Lake Campground, 1.5 miles from the village on Forest Rd. 218 (62 sites); and West Lake Campground, 1 mile

from the village on Forest Rd. 200 (29 sites).

WORTH A PAWS

Doggie Olympics. Do you think you have a potential gold medalist in the Hot Dog Retrieve, just waiting for an opportunity to demonstrate his skills? Or maybe your dog would prefer to strut his stuff in the 25-Yard Dash or the Obstacle Course. Bring him down to Fort Collins's City Park in September for the Doggie Olympics, where he can compete in these and other events, such as Best Tidbit Catcher and the Pentathlon. There are four levels of competition for each event, so the serious canine athlete as well as the habitual couch potato can participate. Proceeds benefit the Larimer Animal–People Partnership (LAPP). You can register in advance or on the day of the competition. Call Lisa Sadar at 970-226-4146 for more information.

Fire Hydrant Five. Held in early May in Edora Park in Fort Collins, the Fire Hydrant Five consists of a 5K run for humans only and a 3K fun run and 5K walk for leashed dogs and their owners. In addition to your registration fee, you and your dog can collect donations, all of which will benefit the Humane Society for Larimer County's pet adoption program. Call the Humane Society at 970-226-3647 for more information.

Flame Out Five. Dalmatian or no, your dog can join you for this 5K run that raises money for the smoke-detector distribution program of the Poudre Fire Authority. It takes place on either the first or second Saturday in October, in conjunction with Fire Prevention Week. The course begins at Fire Station 3, at 2000 Matthews St., and goes through the surrounding residential district. Prizes (including 50 pounds of dog food) are given to the top male and female runners with dogs, and there are treats for everybody. Call 970-416-2867 (the Fort Collins Fire Prevention Bureau) for details.

Annie Walk. This family-friendly canine walk, held the fourth Saturday in August, honors Annie the railroad dog (see sidebar). The 1.5-mile course runs from the Fort Collins library's main branch (201 Peterson St.) through downtown to Annie's grave on Mason St. and back. The registration fees bring in funds for children's books and materials in the Fort Collins library system. Participants also get an Annie T-shirt. Contact the library at 970-221-6526 for more information.

ESA's Walkin' the Dog. The event is part of an annual nationwide campaign of Walkin' the Dogs that raises funds for the St. Jude's Children's Research Hospital in Memphis, Tennessee, which treats children with catastrophic illnesses, especially cancer, from around the world. Epsilon Sigma Alpha International sorority is the sponsor,

Fort Collins's most prominent canine was Annie, a shepherd/collie mix who was adopted by workers for the Colorado and Southern Railroad and became the station mascot.

Annie lived at the railroad depot until her death in 1948. The workers buried her outside the station, and though the depot no longer exists, you can still visit the grave, surrounded by an iron fence, on Mason St. just north of LaPorte Ave.

Annie is also commemorated by a life-size bronze sculpture, by local artist Dawn Weimmer, in front of the Fort Collins Library at 201 Peterson St. The annual Annie Walk (see "Worth a Paws") is held in her honor.

and a black lab named Chuck serves as the national mascot. The Fort Collins 3K walk takes place at the Colorado State University Oval during the third weekend in April. Money is raised through the entry fee and pledges. Call the sorority offices at 970-223-2858 or 800-704-7336 (or click on www.esaintl.com/chuck) for more information.

Fort Collins Frisbee Dog Event. This annual athletic event is usually held the third weekend in June at City Park in Fort Collins (1500 W. Mulberry St.). The competition has two components: the minidistance, in which dogs compete in sixty-second rounds, earning points for catching distance and a bonus for midair catches; and the freestyle, in which they're judged on difficulty, execution, leaping agility, and showmanship while performing tricks. Colorado Disc Dogs puts on the events. For more information, contact Rick Brydum, 303-759-8785 (frflyers@ aol.com), or look at the organization's website, www.varinet.com/~eyebum/noco dido.html.

Doggie Dips and Chips, 265C E. 29th St. (Orchard Center shopping plaza), Loveland, 970-461-1109. The "dip" in the name of this canine emporium refers to the self-service dog wash, which has four tubs with spalike redwood surrounds. A wash is $10 for one dog, $17 for two, and includes shampoo, towels, an apron for you, and use of a professional dryer and grooming tools. The "chips" relates to the in-house biscuit bakery; once he's clean, your dog can sniff out five flavors of all-natural treats, including health mutts (with sunflower seeds), peanut-butter puppers, and vegetabones, for dogs sensitive to corn and wheat. There's also a comprehensive selection of rawhides, toys, beds, and doggie-oriented craft items. Plus Steve Fifer (who owns the store with his wife, Sandy) is a leathersmith who will craft custom collars and leashes. Closed Mondays.

Alfalfa's Dog Wash. This annual event, held in mid-August at Alfalfa's Market (College Ave. and Foothills Pkwy.) gets your pooch a probably much-needed midsummer bath in addition to raising money for the Humane Society for Larimer County (970-226-3647).

Dirty dogs should try one of these do-it-yourself dog washes: In Loveland, stop into **Happy Tails Self-Service Pet Wash and Boutique, 1710 W. Eisenhower, Unit 5B, 970-669-1182.** The $9 fee includes shampoo, conditioner, and a towel. Dryers are available for an extra charge: $1 for the forced-air dryer, and $3 for the kennel-sized walk-in dryer (so your dog can really feel like he's at the beauty salon). Open Tuesday to Saturday. In Fort Collins, try **Laund-Ur-Mutt, 1119 W. Drake (in Cimarron Plaza), 970-223-8225.** Washing-bay rental is $10 for the first half hour and $4 for each additional dog in the same tub. Additional half hours are $6 each. You'll have use of an apron, a scrub mitt, one towel per dog, combs and brushes, and the fur dryer. You'll need to supply your own shampoo or buy it from Laund-Ur-Mutt's stock. Open Tuesday to Sunday.

DOGGIE DAYCARE
Fort Collins
Andelt's Pet Motel, 3200 E. Mulberry, 970-484-5776. $11/day. Open 7:30 a.m.–1 p.m. and 2–5:30 p.m., Monday to Friday; 7:30 a.m.–noon and 3:30–5:30 p.m., Saturday; 8–9 a.m. and 3:30–4:30 p.m., Sunday.

Ashcroft Boarding Kennels, 5020 S. County Rd. 3, 970-221-5689. $9–$12/day, depending on the size of dog. Open 7:30 a.m.–6 p.m., Monday to Friday; 7:30 a.m.–noon, Saturday.

Country Squire Kennels, 3320 N. Shields, 970-484-3082. $8–$10/day,

depending on the size of dog. Open 8 a.m.–6 p.m., Monday to Saturday.

Crystal Glen Kennel, 720 W. Willox Ln., 970-224-3118. $8/day for an indoor/outdoor run. There's a small extra charge if you want to have your dog walked during the day. Open 8 a.m.–6 p.m., Monday to Saturday; 5–6 p.m., Sunday (pickup only).

Dog Planet Daycare, 1015 S. Taft Hill Rd., 970-224-3244. $12/day; $8/half-day (five hours or less). Open 7:30 a.m.–6:30 p.m., Monday to Thursday; 7:30 a.m.–6 p.m., Friday.

Moore Animal Hospital Pet Camp, 2550 Stover, 970-416-9101. $6/day. Open 7 a.m.–6 p.m., Monday to Friday; 7 a.m.–noon, Saturday.

The Pet Lodge (at South Mesa Veterinary Hospital), 3801 S. Mason, 970-226-6526. $6/day. Open 7:30 a.m.–5:30 p.m., Monday to Friday; 7:30 a.m.–noon, Saturday; 5–7 p.m., Sunday (pickup only).

Rocky Mountain Dog Gym and Day Care, 315 W. Hickory, 970-493-0913. Don't worry—your dog won't get put on the Stairmaster here; but he will probably exhaust himself at this indoor/outdoor facility that features lots of toys, activities, and a canine jungle gym. $10/day; $7 half-day (any five or six hours throughout the day). Open 7 a.m.–6 p.m., Monday to Friday.

Rover's Ranch, 4837 Terry Lake Rd., 970-493-5970. $9–$12/day, depending on the size of dog. Open 8 a.m.–6 p.m., Monday and Wednesday to Friday; 8–10 a.m. and 4–6 p.m., Tuesday; 8 a.m.–noon Saturday; by appointment only on Sunday.

Loveland
Creature Comforts Pet Retreat, 808 S. County Rd. 23E, 970-669-2084. $8/day. Optional exercise sessions include a 1-mile

nature hike, for $3.50 extra, or a supervised play session, for $2.50 extra. Open 8 a.m.–5 p.m., Monday to Friday; 8 a.m.–noon, Saturday; 9–10 a.m. and 4–5 p.m., Sunday.

Loveland Veterinary Clinic, 1403 N. Monroe Ave., 970-667-3252. $8–$9/day, depending on the size of dog. Open 8 a.m.–5 p.m., Monday to Friday; 8 a.m.–noon, Saturday.

PET PROVISIONS
Fort Collins
Cache La Poudre Feeds, 1724 N. Overland Trail, 970-482-5092

Feeders Supply South, 4229 S. Mason, 970-223-1364

Petco, 2211 S. College, 970-484-4477

PetsMart, 4330 S. College, 970-228-9502

Poudre Feed Supply, 622 N. College, 970-482-2741; 6204 S. College, 970-225-1255

Vetline, 425 John Deere Rd. (behind the Holiday Inn I-25), 970-484-1900 (800-962-4554). The store carries a complete line of animal vaccines, medications, and other medical supplies.

Loveland
Canine Corner, 1402 W. 8th, 970-663-3293

High Point Feed and Supply, 530 E. Eisenhower Blvd., 970-667-2950

Loveland Feed and Grain, 130 W. 3rd St., 970-667-4567
Sage Valley Feed and Supply, 5623 W. Highway 34, 970-663-1261

Town and Country Pet Center, 130 S. Cleveland Ave., 970-667-9669

CANINE ER
Fort Collins
Colorado State University Veterinary Teaching Hospital (AAHA certified), 300 W. Drake Rd., 970-221-4535. The clinic is staffed 24 hours a day for emergency patients.

Loveland
Animal Emergency Services of Northern Colorado, 201 W. 67th Ct. (off Highway 287 between Loveland and Fort Collins), 970-663-5760. The clinic is open 6 p.m.–8 a.m. the next morning, Monday to Friday; 24 hours on weekends and holidays.

RESOURCES
Canyon Lakes Ranger District, Arapaho and Roosevelt National Forests and Pawnee National Grassland, 1311 S. College Ave., Fort Collins, 970-498-2770

Colorado Welcome Center/Fort Collins Visitor Information Center, Interstate 25 and Prospect Rd. (Exit 268) Fort Collins, 970-482-5821 (800-274-3678; www.ftcollins.com)

FortFIDOS (Friends Interested in Dogs and Open Space), 970-226-2100

Greeley and Northeastern Plains

THE BIG SCOOP

For the most part, the plains of eastern Colorado are travel-through country (although the tourism organizations, which market part of the area as "Colorado's Outback," don't want you to think this). But frankly, unless your dog is fascinated by pioneer history or into long car rides, he'll want to keep heading toward the mountains. You will, however, find plenty of dog-friendly lodgings, most of them lower-priced motels.

Greeley, somewhat of a gateway to the plains and home to the University of Northern Colorado, is a town of great smells—for dogs. When the wind's blowing just right, evidence of the area's agriculture industry permeates the airwaves, so to speak. That's one of the few things dogs will find to enjoy, however, as all parks except one in Greeley are closed to canines. Although there was talk of lifting the ban in 2000, it's been upheld for the time being. The Parks Department is working to create an off-leash area in the city for dogs, however, which could be open in 2001. In the meantime, for a more scenic walk than the average curbside stroll, take your dog to the UNC campus (but be sure to keep him on leash, in compliance with the citywide regulation) or visit Island Grove Regional Park (see description below).

TAIL-RATED TRAILS

The observant dog will note that there are three state parks in the region—Bonny Lake, North Sterling Reservoir, and Jackson Lake—but he might be disappointed to hear that only one (North Sterling) currently has hiking trails of note. They all make great destinations, however, to camp with your dog and hang out by the water on a hot day. Dogs are not allowed on any of the swim beaches, but there are other areas in each park with water access where Fido (on leash) can dip a paw. (For park locations, see the campgrounds section in "Creature Comforts.")

 North Sterling Reservoir State Park. From the Sterling exit off I-76, head west on Highway 14 (3rd Ave.) to 7th Ave. Turn right on 7th, then left at the T-intersection with County Rd. 46. Go right at the next T onto County Rd. 33, which will bring you to the park entrance. *Dogs must be leashed.*

The recently constructed South Shoreline Trail runs for 5.5 miles along the 3,000-acre reservoir's south side. You can pick up the crushed-surface trail at the southernmost boat ramp on the east side of the lake; from there it runs down to the Inlet Grove Campground and then crosses a bridge before following the shore in an otherwise undeveloped section of the park. You'll be able to go as far as County Rd. 29 before the trail ends at private property.

 Pawnee Buttes. 4 miles round-trip. Depending on your starting-out point, head either east or west on Highway 14 to County Rd. 390 (about 13 miles east of Briggsdale or 10 miles west of Raymer). At Keota, head north on County Rd. 105 for 3 miles, then turn right on County Rd. 104 and go another 3 miles to County Rd. 111. Go left for 4.5 miles, then follow the signed road to the trailhead parking area, next to a windmill. *Dogs can be off leash.*

The buttes are two dramatic, 300-foot-tall blocks of eroded sandstone within the Pawnee National Grasslands, a shortgrass prairie preserve. They top out at 5,500 feet elevation. Your dog will enjoy this hike most during the spring or fall, when intense daytime temperatures subside a bit. And you might enjoy it most in the spring, when the abundant wildflowers bloom. Regardless of when you choose to hike, bring plenty of water along. Because the area is home to several species of birds of prey that nest here in the spring, you might want to keep your dog on a leash if he's a wanderer. The easy-to-follow, primarily flat trail goes through a couple of drainages before ending at a fenceline near the buttes. En route, your dog might sniff out yucca, prickly pear cactus, and rabbitbrush, as well as some juniper. If you decide to explore more of the grasslands, be aware that dogs are not allowed on the nature walk at the Crow Valley Recreation Area (in the southwest corner of the campground).

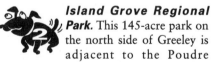 **Island Grove Regional Park.** This 145-acre park on the north side of Greeley is adjacent to the Poudre River, which makes it a nice canine oasis. Drive north on 14th Ave. until it dead-ends at the park. *Dogs must be leashed.*

Your dog will appreciate the park's grassy expanses and huge, old trees in addition to the river. A short section of the paved Poudre River Trail also runs through it. A small lake is under construction on the park's west side, and within the next decade, the park is slated to more than double in size, with plans for a dog training area.

Staying cool—Bismarck lets it fly. (photo by Tim Hancock)

CREATURE COMFORTS

Unless otherwise stated, dogs should not be left unattended in the room or cabin.

Evans

$ Motel 6, 3015 8th Ave., 970-351-6481 (800-4-MOTEL6 [national number]). The Motel 6 policy is one small pet per room (although if your medium- to large-sized dog is well behaved, chances are the motel can accommodate him).

$–$$ Winterset Inn, 800 31st St., 970-339-2492 (800-777-5088). Dogs are allowed with a $20 deposit per pet.

$$ Sleep Inn, 3025 8th Ave., 970-356-2180 (800-753-3746 [national number]). There's a $10 one-time pet fee.

$$–$$$$ Travelodge/Heritage Inn, 3301 W. Service Rd., 970-339-5900 (800-759-7829). A little bit of Las Vegas comes to Greeley in the form of fourteen "Dreamscape" suites, each elaborately decorated according to a particular theme, such as Arabian Nights, Cupid's Corner, Space Odyssey, the Jungle Retreat, and, since this is Colorado, after all, the Broncos Room. Alas, your dog will only be able to stay with you in one of the motel's nonthemed rooms. There's a $5 fee per night, and a dog can be left unattended in the room.

Greeley

$ **Greeley Inn**, 721 13th St., 970-353-3216. There's a $10 fee per night, per pet. Dogs are relegated to the smoking rooms for the most part, and they can be left unattended, but housekeeping won't enter to clean the room during that time.

$$ **Best Western Ramkota Inn**, 701 8th St., 970-353-8444 (800-528-1234 [national number])

$$ **Holiday Inn Express**, 2563 W. 29th St., 970-330-7495 (800-HOLIDAY [national number]). There's a $20 one-time fee, and you can leave your dog unattended in the room.

$$ **Microtel Inn and Suites**, 5630 W. 10th St., 970-392-1530 (888-771-7171 [national number]). Dogs are allowed only in smoking rooms, with a $50 deposit and a $5 per night fee.

Windsor

$$ **Windsor Inn**, 1265 Main St., 970-686-5996 (877-333-5996; www.windsinn.questdex.com). Dogs are allowed at this former Holiday Inn Express for a $6 nightly fee.

Northeastern Plains

Akron

$ **4 B's Motel**, 60 Hickory Ave., 970-345-2028 (888-882-8518). This friendly motel, which used to be a railroad lodge, allows dogs with a credit-card imprint as a deposit if you're paying cash. There's a nearby field where you can exercise Fido on leash.

Brush

$ **Budget Host Empire Motel**, 1408 Edison, 970-842-2876. There's a $2 dog fee per night.

$ **Kozy Kort Motel**, 717 Edison, 970-842-2736. The motel usually takes only small dogs during the summer; dogs of all sizes are accepted in the fall and winter to accommodate hunters. There's a $5 one-time fee.

$$ **Best Western Brush**, 1208 N. Colorado Ave., 970-842-5146 (877-224-6999). It's $10 per dog for the first night of your stay, $5 per dog, per night after that.

$$ **Microtel Inn**, 975 N. Colorado Ave., 970-842-4241 (888-771-7171 [national number]). Dogs are allowed only in smoking rooms, with a $25 deposit and a $5 per night fee.

Fort Morgan

$ **Central Motel**, 201 W. Platte, 970-867-2401. Dogs are allowed in most of the motel's rooms for a $5 one-time fee.

$ **Country Comfort Motel and RV Park**, 16466 W. Highway 34, 970-867-0260. The motel is on 2.5 acres, so your pooch will have a chance to stretch his legs. And you can leave him unattended in the room.

$ **Sands Motel**, 933 W. Platte Ave., 970-867-2453. You can leave your dog unattended in the room.

$–$$ **Best Western Park Terrace**, 725 Main St., 970-867-8256 (800-528-1234 [national number]). With a $25 deposit, dogs can stay in eight of the smoking rooms.

$–$$ **Econo Lodge**, 1409 Barlow Rd. (Exit 82 off I-76), 970-867-9481 (800-55-ECONO [national number]). Dogs are only allowed in three rooms (two of which are nonsmoking), with a $25 deposit, $20 of which is refundable at checkout. But they can be left unattended in the room, and there's a small pond in back that you can bring your dog to visit off leash.

$–$$ **Madison Hotel**, 14378 Highway 34, 970-867-8208 (800-634-6868). This motel has several rooms where dogs can stay with a $25 deposit.

$$ Fort Morgan Quality Inn, 14378 Highway 34, 970-867-8208 (800-634-6868). Dogs are permitted in first-floor smoking rooms with a $25 deposit.

Holyoke
$ Cedar Inn, 525 E. Denver, 970-854-2525 (877-792-5545). Dogs are allowed for $5 per dog per visit.

$ Golden Plains Motel, 1250 S. Interocean Ave., 970-854-3000 (800-643-0451). Dogs are allowed in smoking rooms only, for a $7 one-time fee.

Julesburg
$ Grand Motel, 220 Pine, 970-474-3302

$ Holiday Motel, Highway 138, 970-474-3371

$$ Platte Valley Inn, I-76 and Highway 385, 970-474-3336 (800-562-5166). It's smoking rooms only for dogs here. There is a gravel and grass pet area where they can be walked on leash.

Sterling
$ Crest Motel, 516 S. Division Ave., 970-522-3753. The motel allows dogs in some of its rooms and may charge a nightly fee if you have a long-haired or other type of dog that might require extra cleaning of the room.

$ First Interstate Inn, 20930 Highway 6, 970-522-7274 (800-462-4667 [national number]). Dogs are charged $5 extra per night.

$ Super 8, 12883 Highway 61 (Exit 125 off I-76), 970-522-0300 (800-800-8000 [national number]). Dogs can stay in smoking rooms only.

$–$$ Plains Motel, 1005 S. Division, 970-522-7394. It's mainly smoking rooms for canines here, with a $50 deposit.

$$ Best Western Sundowner, Overland Trail St., 970-522-6265 (800-528-1234 [national number]). Dogs are allowed in smoking rooms only, for $10 per night extra. There's a large yard outside the motel where dogs can exercise off leash.

$$ Ramada Inn, I-76 and E. Highway 6, 970-522-2625 (800-835-7275). Dogs are welcome in outside rooms with a $20 deposit.

Wray
$ Butte Motel, 330 E. 3rd, 970-332-4828. A dog in a travel kennel can be left unattended in the room for a short time.

$ Sandhiller Motel, 411 NW Railway, 970-332-4134 (800-554-7482). Dogs are accepted, but if another guest complains, the offending dog has to pack up his biscuits and go. Only one smoking room is open to furry travelers, with a $25 deposit.

Yuma
$ Harvest Motel, 421 W. 8th Ave., 970-848-5853 (800-273-5853). Quiet dogs are welcome for a $5 one-time fee.

$ Sunrise Inn, 420 E. 8th Ave., 970-848-5465 (800-378-9166). There's a $5 one-time fee.

Central Eastern Plains
Burlington
$ Burlington Inn, 450 S. Lincoln St., 719-346-5555. There's a $5 fee per night, and a dog can be left unattended in the room.

$ Chaparral Motor Inn, 405 S. Lincoln St. (Exit 437 off I-70), 719-346-5361 (800-456-6206). The motel allows small dogs. A field where they can stretch their legs is beside the motel.

$ Hi-Lo Motel, 870 Rose Ave., 719-346-5280. Dogs are allowed in certain rooms for a $5 one-time fee.

$ Western Motor Inn, 2222 Rose Ave., 719-346-5371 (800-346-5330). Small dogs (50 pounds and under, or thereabouts) are allowed in smoking rooms only for $5 per night extra.

$$ Comfort Inn, 282 Lincoln St., 719-346-7676 (888-388-7676). The motel has designated pet rooms for a $50 deposit and a $10 one-time fee.

Byers
$–$$ Budget Host Longhorn Motel, 457 N. Main, 303-822-5205. If you're paying by credit card, a $40 deposit will be put on it for your dog; if you're paying with cash, you'll have to ante up a $10 nightly fee that's nonrefundable.

Flagler
$ Little England Motel, 244 High St., 719-765-4812. This small motel allows dogs that are "housebroken and won't jump up on the bed," says the owner.

Idalia
$ Prairie Vista Motel, 26995 Highway 36, 970-354-7237

Kit Carson
$ Stage Stop Motel, 208 W. Highways 287 & 40, 719-962-3277. Dogs can be left unattended in the room; "squirrely" dogs can be leashed outside, if necessary.

Limon
$ Econo Lodge of Limon, 985 Highway 24, 719-775-2867. There's a $10 one-time fee.

$ K S Motel, 385 Main, 719-775-2072. The motel allows dogs in five of its smoking rooms for a $5 nightly fee. There's a small park area in the back where you can exercise your dog off leash.

$ Safari Motel, 637 Main, 719-775-2363 (800-330-7021). For $4 extra per night, dogs can stay in several of the motel's rooms.

$–$$ Best Western Limon Inn, 925 T Ave., 719-775-0277 (800-528-1234 [national number]). There are seven designated pet rooms; the fee for pets is $10 per night.

$–$$ Preferred Motor Inn, 158 E. Main, 719-775-2385 (800-530-3956). Dogs are allowed in about half of the rooms here, and a third of the pet rooms are nonsmoking. There's a potential $2 fee per night.

$–$$ Super 8 Motel, 937 Highway 24, 719-775-2889 (800-800-8000 [national number]). Dog guests are welcome for a $10 fee per night.

$$ Tyme Square Inn, 2505 6th St., 719-775-0700 (877-900-TYME). There's a $5 to $15 one-time fee, depending on the size of the dog.

Strasburg
$ Denver East/Strasburg KOA and Kamping Kabins, 1312 Monroe St., 970-622-9274 (800-KOA-6538). The campground's management doesn't necessarily like allowing dogs in the cabins because they've had "too many poopy dogs." However, they will consider dogs on a case-by-case basis, so if you're in the area and need to find a place to stay, you might give it a try.

$–$$ Strasburg Inn, 1406 Main St., 303-622-4314. Well-behaved, well-trained dogs are accepted at this historic bed-and-breakfast if they pass muster with "Uncle" Joe, the loquacious manager. The 85-year-old house used to lodge railroad workers and travelers. Next door today is a foundry that restores old train cars. The eight rooms (one with private bath) are decorated in an early American style, with vintage furniture and patchwork quilts. It's possible to leave your well-behaved, well-trained dog unattended for a short period of time in your room.

Stratton
$–$$ **Best Western Golden Prairie Inn**, 700 Colorado Ave., 719-348-5311 (800-626-0043). The motel has several rooms that dogs can stay in. They can be left unattended in the room if they're in a travel kennel.

Campgrounds
Pawnee National Grasslands. The campground is at the Crow Valley Recreation Area, about 25 miles east of Greeley near the intersection of Highway 14 and County Rd. 77. There are ten individual sites (seven single and three double), plus some group sites that must be reserved in advance.

State park campgrounds: **Bonny Lake State Park,** near Idalia, off Highway 385 (200 sites); **Jackson Lake State Park,** northwest of Fort Morgan, off Highway 144 (270 sites); **North Sterling Reservoir State Park,** northwest of Sterling off County Rd. 33 (141 sites).

WORTH A PAWS
Paws and Sneakers. This annual run/walk for dogs and their owners is held on a Saturday during the first half of September. The 2-mile course winds through the area surrounding the Northern Colorado Animal League shelter in Evans. The event's proceeds, raised through registration fees, pledges, and community sponsors, benefit the league. Participation gets you a T-shirt, your pooch a goodie bag, and the both of you a great time.

After the run, stick around for the ten-event Canine Carnival, in which your dog can compete for honors such as best trick or best kiss. For more information, call the Northern Colorado Animal League at 970-506-9550.

DOGGIE DAYCARE
Windsor
Double J Pet Ranch, 14253 Highway 392, 970-352-5330. $8/day. Dogs stay in indoor/outdoor runs and enjoy an outside play area several times a day. Open 8:30 a.m.–5:30 p.m., Monday to Friday; 8:30 a.m.–noon, Saturday.

PET PROVISIONS
Fort Morgan
Grooming Spot, 406½ E. Railroad Ave., 970-867-6007

Pets R People Too, 835 E. Platte Ave., 970-867-4860

Sterling
Cher's Pet Shop & Dog Grooming, 415 N. Front, 970-522-2577

Country General, 155 Cucarola Rd., 970-522-7681

Windsor
Animal Affair Again, 201 4th St., 970-686-6762

CANINE ER
Burlington
Vondy and Powell Veterinarians, 11675 Highway 385, 719-346-7341. Open 7 a.m.–5 p.m., Monday to Friday; by appointment on Saturday.

Fort Morgan
Fort Morgan Veterinary Clinic, 1215 E. Burlington, 970-867-9477. Open 8 a.m.–5 p.m., Monday to Friday; 9 a.m.–noon, Saturday.

Greeley
West Ridge Animal Hospital (AAHA certified), 6525 W. 28th St., 970-330-7283. Open 8 a.m.–5:30 p.m., Monday to Friday; 8 a.m.–noon, Saturday.

Limon
Limon Veterinary Clinic, 1005 Immel, 719-775-9773. Open 8 a.m.–6 p.m., Monday to Friday; 8 a.m.–4 p.m., Saturday.

Sterling

Sterling Animal Clinic, 1331 W. Main, 970-521-0333. Open 8 a.m.–12 p.m. and 1–5 p.m., Monday to Friday.

RESOURCES

Colorado Welcome Center, I-70 near Colorado/Kansas border, Burlington, 719-346-5554

Greeley Convention and Visitors Bureau, 902 7th Ave., Greeley, 970-352-3567 (800-449-3866)

Northeast Colorado Travel Region, 451 14th St., Burlington, 719-346-7019 (800-777-9075)

Pawnee National Grasslands Ranger District, 660 O St., Greeley, 970-353-5004

Estes Park

THE BIG SCOOP

This area's primary tourist draw—Rocky Mountain National Park—becomes a lot less attractive if you're visiting with your dog: You can't bring him on any hikes within the park. To the north, east, and south of Estes Park, however, is a range of national forest trails that you and your furry cohiker can enjoy together.

Dog guidelines to live by when in Estes: (1) remind your owner to keep you leashed within the city limits and not to leave you unattended in front of a store or restaurant; (2) leave the elk alone—they don't want to play with you; and (3) keep your paws off the park trails—otherwise your owner will have to pay a fine, which just might come out of your dog-treat allowance.

TAIL-RATED TRAILS

Several years ago the Forest Service proposed a management plan that would have banned dogs completely from the eastern half of the Indian Peaks Wilderness area, south of Rocky Mountain National Park, if compliance with the mandatory leash law was less than 90 percent five years after the plan's enactment. Although the plan was not approved, *be extra diligent about keeping your dog leashed when in this area* so that the ban idea is not resurrected (none of the trails described here are in the wilderness area). Note that if you decide to hike **St. Vrain Mountain** outside of Allenspark, you're supposed to turn around before reaching trail's end: Part of the trail goes through a short section of Rocky Mountain National Park, and

dogs are not allowed on this part. (You could also skirt this section altogether by heading off-trail, but you didn't hear it from me.) And though the **Twin Sisters Trail** is in a separate location, it's on National Park property and is therefore off-limits to dogs. In addition to the trails listed below, you can hike with your dog in the **Pierson Park** and **Johnny Park** areas (see "Cycling for Canines").

Crosier Mountain. 8 miles round-trip. From the intersection of U.S. Highways 34 and 36 in Estes Park, take Highway 34 west, past the Stanley Hotel. Make a right onto Devil's Gulch Rd. After about 7 miles, you'll reach the hamlet of Glen Haven. Look for the Crosier Mountain Trail sign on the right, just before a horse rental operation. You'll need to park across the street, however, as the road leading to the trailhead is a private drive. *Dogs can be off leash.*

This is a marvelous hike that will capture the interest of both you and your dog with a variety of terrain and landscape. Walk up the private road (you'll probably want to keep your dog on a leash during this part) and hook up with the trail on the right. Be aware that the trail gets high horse use in the summer, which means that if your dog is like most, he'll try to help himself to "snacks" along the way. The trail begins by switchbacking up, though not too steeply, through stands of ponderosa pine. At half a mile, you'll pass a signed turnoff to the H-G Ranch, the first of a couple you'll come to. Shortly after, your dog can pause for refreshment at a small stream. The trail then narrows and leads you to perhaps the most beautiful part of the hike, Piper Meadow, a vast expanse studded with wildflowers in the summer. The Mummy Range and other mountains in the park stretch out to the west. Stay left at the fork, and follow the trail as it crosses above the meadow. After passing another trail junction, you'll climb a series of switchbacks leading up the hillside above the meadow. Hike past another junction atop a small saddle. The final ascent to the peak goes through thick stands of lodgepole pine, passing yet another trail junction. The very last part before the summit is rocky and steep. The trail ends at a spectacular vista atop the 9,250-foot peak.

Coulson Gulch. 5 miles round-trip. From Highway 7 at Lake Estes, drive south on U.S. Highway 36 for just under 10 miles and take the turnoff for Big Elk Meadows on the right. Drive for 3.1 miles and veer left at the fork; you'll then drive about 0.5 mile on the dirt road to the trailhead. The last 0.1 mile is a little rough, so you may want to park on the side of the road if you have a low-clearance vehicle. Otherwise, look for a large parking area to the left (the road continues on as the Johnny Park four-wheel-drive route). *Dogs can be off leash.*

We met a couple of mountain bikers on this quietly scenic trail who had just discovered it the weekend before and referred to it as the "ssshh" trail. After some debate over whether to publicize it, my friend Sean and I were outnumbered by our three dogs, who made a case for sharing it with their canine brethren as another alternative to the forbidden trails of the national park.

The trail begins at an unsigned wooden post next to a signboard (blank when we visited) and heads downhill through a meadow before entering an area of widely

Is Fido craving a cool drink in downtown Estes Park? Bring him to Riverside Plaza, where a fountain and surrounding pool (as well as the nearby Big Thompson River) can provide some relief.

The Shining Mountains group of the Colorado Mountain Club (CMC) includes "doggie hikes" in its annual schedule of trips and activities. For information on joining this CMC group, call 970-586-6623.

spaced ponderosa pine. A small stream runs alongside the trail through the gulch, providing refreshment for thirsty canines. Eventually, a short, steep climb leads you out of the gulch onto a side hill, from which you'll gain a nice view of the surrounding foothills. After switchbacking down again through the pines, you'll come to a small clearing with the remains of a cabin. Next up is a huge expanse of meadow known as Higgins Park (bring a tennis ball if Fido really wants to romp). At the meadow's south end, take a right on the dirt track and continue for about 25 minutes or so to the bridge over rushing North St. Vrain Creek. This makes a good spot for a well-earned doggie paddle and is the turnaround point for this hike. If you're up for a longer excursion, however, you can continue across the bridge and to the right on the North Sheep Mountain Trail, which runs along the creek for 3.5 miles. It's then possible to loop back to the Coulson Gulch trailhead via the Johnny Park four-wheel-drive road, for a total distance of about 8 miles.

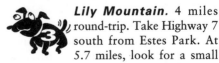

Lily Mountain. 4 miles round-trip. Take Highway 7 south from Estes Park. At 5.7 miles, look for a small parking pullout on the right as well as a small brown "Lily Mountain" sign and blue call-box sign. *Dogs can be off leash.*

A popular hike close to Estes Park, 9,786-foot Lily Mountain lies just outside the park boundary; therefore, dogs are allowed, and because it's on national forest land, they can even explore leash-free. You'll need to bring water for the both of you, as there's none along the trail. Clover liked this hike because it remains primarily in ponderosa and lodgepole pine, which meant she found an ample supply of sticks to carry around. The first half of the trail parallels Highway 7, though as you make the moderate climb, the noise from the busy highway begins to fade. And during the ascent, you'll pass lots of vista points that look down into the Estes valley. The peaks of Twin Sisters rise directly to the east. Stay left at an unmarked fork; from this point, the trail switchbacks up the mountain. As you approach the top, the trail becomes harder to follow; look for the rock cairns. The final ascent involves a bit of rock scrambling, but nothing that an agile dog won't be able to handle. The reward is a panoramic view of the park's lofty peaks.

Frostbite is a local Estes Park trouble-maker. (photo by Cindy Hirschfeld)

Lion Gulch. 5 miles round-trip to Homestead Meadows. From Estes Park, head south on Highway 36 for 8 miles. Then look for the parking area and trailhead on the right. *Dogs can be off leash.*

The hike begins with a short descent down to the Little Thompson River. After crossing this, the trail follows a smaller stream on the ascent up the gulch, criss-crossing it several times via bridges and logs laid across. You'll enjoy the sweet smell of pine as you travel. Shortly before reaching the first meadow—a great spot for summer wildflowers—the trail turns into an old dirt road. Pause to read the trailside sign that will educate you and your dog about the Homestead Act of 1862, in case you've forgotten that part of your high school history class. Once at the meadows, you can hike to as many as eight homesteads or a sawmill (distances range from 0.25 mile to 2 miles one-way). The homesteads, which date from 1889 to 1923, are in various states of degeneration, but you'll still be able to appreciate their scenic settings. Fido, in the meantime, can enjoy the open terrain and, if thirsty, refresh himself at the horse trough in the first meadow.

Lake Estes Trail. 4-mile loop. The easiest place to pick up the trail is behind the Estes Park Chamber of Commerce building, just east of the intersection of U.S. Highways 34 and 36. *Dogs must be leashed.*

Great for a scenic stroll close to town, this newly completed paved path encircles Lake Estes, where your dog can do a bit of on-leash splashing in the water and, perhaps, gaze longingly at the ducks. And you'll get a nice view of the park's eastern peaks. A spur of the trail runs along the Big Thompson River from the lake to Riverside Plaza downtown.

Rocky Mountain National Park. In case your dog missed the explanation at the beginning of the chapter, here's a recap: The park is just not a dog-friendly place. Dogs can come along to campgrounds and picnic areas in the park as long as they're on a leash six feet long or less. And they can venture up to 100 feet from roadways or parking areas. That's it—all trails have been designated canine-free. And in case you're thinking of leaving Fido in the car or tied up at a trailhead or campsite, that's a no-no, too. Your best bet is to stay at a place where you can leave your dog unattended in the room or to board him during the time you plan to be in the park.

CYCLING FOR CANINES

Several four-wheel-drive roads on national forest land provide good spots for taking the pooch for a pedal. The **Pierson Park** area is accessible from Fish Creek Rd., near the east end of Lake Estes. The **Johnny Park** area can be reached from either Highway 36 south (at the Forest Service access sign for Big Elk Meadows; see Coulson Gulch in "Tail-Rated Trails") or from Big Owl or Cabin Creek Rds. off Highway 7 south. To reach **Pole Hill**, follow the Forest Access sign off Highway 36 north, just before the final descent into the Estes valley. The Forest Service office (see "Resources") has maps of all these areas.

POWDERHOUNDS

Finding places to ski and snowshoe with your dog in the Estes Park area generally means having to venture southwest toward Nederland (see Chapter 2). The Estes valley does not hold snow for very long, making national forest trails iffy for skiing. Rocky Mountain National Park,

of course, is off-limits, and trails just south of Estes are in the Indian Peaks Wilderness, where leashes are required.

CREATURE COMFORTS

Unless otherwise stated, dogs should not be left unattended in the room or cabin.

Allenspark

$$ Sunshine Mountain Inn, 18078 Highway 7 (2 miles south of Allenspark), 303-747-2840 (www.sunshinemtninn.com). Dogs are welcome in both the fully equipped one- and two-bedroom cabins or in the main lodge, where dorm space is available (retreat groups usually use the latter). You can leave your dog unattended in the cabin.

$$$$ Lane Guest Ranch, 12 miles south of Estes Park off Highway 7, 303-747-2493 (www.ranchweb.com/laneranch). A vacation at this family-oriented guest ranch is a treat for everyone, including the dog. In operation since 1953, the ranch accommodates up to eighty-five guests and has a staff of about forty-five. There are twenty-five cozy one- and two-bedroom cabin and A-frame units, most with private patios or decks, and more than half with private hot tubs. You can leave your dog unattended inside or on the deck while you go horseback riding or whitewater rafting. Other ranch offerings include guided hikes and fishing trips, outings to Central City and Grand Lake, evening entertainment, and a whole slate of children's activities. And of course there's plenty of hiking and biking nearby that you can do with your dog (you'll need to keep him leashed on the 25-acre ranch property). The best deals are the week-long package plans, which include three meals a day and all activities. And your pooch is sure to salivate when you tell him that free dog meals—steak, prime rib, or chicken breast—are available! Open beginning of June to end of August.

Bruno pauses for refreshment on a trail near Estes Park. (photo by Cindy Hirschfeld)

Estes Park

$–$$ Four Winds Motor Lodge, 1120 Big Thompson Ave., 970-586-3313 (800-527-7509; www.estesparkresort.com/four winds). The motel accepts dogs for a $15 fee per dog, per night. In addition to standard rooms, two- and three-room suites and units with kitchens are available. A three-bedroom house can also be rented.

$–$$ Lazy T Motor Lodge, 1340 Big Thompson Ave., 970-586-4376 (800-530-8822; www.estes-park.com/lazyt). There's a limit of one dog per room, and a credit-card imprint is required as a deposit. Kitchenette units are available. Open May 1 to the end of October.

$$ Aspen Grove Cottages, 238 Riverside Dr., 970-586-4584 (www.estes-park.com/aspengrove). Dogs 20 pounds and under can stay in these fully outfitted cabins close to downtown. There's a $5 fee per night, and you can leave your dog unattended in the room if he's in a travel kennel. Open Memorial Day to October 1.

$$ Cliffside Cottages, 2445 Highway 66, 970-586-4839 (888-643-0203; www.cliff sidecottages.com). The only restriction on dogs at this small resort is that they be walked in a certain area on the property. The three fully equipped cabins vary in size, from sleeping two to six, and all have fireplaces. You can leave your dog unattended inside. Open May 1 through early October.

$$ Inn at Estes Park, 1701 Big Thompson Ave., 970-586-5363 (800-458-1182; www.innatestespark.com). The motel allows dogs 20 pounds and under in its ground-floor rooms and suites for a $20 one-time fee.

$$ Silver Moon Inn, 175 Spruce Dr., 970-586-6006 (800-818-6006; www.silver mooninn.com). Dogs are permitted during the off-season only, from September 15 to June 15, in select units. Lodging options range from motel rooms to suites to older, two-room cabins with kitchenettes. The complex is located on the Fall River, about a block from downtown.

$$ Wonderview Cabins, 540 Laurel Ln., 970-586-6500 (800-324-4149). Formerly known as Anderson's Wonderview Cottages, the property is now a mix of privately owned and short-term rental cabins overseen by a property management company, Ponderosa Realty. Four fully equipped cottages range in size from one to three bedrooms, and all have fireplaces and decks. There's a limit of two dogs per unit, and the fee is $15 per night. Extremely well-behaved dogs or those who stay in a travel crate can be left unattended in the cabin. Be sure to keep your dog leashed on the 7-acre property.

$$–$$$ Castle Mountain Lodge, 1520 Fall River Rd., 970-586-3664 (800-852-7463; www.estes-park.com/castle). Dogs are allowed in about ten of the cottages here, which range from one to three bedrooms, for a $15 fee per night, per dog. The cottages are fully equipped, and many have fireplaces. Your dog will enjoy the scenic location along the Fall River, close to the national park.

$$–$$$ Edgewater Heights Cottages, 2550 Big Thompson Ave., 970-586-8493 (800-530-3942; www.estes-park.com/edge water). For $5 a night extra, your dog can have his pick of nine fully equipped cabins (most are one bedroom), all with fireplaces. "I enjoy having pets," says David, the owner. And you can take Fido to explore the surrounding 15 acres along the Big Thompson River leash-free. Open March to November 1.

$$–$$$ Elkhorn Lodge, 600 W. Elkhorn Ave., 970-586-4416. Though the main lodge does not allow pets, you can stay with your dog in the cottages, studio cabins, or "the woodshed," a detached building with five motel rooms inside. All of these are fully furnished, but most don't have kitchen facilities. Five "alpine homes," with two to four bedrooms and full kitchens, are also available. There's a $10 fee per dog, per night, and you can leave your dog unattended as long as you inform the management. Open May through October.

$$–$$$ Estes Park Center YMCA, 2515 Highway 66, 970-586-3341 (www.ymca rockies.org). The YMCA complex is scenically situated on 860 acres right next to the national park. Although dogs are not permitted in the lodge rooms, you'll be able to choose from more than 200 fully equipped cabins, ranging in size from two to four bedrooms and the majority with fireplaces, that can accommodate Fido. You can leave your dog unattended in the cabin; keep him leashed when outside it.

$$–$$$ Hobby Horse Motor Lodge, 800 Big Thompson Ave., 970-586-3336 (800-354-8253; www.estesweb.com/hobby horse). Dogs are allowed during the summer only in most rooms, for a $5 fee per night, per dog. Many of the rooms are at ground level, providing easy access for dog walking, and the motel is on five acres of wooded property.

$$–$$$ Machin's Cottages in the Pines, 2450 Eagle Cliff Rd., 970-586-4276 (www.estes-park.com/machins). Dogs less than 20 pounds may stay in any of the seventeen fully equipped, quaintly furnished cabins, which have from one to three bedrooms and fireplaces. Because the cottages are surrounded by national park land, you won't be able to walk Fido very far from them. There's a two-night minimum stay. Open from May through the end of September.

$$–$$$ National Park Resort Cabins and Campground, 3501 Fall River Rd., 970-586-4563 (www.natlparkresort.com). The resort is located just outside the Fall River entrance to the park. Your dog is welcome to join you in the motel rooms (two have kitchens), one of the four fully outfitted cabins, or the new lodge building, a fully furnished unit that sleeps groups of up to twelve. There's a limit of two pets in a unit.

$$–$$$ Olympus Motor Lodge, 2365 Big Thompson Ave., 970-586-8141 (800-248-8141; www.estes-park.com/olympus). Teeny dogs (those under 10 pounds) are allowed in certain rooms, with a credit-card imprint as a deposit.

$$–$$$ Palisade Motel, 1372 Big Thompson Canyon (about halfway between Estes Park and Loveland), 970-663-5532 (www.palisademotel.com). The motel's units are more like cabins; some are separate, some share a wall, and all but one have fully equipped kitchens. There's a $5 fee per night, per pet, and you must keep your dog leashed at all times when outside (you'll be able to take him to explore the Big Thompson River at property's edge).

$$–$$$ Skyline Cottages, 1752 Highway 66, 970-586-2886 (www.skylinecottages.com). Your dog will join a long line of canine visitors with a stay at Skyline, as the owner has welcomed pets for more than two decades. The eight fully equipped cottages range in size from one-room units to two bedrooms. Most have fireplaces, and a couple have decks overlooking the Big Thompson River; one even has a separate spa room with a whirlpool bath. There's a $6 fee per night, per pet, and you are able to leave your dog in the cottage unattended. The property also features a large stand-alone riverside deck with picnic tables and other seating. Be sure to bring Fido by the office for a treat from the basket of dog biscuits; poop pickup bags and plastic gloves are also dispensed. Open from the end of May through mid-October.

$$$ Braeside Cabin, 2179 Highway 66, 970-586-6845, (www.rmnp.com/braeside). This renovated studio cabin, which sleeps up to four humans, is a sister property of the Braeside Bed-and-Breakfast (where dogs are not allowed). Done up in a mountain cabin decor, with knotty pine interior, cathedral ceiling, full kitchen, and wood-burning fireplace, it allows you and your dog to enjoy a great vista of the adjacent national park, and specifically Long's Peak, in comfort. Well-behaved dogs can be left unattended inside. Since there's no extra canine fee or deposit, "if the dog redecorates, we'll settle up at check-out," says the friendly owner. "But I've never had that happen," she adds. Make sure you keep it that way! As a cabin guest you'll have access to the hot tub at the B&B, though not the breakfast.

$$$ Mountain Haven Inn and Cottages, 690 Moraine Ave., 970-586-2864 (www.estes-park.com/mountainhaven). Dogs are welcome in four of the six fully furnished two-bedroom cabins at this friendly complex situated on the Big

Bess finds her footing at the top of St. Vrain Mountain. (photo by Connie Oehring)

Thompson River. (The inn itself, a three-bedroom house, is off-limits to canines.) The cabins are among the newer ones that you'll find in Estes. You'll need to keep Fido on his leash when outside on the property.

Campgrounds

Rocky Mountain National Park. The park has four campgrounds on the eastern side, and dogs are permitted at all of them.

National forest campgrounds: Camp Dick Campground (41 sites) and Peaceful Valley Campground (17 sites) are off Highway 72 (via Highway 7 south past Allenspark) at Peaceful Valley; Olive Ridge Campground, off Highway 7, is near the Wild Basin area of the national park (56 sites).

Private campgrounds: National Park Resort Cabins and Campground (see "Creature Comforts").

WORTH A PAWS

International Dog Weight Pull Competition. Bring your dog to drool over the Arnold Schwarzeneggers of the canine world. Sanctioned by the International Weight Pulling Association, this two-day competition, held in mid-February in Estes Park, allows about fifty dogs to show off their pulling prowess. Each dog is put into a competitive class based on his own weight. The competitors then vie to see who can pull the most weight on a sled on snow one day, and the most wheeled weights the next. Contact the Chamber Resort Association at 800-44-ESTES or 970-586-4431 for more information.

DOGGIE DAYCARE
Estes Park
Animal Medical Center of Estes Park (AAHA certified), 1260 Manford Ave., 970-586-6898. $10/day. Open 8 a.m.–5:00 p.m., Monday to Friday; 8 a.m.–noon, Saturday. Later pickups on Saturday and boarding on Sunday can be arranged in advance.

Boarding House for Pets, 863 Dry Gulch Rd., 970-586-6606. $11 for the first dog, $6 for the second. Open 7:30 a.m.–5:30 p.m., Monday to Saturday, and for check-in at 11 a.m. and pickup at 4 p.m. on Sunday (other times available by advance arrangement).

PET PROVISIONS
Estes Park
Boarding House for Pets, 863 Dry Gulch Rd., 970-586-6606

Estes Bark Pet Grooming, 1632 Big Thompson Ave., 970-586-3181

Pets 'N' Nature, Upper Stanley Village, 970-586-8442. There's a self-service dog wash here too.

CANINE ER
Estes Park
Animal Hospital of the Rockies, 1632A Big Thompson Ave., 970-586-4703. Open 8 a.m.–5 p.m., Monday to Friday; 8 a.m.–noon, Saturday.

Animal Medical Center of Estes Park (AAHA certified), 1260 Manford Ave., 970-586-6898. Open 8 a.m.–5:30 p.m., Monday to Friday; 8 a.m.–noon, Saturday.

RESOURCES
Estes Park Chamber Resort Association, 500 Big Thompson Ave., Estes Park, 970-586-4431 (800-44-ESTES; www.estesparkresort.com)

Estes Park Forest Service Office, Arapaho and Roosevelt National Forests, 161 2nd St., Estes Park, 970-586-3440

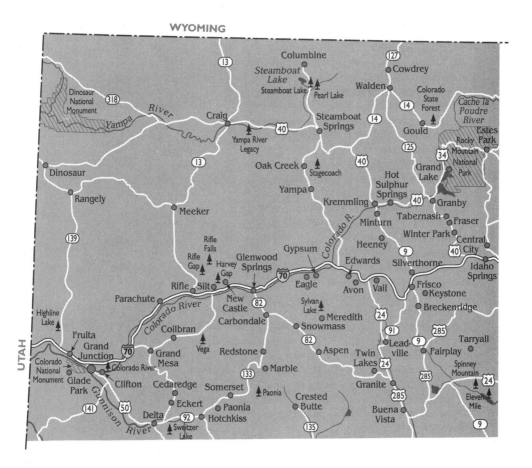

WYOMING

Dinosaur National Monument
318
Yampa River
Craig
13
Columbine
Steamboat Lake
Steamboat Lake
Pearl Lake
Walden
127
Cowdrey
Colorado State Forest
14
Cache la Poudre River
Steamboat Springs
14
Gould
125
34
Estes Park
Rocky Mountain National Park
Dinosaur
13
Oak Creek
Stagecoach
40
Grand Lake
Rangely
Yampa
Hot Sulphur Springs
Meeker
Kremmling
40
Granby
139
Tabernash
Fraser
Minturn
Winter Park
Rifle Falls
Rifle Gap
Harvey Gap
Glenwood Springs
Gypsum
Heeney
Central City
Edwards
Silverthorne
Idaho Springs
70
9
40
Rifle
Silt
Eagle
Avon
Vail
Frisco
Keystone
Parachute
New Castle
82
Sylvan Lake
Breckenridge
Highline Lake
Collbran
Carbondale
Meredith
Snowmass
24
Fruita
Grand Junction
70
Vega
Redstone
Aspen
82
91
285
Tarryall
Spinney Mountain
Grand Mesa
Marble
Twin Lakes
Lead-ville
9
Fairplay
Colorado National Monument
Glade Park
Clifton
Cedaredge
Somerset
133
Paonia
Granite
24
285
141
50
Eckert
Paonia
Crested Butte
Buena Vista
285
Eleven Mile
24
Delta
92
Hotchkiss
135
9
Swetizer Lake

UTAH

Colorado River
Colorado R.
Colorado River
Gunnison River
Yampa
River

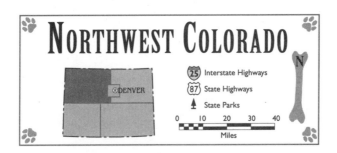

SEVEN

Winter Park, Grand Lake, and Granby

THE BIG SCOOP

The area from Winter Park to the town of Grand Lake, which runs along the western side of the Continental Divide, has fantastic views of the rugged peaks along the Divide, several lakes nestled at the base of the mountains, and abundant recreational opportunities. And Grand Lake itself is Colorado's largest natural lake. So what's in it for Rover? Not quite as much as for you, unfortunately, primarily because dogs are not allowed on any of the trails in Rocky Mountain National Park, which lies adjacent to Grand Lake. And many of the other trails enter the Indian Peaks Wilderness area, where dogs must be leashed. But there are some great trails where your dog can hike off leash with you (including the Never Summer, Byers Peak, and Vasquez Wilderness Areas, where dogs can be under voice command) as well as suitable mountain biking terrain for the both of you. And there's even a backcountry hut you can ski to with your dog!

Within the town limits of Winter Park, Fraser, Tabernash, Granby, Grand Lake, and Hot Sulphur Springs, you'll need to keep your dog leashed. In unincorporated parts of Grand County, you can walk your dog under voice command.

TAIL-RATED TRAILS

For additional trail information, stop by the Sulfur Ranger District office in Granby (see "Resources"), which puts out a few pamphlets with short hike descriptions. Or pay a visit to Flanagan's Black Dog Mountaineering, on U.S. Highway 40 in downtown Winter Park,

which carries a range of guidebooks and maps. (Because the store also sells ice cream, you won't be able to bring Rover inside; bring him a scoop as a reward for waiting.) If you're starting a hike at the Monarch Lake Trailhead, note that dogs are required to be on leash on trails by the lake, even though it's not within the wilderness boundary. And you can hike with your dog at the Winter Park Ski Area as long as he stays on leash.

Baker Gulch. 12 miles round-trip. Note that to access this trail, you will have to enter Rocky Mountain National Park and pay the requisite entrance fee. Even though the first half mile of trail is on park property, dogs are allowed because the rest is on national forest land. Access to the trail is closed for the week before hunting season each fall, so call the park (970-627-3471) first to check on the access if you're hiking in late September or early October. To reach the trail, take U.S. Highway 34 north from Grand Lake to the West Entrance Station of the park. From here it's 6.2 miles to the turnoff for the trailhead. Look for the Bowen–Baker Gulch trailhead sign on the right; a large parking area is on the left. *Dogs can be off leash.*

This beautiful hike, which ascends to the top of Baker Pass, allows you to enjoy the same scenery and terrain as other trails on the western side of Rocky Mountain National Park—but your dog can come too. For the first half mile, hike along a dirt service road that begins by crossing the Colorado River, and stay

Artemis basks in a wildflower-studded meadow near Winter Park. (photo by Karen Pauly)

ditch via the log footbridge up ahead to pick up the trail again. You'll then skirt the flanks of Mount Baker before heading north toward the pass, at 11,253 feet. The trail crisscrosses the creek a few times as it traverses open meadows. The final section is marked by cairns. Directly east of the pass lie Mounts Cumulus, Nimbus, and Stratus, all above 12,000 feet. On the return trip, you'll be treated to a view of the peaks in the park.

Alternate hikes in this area include the **Parika Lake Trail,** which branches off the Baker Gulch Trail at about 5 miles; from there it's 2.4 miles to the lake. The **Bowen Gulch Trail** begins from the same trailhead as Baker Gulch; stay left at the signed fork on the park service road. It's a 16.2-mile round-trip to the top of Blue Ridge to the south.

right at the signed fork; since you're on park property, keep your dog leashed on this section. A sign board marks the entrance into the Arapaho National Forest. (During hunting season, you'll be able to drive up this road to the forest boundary.) The trail itself starts out next to a creek. After a bit you'll head away from the creek but will never be far from its hearty roar during the first few miles of the hike. Aside from an occasional switchback, the trail remains moderate and is well maintained as it winds through lodgepole pine and subalpine fir. About 2 miles from the trailhead, you'll pop out into a treeless area with a grand view of Fairview Mountain ahead, part of a spectacular alpine cirque. The trail crosses a talus slope, then reenters the trees, following the general uphill course of the creek below. You'll come to a dirt road that parallels the Grand Ditch, a water-diversion project planned in 1890 and completed in 1936 that captured snowmelt and brought it to farmers on the eastern side of the Continental Divide. Cross the

High Lonesome Trail. 6 miles round-trip. Take County Rd. 83 off Highway 40 at the south end of Tabernash (you'll see a sign for the Devil's Thumb Ski Area and a forest access/Meadow Creek Reservoir sign). Stay left at the next two forks—the first left will put you on County Rd. 84—following the signs to the reservoir, which is about 9 miles away. About 0.7 mile after Forest Rd. 128 comes in from the right, you'll come to an unmarked fork; stay right. Once you reach Meadow Creek Reservoir, follow the sign to Junco Lake. The parking area and trailhead are by a small Forest Service cabin. *Dogs can be off leash.*

The trail, which is also designated as part of the 3,100-mile-long Continental Divide National Scenic Trail (CDT), brings hikers to Devil's Thumb, a prominent rock feature on the Continental Divide; from here you'll be treated to expansive views of the Fraser River valley, the Indian Peaks Wilderness area to the east, Winter Park Ski Area and surrounding peaks to the west and south, and the Never Summer Range to the north. From the trailhead, head right (south) along the High Lonesome Trail. The trail winds through a fragrant forest of lodgepole pine and spruce. In a half mile you'll come to a road; cross it, following the CDT markers. Soon you'll come to a series of beautiful, high-mountain meadows. Their open expanse allows sensational views of the high peaks that form the Continental Divide.

These meadows also allow you to glean a better understanding of forest succession. They started as beaver ponds (if you look closely you can still see where the waterline was). As the streams feeding the ponds continued to transport waterborne silt and sediments, the ponds gradually filled in, becoming the lush meadows surrounding you. In time, these meadows, too, will change: The rich soil will nourish the same lodgepole pine and spruce through which you've been hiking. And, in the far-off future, some enterprising beavers might take a liking to the landscape and use the trees to dam the stream, creating suitable habitat—and beaver ponds. And so it goes.

After a little less than 3 miles of easy hiking, the trail reaches a junction with

The Dog Trail, so called because the Native Americans who traveled it used dogs to carry their possessions, went through an area between Estes Park and Grand Lake.

A barrier-free nature trail constructed by the Bonfils-Stanton Foundation and the Winter Park Outdoor Center allows a guide dog and his owner to enjoy a wilderness experience. The trail is located off Highway 40, across from the entrance to the Winter Park Ski Resort.

another access trail; stay left on the CDT. After the junction you'll start to climb toward the peaks to the east. Soon you'll be able to spot the Devil's Thumb, a lone spire rising from the ridgeline. The trail ultimately passes just south of the thumb (it makes a good landmark, as the trail becomes faint near the ridgeline) into the Indian Peaks Wilderness area. Stop at the pass and savor the outstanding views in all directions before returning the way you came.

Columbine Lake. 5.6 miles round-trip. Follow the directions to the trailhead for the High Lonesome Trail (see previous entry). *Dogs can be off leash until the wilderness boundary, about 1.75 miles in.*

Begin hiking up an old road, which crosses a couple of streams and then ascends gradually through subalpine fir. At the entrance to a large meadow, you'll cross the wilderness boundary, which means it's time to leash up. Ahead on the right, Mount Neva comes prominently into view. The road skirts the meadow on the left, eventually becoming a narrower trail. Shortly after passing the turnoff for the Caribou Trail, you'll ascend away from the meadow into the woods; you should be on the left side of a creek. The trail then skirts a couple of other meadows before the final ascent to the lake. The last part of the trail is a bit trickier to follow, so you may want to let Rover sniff out the way. You'll ascend the left side of a scree-filled drainage, hiking next to a melodic stream. The trail then crosses a plateau, which includes some marshy areas, as it angles southeast toward the lake. The lake itself is at the base of a cirque and makes for a scenic lunch spot before the return hike.

Jim Creek Trail. About 3 miles round-trip. From Highway 40 west, 0.6 mile past the turnoff for Mary Jane Ski Area, make a right on an unmarked dirt road (it's actually Forest Rd. 128). Drive 1.6 miles, staying left at the fork, to a small parking area by a water diversion dam. The trail begins on the right side of the parking lot, through the bushes. *Dogs can be off leash.*

This hike, which stays below tree line, doesn't include any spectacular vistas of the peaks on the Continental Divide or a specific destination. But your dog will be more interested in the fresh aroma of pine and spruce and the cooling waters of Jim Creek—as well as the fact that he can enjoy them leash-free. During the summer, wildflowers dot sections adjoining the trail; this would also be a nice fall hike, as a hillside of aspen rises above the trail. About the first half mile follows an old roadbed, gradually descending to creek level. The trail then winds uphill of the creek, alternately passing through stands of fir and alpine meadows. Eventually you'll cross a series of small streams coming down the hillside and come creekside again. A small open area makes a good turnaround point; the trail continues but gets increasingly sketchy from here onward.

Rocky Mountain National Park. To reiterate (see Chapter 6), the park is just not a dog-friendly place. Dogs can come along to campgrounds and picnic areas in the park as long as they're on a leash six feet long or less. And they can venture up to 100 feet from roadways or parking areas. That's it—all trails have been designated canine-free. And in case you're thinking of leaving Fido in the car or tied up at a trailhead or campsite, that's a no-no too. Your best bet is to stay at a place where you can leave your dog unattended in the room or to board him during the time you plan to be in the park.

Shadow Mountain and East Shore Trails and part of the Knight Ridge Trail. Dogs are not allowed on the East Shore Trail, which runs along the east shore of Shadow Mountain Lake, or the Shadow Mountain Trail, which branches off it, because both are within Rocky Mountain National Park. Half of the 7-mile-long Knight Ridge Trail, starting at the Green Ridge Recreation Complex, also runs across park land, making it inaccessible to dogs. However, if you begin at the Roaring Fork trailhead at the end of County Rd. 6, your dog can join you on the southern half of the trail, which goes through a portion of the Arapaho National Recreation Area and the Indian Peaks Wilderness area. Though dogs do not have to be leashed on the sections of trail in the recreation complex, keep a leash handy and a sharp eye out for wilderness boundary signs, as you will need to leash your dog on the sections of trail in the Indian Peaks Wilderness.

CYCLING FOR CANINES

Winter Park has developed a reputation for the quality and variety of its mountain-biking trails. But you won't be easily able to bike with Rover on the ski resort's network of trails, as dogs are required to be leashed on them. For a ride near the Divide, set out on the **High Lonesome Trail** (see "Tail-Rated Trails"). The **Creekside** and **Flume Trails** make an approximately 4-mile loop that begins and ends at the St. Louis Camp-ground off County Rd. 73, outside of Fraser. In the same vicinity, you can access the **Chainsaw Trail** (about 2 miles one way) and **Zoom Trail** (about 1.5 miles); the Chainsaw Trail goes out of County Rd. 72 and intersects the Zoom Trail, which can also be accessed from County Rd. 159. Water is available at places along all of these trails. For a different type of cycling adventure, bike 2.5 miles in to the High Lonesome Hut, outside of Tabernash. See "Powderhounds" for more details.

POWDERHOUNDS

Devil's Thumb Cross-Country Center,

3530 County Rd. 83, 970-726-8231. This popular Nordic ski area, at the end of County Rd. 83 out of Tabernash, allows dogs on three of its trails: the 3.5-kilometer **Foxtrot**, the 3.5-kilometer **Left Field**, and the 2-kilometer **Creekside**. A leash regulation is in effect, but there's no restriction on length, so you can outfit Rover with an extra-long leash to make skiing or snowshoeing with him in tow a bit more manageable. You'll have to pay a trail fee to access the dog-friendly routes as well as buy a $10 season pass for your dog.

Grand Lake Touring Center, 1415 County Rd. 48, 970-627-8008. The center, located about 2 miles west of Grand Lake, features a dog loop for skiers and snowshoers as well as their canine companions. The loop begins and ends near the center's main building and goes for about three-quarters of a mile. Dogs can be off leash as long as they don't run over to any of the neighboring Nordic trails. A few laps should tucker out Rover enough that you can check out the rest of the terrain while he snoozes in the car. It's $3 to go on the dog loop only (you'll have to buy a regular trail pass to access the rest of the center); you can also purchase a season dog-loop pass for $15.

High Lonesome Hut. 970-726-4099 (www.lonesome-hut.com). A backcountry hut that your dog can come along to—wonders never cease! Actually, there are some good reasons why dogs aren't allowed at most huts, water supply being one of them (you don't want to be melting yellow snow!). But the High Lonesome has a well—and indoor plumbing—making the water source a moot point. The hut, which sleeps up to eight people, is a gentle 2.5-mile ski or snowshoe in from County Rd. 84 out of Tabernash, in the Strawberry region. You can either go the traditional route, humping your own pack with food and drink, or pay extra for the "hut master service," which includes gear transport and three meals a day. Either way, your dog will love being able to accompany you on a ski tour and telemark adventure. The hut is also available during the summer to hikers and mountain bikers.

Snow Mountain Ranch. Highway 40 north of Fraser, 970-887-2152, ext. 4173 (www.ymcarockies.org). The Nordic ski area at this YMCA center has two dog-friendly trails, and both are even named after dogs. The 2-kilometer groomed **Loppet's Trail** permits skiers with leashed dogs; it's also a popular route for skijoring (your dog, wearing a harness, pulls you along) and dog-sled training runs. **Peter's Trail**, a 5-kilometer loop, is not groomed and is open to skiers and snowshoers; dogs can be off leash. You'll need to pay a fee to use either of these trails, though dogs are free.

CREATURE COMFORTS

Unless otherwise stated, dogs should not be left unattended in the room or cabin.

Fraser

$$$–$$$$ **High Mountain Lodge, 425 County Rd. 50, 970-726-5958** (800-772-9987; www.himtnlodge.com). The homey High Mountain Lodge has thirteen rooms, all with king-size beds and most with fireplaces. Four are designated pet rooms, with a $20 one-time fee. The ranch sits on 180 acres, and you can take your dog hiking off leash if he's a good voice-command listener. He might also want to sniff out the three resident dogs. During the summer, trail rides are offered at the ranch. Winter rates include breakfast and dinner at the on-site Meadow View restaurant; summer rates, from May to October, include breakfast only.

Granby

$–$$ **Blue Spruce Motel, 170 E. Agate** (Highway 40), 970-887-3300 (800-765-0001). Dogs are allowed in smoking rooms only.

$–$$ Homestead Motel, 851 W. Agate (Highway 40), 970-887-3665 (800-669-3605). The motel's flyer advertises the touches of home, including "colored, printed sheets"—you won't find the standard-issue, tissue-thin motel sheets here. (No word on the carpeting, as far your dog is concerned.) Units with kitchenettes are available.

$$$–$$$$ Shadow Mountain Guest Ranch, 5043 Highway 125 (8 miles from Granby), 970-887-9524 (800-64-SHADOW; www.coloradodirectory.com/shadowmtn ranch). The six fully outfitted log cabins at the ranch, which was first opened to guests in 1936, range from studios to three bedrooms, and some have fireplaces or wood stoves. The rates include a full breakfast in the central lodge. You'll pay a $10 fee per night, per dog to bring four-legged guests, and Fido can stay inside unattended, preferably in a travel kennel. But he'd probably rather be out with you, exploring the ranch's 1,100 acres leash-free. Horseback rides are offered during the summer.

Grand Lake
$ Elk Creek Camper Cabins and Campground, 143 County Rd. 48 (near the park entrance), 970-627-8502 (800-ELK-CREEK). Dogs are allowed in the ten camper cabins here with a credit-card imprint as a deposit. "We're doggie people," says the owner, "but we don't want things getting torn up." You'll need to supply your own bedding and cooking gear.

$–$$ Bluebird Motel, 30 River Dr., 970-627-9314. There's a $10 nightly fee per dog, and they're permitted in smoking rooms only. Note that the Peaks Point Cottages, which are affiliated with the motel, do not allow dogs.

$–$$ Inn at Grand Lake, 1103 Grand Ave., 970-627-9234 (800-722-2585). The inn is located in one of Grand Lake's

historic buildings, which dates from 1890, and rooms have antique furnishings. Dogs are accepted on a case-by-case basis— "We like to meet the dog," says the manager—and you'll have a better chance of being able to stay here with Rover in the off-season (i.e., anytime but summer). There's a $10 one-time fee for a dog.

$–$$ Sunset Motel, 505 Grand Ave., 970-627-3318. Dogs are welcome for a $10 fee per night. Be sure to check out the motel's new indoor pool.

$$–$$$ Mountain Lakes Lodge, 10480 Highway 34 (4 miles south of Grand Lake), 970-627-8448 (www.coloradodirectory.com/mountainlakeslodge). "We welcome dogs," say the friendly owners of these rustic log cabins, which are situated in a wooded area on a canal that connects Lake Granby and Shadow Mountain Lake. Eleven connected, fully equipped cabin units (some with gas fireplaces) are available as well as one three-bedroom log house with a fenced yard (for a higher rate). Cabins are comfortably furnished with handmade log furniture and quilts and have vaulted ceilings. There's a $10 nightly dog fee from Memorial Day to Labor Day; it's $5 the rest of the year. If your dog is a nonchewer and nonbarker, you can leave him unattended inside. You'll also be able to walk him on the surrounding 2.5 acres of property, which has great views of the Indian Peaks, and on the pathway that runs along the canal for several miles in each direction.

$$–$$$ Spirit Lake Lodge, 829 Grand Ave., 970-627-3344 (800-544-6593). Dogs are allowed in two of the motel's rooms for $10 extra per night. The lodge was remodeled in 2000, and rooms now have log furniture and fireplaces. The motel is located in downtown Grand Lake.

$$$–$$$$ Rocky Mountain Cabins, 12206 Highway 34, 970-627-3061

(www.coloradodirectory.com/rockymtn cabins). Not your average cabin, the three units here, 2.5 miles south of Grand Lake on the North Fork of the Colorado River, are custom-built log homes. They're all fully equipped, including washer/dryers and fireplaces. Dogs are permitted on a case-by-case basis, usually with a limit of one dog per cabin. "We'd rather rent to pets than to kids," quips the owner. You can leave your dog unattended inside only if he's in a travel kennel, but you can walk him off leash on the six acres that surround the cabins. He may also want to meet the resident dog and cats. There's a two-night minimum stay, which goes up to three nights on holiday weekends and six nights during July and August.

$$$–$$$$ The Stable Cabin, 10480 Highway 34, 303-838-3757 (888-556-2097; www.grandlakecolorado.com/stable cabin). The owner of this log cabin located on the waterway connecting Lake Granby and Shadow Mountain Lake welcomes dogs "with joy," he says. The three-bedroom/one-bath cabin, which can sleep up to fourteen people, has been remodeled, with hardwood floors and lots of interior wood trim. In addition to the full kitchen, there's also an outdoor fire pit for barbecuing. Dogs are $10 per night extra. Plans call for a shed with a dog door that leads into a fenced area so your pooch will have a place to hang out if you need to leave him behind. Four other rental cabins will eventually be built on the 1-acre, forested site.

Hot Sulphur Springs
$–$$ Canyon Motel, 221 Byers Ave., 970-725-3395 (888-489-3719; www.col oradodirectory.com/canyonmotel). Dogs are assessed an $8 nightly fee. Some rooms with kitchenettes are available.

$–$$ Ute Trail Motel, 120 E. Highway 40, 970-725-0123 (800-506-0099).

There's a $10 fee per night, per dog, and a credit-card imprint is required as a deposit. Also, dog guests can't stay for more than three nights at a time.

SolVista (formerly Silver Creek)
$$–$$$$ The Inn at Silver Creek, 62927 Highway 40, 970-887-2131 (800-926-4386; www.silvercreeklodging.com). This resort hotel, located at the base of family-oriented SolVista Golf and Ski Ranch outside of Granby, offers a range of rooms, from standards to studios and lofts with kitchenettes and fireplaces to suites. There's a $12 one-time fee for a dog ($24 if he's staying in a suite), and a credit-card imprint is required as a deposit.

Tabernash
$$$ Devil's Thumb Ranch, 3530 County Rd. 83, 970-726-5632 (800-933-4339; www.devilsthumbranch.com). Dogs are allowed in six out of the ranch's seven cabins (not in the lodge rooms). The one-room cabins include a sleeping area and bathroom; one cabin has four bedrooms. You'll be asked to sign a damage waiver on behalf of your dog. Devil's Thumb Cross-Country Center is on the property, and you can take your dog on three of the trails (see "Powderhounds" for more details). The cabins are open year-round.

Winter Park
$–$$$ Valley Hi Motel, 79025 Highway 40, 970-726-4171 (800-426-2094 [out of state only]; www.valleyhimotel.com/ winterpark). Dogs are permitted on a case-by-case basis in the motel's older rooms, with a $10 deposit. If your dog is in a travel kennel, he can stay unattended in the room. Otherwise, you can tie up Fido outside as long as he's not a constant barker.

$–$$$ Viking Lodge, 78966 Highway 40, (800-421-4013; www.skiwp.com). The

Frostbite, Sunny, Clover, and Bruno enjoy their camp near the Continental Divide with Becky Greer. (photo by Cindy Hirschfeld)

Viking bills itself as a traditional European ski lodge. Room sizes and amenities vary, ranging from the very small "Nordic" rooms to larger "Alpine" rooms, some with lofts and kitchens. There's also a suite with full kitchen and fireplace. Note that during ski season, there are minimum-stay requirements from two to five nights.

$$–$$$ Alpenglo Motor Lodge, 78665 Highway 40, 970-726-8088 (800-541-6130; www.wplodging.com). Under the same management as the Winter Park Super 8 (which doesn't allow dogs), the Alpenglo has mostly been converted to meeting space, but there are still three units available for lodging: a motel room with queen-size bed, a two-bedroom apartment-style unit, and a four-bedroom house. There's a $5 fee per night for a dog.

$$–$$$ Sitzmark Chalets and Cabins, 78253 Highway 40, 970-726-5453 (www.coloradodirectory.com/sitzmark lodgechalets). The lodge offers six units, ranging from motel rooms to cabins (two have kitchens). Dogs are charged $10 per

night extra. An RV park and campground also are on site.

$$–$$$$ The Vintage Hotel, 100 Winter Park Dr., 970-726-8801 (800-472-7017; www.vintagehotel.com). Winter Park's resident upscale hotel, the Vintage offers a variety of lodging options, ranging from regular rooms to studios with kitchenettes and fireplaces, that you can share with your dog. Though the hotel hasn't charged extra for canine guests in the past, it's considering adding a fee. You can leave Fido unattended inside, but housekeeping won't service the room during that time.

$$–$$$$ Winter Park Mountain Lodge, 81699 Highway 40, 970-726-4211 (800-726-3340; www.winterparkhotel.com). Formerly the Raintree Inn, this hotel underwent a major renovation, adding 110 new rooms, underground parking, and a microbrewery and restaurant on site. Rooms range from standards to new mountain suites, which have fireplaces, Jacuzzis, and full kitchens.

$$$ Beaver Village Resort, 79303 Highway 40, 970-726-5741 (800-666-0281; www.beavervillage.com). This old-time ski lodge, with its distinctive A-frame architecture, was first opened in 1939. Dogs are allowed in any of the lodge's hotel rooms, but not in the condos. Rates from mid-December to April include buffet breakfast and dinner (not gourmet style but hearty). You can leave your dog unattended in the room, though housekeeping won't enter during that time.

$$$ Snow Mountain Ranch YMCA, Highway 40 north of Fraser, 970-726-4628 or 303-443-4743 (www.ymcarock ies.org). Located on almost 5,000 acres, the ranch has forty-five fully furnished cabins, ranging from two to five bedrooms, in which you and your dog can stay (dogs are not permitted in the lodge rooms). All the cabins have fireplaces, and you can leave your dog unattended inside. When exploring the ranch property, you'll need to keep Rover on his leash. The complex also offers a restaurant, indoor pool, indoor climbing wall, tennis courts, miniature golf, and a Nordic trail system (see "Powderhounds"). Camping and RV sites are also available.

Campgrounds

Rocky Mountain National Park. The park has one campground, Timber Creek, on its western side.

National forest campgrounds: **Arapaho National Recreation Area,** which includes Lake Granby, Shadow Mount-ain Lake, Monarch Lake, Willow Creek Reservoir, and Meadow Creek Reserv-oir, has several campgrounds, among them **Stillwater Campground,** off Highway 34 (148 sites); **Green Ridge Campground,** off County Rd. 66 (78 sites); **Arapaho Bay Campground,** at the end of County Rd. 6 (84 sites); and **Willow Creek Campground,** off County Rd. 40 at Willow Creek Reservoir (35 sites). Also available are **St. Louis Campground,** 4 miles from Fraser off County Rd. 73 (18 sites); **Byers Peak Campground,** 7 miles from Fraser off County Rd. 73 (6 sites); **Idlewild Campground,** 1 mile south of Winter Park off Highway 40 (26 sites); and **Robbers Roost Campground,** 5 miles south of Winter Park on Highway 40 (11 sites).

Private campgrounds: **Elk Creek Camper Cabins and Campground** in Grand Lake; **Snow Mountain Ranch YMCA** outside of Winter Park; **Sitzmark Chalets and Cabins** in Winter Park (see "Creature Comforts" for details on all).

WORTH A PAWS

K9-5K at SolVista Golf and Ski Ranch. This dog-and-owner trail run is held on a Saturday in early September at the Sol Vista ski area. Both a 2K and a 5K course begin behind the ski area base

lodge and traverse the mountain. Canine participants must be on leash and sport current rabies tags. The money brought in from registration fees benefits local animal organizations. After the race, your pup can cool down in one of the wading pools on hand, then try his skill at the canine agility course. Or if he's more into being seen, he can vie for prizes in contests such as curliest tail, shortest tail, best behaved, and fluffiest fur. You and your dog will also take home a giveaway bag with treats and a T-shirt. Special lodging packages at the dog-friendly Inn at Silver Creek are available for the race. Call the event organizer at 970-887-5203 (or 800-754-7458, ext. 203) for more details.

High Altitude Sled Dog Championships. During the last weekend in February, the heartiest of the huskies gather outside of Grand Lake to compete in these championships, in which winners' points count toward the national championships. More than 100 teams typically compete. The races start at the Winding River Resort and follow 4-mile, 6-mile, and 8-mile routes. A series of cross-country ski and walking trails are set up along the courses for human spectators only. If you'd like to bring your dog to cheer on his fellow tail-waggers, you'll have to stay at the start/finish line—and keep Fido firmly under control. Call the Grand Lake Chamber of Commerce (see "Resources") or Winding River Resort (970-627-3215; 800-282-5121) for more information.

DOGGIE DAYCARE
Fraser
Byers Peak Veterinary Clinic, 360 Railroad Ave., 970-726-8384. $12/day. Open 9 a.m.–12:30 p.m. and 2–5 p.m., Monday to Friday; 10–10:15 a.m. for dropoffs and 6–6:15 p.m. for pickups, Saturday and Sunday.

Granby
Granby Veterinary Clinic, 458 E. Agate (Highway 40), 970-887-3848. $8.50–$9.50/day, depending on the size of dog. Open 9 a.m.–5 p.m., Monday to Friday; 9 a.m.–noon, Saturday.

PET PROVISIONS
Granby
Granby Mart, 62 E. Agate, 970-887-3843

Grand Lake
Rocky Mountain Sports, 711 Grand Ave., 970-627-8124

CANINE ER
Fraser
Byers Peak Veterinary Clinic, 360 Railroad Ave., 970-726-8384. Open 9 a.m.– 12:30 p.m. and 2–5 p.m., Monday to Friday.

Granby
Brooks Veterinary Service, 12 E. Agate (Highway 40), 970-887-2417. Open 8 a.m.–5 p.m., Monday to Friday; 9–11 a.m., most Saturdays.

Granby Veterinary Clinic, 458 E. Agate (Highway 40), 970-887-3848. Open 9 a.m.–5 p.m., Monday to Friday; 9 a.m.–noon, Saturday.

RESOURCES
Fraser Visitor Center, 120 Xerex St., Fraser, 970-726-8312

Grand Lake Chamber of Commerce Visitor Center, intersection of Highway 34 and Grand Ave., Grand Lake, 970-627-3402 (800-531-1019; www.grandlakechamber.com)

Greater Granby Area Chamber of Commerce, 81 W. Jasper, Granby, 970-887-2311

Sulfur Ranger District, Arapaho and Roosevelt National Forests, 9 Ten Mile Dr., Granby, 970-887-4100

Winter Park/Fraser Valley Chamber of Commerce, 78841 Highway 40, Winter Park, 970-726-4118 (800-722-4118)

EIGHT

Steamboat Springs and North Park

THE BIG SCOOP

Steamboat Springs, with its ski-town sensibility (which means lots of dogs) and miles of trails in Routt National Forest close at hand, is a dandy place to take a dog. If you're looking for a truly get-away-from-it trip, head to the North Park area northeast of Steamboat. The region combines ample BLM and national forest land with a location remote enough that your dog can explore leash-free to his heart's content without disturbing other hikers (keep an eye out for wildlife, though).

Leash laws are enforced within the city limits of Steamboat Springs. In Routt County, you can have your dog under voice command only on agricultural land, which basically rules out any areas you're apt to be visiting. In Jackson County (North Park), dogs can be under voice command on county land; individual towns have their own leash laws.

TAIL-RATED TRAILS

For more hiking ideas, pick up a "Trails Map" brochure at the Steamboat Springs Chamber Resort Association (see "Resources") or a copy of *Hiking the 'Boat,* by Diane White-Crane (the author's dog accompanied her on all of the hikes). The three state parks in the Steamboat area—Stagecoach, Pearl Lake, and Steamboat Lake—primarily focus on water recreation, though all offer some lakeside hiking opportunities, with the longest trail following the eastern shoreline of Stagecoach Reservoir. Colorado State Forest, outside Walden, is described in more detail later in this section.

Steamboat Springs

Mad Creek. 7.8 miles round-trip to the Mount Zirkel Wilderness Area boundary. Head west from Steamboat Springs on U.S. Highway 40 to County Rd. 129 (you'll see a sign for Steamboat Lake). Turn right and drive 5.5 miles to the parking area and trailhead on the right. *Dogs can be off leash up until the wilderness boundary.*

Be aware that this trail can get heavy horse use on summer weekends. You'll start out climbing up a rocky hill for the first few tenths of a mile. The trail then meanders along a shelf high above Mad Creek before dropping closer to creek level. After going through a livestock fence, you'll spot a footpath leading down to the creek, a side-trip your dog will no doubt want to take. Shortly after, you'll reach a junction; stay right on Trail 1100 (the sign says "Swamp Park"). A Forest Service building known as the Mad House sits to the south. The trail becomes a narrow single-track rolling through a pasture. When you come to a fork where a split-rail fence curves to the right, stay to the left. You'll hike through a beautiful stretch of open meadow on an old wagon road. The next section of trail meanders through stands of aspen and again parallels the creek, this time at dog's-eye level. At about 4 miles, you'll reach the clearly marked wilderness boundary, the turnaround point for this hike. Remember that if you decide to venture farther, Fido will need to leash up.

Soda Creek. About 3.5 miles round-trip. From downtown Steamboat, take 3rd St. northwest from Lincoln Ave., then make a right at the next block onto Fish Creek Falls Rd. Shortly after, look for a sign for Buffalo Pass and make a left onto Amethyst. Follow Amethyst until it ends in a fork at Strawberry Park Rd.; bear right. You'll see a sign on the right that points toward Buffalo Pass. Drive up Buffalo Pass Rd. to Dry Lake Campground on the left. Park in the large lot across the road. *Dogs can be off leash.*

Begin by walking on a service road just past the campground sign. When the road forks, stay right; you'll come to a gate barring vehicle traffic as well as a small wooden "Soda Creek" sign. After this point, the road turns into a smooth, gentle trail, descending gradually through aspen and ferns toward Soda Creek. When you reach a three-way junction, stay right to follow the trail (though you should consider detouring down the middle path to allow your dog a dip in the creek). You'll eventually reach a large meadow, prime dog frolicking ground and, during the summer, a first-rate place to view wildflowers. The trail, which begins to become less distinct, goes along the meadow's edge. The end of the meadow, where the trail pretty much peters out, makes a good turnaround point.

Steamboat Ski Area. You and your dog can speed on up the Silver Bullet Gondola, which goes about halfway up the mountain, and hike back down. Most of the summer trail network is open to mountain bikers, so if you're out on foot, your best options are the hikers-only Vista Nature Trail, which makes a 1.25-mile loop around near the gondola, and the Thunderhead Hiking Trail, an approximately 3-mile trip down to the gondola base area. Although this is actually national forest land, *the resort*

requests that you keep your dog leashed.

The gondola operates daily from 10 a.m. to 4 p.m. from mid-June through August. In early June and from Labor Day to mid-September, it runs on weekends only. There is a fee.

Spring Creek. 8 miles round-trip. From downtown Steamboat Springs, drive northwest on 3rd St. for one block to Fish Creek Falls Rd. on the right. Turn left onto Amethyst shortly after, then right onto E. Spring St. (which is E. Maple on the left). Park along the road. *Dogs must be leashed.*

"All the dogs come here," says one local dog owner about Spring Creek. Unfortunately, this has also resulted in a bit of controversy over leash laws—there are a lot of noncomplying dogs, and property owners near the trail have been getting upset. So make sure you do your bit not to make things worse. The trail is also a popular mountain-biking route, so ask Rover to keep a nose out for riders flying downhill. The first part of the hike follows a single-lane dirt road for about a half mile to the Spring Creek Reservoirs. The reservoirs make a pleasant destination in themselves, and a separate footpath encircles them. After passing the reservoirs, the road narrows and bends to the left; follow the signs to the right to access a newer, rerouted section of the trail. As you ascend the Spring Creek drainage via a consistent, but moderate, climb, you'll crisscross the creek several times over a series of bridges, giving your dog ample opportunity to hydrate. The Steamboat Ski Area becomes visible to the right as you gain elevation. The trail ends partway up Buffalo Pass, in a parking area across from the Dry Lake Campground.

Yampa Core Trail. Runs for 4 miles along the Yampa River, from West Lincoln Park (next to the Dream

Island mobile home park) to Walton Creek Rd., east of town. *Dogs must be leashed.*

This paved recreation path runs along the river, passing by the southeastern edge of downtown Steamboat Springs, the Howlsen Hill Ski Area, and the rodeo grounds before reaching a more undeveloped area in riparian habitat. It's a great spot for a close-to-town stroll with your dog—just keep an eye out for bicyclists and in-line skaters.

Fish Creek Falls. A little under a mile round-trip to view the falls. From Lincoln Ave. in downtown Steamboat Springs, head northwest on 3rd St. (you'll see a sign for Fish Creek Falls). Take a right at the next block, which is Fish Creek Falls Rd. The falls are 4 miles ahead (there's a fee for parking). *Dogs must be leashed.*

From the main parking lot, take the gravel-surface Fish Creek Falls National Recreation Trail (the other two trails are paved) to the Historic Fish Creek Bridge, where your dog can salivate at the 280-foot-high waterfall. Reward him with a dip in the creek. If you're feeling ambitious (and are suitably prepared), follow the trail 2 miles farther to the Upper Falls or 5 miles total to Long Lake, at 9,850 feet. As dogs are allowed off leash on this national forest trail, this could turn your outing into a three- or four-wag hike.

North Park

Colorado State Forest. Look for a park entrance off Highway 14 west, about 20 miles from Walden and just before Gould. Highway 14 also runs through the park before reaching Cameron Pass. *Dogs must be leashed.*

The forest is actually a state park, and with 70,000 mostly undeveloped acres along 28 miles from north to south, it's by far the biggest of Colorado's state parks. There are only five established

hiking trails throughout the park. The 2-mile round-trip **Lake Agnes Trail** is the most heavily used, as it's short and incredibly scenic, nestled near the 12,400-foot Nokhu Crags and 12,940-foot Mt. Richthoven, the highest peak in the Never Summer Range in nearby Rocky Mountain National Park. The 10-mile round-trip **American Lakes Trail** is nearby. The trailheads for these hikes are off Highway 14 toward Cameron Pass. The least-used trails are those to **Clear Lake** (10 miles round-trip) and **Kelly Lake** (6 miles round-trip). Both lakes are at timberline, and you'll hike through pine and spruce forest to reach them. The trailhead is accessed via a road heading north shortly past the park headquarters. The **Ruby Jewel Lake Trail** is a relatively short 3 miles round-trip if you're able to get all the way up the four-wheel-drive access road to the trailhead. As this road is often not passable to the end, you'll likely end up parking somewhere along it and extending the hike's mileage. During any of these hikes, but especially the less-traveled ones, keep an eye out for moose, the park's "specialty." Note that dogs are not allowed in the park's camper cabins or at the Never Summer Nordic yurt system in the park.

CYCLING FOR CANINES

The **Mad Creek Trail** (see "Tail-Rated Trails") is a scenic ride you can take Fido on. So is the **Coulton Creek Trail**, off Seedhouse Rd. (County Rd. 64) north of Steamboat, though you'll want to ride it as an out-and-back rather than as a loop to avoid 1.5 miles of road riding. A network of jeep roads just west of **Steamboat Lake State Park** and north of **Sand Mountain** is a less-frequented cycling area: Begin on Forest Rd. 42, which runs west out of County Rd. 62, and follow Forest Rd. 480 to the left and around to make a loop. The top of **Rabbit Ears Pass** offers a couple of biking options: You and your dog can take an approximately

Former greyhound racer Spro contemplates a future of recreational running. (photo by Carol Kauder)

6-mile round-trip ride to the distinctive Rabbit Ears Peak by following Forest Service Rd. 291, which branches out of Forest Service Rd. 311 past the Dumont Lake Campground (park at the beginning of Rd. 291). Or drive farther on Forest Rd. 311 to the Base Camp trailhead (Trail 1102). From here you can ride to **Fishhook Lake, Lost Lake,** and **Lake Elmo,** up to a 6-mile round-trip.

POWDERHOUNDS

Rabbit Ears Pass is one of the most popular ski and snowshoe areas around Steamboat. Several trails start here, including the **West Summit Loop,** a 3.5-mile tour that doesn't cross any avalanche terrain. There are also trails off **Seedhouse Rd.** (County Rd. 64) north of Steamboat, out of the Hinman Park and Seedhouse Campgrounds—watch out for snowmobilers in this area. And the road itself is unplowed after a certain point, providing a wide, gentle grade for skiing or snowshoeing. Refer to *Snowshoeing Colorado,* by Claire Walter, for details on these and other routes. Also see **High Meadows Ranch** in "Creature Comforts."

CREATURE COMFORTS

Unless otherwise stated, dogs should not be left unattended in the room or cabin.

Columbine

$$–$$$ Columbine Cabins, 64505 County Rd. 129, 970-879-5522 (www.coloradovacation.com/cabins/columbine/). Columbine, located about 30 miles north of Steamboat, was once an active mining town. The only buildings that remain are these historic cabins (the oldest is from about 1890), which have been renovated to accommodate guests, and a general store. The thirteen rustic cabins are furnished and vary in their amenities: Most have wood-burning stoves to cook on as well as hotplates, though a few have more modern kitchen facilities; most rely on the central showerhouse for bathing and toilet facilities; and a few lack running water. There's a $10 fee per night, per dog, for the first three nights (no charge after that). It'll be a step back in time for you, and your dog is sure to enjoy the surrounding Routt National Forest and miles of trails nearby. Bring your skis or snowshoes to explore in the winter.

Cowdrey

$ Cowdrey Store, Trout Camp & Cafe, 41489 Highway 125, 970-723-8248. This is the only business in Cowdrey, so it'll be hard to miss. Six rustic cabins are for rent; they all have kitchenettes (you'll need to bring your own dishes and utensils) but use a central bathhouse. If your dog sleeps on the bed, you'll need to provide a blanket to put under him.

Gould

$ North Park KOA, 53337 Highway 14, 970-723-4310 (800-KOA-3596). Dogs are allowed in the Kamping Kabins (you'll need to supply your own bedding and cooking gear), and they must be kept leashed when outside. Open end of May through mid-November.

$ Powderhorn Cabins, 35336 County Rd. 21, 970-723-4359 (www.homestead.com/powderhorncabins). There are fifteen cabins, all fully furnished and with kitchens; the "rustic" ones have use of a central bathhouse, and the "modern" ones have their own bathrooms. A $10 deposit is required for a dog, in addition to a $6 fee per night. You'll need to keep your dog leashed on the property. Open May 15 to November 15.

Kremmling
$ Bob's Western Motel, 110 West Park Ave., 970-724-3266. Luckily, Bob likes dogs.

Oak Creek
$–$$ Oak Creek Motel, 400 Willow Bend, 970-736-2343. One dog per room is preferred at this small motel (ten rooms, some with kitchenettes). You can walk your dog off leash on the 1.5-acre property.

$$$ High Meadows Ranch, 20505 RCR 16 (southeast of Stagecoach Reservoir), 970-736-8416 (800-457-4453; www.hm ranch.com). This ranch, about 25 miles from Steamboat, is a perfect place for a getaway with Fido in tow. It's situated on 200 acres, which your dog can check out leash-free with you. Three attractive, modern log buildings are available for guests: one with two bedrooms and two and a half baths; one with three bedrooms and three baths; and one with five bedrooms and two baths. All have kitchen and living areas and woodstoves as well as use of an outdoor hot tub. During the summer, the ranch offers a variety of horseback rides. In winter, you and your dog can explore 12 miles of groomed ski trails. You can leave your dog unattended inside, or he can stay in a small outside kennel with dog house. Meals (for humans) are available for an extra charge.

Steamboat Lake
$ Steamboat Lake Camper Cabins, Steamboat Lake Marina, 970-879-7019.

These five cabins allow dogs for $5 per dog, per night. Each cabin has electric heat, a small refrigerator, and a coffeemaker, but you'll have to bring your own bedding and do any cooking on an outdoor grill.

$$–$$$ Dutch Creek Guest Ranch, 61565 RCR 62, 970-879-8519 (800-778-8519). The ranch, on 100 acres across from Steamboat Lake and bordered by Routt National Forest, offers a total of nine modern, fully outfitted log cabins and A-frames. Dogs are allowed for a $5 fee per dog, per night, with a limit of two dogs per unit. The owners ask that you keep your dog leashed when around the main lodge and cabins and the horse area. The ranch offers horseback rides in the summer and sleigh rides in the winter. Breakfast is included, and dinner is available by reservation.

$$–$$$ Steamboat Lake Outfitters, 60880 County Rd. 129 (7 miles north of Clark), 970-879-5878 (800-342-1889; www.steamboatoutfitters.com). This guest ranch is just across the road from Steamboat Lake State Park. You and your dog have a choice of lodging options, with a $40 one-time pet fee and a two-dog limit per unit: four rustic cabins, all fully equipped, that sleep from two to eight guests; four new fully equipped cabins, with two bedrooms and two baths; or twelve "bunkhouse" rooms, each with two queen beds and private bath. You can leave your dog unattended inside. There's not a strict leash law, though if a lot of other dogs are around, you might be asked to restrain yours. The ranch offers guided horseback rides and ATV tours in summer and snowmobile tours in the winter. A general store is on the premises as well as a full restaurant that serves breakfast, lunch, and dinner.

Steamboat Springs
$–$$ Nite's Rest Motel, 601 Lincoln

Ave., 970-879-1212 (800-828-1780; www.nitesrest.com). The dog fee varies according to time of year: $5 per night from October 1 to December 20 and again from April 1 to June 1. At all other times it's $10 per night. Some units come with fully equipped kitchens.

$$ Nordic Lodge Motel, 1036 Lincoln Ave., 970-879-0531 (800-364-0331). There's a $10 one-time fee for a dog. You can leave yours unattended in the room provided you're certain he'll remain well behaved.

$$–$$$ Alpiner Lodge, 424 Lincoln Ave., 970-879-1430. Dogs are permitted with a $15 one-time fee.

$$–$$$ Best Western Ptarmigan Inn, 2304 Apres Ski Way, 970-879-1730 (800-538-7519). You can stay at this slopeside hotel with your dog during the summer only (from about the end of May to sometime in October). Because the gondola is open for summer hiking, there is still some advantage to being mountainside. The one-time fee for a dog is $25.

$$–$$$ Harbor Hotel, 703 Lincoln Ave., 970-879-1522 (800-543-8888). Dogs are allowed in the summer only (which is broadly defined as mid-April through mid-November) for a $25 one-time fee. Moreover, only motel units and one- and two-bedroom condos are dog friendly; the rooms in the historic hotel building are off-limits. Dogs may be left unattended in the room—you just won't get housekeeping service during that time. And you'll be conveniently located on Steamboat's main street.

$$–$$$ Holiday Inn, 3190 S. Lincoln Ave., 970-879-2250 (800-654-3944). Dogs are welcome year-round with a $25 deposit.

$$–$$$ Rabbit Ears Motel, 201 Lincoln Ave., 970-879-1150 (800-828-7702; www.rabbitearsmotel.com). Your dog may not know what to make of the neon pink bunny head on the motel's sign. But he's welcome to sniff it out any time of the year.

$$–$$$ Scandinavian Lodge, 2883 Burgess Creek Rd., 970-879-0517 (800-233-8102; www.steamboat-springs.com). The lodge consists of condos, from studios to three bedrooms. Dogs are allowed in four of the units—those that have not been recently remodeled. If your dog has an affinity for 1970s-style ski digs, this is the place. And you can leave your pooch unattended inside.

$$$ Perry-Mansfield Log Cabins, 40755 County Rd. 36, 970-879-1060 (800-538-7519). These six rustic cabins are located on the expansive grounds of the Perry-Mansfield Performing Arts Camp. If your dog is a budding thespian, he'll enjoy coming here. Although the cabins are open year-round, dogs are only permitted outside of ski season (generally the end of April to mid-November), for a $25 one-time fee. The fully equipped cabins have from two to five bedrooms and wood-burning stoves. Note that cabin reservations are taken through the Best Western Ptarmigan Inn in Steamboat.

$$$–$$$$ Moving Mountains Chalet, 2774 Burgess Creek Rd., 970-870-9359 (877-624-2538; www.movingmountains.com). This European-style bed-and-breakfast (and more) will consider dogs on a case-by-case basis, with the line drawn at small dogs (or "lap-size yappers," says owner Robin Craigen). This preference is reflected by the resident chocolate lab. The six individually themed rooms have lodgepole furnishings and private baths; the largest includes a Jacuzzi. In summers the chalet operates primarily as a B&B. During ski season (Thanksgiving to mid-April) a Euro-plan is in effect: Rates include three meals a day plus shuttle service. And during February and March, the chalet is rented out only to groups. If you're visiting during ski season, you may be able to borrow a portable kennel from the Craigens so that you can leave your dog in your room or in the heated garage; inquire in advance.

Walden

$ **North Park Motel, 625 Main St., 970-723-4271.** All rooms have kitchenettes.

$ **Roundup Motel, 365 Main St., 970-723-4680.** Dogs are welcome as long as they stay off the beds. Rooms with kitchenettes are available.

$ **Westside Motel, 441 LaFever, 970-723-8589.** You can leave your dog unattended in the room.

$$ **Lake John Resort, 2521 JCR 7A (17 miles northwest of Walden), 970-723-3226.** The resort, located alongside Lake John, has four one-room cabins with kitchenettes and private baths for rent. There's a two-dog limit per cabin, with a $20 one-time fee. The cabins are heated, though the water is shut off in the winter, so you'll have to use the bathrooms in the main building. You'll need to keep your dog leashed on the resort's 14 acres, but dogs do have swimming privileges in the lake. There's a general store on site as well as a restaurant (open from the beginning of May to the end of November), and boat rentals are available.

Yampa

$ **Van Camp Cabins, 303 Rich Ave., 970-638-4254 (www.coloradovacation. com/cabins/vancamp).** There's a $5 one-time fee per dog to stay in one of these six one-room cabins (note that they don't have kitchen facilities). You can also bring your horse.

$–$$ **Royal Motel, 201 Moffatt, 970-638-4538.** The owner emphasizes that

dogs should be well behaved and well trained to stay at this small motel, housed in a building from 1906 that has undergone some recent renovation. Two of the seven rooms have private baths.

Campgrounds

State park campgrounds: Colorado State Forest, off Highway 14 near Gould (104 sites; note that dogs are not allowed in the primitive cabins available for rental at North Michigan Reservoir or the Lake Agnes trailhead); **Stagecoach State Park,** 17 miles southeast of Steamboat Springs on County Rd. 14 off Highway 131 (100 sites); **Pearl Lake State Park,** 26 miles north of Steamboat Springs, via County Rd. 129 to County Rd. 209 (40 sites); **Steamboat Lake State Park,** 27 miles north of Steamboat Springs, via County Rd. 129 to County Rd. 62 (182 sites).

National forest campgrounds: Hinman Park Campground, 20 miles north of Steamboat Springs (13 sites), and **Seedhouse Campground,** 22 miles (25 sites), are off Seedhouse Rd., via County Rd. 129 north; **Dry Lake Campground,** 6 miles east of Steamboat Springs (8 sites), and **Summit Lake Campground,** 15 miles east of town (16 sites), are both on Buffalo Pass Rd.; **Meadows Campground,** 15 miles southeast of Steamboat Springs (30 sites), **Walton Creek Campground,** 18 miles (16 sites), and **Dumont Lake Campground,** 22 miles (22 sites), are all off Highway 40, on Rabbit Ears Pass; **Big Creek Lakes Campground,** west of Cowdrey via County Rd. 6 and Forest Rd. 600 (54 sites); **Aspen Campground** (7 sites) and **Pines Campground** (11 sites) are both on Forest Rd. 740, just outside of Gould.

Private campgrounds: North Park KOA (see "Creature Comforts").

WORTH A PAWS

Silver Bullet Gondola. Bring your dog aboard Steamboat Ski Area's gondola for a bird's-eye view of the surrounding valley. You can either hike down or make a return trip on the gondola. See "Tail-Rated Trails" for more details.

Felix and Fido, 635 Lincoln, Steamboat Springs, 970-870-6400. Felix and Fido bills itself as a dog and cat boutique store. Your dog may just turn up his nose at the abundance of cat-related paraphernalia, but he'll love sniffing out the selection of unique collars and leashes, bowls, dog packs, dog booties, treats, and squeaky toys. You'll enjoy browsing among the dog-theme items, including clothing, jewelry, accessories, and knick-knacks—more than 125 different breeds of dogs are represented.

Crazy River Dog Contest. Part of Steamboat's annual Yampa River Festival, held the second weekend in June, local crazy canines and other river-savvy dogs turn out for this unique twist on stick retrieval. A stick is thrown into the Yampa; once it passes a certain point, a doggie contestant swims out and is timed on how long it takes him to get the stick and get out of the water. Once the field has been narrowed down to the top four dogs, there's a "stick-off": All four dogs go at once, and the winner is the one who comes up with the stick first. The prize? A dog bed, for a well-deserved rest.

There's no entry fee for the contest, which takes place at Yampa River Park on the Saturday of the festival. Any dog is welcome to participate, though "we'd hate for your dog to drown if you show up with a little city dog," quips one of the organizers. Call Back Door Sports at 970-879-6249 for more information.

Fish Creek Sneak. This annual Father's Day run is sponsored by the Ski Haus and starts at the store (1450 S. Lincoln Ave.) You and your leashed dog can compete in either the 5K or 10K (both routes are on paved roads). Register at the store in advance or on the day of the race. For more details, call the Ski Haus, 970-879-0385 (800-932-3019).

DOGGIE DAYCARE
Steamboat Springs
Mt. Werner Veterinary Hospital, 35825 E. Highway 40, 970-879-3486. $15/day. Open 9 a.m.–5:30 p.m., Monday to Friday; 9 a.m.–noon, Saturday. Weekend day boarding available by appointment.

Steamboat Veterinary Hospital, 30278 W. Highway 40, 970-879-1049. $14/day. Open 7:30 a.m.–6 p.m., Monday to Friday; 8 a.m.–noon, Saturday. Weekend day boarding available by appointment.

PET PROVISIONS
Steamboat Springs
Elk River Farm and Feed, 26075 Copper Ridge Cir., 970-879-5383

Paws 'n Claws 'n Things, 1250 S. Lincoln Ave. (in Sundance Plaza), 970-879-6092

CANINE ER
Steamboat Springs
Mt. Werner Veterinary Hospital, 35825 E. Highway 40, 970-879-3486. Open 9 a.m.–5:30 p.m., Monday to Friday; 9 a.m.–noon, Saturday.

Pet Kare Clinic, Sundance Plaza, 970-879-5273. Open 8:30 a.m.–8 p.m., Monday; 8:30 a.m.–5 p.m., Tuesday to Friday; 9 a.m.–noon, Saturday.

Steamboat Veterinary Hospital, 30278 W. Highway 40, 970-879-1049. Open 7:30 a.m.–6 p.m., Monday to Friday; 8 a.m.–noon, Saturday.

RESOURCES
Bureau of Land Management, 2103 Park Ave., Kremmling, 970-724-3437

Hahn's Peak/Bears Ears Ranger District, Routt National Forest, 925 Weiss Dr., Steamboat Springs, 970-879-1870

North Park Chamber of Commerce, Main St., Walden, 970-723-4600

Parks Ranger District, Routt National Forest, 612 5th St., Walden, 970-723-8204

Parks Ranger District, Routt National Forest, 210 S. 6th, Kremmling, 970-724-9004

The Ski Haus, at 1450 S. Lincoln Ave. in Steamboat Springs (970-879-0385; 800-932-3019), has a good selection of trail guides and maps to the area

Steamboat Springs Chamber Resort Association, 1255 S. Lincoln Ave., Steamboat Springs, 970-879-0880 (800-922-2722; www.steamboat-chamber.com)

Yampa Ranger District, Routt National Forest, 300 Roselawn Ave., Yampa, 970-638-4516

NINE

Summit County

THE BIG SCOOP

Summit County is somewhat of a dog paradise, with plenty of great hiking, mountain biking, and skiing opportunities as well as a variety of accommodations that actively welcome four-legged guests. When Denver or other areas along the Front Range become a bit too warm midsummer for those stuck with a permanent fur coat, mountain relief is but an hour's drive away among the towns of Silverthorne, Dillon, Frisco, and Breckenridge. And about 20 miles north of Silverthorne is Green Mountain Reservoir and the hamlet of Heeney (though your dog probably won't want to visit during Heeney's annual Tick Festival in mid-June!).

All of the principal Summit County towns have leash laws within their city limits. On county land, your dog can be off leash if he stays within ten feet of you and is under voice control.

TAIL-RATED TRAILS

What follows are but a few recommendations out of the many hiking options in the region. For more ideas, consult *The New Summit Hiker and Ski Touring Guide,* by Mary Ellen Gilliland.

Chihuahua Gulch. 6 miles round-trip. From Dillon, head east on U.S. Highway 6 past Keystone Resort. Exit onto Montezuma Rd. About 4.5 miles from the exit, turn into a parking area on the left (across from the Western-Skies Bed and Breakfast). Peru Creek Rd. begins just beyond the parking area. Drive 2.1 miles

to a parking pullout on the right; the trailhead is on the left. *Dogs can be off leash.*

With a name like Chihuahua, the hike begs exploration by dogs. When I brought Clover and her hiking companion Tundra here, they had a blast on this spectacularly beautiful trail that ascends between the backside of Arapahoe Basin Ski Area and Grays and Torreys Peaks, a pair of 14,000-foot mountains, to Chihuahua Lake. Because the hike involves several stream crossings, it's best to wait until the spring runoff has subsided before tackling it. Begin by climbing steadily up a four-wheel-drive road. Stay left at a fork, which will bring you to the first stream to ford. The ascent levels off as you enter a vast meadow, with two more stream crossings. After the beaver ponds, take the left trail fork and stay left again after another stream crossing. At the end of the meadow, the trail resumes its climb. The final approach to the lake involves scrambling up a steep, but short, talus slope to the left. You'll first reach a small pond; continue downslope to reach the emerald-green lake, which shimmers at the base of a cirque of rocky peaks.

French Gulch. About 6 miles round-trip. From Frisco, head south on Highway 9 to County Rd. 450 just before Breckenridge (there's a 7-11 store on the corner). Turn left (east) and follow the road as it curves right under a railroad trestle structure marking the French Creek subdivision. Make a left at the stop sign. Then drive past numerous mine tailings and structural remains for about 3.5 miles, until you come to a gate across the road. Park on the side of the road. *Dogs can be off leash.*

French Gulch is a favorite among locals but is less crowded than many of the other Summit County trails, meaning that especially on a weekday afternoon, you and your dog may be able to hike in relative solitude. The "trail" is actually an old mining road, a remnant of the area's past excavation industry. You'll start out walking up the road past the gate, which goes gradually uphill. About 1.5 miles into your hike, you'll pass some beaver ponds on the right—a good place for your dog to take a stick-retrieving break. After crossing a meadow a little farther along, the trail climbs more steeply. Go either way at the fork; the trails rejoin shortly after. Pass an orange metal gate marked "road closed" on the right. You'll cross a small stream twice within a short distance and then will emerge into a beautiful wildflower-strewn meadow. The trail continues up the meadow's right side and eventually crosses another small stream. After passing through a stand of timber you'll come out at yet another glorious meadow, framed by the barren, red-hued slopes of Mount Guyot on the left and Bald Mountain on the right, both 13,000-foot-plus peaks. This was our turn-around point, though you could continue hiking for about 0.75 mile more up the ridge at the head of the meadow to French Pass, just above 12,000 feet, for a vista of both Breckenridge and the peaks to the east.

Buck, Dan Shore, and Clover consult Canine Colorado *for a hike up to Crystal Lake. (photo by Cindy Hirschfeld)*

a small pumphouse farther downhill, toward Copper Mountain). Stand on the access road uphill from the building and look for a small paved path on the right that ultimately leads to the bikeway. From the top of this path you'll also see the faint outline of a footpath through the grass that goes down a hill, crosses a brook, and climbs a gentle hill on the other side. Follow this small path for half a mile; it will bring you to Wilder Gulch. (Although you can also access the trail from the bikeway, you'd spend the first half mile of your hike uncomfortably close to the interstate.) *Dogs can be off leash.*

Turn right at the junction with the Wilder Gulch Trail, which climbs gradually along Wilder Creek. You'll ascend through wildflower-studded meadows surrounded by lodgepole pine. Stop occasionally to enjoy the views of Ptarmigan Hill at the head of the gulch ("hill" is definitely a misnomer), and Jacque Peak, Copper Mountain, and the Tenmile Range to the east. Eventually you'll come to an expansive meadow. Here the slope intensifies somewhat as it climbs through cool and fragrant stands of spruce. If

Wilder Gulch. 6 miles round-trip. Turn off I-70 at the Vail Pass rest area and park by the buildings. Finding the trailhead can be a bit tricky. First, walk down toward a small hexagonal building (not the rest area concession building, which is also hexagonal; this is

your dog's a mycophile, let him know to keep an eye out for the big brown caps of boletus mushrooms, which grow in profusion in August and September. After about another mile you'll come to a junction with four-wheel-drive Wearyman Road; if you're game to keep going, turn left and climb 2 more miles to Ptarmigan Pass, which offers great views of the Gore and Tenmile Ranges.

Crystal Lake. 4 miles round-trip. Drive south from Breckenridge on Highway 9 for 2.5 miles to Spruce Creek Rd. (you'll see a sign for the Crown sub-division). Turn right and continue on Spruce Creek Rd. for 1.2 miles to the trailhead parking area. *Dogs can be off leash.*

This popular hike follows a jeep track up to Lower Crystal Lake, nestled at the base of a cirque. Begin by walking along Spruce Creek Rd. for about a quarter mile, to where the Crystal Rd. takes off to the right. The wide, rocky trail ascends somewhat steeply for about the first half mile through forested terrain of lodgepole pine, Douglas fir, blue spruce, and aspen; it then levels out to a more gradual ascent. As you hike, you'll become aware of Crystal Creek in the gully to the left, though it remains out of paw-dipping range. Not too far from the trailhead, you'll pass the Burro Trail coming in from the north. About a mile later, the Wheeler National Recreation Trail crosses your route. At this point, the trail breaks out above treeline and follows a short, steep ascent onto a shelf. You may glimpse lovely Francie's Cabin off to the right, part of the Summit Huts Association and available for winter use by reservation only (dogs are not allowed). It's then a steady uphill to the lake, through wildflower-filled meadows bordered by craggy Mount Helen to the south. At the lake, your dog can play in the water and sniff out the remains of an old cabin while you savor the scenery. If

you're inspired to make the hike longer, it's possible to climb up on a trail that winds north and then southwest to Upper Crystal Lake, hidden from sight at the base of Crystal Peak, which rises to the west from Lower Crystal Lake.

North Tenmile Trail. 4 miles round-trip to the Eagles Nest Wilderness Area boundary. Head west on I-70 past Silverthorne to Exit 201. Stay right at the end of the exit ramp and park in the gravel lot by the trailhead. If coming from Frisco, drive west on Main St. and cross under I-70 to reach the parking area. *Dogs can be off leash up until the wilderness boundary.*

This pleasant hike follows an old mining road, alternating between stands of pine and spruce and grassy clearings. Follow the dirt road from the parking area. Just before you get to a large green water tank on the left, take the road that branches off to the right. At the next junction, either option works; they both rejoin shortly after. Then stay right at a fork shortly afterward, as the road takes a short climb. From here on, it's easy going. The trail parallels North Tenmile Creek, with many good access points for dogs, including a crystal-clear beaver pond. The wilderness boundary was our turnaround point, though you could continue 1.5 miles more to an intersection with the Gore Range Trail. If you do keep hiking, remember to leash up Fido once you cross that wilderness area line.

Rainbow Lake. Approximately 2 miles round-trip. From Main St. in Frisco, go south on 2nd St. until it terminates; cross the bike path and, if you're driving, park in the dirt lot. *Dogs can be off leash.*

This short hike is great for a close-to-town canine workout. It's also a good place to spot columbine in July and

August. Begin by taking a right on the paved bike path, toward Breckenridge and Keystone, from the parking lot (keep your dog leashed when on the path). Walk about an eighth of a mile to an opening in the trees, on the right. Then go straight across a clearing and pick up the wide path that leads to a boardwalk across fragile wetlands. After crossing a stream, the trail ascends gradually through lodgepole pine, aspen, and blue spruce. You'll cross an old road and another trail before reaching the lake. For a loop option, look for the blue diamond marker at the right of the lakeside clearing. Almost immediately, you'll come to another dirt road; take a right. Stay to the right when the trail converges with another road, right at the fork shortly after, and right at the junction that follows. When you pass a small wooden post on the right, marked with arrows, turn left, and you'll be back at the original trail.

Tenderfoot Trail. 2.5 miles round-trip. Head east on Highway 6 from Silverthorne. At the stoplight turnoff toward Dillon, make a left, then an immediate sharp right. Signed parking for the trail is 0.6 mile ahead on the right. *Dogs can be off leash.*

In this trail's favor are its accessibility and views. However, the constant drone of traffic from I-70 reminds you that you haven't escaped civilization. This is a dry area, so bring water. Walk up the hairpin curve in the road and past the water treatment plant to access the trail. Follow a dirt road for a quarter mile to a trail sign pointing left and uphill. Wend your way through an odd gate contraption, and you'll be on the trail. As you hike, you'll enjoy wonderful views of Buffalo Mountain and the Gore Range to the north, as well as Dillon Reservoir and Peaks 1 through 10 beyond. The trail switchbacks gently up Tenderfoot Mountain, first through sagebrush, then

aspen, and, finally, lodgepole pine. The second bench along the trail, from which you can see Breckenridge and Keystone Resorts, is a good turnaround point. After this, the trail gets considerably steeper and less maintained as it heads to the summit of Tenderfoot.

CYCLING FOR CANINES
Summit County is filled with great riding spots, and because many routes follow trails or old mining roads on national forest property, they're also dog friendly, as long as you keep an eye on distance. **Wilder Gulch, Crystal Lake, Rainbow Lake,** and **North Tenmile Trail** up to the wilderness area boundary (see "Tail-Rated Trails" for more informatiion) all make suitable dog rides. Or try an out-and-back on the jeep road along **Tenderfoot Mountain** (see Tenderfoot Trail in "Tail-Rated Trails"; keep following the dirt road you start out on instead of taking the trail uphill). You can also bike with your dog (with a gondola ride uphill if you're averse to climbing) at Keystone Resort.

For more ideas, check out *The Mountain Bike Guide to Summit County,* by Laura Rossetter.

POWDERHOUNDS
There are many excellent backcountry ski and snowshoe trails throughout Summit County. Some routes that follow roads, which means more room for both skiers/snowshoers and dogs to maneuver,

Woods, a husky, in her natural element near Loveland Pass. (photo by Greg Deranlau)

include **Peru Creek, Webster Pass,** and **Deer Creek,** off the Montezuma Rd.; **Keystone Gulch; French Gulch** and **Sally Barber Mine,** outside of Breckenridge; **North Tenmile Trail** near Frisco; and **Mayflower Gulch,** south of Copper Mountain via Highway 91. Refer to *Skiing Colorado's Backcountry,* by Brian Litz and Kurt Lankford, for detailed route descriptions, and to *Snowshoeing Colorado,* by Claire Walter, for other options.

Breckenridge Nordic Center, 1200 Ski Hill Rd., and **Frisco Nordic Center, 18454 Highway 9 (on Dillon Reservoir), 970-453-6855.** Although dogs are not allowed on the regular groomed trails, each center has devoted one ungroomed trail to skiers or snowshoers with dogs in tow. At Breckenridge, it's the 3.5-kilometer Loop de Poop; at Frisco, the 1-kilometer Fire Hydrant Loop (and the owners hope to eventually expand both). You'll need to buy a trail pass (Fido is free) and keep your dog on his leash (an extendable/retractable leash comes in handy here).

Mountain Creek Ranch, 303-789-1834 (www.ecentral.com/mcr). You can bring your dog on a backcountry adventure at this privately owned ski and snowshoe venue near the hamlet of Jefferson in Park County, adjacent to the Pike National Forest and to southern Summit County. Stay at the restored Homestead Cabin, which dates from the 1890s, or in a new, 18-foot-diameter yurt, each of which comfortably sleeps six people. Both structures have woodstoves and cooking utensils; you'll need to bring food and sleeping bags. There's potable water next to the yurt, but you'll be relying on melted snow at the cabin, so watch where your dog relieves himself. It's a 2.5-mile trek into the yurt; 3.5 miles to the cabin. The ranch's trail system is on gentle terrain, meaning you'll be happiest on lightweight touring skis or on snowshoes. If

you really want to search for turns, you'll have to head farther afield to French Pass or Georgia Pass. "The dogs really have a nice time up here because they can be free," says owner Linda Purdy. And resident yellow lab Jackson is sure to show your dog the best spots to roll in the snow. Open from Thanksgiving to late April, depending on snow cover.

CREATURE COMFORTS

As you get into ski resort territory, it gets more difficult to find lodgings that accommodate dogs. For example, none of the hotels or condos at Copper Mountain Resort accepts pets. However, as you'll see below, several places will welcome your dog as a guest. A little persistent research pays off! And if accommodations are hard to come by, try the town of Fairplay, about a half-hour south of Breckenridge on the other side of Hoosier Pass.

Unless otherwise stated, dogs should not be left unattended in the room or cabin.

Breckenridge

$–$$ Wayside Inn, 165 Tiger Rd., 970-453-5540 (800-927-7669). In addition to comfy motel-style rooms, the inn has a condo that sleeps up to twelve guests. Dogs are permitted in both with either a $20 cash deposit or a credit-card imprint. And they'll be in good company, as three dogs call the inn home (though they're not inclined to share the lobby area with other dogs). You can leave your dog unattended inside, but housekeeping won't enter the room. And be sure to keep him on a leash when outside on the wooded property.

$$$–$$$$ Lodge and Spa at Breckenridge, 112 Overlook Dr., 970-453-9300 (800-736-1607; www.thelodgeatbreck.com). This luxury lodge, located off the road to Boreas Pass, accepts dogs for a $50 nightly fee. Rooms are furnished in an upscale rustic style, with peeled log furniture and beams. Deluxe rooms, with hand-painted armoires, nicely appointed kitchenettes, and gas fireplaces, are definitely the nicest of the bunch. The one-notch down superior rooms are on the small side. All upper-level rooms have balconies; if you appreciate views, ask for a room with a dramatic vista of the Tenmile Range. You can leave your dog unattended inside as long as he's well behaved and quiet, perhaps while you visit the on-site spa for an herbal wrap or reiki treatment.

$$$–$$$$ Tannhauser Condominiums, 420 S. Main St., 970-453-2136 (800-433-9217). Serviceable but not luxurious, these condos are conveniently located in downtown Breckenridge. Select one- and two-bedroom units in the complex allow pets with a $25 one-time fee. You can leave your dog unattended inside. Available from the beginning of November to the beginning of May (during the summer, rentals are long-term only).

Dillon
$$–$$$ Best Western Ptarmigan Lodge, 652 Lake Dillon Dr., 970-468-2341 (800-842-5939). The motel, located across from the Dillon Marina and a lakeshore path, accepts dogs in two of its buildings for a $15 one-time fee per pet.

Fairplay
$–$$ Hand Hotel Bed and Breakfast, 531 Front, 719-836-3595 (www.hand hotel.com). Built as a hotel in the 1930s, the Hand has been converted to a B&B. The eleven rooms, all with private bath, are individually decorated with a Western theme that commemorates Fairplay's history. Canine guests pay $5 extra per visit, and particularly quiet, well-mannered dogs may be left unattended inside if they're in a travel kennel.

$$ Fairplay Hotel, 500 Main, 719-836-2565 (888-924-2200). This recently renovated Victorian-era hotel is dog friendly so long as you put down a $100 deposit. The twenty-one rooms are furnished with antiques, and you can leave your dog unattended inside as long as he behaves responsibly.

$$ Gold Miner's Inn, 801 Main, 719-836-3278 (www.goldminersinn.com). The motel allows dogs for $10 extra per night. All rooms are equipped with refrigerators and microwaves.

$$ Western Inn Motel & RV Park, 490 W. Highway 285, 719-836-2026. Dogs are welcome for $5 extra per night, along with a $25 deposit.

Frisco
$–$$ 5 Mtns. Inn, 211 Main St., 970-668-8868 (888-850-8868; www.5mtnsinn.com). It's not luxe, but the motel is certainly one of Summit County's lower-priced lodging options. There's no extra charge for dogs, but motel management emphasizes that dogs can't be left unattended.

$–$$ New Summit Inn, 1205 N. Summit Blvd., 970-668-3220 (800-745-1211). The motel accepts dogs with a $20 deposit, of which you'll get $15 back if your dog leaves the room damage-free.

$–$$ Snowshoe Motel, 521 Main St., 970-668-3444 (800-445-8658; www.snow shoemotel.com). This older motel has some designated pet rooms where dogs can stay for a $20 deposit, $10 of which is refundable if your dog leaves the room as he found it. You can leave your dog unattended in the room if he's in a travel kennel and promises not to bark.

$$ The Finn Inn, Highwood Terrace, 970-668-5108. A homey B&B in a residential neighborhood, the Finn Inn tends to keep a low profile these days, but the owners do accept pets. And there's a resident

dog, Mustaa, whom Clover took a shine to when we visited. Check with the owners about leaving your dog unattended inside.

$$–$$$ **Ramada Ltd., 990 Lake Point Dr., 970-668-8783 (800-2-RAMADA [national number]).** The motel allows dogs for $10 per night extra.

$$–$$$$ **Best Western Lake Dillon Lodge, 1202 N. Summit Blvd., 970-668-5094 (800-727-0607).** Dogs are allowed in smoking rooms only, with a $50 deposit.

$$–$$$$ **Holiday Inn Frisco, 1129 N. Summit Blvd., 970-668-5000 (800-782-7669 [national number]).** Dogs are allowed in designated pet rooms for a $20 one-time fee. You can leave your dog unattended in the room if you need to, but housekeeping won't enter during that time.

Heeney (Green Mountain Reservoir)
$$–$$$ **Melody Lodge, 1534 County Rd. 30, 970-468-8497 (800-468-8495; www.melodylodgecabins.com).** The lodge accepts "mature" dogs (i.e., those older than one year) for $10 per night, per pet. There are eight one- and two-bedroom, fully equipped cabins (five newly built in 2000), one of which is actually a two-bedroom suite upstairs in the main building (which used to be a saloon and brothel in the 1940s). It's about a two-minute walk to the reservoir. You must keep your dog on a leash on the lodge's property. Note that there's a two-night minimum stay on weekends from May to November.

A visit to the Pika Bagel Shop (401 Main St. in Frisco and 500 S. Main in Breckenridge) will not only net you a tasty treat but score one for Fido as well. The shops hand out day-old bagel pieces for dogs to nosh on.

Keystone
$$–$$$$ **Arapahoe Motel, 22859 Highway 6, 970-513-9009 (888-513-9009; www.arapahoemotel.com).** For $20 extra per night you can stay with your dog at this motel next to the Keystone base village. There are three pet-friendly rooms. Check with the front desk about whether you can leave your dog unattended in the room.

Silverthorne
$–$$ **First Interstate Inn, 357 Blue River Pkwy., 970-468-5170 (800-462-4667 [national number]).** The motel accepts small to medium-sized dogs for $5 extra per pet, per night.

$$ **Home and Hearth Bed and Breakfast, 1518 Rainbow Dr., 970-468-5541 (800-753-4386; www.colorado-bnb.com/hhearth).** Located in a residential neighborhood, this homey, antique-filled five-room B&B allows dogs on a case-by-case basis. If your dog passes muster, he can also hang out with the resident lab, Chaco.

$$–$$$ **Days Inn, 580 Silverthorne Ln., 970-468-8661 (800-520-4267).** There's a $10 charge per dog, per night.

Campgrounds
National forest campgrounds: **Blue River Campground,** 9 miles north of Silverthorne off Highway 9 (24 sites); **Dillon Reservoir** has four campgrounds, for a total of 314 sites, plus one group campground; **Cataract Creek Campground** (4 sites), **Elliot Creek Campground** (64 sites), **McDonald Flats Campground** (13 sites), and **Prairie Point Campground** (44 sites) are all at Green Mountain Reservoir in Heeney.

WORTH A PAWS
Keystone Resort Gondola. Enjoy a scenic summertime trip on the Keystone gondola with your dog. Once at the top, you can hike or bike down the mountain (or

download on the gondola). Dogs can be off leash. The gondola runs from the end of June to the beginning of September, 9:30 a.m.–7:00 p.m., Wednesday to Sunday, and 9:30 a.m.–3:30 p.m., Monday and Tuesday. Call the Keystone Activities Desk (970-496-4386) for information on ticket prices.

Canine 4K Walk/Run. This annual race, held the first Saturday of August, is a fundraiser for LAPS (League for Animals and People of the Summit). You and your leashed dog will follow a course that begins and ends at the Frisco Town Hall. Registration fee (around $20; slightly more on race day) includes a T-shirt for you and a bandanna for your canine companion. Participants also are encouraged to collect money from sponsors to turn in at the race. Following the race, stick around for the Mountain Mutt contest, in which your dog can vie for prizes in categories such as biggest and smallest dog and closest pet-owner lookalike. You can register in advance of the race at the Summit County Animal Shelter (970-668-3230) or at Frisco Town Hall; race-day registration is also available. Your dog must show proof of current rabies vaccination to participate.

Marina Mutt Contest. Started in 1997, this fun land-based social event is put on for dogs and their owners by the Lake Dillon Marina during Labor Day weekend. There are three categories of canine competition: best trick, best pet/owner lookalike, and best howl. No entrance fee is required, but your dog can win cool prizes from local businesses. Even if your dog is the noncompetitive type, bring him down just to socialize. The marina is located at 150 Marina Dr. (take a right on Lake Dillon Dr. when heading east on Highway 6, then a left on Lodgepole, which will bring you near the marina). Call 970-468-5100 for time and date specifics.

Snowshoe with Spot. This mid-March canine get-together is sponsored by LAPS (League for Animals and People of the Summit), and the registration fees benefit the animals at the Summit County shelter. You and your leashed dog can either hike or snowshoe at your leisure along a 2-kilometer course that begins at the Iron Springs trailhead in Frisco (near the shelter). Coffee and bagels are on hand for humans; dogs get a goody bag for participating. The Spring Fever contest that follows awards prizes for fluffiest dog, dog with the bushiest tail, best-dressed dog, and the like. Bring proof of your dog's rabies and other vaccinations. For more details, contact event organizer Lisa Dossey at 970-547-1071.

Colorado Disc Dog Frisbee Competition. The newest addition to a series of canine Frisbee events in the state, this annual competition takes place in Breckenridge's Carter Park in July. Dogs participate in the minidistance, earning points for catching distance and a bonus for mid-air catches; and the freestyle, in which they're judged on difficulty, execution, leaping agility, and showmanship while performing tricks. Colorado Disc Dogs puts on the events. For more information, contact Rick Brydum, 303-759-8785 (frflyers@ aol.com), or look at the

Even dogs can pose for tourist shots. (photo by Cindy Hirschfeld)

organization's website, www.varinet.com /~eye bum/nocodido.html.

DOGGIE DAYCARE
Breckenridge
DnR Kennels, 0115 Gateway Dr. (SCR 950), 970-453-6708. $10/day. Open 8 a.m.–6 p.m., daily.

PET PROVISIONS
Breckenridge
Paws & Claws Pet Supply, 118 S. Ridge, 970-547-9633

Frisco
The Barnyard, 104 Main, 970-668-0238

Silverthorne
Summit Feed and Mountain Supplies, 457 Blue River Pkwy., 970-468-1669

CANINE ER
Frisco
Animal Hospital of the High Country (AAHA certified), 700 Granite St., 970-668-5544. Open 7:30 a.m.–6:30 p.m., Monday and Wednesday; 7:30 a.m.–5:30 p.m., Tuesday, Thursday, and Friday; 8 a.m.–noon, Saturday.

RESOURCES
Breckenridge Information Center, 309 N. Main, Breckenridge, 970-453-6018

Breckenridge Resort Chamber, 555 S. Columbine St., Breckenridge, 970-453-2918 (800-221-1091; www.gobreck.com)

Dillon Ranger District, White River National Forest, 680 Blue River Pkwy., Silverthorne, 970-468-5400

South Park Ranger District, Pike National Forest, 320 Highway 285, Fairplay, 719-836-2031

Summit County Chamber of Commerce Visitor Centers: in Frisco at the Antlers Shopping Center, 916 N. Summit Blvd., 970-668-2051 (800-530-3099); in Silverthorne at the Summit Shopping Center, just south of the intersection of Highway 6 and I-70 (look for the Office Max)

TEN

Vail, Leadville, and Vicinity

THE BIG SCOOP

Situated smack-dab in the middle of the mountains, Vail and Leadville offer the avid outdoor canine lots of trail mileage to sniff out. The more refined dog might prefer Vail, with its faux-Tyrolian decor and upscale boutiques—and where the arm that reaches out to pet him is likely to be sporting a Rolex. The dog with an interest in Colorado's past will relish a visit to Leadville, whose ties to its mining roots are still strong. About the only place your dog won't enjoy is Beaver Creek Resort—because he can't. Dogs are not allowed anywhere in Beaver Creek unless they belong to property owners at the resort. Rumor has it that even Olympic gold medalist Picabo Street was deterred when she tried to bring her pooch along.

In Vail, dogs must be on a leash in Vail Village, Lionshead, and West Vail (specifically, the neighborhood around the Safeway); on any bike path; and in all public parks. Anywhere else in the city limits, as well as in unincorporated areas of Eagle County, dogs can be under voice control as long as they're within ten feet of their owners. In Leadville, a leash law is in effect within the town and in Lake County. There's also a law against public tethering, meaning you can't tie up your dog in front of a store or restaurant, for example, and leave him unattended, even for a few moments.

TAIL-RATED TRAILS

If you're looking for a place to wander in Vail that's close at hand, bring your dog to the paved walkway/bike path that follows **Gore Creek** (from Vail Village to Lionshead, the route parallels W. Meadow Dr. instead of the creek). Or check out the **Vail Nature Center,** next to Ford Park, where a network of four short interpretive trails goes through a meadow and riparian habitat (your dog can be under voice command here). For more hiking options in the beautiful mountains surrounding Vail, refer to *The Vail Hiker and Ski Touring Guide,* by Mary Ellen Gilliland. In Leadville, stop by the Chamber of Commerce (see "Resources") and pick up a copy of the Chamber-issued hiking guide.

Leadville

 Douglass City and Hagerman Tunnel. 5.5 miles round-trip. From U.S. Highway 24 in Leadville, take 6th St. west. In approximately 2 miles, you'll come to a T-intersection (Leadville's recreation center will be on your right). Turn right and continue straight on the paved road to Turquoise Lake. As you reach the lake, continue past the dam. You'll climb two separate hills that afford wonderful overlooks of the lake before coming to Forest Rd. 105, a dirt road bearing to the left. Turn

If your dog stays in Vail for more than two weeks, you'll have to get him a local license. Call the animal shelter in Eagle at 970-328-DOGS for details.

here. You'll drive for approximately 3.5 miles before coming to a sharp turn in the road; proceed another quarter mile to a parking area on the right. Across the road is the trailhead and a sign describing the Colorado Midland Railroad. *Dogs can be off leash.*

This hike will let your dog sniff around one of the ghost towns for which Colorado is renowned. Many of these former towns have some connection to the state's fabled mining past. This one does, too, but in a roundabout way.

Douglass City was a wild and woolly construction camp built high above Turquoise Lake and Leadville to house workers building the Hagerman Tunnel. The tunnel was built in 1888 and used until 1897 as a route for the Colorado Midland Railroad between the silver mines of Aspen and the smelters of Leadville. At 11,528 feet, the tunnel was the highest ever built, featuring an 1,100-foot-long curved trestle (both the trestle and the tunnel were engineering marvels at the time). The path to Douglass City and the Hagerman tunnel follows the former railroad grade.

The trail starts out over rough cobble and rocks, but it soon smooths out to a gradual doubletrack. Throughout the ascent, you'll enjoy spectacular views of the valley you just traveled through as well as the northern flank of Mount Massive. After about a mile the grade comes to an abrupt end; this is where the long trestle once stood. If you look hard, you can see where the railroad grade resumes 1,100 feet across the valley. Don't hike to it! Instead, turn around to see a small trail climbing the hill to the left 50 feet behind you. Continue up this trail, which is a bit steeper and more rocky. At the four-way intersection in the trail shortly after, turn left to take a shortcut to the site of Douglass City. No standing structures remain; in fact, many of the "buildings" of Douglass City were tents. Eight saloons and one dance hall

were among the first buildings up and among the busiest as long as the work lasted. You'll see a few of their remains among the rocks and wildflowers.

Continue climbing past the town, toward a steep rock wall. Soon you'll come to remnants of the tunnel-making operation; high above and to the right is the old railroad grade leading to the tunnel. Follow the trail up the hill to the railroad grade and turn left. In less than a hundred yards you'll see the entrance to the tunnel, and, just inside, ice. The tunnel was used only briefly by the Colorado Midland. It cost James J. Hagerman, the tycoon who owned the rail line, millions to construct and almost as much to keep open. The high elevation and fierce winter conditions caused so many problems that the Midland was soon routed through another tunnel, the Busk-Ivanhoe (now called the Carlton), which allowed the trains easier passage. Enjoy the coolness of the tunnel's mouth and the quiet dripping sounds from deep within. Your pooch may be tempted at the sight of emerald-green Opal Lake below, which can provide a welcome splash on the hike down.

Turquoise Lake Trail. Runs 6.4 miles along the lakeshore. From Highway 24 in Leadville, take 6th St. west. In approximately 2 miles, you'll come to a T-intersection (Leadville's recreation center will be on your right). Turn right and continue straight on the paved road to Turquoise Lake. As you reach the lake, continue toward the dam, but don't drive onto it. Park at the pullout on the left immediately before it. Cross the road and start down the singletrack that contours along the shoreline. The other main access point for the trail is at the May Queen Campground, though you can also pick up the trail at various points along it. *Dogs can be off leash (though you may want to leash* *your dog when in the vicinity of the campgrounds the trail skirts).*

This beautiful trail is a great hike. It never strays farther than 25 yards from the water—most times it's a lot closer than that—and winds around several secluded coves with sparkling water and sandy beaches. During the summer, the trail is fairly popular, especially close to the dam. Expect to see plenty of other hikers and cyclists if you go on a holiday weekend. (Hint: Go off-season if you can. On a beautiful autumn day, we had the trail completely to ourselves.) You'll savor spectacular views of the two highest peaks in the Rocky Mountains, Mounts Elbert (14,433 feet) and Massive (14,421 feet), which dominate the skyline across the water.

After approximately 4 miles, you'll encounter the remains of some abandoned mines—remnants of Leadville's rip-roaring mining heyday. A sign alongside the trail enumerates many of the dangers posed by the abandoned mine shafts and suggests you turn around here. Don't, but take the warnings to heart, and make sure your dog (and you) stay on the trail, which passes safely through the dilapidated remains. (While you're in Leadville, you may want to stop by the National Mining Hall of Fame and Museum, 120 W. 9th St., which offers fascinating displays and artifacts on mines and mining. Your dog won't be able to accompany you inside, however.)

After 6.4 miles, the trail reaches the May Queen Campground at the northern terminus of the lake. The Charles Boustead tunnel empties water collected from the Fryingpan River into this end of Turquoise Lake. The tunnel is one of many that brings water from the Western Slope underneath the Continental Divide for burgeoning Front Range population centers. Water, it turns out, is ultimately the most precious resource—more valuable than all of the gold and silver ever mined in this area.

Clover and Peter Hirschfeld pause for a pose atop the Continental Divide near Twin Lakes. (photo by Cindy Hirschfeld)

Vail

 Meadow Mountain. 7 miles round-trip. From the Minturn exit off I-70, drive for half a mile to the Holy Cross Ranger District Forest Service office on the right. There's ample parking in the large lot. You'll find the trailhead at the parking lot's southwest corner. *Dogs can be off leash.*

This area use to be the location of the short-lived Meadow Mountain Ski Area, which operated only from 1966 to 1969, when it was purchased by Vail and the lifts were sold to A-Basin. What a beautiful ski area it must have been! From late spring (after the mud dries up) through early autumn, the trail, actually an old road, is a great venue for hiking and mountain biking. In the winter months, it's shared by snowshoers, cross-country skiers, and snowmobilers. And the mountain lives up to its name, providing plenty of meadows for Rover to romp in and chase down a few sticks.

Begin by walking through a gate and heading south on the trail/road. The trail starts to switchback soon after, although the climb is continuously gradual as you ascend through sagebrush and stands of aspen. Inside thirty minutes, you'll find

Highways 24 and 82, 719-486-0785 (800-6-WINMAR; www.coloradodirec tory.com/winmarcabins). These fully equipped cabins, situated at the turnoff for Independence Pass, aren't in the most scenic setting, but the location—about halfway between Leadville and Buena Vista—is convenient. Small dogs are permitted with a $10 one-time fee. From May to mid-November, all cabins are available; during the winter only a couple are kept open.

Leadville

$ Avalanche Motel, 231 Elm St., 719-486-0881 (888-462-1910). You can leave your dog unattended in the room here for a short time; for example, to get a meal.

$ Hitchin' Post Motel, 3164 Highway 91 (3 miles north of Leadville), 719-486-2783. Your dog is welcome to hang his hat here. The motel is on 7.5 acres, with some frontage on the East Fork of the Arkansas River, and you can exercise your dog off leash on the property, away from the main area.

$ Leadville Hostel, 500 E. 7th St., 719-486-9334 (www.leadvillehostel.com). This small, friendly hostel welcomes dogs "provided that the owners are nice, they have the dog under control, and the dog gets along with other people," says owner "Wild" Bill Clower. Of the eight rooms, some are private with their own bathroom; others are dormitory style with several beds and shared bath. Guests have use of the kitchen too. You can leave your dog unattended in the room for a short time if you have to, but the owner prefers that you leash up your dog outside, where there's plenty of space to do so. This is a popular place for runners to stay while they engage in high-altitude training, and some bring their dogs. Perhaps yours will be inspired to shed that puppy fat in the company of such athletic canines.

$ Mountain Peaks Motel, 1 Harrison Ave., 719-486-3178 (888-771-4470; www.mountainpeaksmotel.bizland.com). There's a $10 fee per night, per dog as well as a $25 deposit.

$–$$ Alps Motel, 207 Elm St., 719-486-1223 (800-818-ALPS; www.alpsmotel.com). Dogs are allowed in smoking rooms only, with a $7 nightly fee and a credit-card imprint as a deposit. Note that long-haired dogs are not welcome (so if you're set on staying here with your English sheepdog, you'll probably have to get him shaved!).

$–$$ Silver King Motor Inn, 2020 N. Poplar, 719-486-2610 (800-871-2610). This inn offers about six pet rooms, with a choice of smoking and nonsmoking, for a $10 nightly fee for your dog.

$–$$ Timberline Motel, 216 Harrison Ave., 719-486-1876 (800-352-1876). There's a $5 fee per night, per dog. You can leave your dog unattended in the room if he's in a travel kennel and doesn't bark when left alone.

$$–$$$ Moose Haven Condos, 5827 Highway 24 (9 miles south of Leadville), 719-486-1063. Formerly the Pan Ark Lodge, these condos range in size from studio to three bedrooms, and all have fireplaces and fully outfitted kitchens. Some of the units have been upgraded, with amenities such as dishwashers and Jacuzzi tubs. There's a $20 one-time pet fee.

$$$ Alpine Realty, 135 E. 13th St., 719-486-1866 (800-600-5663; www.moun tainhideaway.com). This property management company has a pool of about 40 houses for short-term rentals, some of which allow dogs. There's a three-night minimum stay.

Minturn

$$$ Pando Cabins, Highway 24 at Camp

Hale, 970-827-4232 (888-949-6682; www.novaguides.com). Your dog can step back in history during a stay at these cabins located near Camp Hale, the one-time ski-training ground for the Tenth Mountain Division troops, who courageously fought in the Alps during World War II. The three two-bedroom log cabins (which are almost brand-spanking new) come fully equipped with kitchens, gas fireplaces, decks overlooking Camp Hale, and southwestern decor. There's a $20 one-time fee to bring your dog along. And if he's not into the historical aspect, he'll certainly enjoy romping leash-free on the surrounding eighty acres. The cabins are operated by Nova Guides, which runs rafting, fishing, jeeping, all-terrain vehicle (ATV), and mountain bike trips in the summer and rents snowmobiles in the winter.

Twin Lakes

$–$$ Twin Lakes Nordic Inn, 6435 Highway 82, 719-486-1830 (800-626-7812; www.twinlakesnordicinn.com). Here's another opportunity to take a step back in time, as this historic inn was previously a stagecoach stop and then a brothel. The thirteen rooms, most of which have shared baths, are individually furnished with antiques and European featherbeds. But they're not necessarily plush; you'll probably want to spend time hanging out in the cozy lobby and bar area, where your pooch can join you whenever food is not being served in the adjoining restaurant. There's a $10 one-time fee for a dog, with a limit of one dog per room. From Thanksgiving through Memorial Day, the inn is open on weekends and holidays only.

$–$$ Twin Peaks Cabins, 6889 Highway 82 (one-half mile west of Twin Lakes Village), 719-486-2667. Located on the road to Independence Pass, Twin Peaks offers two fully equipped cabins as well as a four-bedroom mobile home

for rent. Well-mannered dogs are allowed, with a $10 charge per night. The owner, who loves dogs but not necessarily the messes they make, emphasizes that they should be kept on a leash at all times outside and that you should walk Fido away from the property to do his business. Open mid-May to mid-October.

$$–$$$ Mount Elbert Lodge, Highway 82 (4 miles west of Twin Lakes Village), 719-486-0594 (800-381-4433; www.mount elbert.com). This lodge, a former stagecoach stop with an idyllic setting on the banks of Lake Creek, makes a great dog destination. Though dogs are not allowed in the B&B rooms of the main lodge, they are welcome in any of the eight cozily decorated, fully furnished cabins, for $10 per night, per pet. Cabins range from one to four bedrooms. If your dog would like to explore Mount Elbert itself—Colorado's highest peak—the Black Cloud Trail to the summit starts right outside the door.

Vail

$$–$$$ Roost Lodge, 1783 N. Frontage

When in Vail, bring your dog to see and be seen at Bart & Yeti's restaurant, named after Bart, a golden retriever, and Yeti, a spaniel mix, who used to frequent the place. Woodrow, a cocker spaniel, carries on their legacy. Bart mixed with the movers and shakers, siring dogs belonging to Henry Kissinger, Nelson Rockefeller, and Clint Eastwood (Liberty, former President Ford's dog, was the lucky gal). Enjoy a meal with your dog on the outside patio (though a local dog or two has also been known to sneak into the bar area).

113

Rd. West, 970-476-9158 (800-873-3065; www.roostlodge.com). The Roost is known as Vail's "budget" accommodation, a relative term, of course. It's a cozy place—just don't expect a lot of amenities. The prime draw is that the motel allows dogs, "from a chihuahua to a St. Bernard," according to the desk clerk; however, they can only stay in smoking accommodations, which don't include any of the much larger deluxe rooms. Ask for a back-facing room, as you'll be farther from the noise of I-70 traffic.

$$–$$$$ Lift House Condominiums, 555 E. Lionshead Circle, 970-476-2340 (800-654-0635; www.changeinaltitude.com). These studio condos, just steps from the gondola, allow dogs from the beginning of April through mid-December only, which doesn't help out the skiing dog much. Each condo is equipped with a gas fireplace and kitchenette. There's a $25 one-time pet fee if you're staying one to two nights; a $50 fee for stays of three to four nights; and a $100 fee for four nights and up. If you leave your dog unattended in the room, management prefers that you contain him in a travel kennel. Bart & Yeti's restaurant (see sidebar) is just downstairs.

$$–$$$$ West Vail Lodge, 2211 N. Frontage Rd. West, 970-476-3890 (800-543-2814; www.vail-biz.com/westvaillodge). You'll feel like you're staying in a big-city motel here. In addition to standard hotel rooms, the lodge offers one- and two-bedroom condos, which, with two levels, fireplaces, and homier decor, are the best option for the money. Dogs can stay in rooms and condos for a $25 one-time fee.

$$$–$$$$ Antlers at Vail, 680 W. Lionshead Pl., 970-476-2471 (800-843-VAIL; www.antlersvail.com). About a third of the individually owned condos in this very-near-to-slopeside complex allow dogs. For $10 per night in summer ($15

in winter), you and your dog can stay in comfort in units that range from studios to three bedrooms. According to the general manager, "friendly, quiet—with a capital Q—dogs" can be left unattended in the condos. The Antlers is located alongside Gore Creek; a creekside trail runs right behind the building. And the staff is more than willing to dispense free dog biscuits at the front desk.

Campgrounds

State park campgrounds: **Sylvan Lake State Park**, 16 miles south of Eagle on West Brush Creek Rd. (50 sites).

National forest campgrounds: **Gore Creek Campground**, Highway 6, 2 miles from the East Vail exit off I-70 (24 sites); **Camp Hale Memorial Campground**, Highway 24, south of Minturn at Camp Hale (21 sites); **Turquoise Lake**, outside of Leadville (see "Tail-Rated Trails" for directions), with eight campgrounds, for a total of 368 sites; **Lakeview Campground**, Forest Rd. 125, off Highway 82 near Twin Lakes (59 sites).

WORTH A PAWS

Leadville, Colorado & Southern Rail-road Company. Bring Fido on a scenic, open-passenger-car train ride along the old Colorado & Southern high line. Though it's ultimately up to each day's conductor to give the final say on whether a leashed dog is allowed, chances are good yours will make the grade. The two-and-a-half-hour round-trip brings you north of Leadville toward Fremont Pass, up to the Climax molybdenum mine, and back again, with a short stop at the French Gulch water tower. The train runs daily from the end of May to the beginning of October, with two runs a day between mid-June and the beginning of September. Catch it at the historic depot, 326 E. 7th St. in Leadville. For price information, call 719-486-3936.

Paws for Breast Cancer. Every other September, dogs and their owners gather at the base of the gondola in Lionshead at Vail for this fund-raising walk. A 1-mile course goes through Lionshead; there's also a 3-mile option that loops partway up and down Vail Mountain. The event highlights the value of animal love in the healing process; proceeds from the registration fees are equally split between the Vail Breast Cancer Awareness Group and the Eagle Valley Humane Society. In addition to the walk, refreshments, entertainment, and prizes are part of the fun. For more information, call 970-479-8595.

DOGGIE DAYCARE
Avon
Avon Pet Centre, 730 Nottingham Rd., 970-949-6467. $12.50/day. Open 8 a.m.–5:30 p.m., Monday to Friday; 9 a.m.–4 p.m., Saturday.

Eagle–Vail
Animal Hospital, 40843 Highway 6, 970-949-4044. $17.50/day. Open 8 a.m.–5:00 p.m., Monday to Friday; 8 a.m.–noon, Saturday and 4 p.m. for pick-up and dropoff; 9 a.m. and 4 p.m. Sunday for pick-up and dropoff.

Minturn
Animal Hospital of Vail Valley, 23798 Highway 24, 970-949-7733 or 970-949-HELP. $18/day. Open 8 a.m.–6 p.m., Monday to Friday; 8 a.m.–noon, Saturday.

PET PROVISIONS
Avon
Avon Pet Centre, 730 Nottingham Rd., 970-949-6467

Eagle–Vail Animal Hospital, 40843 Highway 6, 970-949-4044

The Pet Spot, 0429 Edwards Access Rd., Suite 204, 970-926-5786

Leadville
Mountain Feed and Coal Company, 329 S. Highway 24, 719-486-3566

CANINE ER
Avon
Avon Pet Centre (AAHA certified), 730 Nottingham Rd., 970-949-6467. Open 8 a.m.– 6 p.m., Monday to Friday; 9 a.m.–6 p.m., Saturday.

Eagle–Vail Animal Hospital, 40843 Highway 6, 970-949-4044. Open 8 a.m.–5 p.m., Monday to Friday; 8 a.m.– 12 p.m., Saturday.

Leadville
Leadville Veterinary Clinic, 728 Front St., 719-486-1487. Open 9 a.m.–5 p.m., Monday to Friday (closed Thursday).

Minturn
Animal Hospital of Vail Valley, 23798 Highway 24, 970-949-7733 or 970-949-HELP. Open 8 a.m.–6 p.m., Monday to Friday; 8 a.m.–noon, Saturday.

RESOURCES
Greater Leadville Area Chamber of Commerce, 809 Harrison Ave., Leadville, 719-486-3900 (800-933-3901; www.leadvilleusa.com)

Holy Cross Ranger District, White River National Forest, 24747 Highway 24, Minturn, 970-827-5715

Leadville Ranger District, San Isabel National Forest, 2015 N. Poplar, Leadville, 719-486-0749

Vail Valley Tourism and Convention Bureau, two locations: at the Vail Transportation Center and on top of the Lionshead parking structure, 970-479-1394 (800-525-3875; www.visitvail valley.com)

ELEVEN

Aspen

THE BIG SCOOP

Aspen is one of the dog-friendliest towns we've visited. So friendly, in fact, that Clover and I moved here shortly after the first edition of *Canine Colorado* came out. A comment I overheard one day while strolling downtown sums it up: "All the dogs here seem so happy," said a woman to her companion, glancing at Clover.

Dogs are welcome on the downtown pedestrian mall, which includes several fountains. The one at the corner of Hyman and Mill—columns of water of varying heights that spurt unpredictably through a grate—is especially appealing to dogs. And your dog need not worry about missing out on any of the chi-chi shopping opportunities for which Aspen is renowned; almost every store allows Clover as a customer (and she knows exactly where some of them keep a stash of dog biscuits).

The leash situation in Aspen and environs merits some explanation. Technically, a leash law is in effect in Aspen and Snowmass as well as throughout Pitkin County. Historically, it hasn't been rigorously enforced on a consistent basis. But as more people (and dogs) move into Aspen, and trail use increases, conflicts have been on the rise. The trail descriptions here reflect the leash laws as they're written, but as you and your dog are out and about, you'll certainly notice a large contingent of off-leash dogs. So with this information in mind, use your common sense and discretion as to how you control your dog.

TAIL-RATED TRAILS

This is only a small sampling of the many gorgeous trails in the Aspen area. For more ideas, consult *Aspen Snowmass Trails,* by Warren Ohlrich, or the "Aspen/Crested Butte/Gunnison Recreation Topo Map," put out by Latitude 40°. And if your dog wants an instant "in" with Aspen's canine social scene, take him up the Smuggler Mountain Rd., on the east side of town near the Centennial condo complex. Especially after work, there's a steady parade of hikers, mountain bikers, and dogs heading up and down this dirt road. The most popular destination is a viewing platform about 1.5 miles up, from which you can catch your breath and enjoy a vista of Aspen and, beyond, Mount Sopris.

 Hunter Creek/Hunter Valley Trail. About 4 miles round-trip. Take Main St. to Mill St. north, bear left onto Red Mountain Rd. after the bridge, then take an immediate right onto Lone Pine Rd. Trail access is via the first left, into the Hunter Creek condos parking lot (you'll

Retrievers and German shepherds are the most common breed for search-and-rescue dogs, but a rescue poodle? Sure enough, Aspen is home to Cassidy, a standard poodle that has been trained to find avalanche victims. She works with Mountain Rescue, a volunteer organization that helps find and evacuate stranded backcountry skiers and hikers.

need to park on the street, however). The trailhead is close enough to town that you can walk to it. There is an upper access point farther up Red Mountain Rd., via a right turn onto Hunter Creek Rd.; however, the lower access offers proximity to the creek. *Dogs must be leashed up until the Forest Service boundary.*

This trail has it all for dogs: water, trees, and a meadow to frolic in. Begin by following Hunter Creek, crossing it via bridges several times. As you ascend, you'll get increasingly better views of Aspen Mountain. The trail becomes steeper and more rocky before reaching the Benedict Bridge, where it merges with the trail from the upper access. Shortly after the bridge, consider a short detour up the hillside to Verena Malloy Park (look for the spur trail to the right and the park sign), where you'll find an overlook, with bench, that provides great views of Aspen and the Elk Mountains. Then continue on the now-wide main trail as it climbs steeply (stay straight at the three-way intersection; a blue blaze marks the way). At the national forest boundary sign (where you can de-leash as long as your dog stays under voice control), the trail opens up into the spacious meadows of the Hunter Valley. Follow the wide trail through and to the left, where you'll come to the Tenth Mountain Bridge, 1.5 miles from the trailhead. The meadow beyond is home to several old cabins. To make a short loop, follow the trail east through this meadow. When you come to another smaller bridge, cross over and come back down the path along the south side of the creek. Rejoin the main Hunter Valley Trail near the Tenth Mountain Bridge. Head back to the trailhead the way you came up.

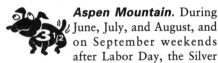

Aspen Mountain. During June, July, and August, and on September weekends after Labor Day, the Silver Queen Gondola whisks hikers to the top of 11,212-foot Aspen Mountain. Not only can your dog accompany you (at no charge) but you can purchase a souvenir dog gondola pass with your loved one's picture on it for $5 at the gondola ticket office.

Once at the top, you can choose to stroll out along Richmond Ridge (there's a short nature walk loop, but you could literally hike for miles on a four-wheel-drive road), hike 4.5 miles to the bottom of the gondola via the Summer Road, or take the shorter (2.5 miles) but more precipitous Ute Trail down. A popular locals' routine is to hike up Aspen Mountain, then ride the gondola down. You can also dine al fresco with your dog at the Sundeck Restaurant; on Saturdays at 1 p.m. during the Aspen Music Festival, students give free concerts mountaintop. *Dogs must be leashed near the restaurant and gondola unloading station, and you'll see signs to that effect, but once you begin hiking on the ridge or down the mountain, you'll be on national forest land more often than not and leashing your dog is at your discretion.*

The gondola operates from 10 a.m. to 4 p.m., and there is a fee.

Difficult Creek. 4.8 miles round-trip. Head east on Highway 82 from downtown; from the spot where you must turn left to follow the highway (at Original St.), it's 3.5 miles to the Difficult Campground parking area on the right. When the campground is open (generally from the end of May to the end of September), drive down to the picnic area day-parking lot on the right; the trailhead is at the southeast corner of the lot. When the campground is closed, you'll have to walk 0.6 mile down a paved road to the trailhead. *Dogs must be leashed (this is wilderness area).*

Don't let the name of this trail mislead you—it's actually a moderate hike. And

In summer, dogs can ride the Silver Queen gondola to the top of Aspen Mountain. (photo by Maryclare Scerbo)

The first 2 miles of this popular path along the Roaring Fork River are paved, and because the trail follows the old Denver & Rio Grande railroad bed, it remains fairly level throughout. If your dog is into jogging, this trail would be a perfect venue. At Cemetery Ln., the trail surface switches to gravel. (To reach the unpaved portion by car, drive on Highway 82 west out of Aspen. Just after the road jogs right, then left, you'll cross Castle Creek; turn right at the traffic light, onto Cemetery Ln. After crossing the Roaring Fork River at about 1 mile, look for the parking area on the left.) About a mile from this juncture, look for the small, tropical-style waterfalls cascading down a rock face next to the trail. Your dog will probably want to take a dip or sip from the crystal-clear pool at the bottom. As you travel farther west, the Roaring Fork drops away into a canyon while the trail comes out onto a plateau behind the Aspen Airport Business Center (a hot, dry stretch on a summer afternoon). After traversing the sagebrush-filled expanse on the wide trail for a mile or so, you'll cross McLain Flats Rd. and pick up a singletrack trail on the other side. If you and your dog are industrious hikers, continue until the trail dips down near the funky Woody Creek Tavern across the road. Enjoy lunch on the patio, then call a taxi to shuttle you back to Aspen.

because the route is mostly in pine and fir forest, this is a good hike for dogs on a hot day. After leaving the parking lot, stay left at the first fork, then follow the brown-and-white "designated route" markers to a wooden bridge that spans the Roaring Fork River. The trail leads to Difficult Creek, then climbs away from the creek for a while before rejoining it (you'll cross another small stream en route). You'll eventually pass through a clearing, where your dog may be able to spot the remains of some log cabins, and arrive at a sign indicating that the trail is not maintained beyond this point. This is the "official" turn-around spot.

Rio Grande Trail. Runs about 9 miles from Neale St. in Aspen to the neighboring town of Woody Creek. To reach the main access point, which is an easy walk from downtown, take Main St. to Mill St. north, then left on Puppy Smith St. The trail begins across the street from the post office. *Dogs must be leashed.*

Sunnyside Trail. About 4 miles round-trip. Take Highway 82 west out of Aspen. Just after the road jogs right, then left, you'll cross Castle Creek; turn right at the traffic light, onto Cemetery Ln. After 1.5 miles you'll see a small parking area on the left; the trail begins on the right. You can also access the trail via a new extension that begins off the Rio Grande Trail. Doing so will add about a mile round-trip to your hike, but parking is more prevalent. After

118

turning onto Cemetery Ln., drive for about 1 mile and look for the large parking area on the left, just after you cross the Roaring Fork River. Hike west on the Rio Grande Trail for a few minutes and look for the signed Sunnyside Trail heading up on the right. *Dogs must be leashed.*

This trail features easy access from town as well as scenic views. Because it climbs up a dry, south-facing slope, dogs would enjoy it most in the early morning or evening on warm days (or anytime on cooler days). However, a recent rerouting of the trail's middle section does bring four-leggers closer to water for at least part of the way. The narrow trail ascends steeply up the hillside. Your dog may want to pause for a drink at an irrigation ditch you'll cross a few minutes into the hike. After crossing a second irrigation ditch, the trail levels out briefly before continuing to climb. As you hike, you'll gain great views of Aspen Mountain, Aspen Highlands, and Buttermilk; the Maroon Bells will soon reveal themselves behind Buttermilk. You'll eventually reach another irrigation ditch, where the trail turns right. This level section follows the ditch for a stretch, giving your dog a perfect wading opportunity. After crossing another irrigation ditch, you'll resume climbing as the trail traverses and switchbacks up the side of Red Mountain.

A good turnaround spot is the radio tower, which you'll come to shortly after entering a large aspen grove, where the trail temporarily levels out again. If you're up for a longer hike, continue uphill until you reach a signed intersection with the **Shadyside Trail**, which peels off to the left. At this point, you're on national forest land, so you can let your pooch romp off leash (but keep him under voice control). The Shadyside Trail, which lives up to its name, follows a not-quite 2-mile loop through the forest; stay right at the first two trail intersections to rejoin the Sunnyside Trail, from which you can retrace your route back down the mountain. The Shadyside extension is particularly appealing because, though it's relatively close to town, you and your dog's chances of encountering other hikers are about as good as finding a hotel room for under $75 in Aspen.

Ute Trail. About 2 miles round-trip. This trail is also within walking distance of downtown. Head east on Ute Ave. for about 0.4 mile. Shortly after you come to a house with a multitude of windows, look for the small wooden trail sign on the right (across from a parking pullout for Ute Park). *Dogs must be leashed.*

Because of its proximity to town and its low mileage, the Ute Trail is an efficient way to exercise your dog (as well as yourself). This short trail switchbacks steeply up the lower third of Aspen Mountain. The reward is a bird's-eye view of town from the rock outcroppings at the end. Don't forget water for your dog, as there's no source on the trail—actually, you'll both need it after tackling the 1,700-foot elevation gain. You can also hike all the way to the top of Aspen Mountain from the Ute, if your dog is up for an even more intense workout; follow the trail to the left just before the rock outcroppings and stay left at the fork shortly after. Farther up the mountain you'll join up with some of the ski area service roads. And if you're tuckered out after topping out, two-leggers and four-leggers alike can ride the gondola down.

Maroon Bells. Take your dog to view two of Colorado's best-known peaks, the 14,000-foot-plus Maroon Bells. From mid-June to Labor Day and on weekends in September, cars are not permitted to drive up to the Bells between 8:30 a.m. and 5 p.m. (As of summer 2000, a $10 per car pass, good for five days, is required for cars visiting before and after these hours.) The best way to get there is to board a Roaring Fork Transit Authority bus (at the Rubey Park Bus Station in downtown Aspen) bound for the Maroon Bells. Dogs are allowed to ride the bus for free (though they're not allowed on any other local buses). Call 970-925-8484 for more information.

Once you're at Maroon Lake, dogs must be leashed due to the heavy use of the area. The 1.5-mile **Maroon Lake Scenic Trail** lives up to its name, providing stunning views of the nearby Bells. (Note that dogs are not allowed within 100 feet of Crater Lake, which is 1.75 miles up the Maroon-Snowmass Trail.) To give your dog a chance to enjoy the beauty of this area while encountering relatively few people, hike the beautiful **Maroon Creek Trail,** which runs 4.5 miles from the upper Maroon Lake parking lot down the valley to the East Maroon Portal. The bus can then pick you up along Maroon Creek Rd. for the trip back to town.

 Conundrum Creek Trail. 17 miles round-trip. The only reason this extremely popular backpack route is included here is so you'll be aware of its restrictions. The trail leads up a scenic valley to a pair of wonderfully situated hot springs pools (and eventually to Gothic, near Crested Butte), but the trip is not a lot of fun for dogs. For starters, *dogs must be leashed because of the wilderness area designation,* and neither Clover nor I (with both of us wearing packs) enjoyed being linked to each other for 8.5 miles. Because the hot springs see heavy use, camping is limited to designated sites, which become even more limited if you're with a dog. And dogs cannot be brought over to the east side of Conundrum Creek, where the hot springs are. So if the thought of tying your dog to a tree, out of sight, while you luxuriate in the springs evokes a pang of guilt, leave Fido at home for this one.

 Ashcroft Ghost Town. The town of Ashcroft, 10 miles up Castle Creek Rd., was established by silver prospectors in 1880, and today some remaining structures, including a couple that have been rehabilitated enough for you to walk into, provide a glimpse into the past. Your dog, unfortunately, will have to stay behind. But you can probably walk around Ashcroft in a short enough amount of time that leaving him in the car wouldn't be problematic. And then you can take him for a hike on one of the nearby trails in the Castle Creek valley.

 Hallam Lake Nature Preserve. As might be expected, dogs are not allowed at this 25-acre oasis that is home to the Aspen Center for Environmental Studies.

Lake Christine and Toner Creek State Wildlife Areas. These two areas near Basalt—the first a 4,000-acre preserve on Basalt Mountain, the second up the Fryingpan Valley—are managed by the Colorado Department of Wildlife. Lake Christine was a popular dog-walking spot in the past; however, the DOW banned dogs in May 2000 from both areas because too many dog owners were ignoring the leash requirement.

North Star Nature Preserve. Dogs are prohibited from this 175-acre open-space-area-cum-nature-preserve on the east side of Aspen (though somehow cross-country ski trail grooming machines and paragliders alighting from the sky are not considered disruptive to the nature idyll). Ironically, the private development of 15,000-square-foot houses that abuts the preserve also bans dogs from entering. You can walk with your leashed dog on the **East Aspen Trail,** which runs adjacent to the preserve's north boundary; just keep Fido from crossing the fence.

CYCLING FOR CANINES

Some of the more popular Aspen biking routes—Smuggler Mountain Rd. and the Government Trail—are not suitable to do with dogs due to leash requirements (Smuggler because it's a county road; the Government Trail for wildlife protection). And because the national forest trails near town start out on county land, where leashes are required, it's not easy to find a place to legally bike with your dog off leash. The **Hunter Valley Trail** (begin from the upper access—Red Mountain Rd. to Hunter Creek Rd.) is Aspen's bike central, and it leads to several great rides in the Four Corners area (see "Tail-Rated Trails"). To comply with the leash regulation, walk your bike and dog up the first part of the trail.

Other options are the 10-mile round-trip ride on **Lincoln Creek Rd.** from Grizzly Reservoir to the ghost town of Ruby, and the unpaved continuation of **Castle Creek Rd.** (a couple of miles past Ashcroft) toward Pearl Pass, for as long as you want to ride. For more detailed information about these routes, look at the single-sheet ride descriptions issued at the Aspen Ranger District office (see "Resources") or check with one of the bike shops in town.

POWDERHOUNDS

In addition to the suggestions below, the **Hunter Creek/Hunter Valley Trail** (see "Tail-Rated Trails") makes a great ski or snowshoe outing.

Though dogs are not allowed on the trails at the Ashcroft Ski Touring Center, they can accompany their skiing or snowshoeing owners on the unplowed section of **Castle Creek Rd.,** which begins at the Nordic center and eventually passes a couple of the Alfred E. Braun system backcountry huts (some avalanche slide paths

do cross the route). Dogs can be off leash provided they refrain from trotting over to any of the nearby Nordic trails. And you can lunch at the Pinecreek Cookhouse as long as you access it via the road (as opposed to the trails) and tie up your dog at least 100 yards from the restaurant.

The Snowmass Club Cross-Country Ski Center grooms two dog-friendly Nordic trails: Village Way and the Ditch Trail. Call the center at 970-923-3148 for details.

During the winter and much of the spring, **Independence Pass Rd.** is closed to vehicles just past the Difficult Creek Campground, 3.5 miles east of Aspen. One of the better doggie social scenes occurs here. There is some potential for avalanches the farther up the pass you venture, but for the first couple of miles the danger is minimal.

If you're visiting Aspen without your dog and are yearning for some canine company, visit Krabloonik, above Snowmass Village. The kennel is home to 250 Alaskan huskies (*Krabloonik* is a native Alaskan term meaning "big eyebrows") and offers twice-daily tours during the summer. The hour-long guided tours include a brief video about dog sledding as well as information about the dogs' diet and training and sled-building techniques. And you will be able to interact with the dogs. During the winter the kennel runs dog-sled tours.

Krabloonik is owned by Dan MacEachen, a seven-time Iditarod competitor who worked for Ashcroft-based dog-sledding pioneer Stuart Mace. In 1974 MacEachen took over Mace's dogs full-time and moved them from the Castle Creek valley to the Snowmass location.

For those into uphill snowshoeing, you can bring your leashed dog with you to the Snowmass ski area to ascend the trails.

CREATURE COMFORTS

Unless otherwise stated, dogs should not be left unattended in the room or cabin.

Aspen

$$–$$$$ Limelite Lodge, 228 E. Cooper Ave., 970-925-3025 (800-433-0832). Dogs are allowed both in the nicely furnished motel rooms at the Limelite and at its sister property down the block, the Deep Powder. The older apartment-style units at the Deep Powder, for many years an Aspen ski lodge on its own, have full kitchens. The motel's location, across from Wagner Park, is a plus.

$$$–$$$$ Hotel Aspen, 110 W. Main St., 970-925-3441 (800-527-7369; www.aspen.com/ha). The hotel has sixteen dog-friendly rooms, each with a small, semi-enclosed patio area or, for second-level rooms, a balcony. Rooms are on the large side, and all have microwaves; some have wood-burning stoves. Paepcke Park, across the street, offers your dog a chance to stretch his legs.

$$$$ Aspen Club Lodge, 709 E. Durant Ave., 970-925-6760 (800-882-2582; www.aspenclublodge.com). One of Aspen's larger hotels, this almost-mountain-side lodge has several of its plush, pine-accented rooms set aside for dogs and owners, with a $200 deposit. All of these quarters are smoking rooms, but the hotel will try to accommodate dogs with an aversion to cigarette smoke. The concierge keeps a list of local dog sitters at the ready for when you have to leave Fido behind. As the lodge management was recently taken over by the exceedingly pet-friendly Kimpton Hotel Group (which runs the Hotel Monaco in Denver), look for more canine-oriented amenities on the horizon.

$$$$ The Brand, 205 S. Galena, 970-920-1800. One of the more unusual places you can stay with your dog, the Brand has six apartment-style suites, each one decorated with exquisite furnishings and art in styles from Southwestern to English country to Soho loft. (The hotel has been featured in *Architectural Digest*.) You can even leave your dog unattended in them—but better warn him against knocking down that pre-Columbian vase with his tail! The staff can sometimes be called on for dog walking as well. There is a three- to four-night minimum visit. Closed from early October to Thanksgiving and from mid-April to Memorial Day.

$$$$ Hotel Jerome, 330 E. Main St., 970-920-1000 (800-331-7213; www.hotel jerome.com). This Aspen landmark dates back to 1889, when Jerome B. Wheeler, one of the town's founding fathers, created a hotel to rival the Ritz in Paris. It has since been restored to its former opulence, and canine guests are welcome. There's even a ready stash of biscuits at the outside bellperson's stand. A $75 cleaning fee is charged per visit, and you can leave your dog unattended in your large Victorian-style room so long as you hang the "pet in room" sign to alert housekeeping.

$$$$ The Little Nell, 675 E. Durant, 970-920-4600 (800-THE-NELL; www.the littlenell.com). If you have the money, there are few better places than the Little Nell to take a dog. Clover slept in style at this luxury hotel, where dogs are presented with welcome biscuits upon check-in. All of the spacious rooms, which start at 600 square feet, have gas fireplaces, and some have balconies. Dogs can be left unattended in the rooms; put up the "privacy" sign to let the housekeepers know. The staff is also willing to watch your dog down in the lobby, if things aren't too hectic, or periodically take him for a short walk. And Glory Hole Park, a pleasant oasis with two small ponds, is down the street, at the corner of Original St. and Ute Ave.

$$$$ The Residence, 305 S. Galena, 970-920-6532 (www.aspenresidence.com). With the benefit of a $1,500 deposit, your pampered pooch can luxuriate in one of this small, centrally located boutique hotel's seven apartment-style suites. Each one is lavishly furnished with antiques, museum-quality artwork, Ralph Lauren linens, and upholstered walls and ceilings. All have full kitchens. Just don't leave your dog unattended in them; you don't really want to have to use that deposit, do you? Max, a Chinese crested (a small, white, fluffy-type dog) is the "resident" canine.

$$$$ The St. Regis Aspen, 315 E. Dean St., 970-920-3300 (800-454-9005; www.stregis aspen.com). It's no longer the Ritz-Carlton, but the hotel and the pet policy are very much the same. First-class Fidos are welcome in any of the rooms, newly redecorated in a luxury mountain style, for a $50 one-time fee. Dogs cannot be left unattended in the rooms, but you can arrange for pet-sitting through the concierge. For $16 an hour, a staff member will either sit with your dog in the room or take him for a walk. Wagner Park, where your dog can spectate at a rugby game, is a block away.

Meredith (Ruedi Reservoir)
$$–$$$ Double Diamond Ranch Bed & Breakfast, 23000 Frying Pan Rd., 970-927-3404. If your dog can play well with others, he can stay with you at this 85-acre ranch surrounded by the White River National Forest and about five minutes from Ruedi Reservoir. He'll have his pick

Though Aspen's Flying Dog Brew Pub no longer exists as a restaurant, this local microbrewery continues to produce quality beer for sale at liquor stores. Quaff an aptly named Road Dog Ale in your pooch's honor.

of two rooms in the main ranch house, each with private bath; a cabin with full kitchen (as well as a Jacuzzi); or the "wilderness" cabin, which is equipped with both gas and wood stoves but no electricity or plumbing. And he can even run leash-free on the ranch as long as he doesn't bother the resident horses or mules.

Snowmass
$$–$$$$ Snowmass Mountain Chalet, 115 Daly Ln., 970-923-3900 (800-843-1579; www.mountainchalet.com). This small slopeside hotel recently started accepting dogs for a $20 one-time fee in the summer, $50 in the winter. You and your dog will usually be booked in a ground-floor room for easy walking access. The recently remodeled rooms are comfortably furnished with log furniture. Rates include a hot breakfast year-round and in winter a light soup lunch. You can leave your dog unattended in the room as long as you're sure he won't bark so much as to disturb other guests.

$$–$$$$ Wildwood Lodge, 40 Elbert Ln., 970-923-3550. (800-525-9402; www.wild wood-lodge.com).The Wildwood is affiliated with the Silvertree and has the same pet regulations (see below). And you can enjoy many of the Silvertree's amenities such as access to the health club. Motel-style rooms are furnished with dark wood furniture and plaid fabric accents, and a few rooms have fireplaces.

$$$–$$$$ Silvertree Hotel, 100 Elbert Ln., 970-923-3520 (800-525-9402; www.silver-treehotel.com). The Silvertree is a full-service slopeside hotel with a three-story atrium lobby and lots of steel-and-glass accents. The rooms are of average size and are comfortable though not ultra-luxe. You must sign a pet waiver when you check in, assuming liability for any damage your dog may inflict during your stay.

Campgrounds
Forest Service campgrounds: Difficult

Campground, 3.5 miles east of Aspen on Highway 82 (47 sites). **Weller** (11 sites), **Lincoln Gulch** (7 sites), and **Lost Man** (10 sites) campgrounds are farther east on Highway 82, as the road ascends Independence Pass.

WORTH A PAWS

Borrow-a-Dog. If your dog wants a friend to play with, or even if you're in Aspen without your dog and could use some surrogate canine companionship, check out this popular year-round program at the Aspen Animal Shelter (212 Aspen Airport Business Center). For nothing more than your signature on a release form, you can borrow a shelter dog, for a few hours or a whole day. Seth Sachson, shelter director, will match you with an appropriate dog. Mention that you read about the program in *Canine Colorado* and you'll get a free T-shirt. Call 970-544-0206.

Snowpaws. Your dog will definitely want to pay a visit to this pet emporium on the Snowmass Village Mall's second level and perhaps exchange sniffs with shop dogs Blue, Marley, and Miles. Owner Colleen Tuohy stocks an inviting selection of unusual toys, chews, collars, leashes, bowls, dog-themed housewares, and books, as well as items for the feline you left at home. Clover gives it a big paws up (snow or no) for best store on the Snowmass Mall. And if you're visiting during Mardi Gras, check out the Snowpaws-sponsored contingent of costumed dogs and owners in the annual Snowmass parade. Call 970-923-7755.

Silver Queen Gondola. Take your dog on the ski gondola up Aspen Mountain. See details in the "Tail-Rated Trails" section.

Golden Retriever Parades. Aspen salutes its furriest finest twice a year, during the annual Wintersköl Carnival in January and on the Fourth of July. Dogs and owners parade down Main St., and local lore has it that the canine marching formation once disintegrated into chaos when spectators threw tennis balls from the roof of the Hotel Jerome. Recently, the goldens have been challenged by an upstart Jack Russell terrier contingent and a poodle brigade.

Canine Fashion Show. If your dog has a penchant for dressing up, and you're in town during January Wintersköl festivities, enter him in the annual fashion show at Aspen's Paepcke Park. Judges award prizes for categories such as most humorous and most original outfits. There's no fee; just show up with your decked-out pooch.

K-9 Uphill. Aspen local Erik Skarvan organizes this annual snowshoe climb for dogs (on leash) and people up Buttermilk Mountain. It takes place the weekend after Buttermilk Ski Area closes for the season, usually in mid-April. Your dog can choose between the competitive and the recreational divisions and look forward to treats at the top of the 2,000-vertical-foot course. This is the one time you *want* your dog to be a puller! After the uphill (you'll also need to walk downhill), there's a barbecue and a raffle with both dog and human prizes at the base area. Registration fee is about $20 in advance, $25 on event day, and proceeds benefit the Aspen Animal Shelter and the Valley Dog Rescue in Basalt.

Aspen Music Festival Concerts. Is your dog a closet Chopin fan? Does he like to snooze to Brahms? Give him a little cultural exposure by bringing him to the David Karetsky Music Lawn, the grassy area outside Aspen's Benedict Music Tent, to hear any of the world-class concerts that take place almost daily from mid-June to mid-August. Dogs are welcome provided they are on leash and cleaned up after (and preferably don't howl during the performance). The best part for humans is that it doesn't cost anything to bring a blanket and listen to the concert—the tent's louvered sides let the music clearly emanate.

Independence Ghost Town. Your dog can envision what life might have been like for a miner's dog in the late 1800s at this former gold-mining community, which dates from 1879 and is believed to have been Aspen's first mining camp. Several tumbledown cabins dot the site, scenically situated beneath the Continental Divide. You can find the ghost town by driving 13.5 miles up Highway 82 from Aspen on Independence Pass. There are no official interpreters on site, but a brochure available in a dispenser at the parking pullout details the town's history.

DOGGIE DAYCARE
Aspen
The Aspen Boarding Kennel, 212 Aspen Airport Business Center, 970-544-0206. $18/day, with two walks a day and feeding, if requested; $32/day for two dogs. Open 9 a.m.–12 p.m. and 2–6 p.m., Monday to Friday; 9–10 a.m. and 5–6 p.m., Saturday and Sunday.

Basalt
Bode's Alpine Meadows Ranch and Kennel, 0329 Holland Hills Rd., 970-927-2688. $10/day for a stay in the heated kennels, with feeding and ball-playing sessions or a short hike as well. Open 9 a.m.–6 p.m., Monday to Friday; 10 a.m.–5 p.m., Saturday and Sunday.

Old Snowmass
Aspen Valley Kennels, 30875 Highway 82, 970-923-7387. $14–18/day, depending on the size of dog. Open 7 a.m.–5 p.m., Monday to Friday; 7–10 a.m. and 2–5 p.m., Saturday and Sunday.

PET PROVISIONS
Aspen
C. B. Paws, 420 E. Hyman Ave., 970-925-5848

Rocky Mountain Pet Shop, 107 S. Monarch, 970-925-2010

Tailwaggers, 212 Aspen Airport Business Center (next to the Aspen Boarding Kennel), 970-925-6076

El Jebel
RJ Paddywacks, 19400 Highway 82 (next to City Market), 970-963-1700

CANINE ER
Aspen
Aspen Animal Hospital, 301 Aspen Airport Business Center, 970-925-2611. Open 7:45 a.m.–5:30 p.m., Monday to Friday; 9 a.m.–12 p.m., Saturday.

Basalt
Basalt Veterinary Clinic, 23286 Two Rivers Rd., 970-927-2684. Open 8 a.m.–5:30 p.m., Monday to Friday; 9 a.m.–12 p.m., first and third Saturday of every month.

Old Snowmass
Aspen Valley Veterinary Hospital, 30875 Highway 82, 970-923-2022. Open 8:30 a.m.–5:30 p.m., Monday to Friday.

RESOURCES
Aspen Central Reservations, 970-925-9000 (800-262-7736; www.aspen4u.com)

Aspen Chamber Resort Association, 425 Rio Grande Pl., 970-925-1940 (888-290-1324; www.aspenchamber.org)

Aspen Ranger District, White River National Forest, 806 W. Hallam, 970-925-3445

Snowmass Resort Association, 970-923-2000 (800-598-2006; www.snowmass village.com)

The Ute Mountaineer, at 308 S. Mill St. (970-925-2849)—with a helpful, friendly staff, a good resource for trail maps and hiking/biking guides

Glenwood Springs and Vicinity

THE BIG SCOOP

Three hours west of Denver and just about an hour down the road from Aspen, Glenwood Springs makes a pleasant destination in and of itself or a more affordable base camp for exploring the mountains around its tonier sister city. (Your dog, however, will have to sit out the natural hot springs for which Glenwood is famed.) About forty minutes south of Glenwood Springs, the one-street town of Redstone—lined with galleries and antiques stores—and the funky hamlet of Marble also invite a visit. While in Glenwood, be sure to stop by the canine-loving Chamber Resort Association, where Clover scored lots of complimentary dog biscuits.

Leashes are the law within Glenwood city limits, but they are optional in unincorporated Garfield County. Be sure to note that the leash law includes an ordinance against "public tethering" (i.e., you can't leave your dog tied up and unattended outside a store or other business), which can make getting food when it's too warm to leave Fido in the car—on most summer days—problematic.

TAIL-RATED TRAILS

Because Glenwood Springs is in a canyon, most of the nearby trails offer vertical climbs. For strolling on the flats, try the paved Glenwood Canyon Recreation Path (see specifics below). A helpful resource is the "Trails Guide to Glenwood Springs, CO," a map that you can pick up at the Forest Supervisor's Office or the Glenwood Springs Chamber Resort Association.

Jesse Weaver/No Name Creek Trail. About 6 miles round-trip. From Glenwood Springs, head east on I-70 to Exit 119 ("No Name"). Make a left at the top of the exit ramp, then follow the paved road to the signed trailhead parking area. *Dogs can be off leash.*

This trail is usually less crowded than the neighboring one up Grizzly Creek, and since it parallels No Name Creek, it's a good pick for a hot day. Begin by walking uphill on a narrow dirt road, past a couple of houses. A short trail diversion to the right bypasses a green gate (if the gate is open, you can stay on the road). No Name Creek rushes by on the left—as it constitutes part of the Glenwood water supply, make sure Fido doesn't relieve himself near the water. If you look above the creek, you'll see some mining remains. Cross the creek on a concrete bridge, then continue following the dirt road to the right (the left track ends at a boarded-up tunnel). The trail narrows immediately after and runs close to the creek. It eventually switchbacks up and away from the creek at a signed fork; to the right is a scenic, but precipitous, overlook above the water, which would make a good turnaround point for a shorter hike. The trail then continues as a steady, though not strenuous, uphill, with the rush of rapids in the creek below a constant companion. Although you can hike for several more miles, our goal was the bridge over the cascading falls, a little more than 3 miles from the trailhead. When it's time to head back, return the way you came.

Red Mountain Trail. The "Trails Guide" map gives the one-way mileage for Red Mountain as 2 miles; the sign at the trailhead indicates 3.5 miles. A Parks Department representative says 3 miles is likely, so count on approximately 6 miles for the round-trip. Take 7th St. west from Grand Ave. to the T-stop at Midland. Make a left, and then a right on 10th St. (at the stop sign). Go up 2 blocks to Red Mountain Dr., take a right, cross the one-lane bridge, then take a left on W. 9th St. (not Pl.). There's a parking pullout at the end of the road, adjacent to the trailhead. *Dogs can be off leash.*

This hike follows a dirt road through what was once the Glenwood Springs ski area. The area closed in the early 1950s, but some of the lift structures remain. Begin by following the road; then cut through an open area to the left of the first water tank you'll come to. (This advised shortcut allows you to avoid walking through the city's water plant.) Hike up the narrow footpath at the far end—a real lung-buster. You'll soon meet up again with the road. The road keeps to a gradual grade; as you ascend, Glenwood Springs unfolds below. About two-thirds of the way up, a bench provides a rest spot with a panoramic view of almost-13,000-foot Mt. Sopris and the Elk Mountains. The road ends at the summit, where the old ski lift used to unload. You'll encounter some shady areas along the way, but this hike is primarily hot and dry (a stream does flow by the trailhead). Your dog might enjoy it most in the early morning or evening.

Boy Scout Trail. About 3.5 miles round-trip. From Grand Ave., take 8th St. four blocks east to the end. There's no trailhead parking lot—just a couple of spaces on the street—so if you're staying downtown, consider walking to the trail. *Dogs can be off leash,*

keeping in mind the following: Although the first 1.5 miles are within city limits, the trail is not regularly patrolled by Animal Control. If your dog harasses or injures another hiker or biker, however, you may be cited, among other things, for having a dog off leash. If you're sharing the trail with a lot of other users, it's probably best to keep your dog leashed.

Because this hike is dry and largely unshaded, it's best for dogs as an evening outing during the summer. Begin by walking down the driveway on the left of 8th St. to the actual trail. You'll face a short, steep climb before the trail levels off to a more gradual ascent as it snakes around the hillside. Enjoy the bird's-eye view into Glenwood Canyon below. After about half a mile, your dog will find brief respite in the shade of piñon pines. The trail continues to ascend, making a large switchback through sage and oak brush. At the T-intersection, go left; the trail continues switchbacking up to the right about 200 feet ahead. In about a third of a mile, you'll end up near the top of Lookout Mountain, by the radio towers and an old campground. Savor the views before returning the way you came.

Instead of doing an out-and-back hike, you can take an alternate route that adds several miles but allows you to loop back into Glenwood Springs. At the T-intersection mentioned above, go right instead. You'll then be following a dirt track that wraps around a ridge on the west side of Lookout Mountain, which eventually brings you to a splendid panorama of Mount Sopris and the Elk Range. Once you contour around the ridge and begin heading downhill, you'll reach a four-way intersection of dirt roads. Stay right and follow a somewhat overgrown dirt track northwest along wide switchbacks down a hillside of sagebrush, juniper, and gambel oak. You'll have a vista of Glenwood Springs below and Red Mountain across the valley. At the distinct intersection with the wide dirt Cemetery Rd., almost at the bottom of your descent, head downhill (left). You'll shortly intersect with the end of Palmer Ave., just a few blocks east of Glenwood's main street, Grand Ave.

 Glenwood Canyon Recreation Path. Runs 16 miles from the Vapor Caves, at the east end of 6th St., to about 2 miles west of the Dotsero exit off I-70. *It's suggested, but not required, that dogs be leashed.*

This paved multiuse trail runs the length of spectacular Glenwood Canyon, bordering the Colorado River. Although your dog probably won't appreciate the much-touted engineering marvels of the highway above, he may well enjoy a walk by the water. If you have a car, the best place to access the path is at the No Name exit (119) just east of Glenwood Springs, as the first section (about a mile) runs directly adjacent to the highway. There are some great doggie play spots in the river accessible from here.

 Rifle Falls State Park. Since you can't take your dog to Hanging Lake (see below), bring him here to see a triple waterfall. From the Rifle exit off I-70, west of Glenwood Springs, travel north on Highway 13. After about 5 miles, take a right on Highway 325; the park is 9.8 miles ahead on the right. *Dogs must be leashed.*

Once inside the park, go left to access the falls; there is a day-use parking area where the road ends. From there, it's a short walk to the falls. Your dog will appreciate their spray on a hot day. After viewing the plunging water, hike on the Coyote Trail, a short twenty- to thirty-minute walk that meanders past limestone grottos and a small stream before taking you to the top of the falls (you'll be glad to have your dog on a leash here!). Descend via the trail marked "difficult" (it's not,

really), and you'll come out by the drive-in campsites. If your dog is into botany, he'll appreciate the trailside markers that identify native plants and trees. The Squirrel Trail (did Rover's ears just prick up?), which follows streams for most of its length, is another option for a short walk; it's part dirt road, part path. If you decide to overnight in the park, stay at one of the walk-in campsites, which you'll pass along the Squirrel Trail.

 Hanging Lake. This is a great hike up to a gorgeous tropical-style waterfall with—well, never mind, because your dog can't see it anyway. Because of the immense popularity of this trail, dogs are not allowed, period.

 Harvey Gap State Park. With the exception of hunting dogs during hunting season, dogs are not allowed in this park, which contains Harvey Gap Reservoir. There are no hiking trails here anyway, so your dog probably won't regret the lack of access.

CYCLING FOR CANINES

The **Red Mountain Trail** is easy to bike, as it follows a dirt road in fairly good shape. Just remember to allow your dog time to catch up with you on the ride down. You can conceivably bike with your dog on the **Glenwood Canyon Recreation Path**, since leashes are not a requirement. Another option is the 7-mile round-trip **Burnt Tree Ridge Trail** (#18 on the "Trails Guide to Glenwood Springs, CO" map), which follows an old four-wheel-drive road about 15 miles east of Glenwood Springs. Or investigate the **Roan Cliffs** area outside of Rifle. A biking map is available at the Bureau of Land Management office in Glenwood Springs (see "Resources"); the northwest section, accessible from Piceance Creek Rd. outside of Rio Blanco, is generally less used by motorized vehicles than the eastern section.

POWDERHOUNDS

It's primarily backcountry as far as finding a good location near Glenwood Springs to ski with your dog. The Ski Sunlight Nordic Center discourages dogs on its trails, and the Four Mile Park area, which is on national forest land, is popular for snowmobiling, making it less than ideal for the four-legged set. See *Snowshoeing Colorado,* by Claire Walter, for a couple of ideas.

Ute Meadows Nordic Center, 2880 County Rd. 3, 970-963-7088 (888-883-6323; www.utemeadows.com). Operated by the Ute Meadows Bed and Breakfast (see "Creature Comforts"), the Nordic center has about 15 kilometers of tracks set for both classic and skate skiing, and dogs are allowed on all of them, leash free. There are also three separate snowshoe trails, also dog friendly. A dog trail pass is $3 per dog, per day, and there's a limit of two dogs per skier. You can even buy your dog a season pass for $15. And the Nordic center provides plastic scoopers and an unlimited supply of doggie bags so you can keep the snow pristine.

CREATURE COMFORTS

Unless otherwise stated, dogs should not be left unattended in the room or cabin.

Carbondale
$–$$ Thunder River Lodge, 0179 Highway 133, 970-963-2543. A $20 deposit and a $5 fee per night lets your dog stay at this motel.

A nice place to eat in the company of your dog is Kiwanis (or Veltus) Park, off of Midland Ave. between 8th and 10th Sts., on the banks of the Roaring Fork River.

Lewis checks out David Wallace's catch of the day. (photo by Bevin Wallace)

$$–$$$ Days Inn, 950 Cowen Dr. (near the intersection of Highways 82 and 133), 970-963-9111 (800-944-3297). This pet-friendly Days Inn permits dogs in designated pet rooms for $8 per night, per dog.

Glenwood Springs
$–$$ Red Mountain Inn, 51637 Highway 6 & 24, 970-945-6353 (800-748-2565; www.redmountaininn.com). The inn offers cabins or motel rooms, and dogs are allowed in both. The rooms are modern, clean, and comfortable. There's a small pet-walking area on the premises where well-behaved dogs can be unleashed. A $100 deposit is required. You can leave your dog unattended in your room, but housekeeping will not clean it during that time.

$$ Affordable Inns, 51823 Highway 6 & 24, 970-945-8888 (800-292-5050; www.afford ableinns.com). A $5 per stay fee is required, and a dog can be left unattended in the rooms.

$$ Budget Host, 51429 Highway 6 & 24, 970-945-5682 (800-283-4678 [national number]). There's a $5 fee per night, per dog.

$$ Buffalo Valley Inn, 3637 Highway 82, 970-945-5297. Rooms with kitchenettes are available at this motel, which also has a steakhouse and bar with live music on weekends. There's a $10 one-time fee per dog.

$$ Caravan Inn, 1826 Grand Ave., 970-945-7451 (800-945-5495; www.caravan.com). A $5 fee per pet, per night is charged as well as a $50 deposit. You can leave your dog unattended in the room, but housekeeping won't come in during that time.

$$ Frontier Lodge, 2834 Glen Ave., 970-945-5496 (800-366-2285). The lodge has only a couple of rooms set aside for pets. Expect to pay a $10 cleaning fee for your dog.

$$ Mama Bear's Cottage, 953 County Rd. 117, 970-945-0830 (888-945-7547). Dogs are welcome at this studio cabin that sleeps up to four, which is the guest cottage of the owner's main residence on the road to Sunlight ski area. The cottage contains a full kitchen, wood-burning stove, and deck, and its decor includes quilts and teddy bears (which your dog shouldn't make into his personal fluffy toys!).

$$ Ponderosa Cabins, 51793 Highway 6 & 24, 970-945-5058 (800-843-5449). Most of the Ponderosa's cabins have kitchenettes. Dogs will like the nice grassy areas outside. There's a $10 one-time dog fee, and a dog can be left unattended in the cabin.

$$ Riverside Cottages, 1287 Road 154, 970-945-5509 (800-945-5509; www.riversidefun.com). These cottages are a throwback to the 1960s as far as furnishings go, but the setting along the Roaring Fork River can't be beat. A one-time $10 fee per dog is charged. Your dog can romp unleashed to his heart's content, with supervision of course, outside the cottages.

$$ Silver Spruce Motel, 162 W. 6th St., 970-945-5458 (800-523-4742; www.silversprucemotel.com). The motel's rooms are modern and spacious. A $5 fee per pet is charged per night, and dogs can be left unattended, but housekeeping won't clean the room during that time.

$$ Starlight Lodge, 121 W. 6th St., 970-945-8591 (www.glenscape.com). The motel, a block from the hot springs, allows dogs in designated rooms, including some with kitchenettes. Quiet dogs can be left unattended in the room.

$$ "The" Bed and Breakfast on Mitchell Creek, 1686 Mitchell Creek Rd., 970-945-4002. Though this B&B is technically outside the parameters of this book in that dogs are not allowed in the room, I've included it because the owners of this bucolic haven are nonetheless accommodating to pets. Your dog is welcome to sleep on the patio or in the garage (either leashed or in a travel crate), and a private hiking trail that begins behind the house is open to you and your dog to venture on leash-free. Because the accommodations are for only one set of guests per night, your dog won't run the risk of bothering anyone else. So if you have a dog used to spending time outside, this is an option to consider.

$$-$$$ Hotel Denver, 402 7th St., 970-945-6565 (800-826-8820; www.thehoteldenver.com). We give this hotel high marks for dog friendliness as well as value. The rooms are modern and comfortably furnished, though the building dates from the early 1900s, and you can leave your dog unattended in them. The Glenwood Canyon Brewing Company, which serves its own microbrews and a full menu, is conveniently located off the lobby. In fact, the aroma of hops pervaded the hotel when we arrived.

$$–$$$ **Quality Inn and Suites**, 2650 Gilstrap Ct., 970-945-5995 (800-228-5151 [national number]). Dogs are allowed in smoking rooms only (none of them suites), with a $25 deposit and a $10 nightly fee.

$$–$$$ **Ramada Inn and Suites**, 124 W. 6th St., 970-945-2500 (800-332-1472; www.ramadaglenwood.com). Dogs are allowed in smoking rooms only, and you must put down a $50 deposit per dog, as well as pay a $10 fee per night, per dog. Dogs may not be left unattended in the room for long periods of time.

$$$–$$$$ **Hotel Colorado**, 526 Pine St., 970-945-6511 (800-544-3998; Denver direct line is 303-623-3400; www.hotel colorado.com). Let your dog be part of history with a stay at this elegant hotel, listed on the National Register of Historic Places, which boasts many past luminaries among its guests, including President Theodore Roosevelt. Clover turned up her nose at the lowest-priced standard rooms but decided that the parlor rooms and suites, recently refurbished and individually decorated with Victorian-style furniture, would more than suffice. Guest dogs receive biscuits on check-in. There's a $10 one-time pet fee, and you can leave a dog unattended in the room only if he's safely contained in a crate.

Gypsum
$$ **A. J. Brink Outfitters at Sweetwater Lake**, 3406 Sweetwater Rd. (25 miles west of Gypsum), 970-524-7344 (www.brink outfitters.net). This well-established rustic resort and stables are on 400 acres adjoining the Flattops Wilderness. Four motel rooms as well as seven one- to three-bedroom cabins, all with kitchen facilities, are available to you and your dog. They're outfitted in a style that the woman I spoke with laughingly referred to as "early American garage sale." Dogs must be kept leashed on the property, though they're certainly welcome to dip a paw in the lake. Quiet dogs can be left unattended in their rooms. In addition to horseback riding, the resort rents out rowboats and canoes to use on Sweetwater Lake, and there's a restaurant too. Open mid-May to November 15 (a few cabins remain open in the winter).

Marble
$ **Beaver Lake Lodge**, 201 E. Silver St., 970-963-2504. There are five rooms in the main lodge building and five rustic cabins, with kitchens. Your dog is welcome to stay with you in either, and he can be left unattended. The lodge is open from mid-May through the end of October.

$$ **Chair Mountain Ranch**, 0178 County Rd. 3, 970-963-9522. The ranch is situated on 8 acres by the Crystal River, and dogs are allowed in any of the five cabins for a $5 fee per night. You can even leave your dog unattended for a few hours or tie him up outside. The owners do ask that you keep your dog leashed on the ranch property because of the abundance of chickens and ducks. Open June through October.

$$–$$$ **Ute Meadows Bed and Breakfast**, 2880 County Rd. 3, 970-963-7088 (888-883-6323; www.utemeadows.com). This newer bed and breakfast allows dogs in two of its seven rooms—all have private baths and are furnished in a modern, casual Western style—for $15 per night, per dog, with a limit of two dogs per room. You can leave your dog unattended inside only if he's in a travel crate, but outdoor kennels are also available if you need to leave Fido behind. If you visit in winter, your dog can join you on the trails at the adjacent Nordic center (see "Powderhounds").

New Castle
$ **New Castle/Glenwood Springs KOA & Kamping Kabins**, 0581 County Rd. 241,

131

970-984-2240 (800-KOA-3240). Dogs are allowed in the camping cabins for $5 extra per night, as well as at the campground as long as they're leashed (you'll need to provide your own sleeping and cooking gear). And "if you leave the campground, your pet goes with you," the owner emphasizes. An enclosed dog area is available, and your dog can run off leash here, but you must supervise him.

Parachute

$ **Super 8**, 252 Green St., 970-285-7936 (800-800-8000 [national number]). With a $20 deposit and $5 extra per night, it's smoking rooms only for dogs here. They can be left unattended in the room as long as they're in a travel kennel.

Redstone

$$ **Redstone Cliffs Motel**, 433 Redstone Blvd., 970-963-2691 (888-652-8005; www.redstonecliffs.com). The motel offers studio and one-bedroom apartments with kitchenettes in an older, log-cabin–style setup. For $10 a night, your dog can join you. There's a limit of one dog per unit, which is strictly enforced.

$$–$$$ **Avalanche Ranch**, 12863 Highway 133, 970-963-2846 (877-963-9339; www.avalancheranch.com). You've got to love a place that advertises "pets welcome" on the front of its brochure. Owner Sharon Boucher says it's her "mission" to provide lodging that you can enjoy with your dog. Fourteen rustic-style cabins are situated on 45 acres where dogs can romp unleashed. The decor is mountain themed, and while the cabins are not upscale, they're cozy and spotless. There is a $10 fee per pet, per night, with a maximum of two dogs per cabin. Along with full kitchens for human convenience, doggie towels are provided in each cabin, and dogs receive biscuits on check-in. The ranch's annual October Apple Festival, with a pig roast and band, is a great time for both dogs and people. And if your dog really enjoyed his stay, buy him a leash at the on-site antiques shop that proclaims, "I vacation at Avalanche Ranch."

$$–$$$ **Redstone Inn**, 82 Redstone Blvd., 970-963-2526 (800-748-2524; www.redstoneinn.com). Dogs are permitted in the "terrace" rooms at this turn-of-the-century hotel, a member of the Historic Hotels of America, for $15 per stay. You can leave your dog unattended in the room, but housekeeping won't come in to clean during that time. The terrace rooms are in a 1950s-era addition to the hotel, and they're large and comfortable but don't feature the Arts and Crafts decor (with original Stickley furniture) of the rooms in the hotel's main section. They do open on to a parking lot for easy dog-walking access. And dogs can romp, leashed, on the inn's 22 acres, which include a pool and tennis courts. The inn has specials during the annual Sled Dog weekend, held in January or February, when races take place near Redstone.

Rifle

$–$$ **Buckskin Inn**, 101 Ray Ave., 970-625-1741 (877-BUCKSKIN; www.buckskininn.com). Most of the motel's rooms are pet friendly. It's possible to leave your dog unattended in the room for under an hour (say, to grab a bite to eat) if you check first with management.

$–$$ **Red River Inn**, 718 Taughenbaugh Blvd., 970-625-3050 (800-733-3152). Dogs are allowed in smoking rooms only for a $10 one-time fee.

$$ **Rusty Cannon Motel**, 701 Taughenbaugh Blvd., 970-625-4004. Four smoking rooms are set aside for guests with pets. There's a $20 deposit, and management says it will call the police if you leave your dog unattended in the room. You've been warned.

Silt

$–$$ Red River Motel, 1200 Main St., 970-876-2346. The motel allows small dogs with a $10 deposit.

Campgrounds

State park campgrounds: **Rifle Falls State Park**—see "Tail-Rated Trails" for directions (18 sites); **Rifle Gap State Park,** on Highway 325 outside of Rifle, just a few miles before Rifle Falls State Park (46 sites).

National forest campgrounds: There are a number of campgrounds along Coffee Pot Rd. (Forest Rd. 600), 2 miles north of Dotsero off I-70, including **Coffee Pot Spring Campground** (15 sites) and **Deep Lake Campground** (45 sites); **Bogan Flats Campground,** on the Marble road off Highway 133 (37 sites); and **Redstone Campground,** about a mile north of Redstone (37 sites).

Private campgrounds: **New Castle/ Glenwood Springs KOA** in New Castle (see "Creature Comforts").

DOGGIE DAYCARE
Carbondale

The Little Tail, 955 Cowen Dr., 970-704-0403. $12/day. Affiliated with the Red Hill Animal Health Center, this boarding facility bills itself as the "five paw pet resort of the Rockies." A stay includes time in the play yard. Open 7 a.m.–7 p.m., Monday to Friday; 8 a.m.– 4 p.m., Saturday.

Mid-Valley Kennel, 16478 Highway 82 (west of Carbondale), 970-963-2744. $13/day. A stay here includes the use of indoor and outdoor runs as well as exercise and play time. Open 8 a.m.–5 p.m., Monday to Saturday; 2–5 p.m., Sunday.

Skyline Ranch and Kennels, 0356 County Rd. 101, 970-963-2915. $12/day for the first dog, $10/day for the second. Open 7:30 a.m.–5:30 p.m., Monday to

Saturday; 8 a.m.–3 p.m., Sunday.

PET PROVISIONS
Glenwood

Glenwood Veterinary Clinic, 2514 Grand Ave., 970-945-5401

Rifle

Nola's Ark Pet Shop, 100 E. 11th, 970-625-3868

CANINE ER
Carbondale

Alpine Animal Hospital, 17776 Highway 82, 970-963-2371. Open 9 a.m.–noon and 1–5 p.m., Monday to Friday; 9 a.m.–noon, Saturday.

Carbondale Animal Hospital, 234 Main St., 970-963-2826. Open 8 a.m.–5:30 p.m., Monday to Friday; 9 a.m.–noon, Saturday.

Red Hill Animal Health Center, 955 Cowen Dr., 970-704-0403. Open 7 a.m.–7 p.m., Monday to Friday; 8 a.m.–4 p.m., Saturday.

Glenwood Springs

All Dogs and Cats Veterinary Hospital, 1605 Grand Ave., 970-945-6762. Open 8 a.m.–5:30 p.m., Monday to Friday.

Birch Tree Animal Hospital, 1602 Grand Ave., 970-945-0125. Open 8 a.m.–5:30 p.m., Monday to Friday.

Glenwood Veterinary Clinic, 2514 Grand Ave., 970-945-5401. Open 8 a.m.–5 p.m., Monday to Friday; 8 a.m.–noon, Saturday.

Parachute

Parachute Veterinary Clinic, 120 W. 1st St., 970-285-0356. Open 9 a.m.–5 p.m., Monday to Friday; 9 a.m.–12 p.m., Saturday.

Rifle

Town and Country Veterinary Hospital,

1595 Railroad Ave., 970-625-2971. Open 9 a.m.–5 p.m., Monday to Friday; 9 a.m.–12 p.m., Saturday.

RESOURCES
Bureau of Land Management, 50629 Highway 6 & 24, Glenwood Springs, 970-947-2800

Eagle Ranger District, White River National Forest, 125 W. 5th St., Eagle, 970-328-6388

Forest Supervisor's Office, White River National Forest, 900 Grand Ave., Glenwood Springs, 970-945-2521

Glenwood Springs Chamber Resort Association, 1102 Grand Ave., Glenwood Springs, 970-945-6589 (888-4-GLEN-WOOD; www.glenwoodsprings.net)

Rifle Ranger District, White River National Forest, 0094 County Rd. 244, Rifle, 970-625-2371

Sopris Ranger District, White River National Forest, 620 Main St., Carbondale, 970-963-2266

Summit Canyon Mountaineering, 8th and Grand Ave., Glenwood Springs, 945-6994 (800-360-6994), has an extensive collection of guidebooks and maps

THIRTEEN

Northwestern Colorado

THE BIG SCOOP

The area of Colorado that's west of Craig and north of I-70 embodies the wide open spaces of the West. This is desert and canyon country, though even in the summer temperatures are cooler than in the Grand Junction area, for example, usually topping out in the 80s. But the very characteristic that can make it an appealing place for you and your dog to visit can also be its downfall—there's not a lot here. The principal towns are Craig, Meeker, and Rangely, all small, with just a few even smaller ones dotting the landscape. There's lots of BLM land where you can hike with your dog off leash, but the developed trails are few (and you can't bring your dog on the trails in Dinosaur National Monument). For forested, mountainous terrain, head east of Meeker into the White River National Forest and the Flat Tops Wilderness Area—one of the few wilderness areas in the state where dogs can hike off leash as long as they're under voice control. Several guest ranches in this region welcome canine visitors, and one even offers a dog-friendly backcountry yurt.

TAIL-RATED TRAILS

 BLM land. Almost all BLM land in this part of the state is undeveloped, meaning there aren't established trailheads or regularly maintained trails. *But you can bring your dog anywhere, and he can be off leash.* Just be sure to bring a topo map along, as well as lots of water.

The land on either side of Harpers Corner Rd., which leads from the Dinosaur National Monument visitor center outside of Dinosaur to the park itself, is BLM managed. On the west side of the road is the **Bull Canyon Wilderness Study Area,** and on the east side is the **Willow Creek Wilderness Study Area.** From the Plug Hat Butte picnic area, 3.5 miles up Harpers Corner Rd. from the visitor center, you can take a 4- or 5-mile round-trip hike into **Lower Buckwater Draw;** you'll find a waterfall in the draw during spring. For more hiking suggestions, stop by the BLM office in Meeker (see "Resources"), which has some printed route descriptions. *Exploring Colorado's Wild Areas,* by Scott S. Warren, also has information about hiking routes on BLM land in northwestern Colorado as well as for other areas throughout the state.

 Dinosaur National Monument. The monument straddles Utah and Colorado and includes Echo Park, at the confluence of the Green and Yampa Rivers, the site of a proposed dam that was scuttled in a celebrated showdown between the federal government and the Sierra Club in the 1960s. Although the monument's name comes from dinosaur bones discovered in the area, you can only actually see the fossils at the Dinosaur Quarry, 7 miles north of Jensen, Utah. The park's Headquarters Visitor Center is 2 miles east of Dinosaur, Colorado. Dogs are not allowed on trails, anywhere else in the backcountry, or on river trips through the park. You can bring your dog to the quarry, though you'll have to leave him tied up outside while you view the fossil exhibits. And he can come to the campgrounds and picnic areas as long as he's always on a leash.

CYCLING FOR CANINES

The BLM office in Craig (see "Resources") has a handy pamphlet called "Mountain Bike Routes of Moffat County." Note that there's a leash law throughout Moffat County, so unless a bike route is actually on BLM or national forest land (and not all of the ones listed in the pamphlet are), it won't be practical for Fido to come along. The Yampa Valley Trail runs for 100 miles from the town of Maybell to within Dinosaur National Monument. You can access a singletrack section of it from Deerlodge Rd., about 20 miles west of Maybell, near the Cross Mountain turnout.

POWDERHOUNDS

Pollard's Ute Lodge, 30 miles east of Meeker in the White River National Forest, has its own yurt that you can ski or snowshoe to and overnight at in the company of your dog. See "Creature Comforts" for details.

CREATURE COMFORTS

Unless otherwise stated, dogs should not be left unattended in the room or cabin.

Craig

$ Trav-O-Tel, 224 E. Victory Way, 970-824-8171 (888-824-8171)

$ Westward Ho Motel, 517 E. Victory Way, 970-824-3413. There's a $3 fee per night for dogs.

Canine spectators are discouraged from attending one of Meeker's most famous events—the Meeker Classic Sheepdog Championship Trials, in early September. Leave Fido at home and promise him you'll share some good tips.

$$ Bear Valley Inn of Craig, 755 E. Victory Way, 970-824-8101

$$ Holiday Inn, 300 S. Highway 13, 970-824-4000 (800-HOLIDAY [national number]). There's a $50 pet deposit, and you can leave your dog unattended in the room.

$$ Ramada Limited, 262 Commerce St., 970-824-9282 (800-2-RAMADA [national number]). A $50 pet deposit is required.

$$ Travelodge, 2690 W. Highway 40, 970-824-7066 (800-458-7228). Dogs are welcome for $10 extra per night, though they're not allowed in the front desk area. The motel is on 2 acres where you can walk your dog off leash.

Dinosaur

$ Hi-Vu Motel, 122 E. Brontosaurus Blvd., 970-374-2267 (800-374-5332). This is the only place in Colorado where your dog can stay at an address that sounds like it's out of *The Flintstones*. The motel allows dogs in six of its eight rooms for a $5 fee per night. Open April 1 to December.

Meeker

$ Ducey's White River Resort, 12830 County Rd. 8 (14 miles east of Meeker), 970-878-4378. This small resort has four one-bedroom cabins, equipped with kitchenettes but not bathrooms (those are in separate buildings), as well as four motel-style rooms. You must keep your dog leashed at all times on the property and be sure to clean up after him. The White River runs through a part of the property. Open April 1 to November 15.

$ Valley Motel, 723 Market St., 970-878-3656. Dogs can stay in smoking rooms at no extra charge; if you prefer a nonsmoking room, there's a $25 nightly fee.

$–$$ Buford Store and Lodge, 20474 County Rd. 8 (22 miles east of Meeker), 970-878-4745. This historic lodge is located on 235 acres along the North Fork of the White River, bordering the national forest. Ten rustic log cabins are fully furnished but have no bathrooms or running water; there's a central bathhouse for guests. And you'll prepare your meals on a wood-burning cookstove. The oldest of the cabins is more than 100 years old; the "youngest" is about seventy-five years old. You can also rent two modern cabins, which do have full baths. In addition to the cabins, the lodge has a grocery store, gas station, and small museum on the premises. There's a $5 one-time fee for a dog. And with hiking trails nearby, as well as off-leash privileges on the lodge's property, you won't have any reason to leave Rover behind. Open May 1 to November 15.

$–$$ Meeker Hotel and Cafe, 560 Main St., 970-878-5255 (800-847-6470). No doubt your dog will be intrigued by the numerous elk and deer heads adorning the lobby walls. The hotel, built in 1896, is on the National Register of Historic Places, and the rooms, though not incredibly luxurious, are cozy and furnished with antiques. Several of the twenty-four rooms are dog friendly if you pay the $10 nightly fee.

$–$$ Pollard's Ute Lodge, 393 County Rd. 75 (30 miles east of Meeker), 970-878-4669 (888-414-2022; www.utelodge.com). Eight cabins, from one to three bedrooms, are at the lodge, which is on 324 acres near the Flat Tops Wilderness Area. Six of the rustic yet cozy log cabins are fully outfitted; two are without kitchen facilities and share a bathhouse. Dogs are $5 extra per night, or $15 extra for a week's stay. Your dog can explore the property, which includes a private fishing lake and a creek, off leash under your supervision. Horseback riding is also available from the lodge, and during the winter you can ski or snowshoe with your dog to the lodge's own yurt, about

1.25 miles from the main complex. The yurt sleeps up to ten people, for $20 per person.

$–$$ Rustic Lodge, 173 1st St., 970-878-3136. The six cabins here (with kitchenettes) are actually not quite as rustic inside as they look on the outside. The owner emphasizes that "mean, aggressive" dogs will not be welcome. There's a resident three-legged dog with whom yours might like to socialize.

$$ Adams Lodge, 2400 County Rd. 12 (30 miles east of Meeker), 970-878-4312. The lodge offers ten fully furnished cabins, and the owners emphasize that visiting dogs cannot lie on the beds. You can walk your dog off leash around the cabins, but be aware that there is a lot of wildlife, in addition to llamas and cats, around. Two of the cabins stay open year-round; the others are open from Memorial Day to November 1.

$$ The Aspens Bed and Breakfast, 1077 County Rd. 10 (20 miles east of Meeker), 970-878-0018 (www.bbonline.com/co/aspens). Your dog can stay with you in one of four rooms, all with private bath, at this nicely appointed B&B in a modern log house along the White River. Each room is individually furnished in an upscale rustic style (e.g., handcrafted log beds) with artisan touches throughout.

$$ Sleepy Cat Guest Ranch, 16064 County Rd. 8 (17 miles east of Meeker), 970-878-4413. Before your dog gets all excited about some unsuspecting cat he can chase around, tell him that Sleepy Cat is actually the name of a mountain in the area. The ranch has seventeen cabins in a variety of styles, all fully equipped, as well as six motel units, and dogs can stay for $10 per pet, per visit. A full-service restaurant on the premises gets great reviews. Your dog can sniff out 110 acres, some bordering the White River, off leash. From the end of

November to the beginning of June, the restaurant is open on weekends only.

$$ Trappers Lake Lodge, 7700 Trappers Lake Rd. (50 miles east of Meeker), 970-878-3336 (www.trapperslake.com). Located waaayy out there, the lodge is surrounded by the Flat Tops Wilderness. You and your dog can stay in one of seventeen primitive cabins; some have propane heat, some wood-burning stoves, and all share a central bathhouse. You can leave your dog unattended inside the cabin. Dogs are not allowed in the lodge lobby, however, and they need to be kept leashed on the lodge's 11 acres so as not to interfere with the resident working dogs. And make sure your dog stays off the bed! Activities at the lodge include horseback riding, fishing, and boating. There's a restaurant too. Open year-round, except from mid-November to mid-December and parts of April and May, depending on the weather. During the winter, one of the lodge's two snow coaches will transport you over the last 17 miles of road.

Rangely
$-$$ 4 Queens Motel, 206 E. Main St., 970-675-5035. Dogs can stay for $5 extra per night.

Campgrounds
Dinosaur National Monument. The park has six established camping areas, three in Colorado: **Gates of Lodore, Deerlodge Park,** and **Echo Park** (38 primitive sites total).

Bureau of Land Management campgrounds: Camping is allowed anywhere on BLM land.

DOGGIE DAYCARE
Craig
McCandless Animal Hospital, 2430 E. Victory, 970-824-5964. $9/day. Open 8 a.m.–5:30 p.m., Monday to Thursday; 9 a.m.–5:30 p.m., Friday; 8 a.m.–12 p.m., Saturday.

PET PROVISIONS
Craig
Country General, 2355 W. Victory Way, 970-824-5633

CANINE ER
Craig
High Country Veterinary Clinic, 356 Ranney, 970-824-2243. Open 10 a.m.–6 p.m., Monday to Friday.

McCandless Animal Hospital, 2430 E. Victory, 970-824-5964. Open 8 a.m.–5:30 p.m., Monday to Thursday; 9 a.m.–5:30 p.m., Friday; 8 a.m.–12 p.m., Saturday.

Meeker
W R Veterinary Clinic, 338 E. Market, 970-878-5647. Open 8 a.m.–5 p.m., Monday to Friday.

RESOURCES
Blanco Ranger District, White River National Forest, 317 E. Market St., Meeker, 970-878-4039

Bureau of Land Management, 455 Emerson St., Craig, 970-826-5000

Bureau of Land Management, 73544 Highway 64, Meeker, 970-878-3601

Colorado Welcome Center, 101 Stegosaurus Freeway (Highway 64), Dinosaur, 970-374-2205

Moffat County Visitor Center, 360 E. Victory Way, Craig, 970-824-5689 (800-864-4405)

Sometimes charm can get you in anywhere. (photo by Tim Hancock)

Rose Picnic Area on the right. The trail begins at the far side of the parking lot. To reach the upper trailhead, head west on Lands End Rd. (sometimes referred to as Rim Dr.) from Highway 65 for 3.1 miles; turn left onto Carson Lake Rd. Stay on the road until its end at Carson Lake. The trail begins just below the lower parking area. *Dogs can be off leash.*

From the lower trailhead, the well-maintained trail climbs at a fairly gradual pace toward the rim of the mesa. You'll cross several streams in the first half mile or so. Have your dog stop long enough so you can admire the wonderful vista of the Kannah Creek Basin below and the Uncompahgre Plateau to the southwest. As the trail ascends the mesa, it winds by large stands of aspen—making this a good candidate for a fall hike—as well as small, scrubby oakbrush. Unless you've arranged a car shuttle at Carson Lake, you'll probably want to turn around before reaching the mesa top.

Whitewater Creek Trail.

7.5 miles one-way to rim of Grand Mesa; 3.5 miles farther to West Bench Trail. Take Highway 50 south from Grand Junction. When you reach the town of Whitewater (about 12 miles outside of Grand Junction), turn left onto Reeder Mesa Rd. (past the abandoned Whitewater General Store). After 2.2 miles, make a left onto Whitewater Creek Rd. From there, it's 2.5 miles to the trailhead on the right side of the road (if you reach Lumbardy Ranch, you've gone a little too far). There's no parking area, but you'll be able to pull over at the side of the road. Look for a brown carsonite stake that marks the start of the trail. *Dogs can be off leash, but watch for cows in early spring and late fall.*

This is an excellent fall hike. During the summer the lower reaches are hot, though the climate becomes pleasant when you reach the higher elevations.

When hiking in the summer, remember to bring lots of water. If you traveled the entire length of this trail, you'd hike from desert to subalpine zone, as it eventually climbs steeply up a basin to the top of Grand Mesa, connecting to the West Bench Trail. Chances are, however, that you and your dog will stick to the sand and sage of the first several miles. And you may well be able to enjoy some quality solitary hiking time together, as the trail is not heavily used. Moreover, it's free from the dirt-bike and ATV traffic of nearby areas because it's designated for hiker use only. The trail is well marked at regular intervals with wooden stakes indicating "WWC." Pay attention to your route, however, so you can return the same way—there's a network of cow trails that could get confusing. Whitewater Creek is, despite its name, slow moving and green. But Clover didn't seem to mind; it gave her a respite from the arid surroundings.

McDonald Creek.

About 4 miles round-trip. The McDonald Creek Cultural Resource Area is part of the BLM's Rabbit Valley Recreation Management Area. One of the beauties of this trail is that no motorized vehicles—or even bikes—are permitted. As you'll quickly surmise from driving to the trailhead, the rest of the Rabbit Valley area is a vast playground for ATVs, jeeps, and motorcycles. From Grand Junction, head west on I-70 for 30 miles to the Rabbit Valley exit (Exit 2). Cross over the highway and pass a parking area for Rabbit Valley Recreation Area. Take the next right. Although the dirt road is narrow and bumpy, my low-clearance Toyota Celica did just fine. Follow the small Kokopelli's Trail decals on brown posts along the road for about 2.3 miles. Just after a small parking pullout on the right, watch for a sign to McDonald Creek and a road to the left. After taking this left, follow the road all the way to a small parking area at the trailhead. *Dogs can be off leash.*

First of all, don't be fooled by the name—there's no actual creek here, just a sandy wash, so bring along plenty of water on this desert hike. The trail allows for some exploring, as several paths wind through the wash, though you'll always be heading south. You'll soon be immersed in a landscape of sculpted sandstone, red sand, and pungent sage. Keep an eye out for rock art as you hike; four panels supposedly grace the canyon (we only spotted three). The trail ends at a set of railroad tracks (stay alert) along the Colorado River. Though it would be difficult to access the river from here, a small tributary comes in near the trail's end, and your dog can take a well-deserved dip.

For another hikers-only venue in the area, try the 5-mile round-trip **Rabbit's Ear Trail**, which leads to the Ruby Canyon overlook of the Colorado River. You can reach it by staying on the road from the I-70 overpass instead of turning right as for McDonald Creek. Drive 4.4 miles to the signed trailhead on the right, where there's also a small parking area.

Old Spanish Trail. Runs about 4 miles along the Gunnison River bluffs.

Situated in the Orchard Mesa section of Grand Junction, this area has some historical significance: The North Branch of the Old Spanish Trail, which was used first by traders and trappers and then by wagon trains in the 1800s, passed through. To reach the present-day trail, head south on Highway 50 from downtown Grand Junction. About 2.5 miles from the bridge over the Colorado River, look for a sign that reads "Fairgrounds Livestock entrance" and make a right (you'll also see Lions Park). Drive one block and then turn left on 28½ Rd. Look for the brown-and-white "Old Spanish Trail" sign immediately on the

right. Pull into the gravel parking area. This trail can also be accessed from a southern trailhead near the town of Whitewater: Drive about 2 miles farther on Highway 50, make a right onto the landfill access road, and follow Old Whitewater Rd. about 1.5 miles to the trailhead. *Dogs can be off leash.*

Don't pack up your dog's leash just yet; you'll have to walk through a few neighborhood streets to actually reach the trail. Once there, the route follows a wide dirt track that stretches off into the distance. This is not the most scenic hike—there are no trees, and you won't actually see much of the river—but it's a great place that's close to town for exercising your dog. And although there's no shade, your dog may enjoy a stiff breeze off the river rippling through his fur. The **Gunnison Bluffs Trail** is also directly accessible from the southernmost trailhead described above as well as by taking various small unmarked paths from the Old Spanish Trail, heading toward the river. The trail seems promising, as it runs directly above the river, but will have to wait for a return visit to get our tail-wag evaluation.

Colorado River Trails. Varying lengths. An extensive trail system has been developed in the past decade

at various points along the Colorado River. The system is divided into six main portions: the **Palisade Trail**; the **Corn Lake** section of Colorado River State Park; **Watson Island**; and the **Audubon Trail, Blue Heron Trail,** and **Connected Lakes** sections of Colorado River State Park, collectively known as the **Redlands Loop**. For more detailed information on specific trails, including access points and mileages, pick up the "Colorado River Trails" brochure, produced by the Colorado Riverfront Foundation, at the Grand Junction Visitor Center or Chamber of Commerce (see "Resources").

One recommended hike begins at the Audubon trailhead and continues to Connected Lakes, a series of reclaimed gravel pits that have been turned into lakes. It's about 4 miles round-trip. To access the Audubon Trail, take Grand Ave. west from downtown. Cross the Colorado River; at the intersection with Dike Rd., turn right into the Brach's Corner shopping plaza. Signed parking for the trail is at the far end of the lot. *Dogs must be leashed.*

Clover and I enjoyed a pleasant amble along this paved trail, which is partially shaded by cottonwoods and borders riparian habitat as it runs along the Redlands Canal. Once at Connected Lakes, your dog will have his choice of gravel trails that wind around and between the lakes. There's lots of water here, obviously, as well as cooling breezes off the river. Note that if you drive into the park rather than hike in via the Audubon Trail, you'll have to pay the standard entrance fee.

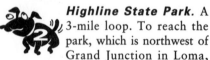

Highline State Park. A 3-mile loop. To reach the park, which is northwest of Grand Junction in Loma, take I-70 west to the Loma exit (Exit 15). Head north on Route 139 for about 5 miles to Q Rd.; turn left and drive 1.2 miles to 11.8 Rd. Turn right; the park entrance is about 1 mile ahead. *Dogs must be leashed.*

The park is a welcome oasis of grass, trees, and water in the midst of arid surroundings. The Highline Lake Trail is an easy, level stroll along a combination of dirt road and wide gravel path that circles the lake. While you gaze at the Book Cliffs to the northeast, your dog can amuse himself by splashing in the water and watching the water-skiers go by. Clover particularly enjoyed our evening walk here. There are several bird-watching blinds at the far side of the lake, so take care that your pooch doesn't disturb any

birders who may be present (as well as the birds they're watching). Note that dogs are not allowed on the park's swim beach.

Rabbit Valley Trail Through Time. A 1.5-mile loop. From Grand Junction, head west on I-70 for 30 miles to the Rabbit Valley exit (Exit 2). Turn right and drive to the trailhead parking area straight ahead. *Dogs must be leashed.*

This is the only dinosaur-related activity in the Grand Junction area in which your dog is welcome to participate. In addition to a working dinosaur quarry on the premises, an interpretive trail highlights dinosaur fossil imprints as well as the geology of the area. Do keep your dog on his leash so he's not tempted to start his own quarry excavation—and remind him that fossil collecting is prohibited by law on all BLM lands.

Colorado National Monument. Your dog can view the wondrous cliffs and canyons of the monument out the car window or from within the confines of the campground, but he's not allowed to set paw on any of the trails.

Riggs Hill and Dinosaur Hill. Dogs are not allowed at either of these outdoor dinosaur fossil-viewing sites.

CYCLING FOR CANINES

The area around Grand Junction offers lots of riding opportunities, and nearby Fruita is becoming something of a mountain-biking mecca. The good news is that many of the rides are on BLM land, so your dog is free (literally) to accompany you. The bad news is that you'll definitely want to keep your rides on the shorter side so that your dog doesn't die of heatstroke in the desert. For descriptions and maps of some of the classic routes, pick up a copy of *River City Rides,* by Toby Gold and Alix Craig, at a local bike shop. Over the Edge Sports, 202 E. Aspen Ave. in downtown Fruita, is a helpful source of maps and information.

Approximately 7.8-mile-long **Lions Loop** is a popular ride west of Grand Junction that begins near the Mack exit (Exit 11) off I-70. It follows Kokopelli's Trail (which goes all the way to Moab, Utah) for part of its length. Look for a flyer with detailed route information on this ride (along with Mary's Loop and tips for Kokopelli's Trail) at a cycle shop.

Grand Mesa is another good biking choice, and it offers the advantage of fir, spruce, and aspen to make your ride (and your dog's run) a little cooler. Try the **West Bench Trail**, which runs about 5.5 miles from the Mesa Lakes Ranger Station to Powderhorn Ski Area, or the 11.5-mile (round-trip) **Lake of the Woods Trail**, which ends at Cottonwood Lake, allowing your dog to go for a welcome swim.

POWDERHOUNDS

The Grand Mesa is the place to head for wintertime recreation with your dog. The **Mesa Lakes Resort** (near milepost 36 on Highway 65) maintains 6 to 8 miles of groomed trails that can be accessed from the lodge or at the Jumbo National Forest Service Campground. There's no trail fee, and the lodge's owners graciously allow anyone, including those who aren't guests at the lodge, to use the trails. The lodge also operates a ski rental shop.

Some recommended backcountry trail areas on the mesa (none of which cross through avalanche terrain) include **Water Dog Reservoir, Griffith Lakes,** and **Deep Creek.** The 11-mile round-trip **West Bench Trail,** which starts from the Mesa Lakes Ranger Station, is also a popular winter ski or snowshoe tour. Stop in at the Forest Service office in Grand Junction (see "Resources") or at the Mesa Lakes Lodge for maps and more trail information.

The Grand Mesa Nordic Council

maintains trails at three different sites on the mesa—Ward Creek, County Line, and Skyway; however, the council asks that you leave your dog at home.

CREATURE COMFORTS

If you can trust your dog on his own, it's a good idea to find lodging where you can leave him unattended while you go out to eat, for example. The high temperatures in the Grand Junction area make it especially inadvisable to leave your dog in the car.

Unless otherwise stated, dogs should not be left unattended in the room or cabin.

Cedaredge

$ Aspen Trails Campground, Store, and Cabins, 1997 Highway 65 (3 miles north of Cedaredge), 970-856-6321. Dogs can stay in either of the two camper cabins here with a $25 deposit. You'll have to bring your own sleeping bag; the cabins do have electricity. A soda fountain, gift shop, and deli are on site. Open April through the end of October.

$ Bryce's Spaulding Mountain Lodge, 2296 2500 Dr. (about 5 miles north of Cedaredge), 970-856-7349 or 970-874-4134 (www.sportsmansdream.com/bryce). Dogs and their owners are welcome to stay in either of two rustic cabins, which sleep four to six and have kitchenettes but no

Looking for a shady respite in Grand Junction? Take your dog to Hawthorne Park, just a few blocks north of downtown west of 5th St., or Whitman Park, a few blocks in the other direction of downtown, also west of 5th St. Sherwood Park, bounded by Orchard Ave., 5th St., North Ave., and 1st St., is a popular dog spot, with its grassy expanse and paved path on its perimeter.

running water, or two rooms in the main lodge, with shared bath. You're welcome to use the main lodge's kitchen if you're staying there. The lodge, at the base of Spaulding Peak, offers horseback rides during the summer and is also a hunting outfitter during big-game season. Winter access requires either a snowmobile or four-wheel-drive.

$–$$ Super 8 Motel, 530 S. Grand Mesa Dr., 970-856-7824 (800-800-8000 [national number]). Several designated pet rooms are available. There's a $10 fee per night for large dogs (lab sized), $5 for small dogs (a little harder to define), as well as a $20 deposit. You'll also be asked to sign a "pet rules" form.

Clifton

$$ Best Western Clifton Inn, 3228 I-70 Business Loop, 970-434-3400 (800-528-1234 [national number]). Dogs 25 pounds and under can stay here, and management emphasizes that only adult dogs are welcome. There's a $5 fee per stay, per dog.

Collbran

$$ Alpine Motel, 102 Spring St., 970-487-3220 (877-557-7173). All the motel requires for dog guests is a credit-card imprint as a deposit. Two of the rooms have kitchenettes.

$$ Wallace Guides & Outfitters, 20781 Kimball Creek Rd. (5 miles north of Collbran); 970-487-3235 (800-770-0186 [enter "44" at the prompt for a code]; www.onlinecolorado.com/wal/003.html). This guest ranch has three rooms in the main lodge as well as several cabins (without baths). You can leave your dog unattended inside, though he'd probably prefer to be out with you, exploring the 90 acres of property off leash or getting to know the resident Boston terrier. The ranch offers horseback riding in summer, and in addition to the included breakfast, you can arrange for family-style meals at a small additional cost.

Eckert

$$ Braham's Inn Bed and Breakfast, 1258 Highway 65, 970-835-3357 (888-995-8008; www.coloradodirectory.com/brahamsinn). This B&B south of Cedaredge, housed in a former fruit-packing shed, has a total of five rooms, and dog guests are allowed in one: The "grape" room has hardwood floors, two queen beds, and a private bath. Your dog can explore the surrounding 10 acres with you as long as he stays on leash (there are resident chickens) and you clean up after him.

Fruita

$ Balanced Rock Motel, 126 S. Coulson, 970-858-7333. There's a $5 one-time fee.

$ Park Hotel, 150 S. Park Sq., 970-858-3917 (800-878-3917). A funky combination of rooming house and overnight lodging, this small 100-year-old hotel has cozy rooms nicely furnished with antiques. (All rooms have shared baths.) If you don't mind the comings and goings of the people who actually live here, it's a nice change for you and your dog from the chain-motel lodging that dominates the area. And the rates can't be beat.

$–$$ H Motel, 333 Highways 6 & 50, 970-858-7198. There's a $5 fee per night, per dog. You can leave your dog unattended in the room.

$$ West Gate Inn, 2210 Highways 6 & 50, 970-241-3020 (800-453-9253). The motel has several pet rooms, and you can leave your dog unattended unless he causes an audible problem.

$$–$$$ Grapeland Bed and Breakfast, 1763 K 6/10 Rd., 970-858-0741 (www.gj.net/~grapebed). This downhome B&B is popular with mountain bikers who come to enjoy Fruita's fine selection of riding. The four rooms, one of them a suite with sitting area, are decorated country style;

FOURTEEN

Grand Junction and Vicinity

THE BIG SCOOP

The Grand Valley is dinosaur country. The legacy of these giant reptiles that roamed the area millions of years ago lives on in museums and fossil sites. But if your dog is already panting at the thought of humongous bones, you'll have to break the news to him that most of the dinosaur-related attractions don't allow dogs. Still, there's plenty to do. Spring and fall are the best times to visit Grand Junction and points west if you're a dog; the summer can be just too darn hot, and there aren't very many trees under which to seek respite or creeks to jump into in the desert. If you are in the area during the "nondog"-day months of June, July, or August, consider escaping to the forested lakes of Grand Mesa for the sake of your fur-coated companion.

In addition to the expected leash law throughout Grand Junction, there's an enforced "pooper scooper" law in all city parks. (Of course, you should be cleaning up after your dog on the sidewalks as well.) Neighboring Fruita allows dogs to be under voice command but requires that they be leashed in all city parks. You don't have to go far, however, to find miles of unrestricted dog territory. One of the least regulatory land overseers—the Bureau of Land Management—manages much of the area surrounding Grand Junction, making it a particularly good bet for leash-free dog hikes.

TAIL-RATED TRAILS

There are hundreds of miles of trails on Grand Mesa, which contains the Grand Mesa National Forest. Unfortunately, many of them are open to ATV use as well as to hikers, bikers, and horseback riders. For good dog-hike options, consider the **Coal Creek Trail** (described here) or the **Kannah Creek Trail** (12 miles one way), neither of which permits motorized use. Both can be accessed from Carson Lake off of Lands End Rd. The **Lake of the Woods Trail** (about 11.5 miles round-trip to Cottonwood Lake #1) is another good possibility. Note that on the immensely popular **Crag Crest Trail**, dogs must be leashed.

Coal Creek Trail. 9 miles one way. The trail, which heads up (or down) the Grand Mesa, can be accessed from a lower or an upper trailhead. Hiking from the upper access is not usually available until June, when the snow has melted enough to open the top section of Lands End Rd. To reach the lower trailhead, drive south on U.S. Highway 50 from Grand Junction for about 12 miles to the Lands End Rd. turnoff to the left. Go about 14 miles (the road turns to dirt after 9 miles) to the Wild

---

Heatstroke is a real risk to your dog when exercising in desert country. If you notice him having difficulty breathing, panting to excess, or refusing to go any farther, get him water immediately; even better, immerse him in cool water (e.g., a stream), if possible.

two have private baths. Thanks to some careless owners of large dogs that caused damage, only small (about lap-size), non-shedding dogs are now allowed. But if your dog is within the size limit, he'll have plenty of company here, as the animal-loving owners have three yorkies and four cats. The B&B also hosts "murder mystery weekends" in which your dog can play a part in sniffing out who done it.

$$–$$$ Super 8 Motel, 399 Jurassic, 970-858-0808 (800-800-8000 [national number]). Dogs can stay in pet-designated rooms with a credit-card imprint as a deposit.

Glade Park
$ Glade Park Store, 1644 DS Rd., 970-242-5421. The owner of this general store/post office in the hamlet of Glade Park, south of the Colorado National Monument, has two guest rooms available in an adjacent building. Each has a private bath and kitchenette and is furnished with antiques. The fee and deposit for a dog is negotiable with the owner, as is leaving your dog unattended in your room.

Grand Junction
$ Columbine Motel, 2824 North Ave., 970-241-2908. The motel charges $5 per night, per dog.

$ El Rio Rancho Motel, 730 Highway 50 South, 970-242-0256. There's a $5 fee per night, per dog.

$ Peachtree Inn, 1600 North Ave., 970-245-5770 (800-525-0030; www.peachtree motel.com). There are designated pet rooms for canine guests; a $25 deposit is required.

$ Prospector Motel, 547 Highway 50 South, 970-242-4891. Dogs are allowed in smoking rooms only for a $5 fee per night.

$–$$ Budget Host Inn, 721 Horizon Dr., 970-243-6050 (800-888-5736). Dogs can stay in designated pet rooms with a $50 deposit. You can leave your dog unattended in the room if he's in a travel kennel.

$–$$ Country Inns of America, 718 Horizon Dr., 970-243-5080 (800-990-1143). The motel has several designated pet rooms available for a $5 one-time fee.

$–$$ Mesa Inn, 704 Horizon Dr., 970-245-3080 (888-955-3080). The motel has designated pet rooms, available with either $50 or a credit-card imprint as a deposit.

$–$$ Motel 6, 776 Horizon Dr., 970-243-2628 (800-466-8356 [national number]. The policy is one small dog per room (with "small" being interpreted to include labrador-sized dogs, for example).

$–$$ Two Rivers Inn, 141 North 1st St., 970-245-8585 (888-TRI-STAY; www.two riversinn.com). This family-owned motel allows dogs for $10 extra per visit.

$$ Best Western Horizon Inn, 754 Horizon Dr., 970-245-1410 (800-544-3782). Note that the Best Western Sandman, down the street, does not accept pets.

$$ Days Inn of Grand Junction, 733 Horizon Dr., 970-245-7200 (800-790-2661). The motel has eight pet rooms and requires a $50 deposit.

$$ Grand Vista Hotel, 2790 Crossroads Blvd., 970-241-8411 (800-800-7796; www.grandvistahotel.com). Dogs 25 pounds and under are welcome here (formerly the Ramada), where they usually stay in ground-floor rooms. (If you have a well-behaved dog who exceeds the size limit, check with management, as exceptions are occasionally made.) There's a $10 one-time fee. You can leave your dog unattended inside as long as he's not a constant barker.

$$ Holiday Inn Grand Junction, 755 Horizon Dr., 970-243-6790 (800-HOL-IDAY [national number])

$$ Ramada Inn, 752 Horizon Dr., 970-243-5150 (800-2-RAMADA [national number]). Dogs are allowed for a $10 one-time fee. You can leave your dog unattended in the room unless the front desk gets complaints about noise.

$$ Super 8 Motel, 728 Horizon Dr., 970-248-8080 (800-800-8000 [national number]). With a $5 nightly fee and a $25 deposit, dogs are allowed to stay in designated pet rooms.

$$–$$$ Hawthorn Suites, 225 Main St., 970-242-2525 (800-922-3883). You can stay with your dog in any of the suites here, which range from studio to two bedroom, some with full kitchen and others with kitchenette. The shocker comes with the $125 one-time pet fee, imposed because the Hawthorn national corporate office requires that after a dog guest leaves, the room be shut down for 24 hours and deep cleaned. At least you know your room will be pristine! And you can leave your dog unattended in the room as long as you let the front desk know.

$$–$$$ La Quinta Inn and Suites, 2761 Crossroads Blvd., 970-241-2929 (800-687-6667 [national number]). The highest end of the price range here is for the two-room suites. You can leave your dog unattended in the room.

Grand Mesa
$–$$ Mesa Lakes Resort, Highway 65 (near milepost 36), 970-268-5467 (888-420-MESA; www.coloradocampgrounds. com). Water dogs will love visiting this resort, as it lives up to its name by being within walking distance of six lakes. Motel rooms, rustic cabins (no running water, but there is electricity), and modern cabins are available, and dogs can stay in

any of them for a $5 one-time fee per dog. The resort offers guided horseback rides in the summer and snowmobile tours in the winter. The owners groom a small selection of Nordic ski trails in the winter close to the resort, and miles of backcountry trails are readily accessible. There's an on-site cafe with homestyle meals that serves breakfast, lunch, and dinner.

$$ Alexander Lake Lodge, 2121 AA50 Rd. (near milepost 21), 970-856-2539 (www./coloradodirectory.com/alexan derlakelodge). The lodge, first opened in the early 1900s, is under new ownership after having been closed for a few years. The owners are doing extensive renovations on the 10-acre property, which should be completed by summer 2001. You and your dog can stay in one of fifteen log cabins that sleep from two to seven people. All have kitchens and fireplaces and are creatively decorated in a rustic Western theme. There's a $10 one-time fee for your dog, and you'll be asked to sign a pet waiver. When you're not out exploring Grand Mesa's numerous lakes and trails, you can refuel at the lodge's Hungry Bear restaurant or ice cream parlor and bakery, have a cold one at the Mosquito Bar, or soak in the hot tub. Boat and mountain bike rentals are available.

$$ Grand Mesa Lodge, Highway 65 (near milepost 28), 970-856-3250 (800-551-MESA; www.coloradodirectory. com/grandmesalodge). Your dog will be greeted here by canine residents Buffy and Storm. The lodge offers motel rooms as well as one- and two-bedroom cabins, but dogs are allowed only in the cabins, for a $5 one-time fee. You can leave your dog unattended if you have to, though the owners prefer that you rent one of their portable outside kennels. Your dog may want to explore Island Lake, the largest lake on the mesa, just behind the lodge buildings; be sure to keep him leashed at all times.

$$ Spruce Lodge Cabins, 2120 AA50 Rd. (near milepost 22), 970-856-6240 (866-2SPRUCE). For $5 extra per night, your dog can stay with you in one of the lodge's eleven one-bedroom cabins, all recently remodeled, with kitchenettes and private baths. There's also an on-site bar and restaurant, and you can leave your dog unattended in the cabin while you check them out. Seven acres surround the cabins for your dog to sniff out off leash, and during the winter he can watch you ice skate on the lake across the road.

Mesa
$$ The Wagon Wheel Motel, 1090 Highway 65, 970-268-5224

Campgrounds
Colorado National Monument, just west of Grand Junction, access off Highway 340, or off I-70 at the Fruita exit. The Saddlehorn Campground, near the visitor center, has 80 sites.

State park campgrounds: Highline Lake State Park—see "Tail-Rated Trails" for directions (26 sites); Colorado River State Parks/Island Acres, Exit 47 off I-70, 5 miles east of Palisade (60 sites); Vega State Park, Highway 330, 12 miles past Collbran (110 sites).

BLM campgrounds: Rabbit Valley—see McDonald Creek in "Tail-Rated Trails" for directions.

National forest campgrounds: Grand Mesa has fourteen campgrounds with a range of 5 to 42 sites each.

WORTH A PAWS
Dog Jog. Sponsored by the Grand Valley Veterinary Medical Society, this annual run, usually held the second weekend of October, raises money for Project Pups, a low-cost spay and neuter program. You and your four-legged running partner have your pick of a 1-mile or 3-mile course, both in Grand Junction's Sherwood Park. Your entry fee also includes a T-shirt for you and a bandanna for your dog. Call 970-242-4646 (animal control, which helps put on the race) for details.

DOGGIE DAYCARE
Clifton
Upper Valley Kennels, 3460 G Rd., 970-464-5713. $8/day ($13 for two dogs) lets your dog choose between inside and outside runs and includes feeding. "We can be accommodating and flexible, because we live here," says owner Donna Bondurant. She'll even do pickup and delivery of your dog if necessary. Open 7 a.m.–6 p.m., Monday to Saturday; 4 p.m.–6 p.m., Sunday.

Fruita
Pet Particulars, 242 S. Mulberry, 970-858-0818. $10/day ($18 for two dogs). Open 7:30 a.m.–6 p.m., Monday to Friday. You can also board your dog on weekends with prior arrangement.

Grand Junction
All Pets Center, 424 S. 5th, 970-241-1976, $7/day. Open 7 a.m.–6 p.m., Monday to Friday; 8 a.m.–5 p.m., Saturday.

Animal Medical Clinic, 504 Fruitvale Ct., 970-434-4094. $7/day. Open 7 a.m.–7 p.m., Monday to Friday; 8 a.m.–5 p.m., Saturday.

Appleton Boarding Kennels, 2388 F Rd. (next to Mesa Mall), 970-242-1285. $5/day. Open 8:30 a.m.–5:30 p.m., Monday to Friday; 8:30 a.m.–noon, Saturday.

The Pet Spa, 2509 Industrial Ct., 970-241-8499. $4.50/day. Open 8 a.m.–6 p.m., Monday to Saturday; 9–9:30 a.m. (for dropoff) and 5–5:30 p.m. (for pickup) Sunday.

Your Best Friends Boarding Kennel and Grooming House, 2708 Highway 50, 970-244-8865. $5/day. Open 7 a.m.– 5 p.m., Monday to Friday; 8 a.m.–10 p.m. and 5–6 p.m., Saturday.

PET PROVISIONS
Clifton
Animal Feed & Supply, Inc., 3261 F Rd., 970-434-8830

Fruita
Pet Particulars, 242 S. Mulberry, 970-858-0818

Grand Junction
Green Fields Seed and Feed, 520 S. 9th St., 970-241-0979

Mesa Feed and Farm Supply, 715 S. 7th St., 970-242-7762

The Pet Spa, 2509 Industrial Ct., 970-241-8499

PetsMart, 2428 F Rd., 970-255-9305

CANINE ER
Grand Junction
All Pets Center (AAHA certified), 424 S. 5th, 970-241-1976. Open 7 a.m.–6 p.m., Monday to Friday; 8 a.m.–5 p.m., Saturday.

Animal Medical Clinic (AAHA certified), 504 Fruitvale Ct., 970-434-4094. Open 7 a.m.–7 p.m., Monday to Friday; 8 a.m.–5 p.m., Saturday.

RESOURCES
Bureau of Land Management, 2815 H Rd., Grand Junction, 970-244-3000

Colorado Welcome Center, 340 Highway 340, Fruita, 970-858-9335

Fruita Chamber of Commerce, 325 E. Aspen, Fruita, 970-858-3894

Grand Junction Chamber of Commerce, 360 Grand Ave., Grand Junction, 970-242-3214

Grand Junction Visitor and Convention Bureau, 740 Horizon Dr. (at I-70), Grand Junction, 970-244-1480 (800-962-2547; www.grand-junction.net)

Grand Valley Ranger District, Grand Mesa National Forest, 218 E. High St., Collbran, 970-487-3534

Grand Valley Ranger District, Grand Mesa/Uncompaghre/Gunnison National Forests, 2777 Crossroads Blvd., Suite A, Grand Junction, 970-242-8211

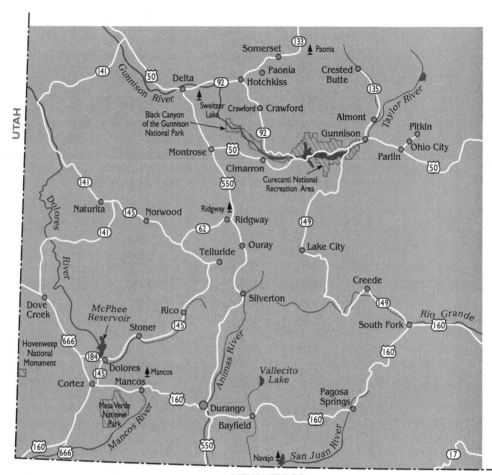

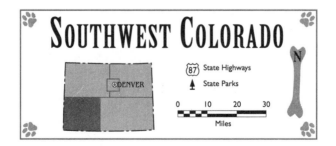

SOUTHWEST COLORADO

⊗DENVER

87 State Highways
🔺 State Parks

0   10   20   30
Miles

N

Black Canyon Area

THE BIG SCOOP

Not quite desert, not quite mountains, the area surrounding the Black Canyon of the Gunnison River will give your dog a taste of high plateau country. And the eponymous national park is one of the few where dogs can actually do something besides sit in the car.

The hub towns are Montrose and Delta, about half an hour's drive apart. Montrose has a leash law in both the city and county. Delta's leash law is imposed within city limits but not on county land. And "things are a little different out here," cautions Delta's Animal Control officer. If you tie your pooch outside a store while you run in, keep a close eye on him; apparently dogs are in high demand in the area. If you're out running your dog in the Adobe Hills that encircle the town, tell him to keep a nose out for people taking target practice. And, finally, note that if your dog is in Delta for more than seven days without a current license and rabies tag, you'll be required to purchase those items for him in town.

TAIL-RATED TRAILS

FYI, the three state parks within this region—Paonia, Crawford, and Sweitzer Lake—focus on water recreation. Hiking opportunities are limited to a half-mile nature trail at Crawford and a short canal road at Sweitzer. For some trail ideas in the West Elk Wilderness area east of Crawford and the western part of the Curecanti National Recreation Area (dogs must be leashed in both locations), pick up the "North Fork Trails Network" brochure at the Delta Visitor Center or the Forest Supervisor's Office in Delta. Or ask for trail descriptions for the Uncompahgre Basin Resource Area at the BLM/Forest Service office in Montrose (see "Resources").

Delta

Confluence Park. There are about 5 miles of trails in this 265-acre park, formerly an abandoned industrial site, situated at the junction of the Gunnison and Uncompahgre Rivers. Head south on Gunnison River Dr. from Main St. to reach the park entrance. *Dogs must be leashed.*

If you're driving through Delta on a longer trip, a visit to this recently constructed park (1993) is a great way for your dog to stretch his legs. It's also a good destination for a late afternoon or evening stroll. The nicest section of the wide gravel trails that loop around and through the park is by the waterfowl habitat area. For the most direct access, begin walking from the boat ramp on the Gunnison River (at the end of Gunnison River Dr., within the park, turn right and follow the road into a parking area). Another section of trail encircles Confluence Lake. Make sure to keep your dog on the trail with you throughout the park; he may encounter some hazards if he frolics in the water.

Montrose

Duncan Trail. 3 miles round-trip. Note that because this trail is part of an area designated as the Gunnison

Gorge Wilderness (under BLM oversight) in 1999, there's a $3 day-use fee per person, payable via a self-service fee station at the trailhead. Drive north out of Montrose for 9 miles on U.S. Highway 50 and turn right onto Falcon Rd., on the right just before Olathe. Travel 3.6 miles to the end of the paved portion of the road, then follow it left as it turns into Peach Valley Rd. Staying left at the next fork you come to, drive 4.8 miles to the BLM sign for access to the Duncan Trail on the right. It's about 1.7 miles to the trailhead, where there's a parking area; stay left at the one fork you'll come to. It's inadvisable to drive on the dirt roads when they're muddy; apparently they turn into a sort of quicksand that will trap your car. And though four-wheel-drive is recommended for the access road off Peach Valley Rd., my low-clearance Toyota Celica made it all the way to the trailhead. *Dogs can be off leash (even with the wilderness designation).*

Less heavily used than the neighboring Chukar Trail, this is a rewarding hike for the intrepid dog. And it provides the access to the Gunnison River Gorge that your dog is unable to enjoy in the national park. The trail begins by traversing a hillside for a half mile or so before beginning the descent to the river. At this point, it gets rather steep—a pair of hiking boots or good shoes are a must. Navigation also gets a little tricky before the final descent to the river. Look for the path of least resistance, as there seem to be several options. To avoid getting minicliffed-out right before the river, stay to the left and somewhat high in the last gully (you'll be able to see the river from here). Once at the river, your dog can cool off in the current while you relax to the water's soothing rush and muster the energy for the climb back up. Try the nearby Ute Trail if you want a more gradual but longer (9 miles round-trip) hike; the access road is about 2.4 miles past the Duncan Trail turnoff.

Black Canyon of the Gunnison National Park. This spectacular canyon reaches depths of up to 2,689 feet. It's 15 miles east of Montrose via Highways 50 and 347. *Dogs must be leashed.*

Unlike at many other sites managed by the National Park Service, dogs actually have a few—albeit short—hiking options at the park. I'll start with the no-no's. Pets are not permitted on the North Vista and Deadhorse Trails (both on the canyon's north rim), on the Oak Flat and Uplands Trails (near the visitor center on the south rim), or on the Warner Point Trail (at the end of the South Rim Rd.). They are also not allowed in the inner canyon or designated wilderness areas. You can bring your pooch along on the approximately 1-mile-long **Rim Rock Trail**, which leads from the South Rim Campground to the visitor center, and on two very short nature trails: **Chasm View**, by the North Rim Campground; and **Cedar Point**, off the South Rim Rd. (dogs are no longer allowed on any section of the Warner Point Nature Trail). Your dog is welcome to gaze down to his heart's content from any of the overlooks—just be sure to keep a tight rein on him if he suffers from vertigo! Bring plenty of water to share for hiking.

In the winter, the South Rim Rd. is unplowed past the visitor center and is open for cross-country skiing, but not for dogs.

CYCLING FOR CANINES

The Uncompahgre Plateau west of Montrose offers lots of varied biking opportunities, including the originations of the **Tabeguache Trail**, which travels 142 miles to Grand Junction, and the **Paradox Trail**, which links up with Kokopelli's Trail 100 miles later in Utah. (Of course, I recommend just biking a few miles of these multiday trails if Fido is in tow.) Because the BLM and Forest

Service oversee the land on which the trails pass, your dog will be able to run leash-free beside your bike. For route descriptions, look for pamphlets on the Tabeguache and Paradox Trails at the BLM/Forest Service office in Montrose (see "Resources") or check out *Bicycling the Uncompahgre Plateau,* by Bill Harris.

CREATURE COMFORTS
Unless otherwise stated, dogs should not be left unattended in the room or cabin.

Cimarron
$–$$ Pleasant Valley Cabins and Campground, 84100 E. Highway 50, 970-249-8330. There's a $5 nightly fee for your dog to stay with you in one of the seven one-room cabins, all with kitchenettes. Open May 1 to November 15.

$$ Cimarron Lodge, Highway 50 (look for the lodge sign in Cimarron), 970-249-8579. The lodge, on 100 acres, has four fairly new motel rooms with kitchenettes and welcomes dogs. The resident Border collie can show your dog the ropes. Open April through November.

Crawford
$–$$ Tyler's Country Store and Motel, 313 Highway 92, 970-921-4575. This small motel (six rooms) is in the heart of Crawford.

$$ Bid-U-Well Guest Ranch, 3396 B 25 Rd., (9 miles out of Crawford), 970-921-7070. The ranch has a building with two bedrooms (both nonsmoking), a sitting room and shared bath, as well as tent and RV sites. You'll get a full homemade breakfast that can be served either near your room or in the main house (other meals are available on request). Each dog you bring will cost you $2 extra per night, and you'll need to keep them leashed outside, but during the day you can explore 122 acres, with some hiking trails. The ranch is home to an assorted

Quinn enjoys a plunge in the Gunnison River. (photo by Amy Ditsler)

populace of horses, cows, goats, chickens, cats, and dogs; you're welcome to bring your own horse too. Owner Ann Critchley touts the ranch's panoramic views and relaxing atmosphere. "We treat everybody like family," she says.

$$ Black Canyon Ranch, 76400 B 76 Rd. (5.5 miles south of Crawford), 970-921-4252 (www.discovercolorado.com/bcranch). The 75-acre ranch accepts canine visitors "as long as they're good dogs," for a $10 nightly fee. A large log home has five bed-and-breakfast rooms, with a combination of shared and private baths, or you can rent the house as a whole (which sleeps up to sixteen). Dogs can be left unattended inside or tied in the yard. And there's a plethora of activities at hand, including horseback riding, mountain biking trails that start on the property, laser tag, and jet ski, boat, and water-ski rentals to use on nearby Crawford Reservoir.

$$ Steward Homestead Cabin, Onion Valley (8.5 miles southeast of Crawford), 970-921-6751. The Homestead Cabin is a vacation house to rent; the owners live nearby but off-site. Your dog is welcome for a $5 nightly fee. In addition to a full kitchen and living space, the cabin has one bedroom and a loft. You can walk your dog leash-free on the surrounding 160 acres.

Delta

$ El-D-Rado Motel, 702 Main, 970-874-4493. There's a $5 fee per night for dogs.

$ Four Seasons River Inn and RV Park, 676 Highway 50, 970-874-9659 (888-340-4689; www.fourseasonsriverinn.com). The motel has eight pet-specific rooms, all of which are two-room units with full kitchens. There's a $5 per-night fee, or $10 per week.

$ Southgate Inn, 2124 S. Main, 970-874-9726 (800-621-2271). This friendly motel allows one adult dog per room (it has ten pet rooms) for a $5 fee per night.

$–$$ Best Western Sundance, 903 Main, 970-874-9781 (800-626-1994). Dogs are $5 per night extra, and you can leave your dog unattended in the room for a short time—for example, to grab the full breakfast that's included in the room rate.

$$ Escalante Ranch Bed and Breakfast, 701 650 Rd., 970-874-0711 (www.escalanteranch.com). Your dog can have a field day at this working cattle ranch; you and he won't run out of room to roam together on the ranch's 100,000 acres along the Gunnison River. And, as long as he doesn't chase cows, your dog can be off leash. The B&B has four rooms, and the owners prefer small to medium-sized dogs. The ranch also offers some rustic cabins equipped with stoves, refrigerators, and propane lamps. You'll need a four-wheel-drive vehicle or, in the winter, skis, to access them.

Hotchkiss

$$ Hotchkiss Inn, 406 Highway 133, 970-872-2200 (800-817-1418; www.hotchkissinn.com). The motel offers four pet rooms, two nonsmoking and two smoking. There's a $5 one-time fee, and you can leave your dog unattended in the room as long as you're sure he won't attack the housekeepers.

$$$ Casa Encatada Bed and Breakfast, 2690 O Road (11 miles from Hotchkiss), 970-835-3658 (800-653-0096; www.fourdmarketing.com). "We're user-friendly with dogs," says owner Marilee Gilman. The accommodation here is actually a separate casita, enclosed in an adobe courtyard, that sleeps up to four. There are two bedrooms and baths, a full kitchen, and a living room with a kiva-style fireplace, furnished in Southwestern decor. You can leave your dog unattended inside, though the owners prefer you use the on-site outdoor kennels. The Gilmans also raise organic produce, offer guided fly-fishing outings, and operate the Upland Game Club for bird hunters on their Four Directions Farm.

Montrose

$ Log Cabin Motel, 1034 E. Main, 970-249-7610. Three or four rooms are set aside for dog guests. There's no deposit for small (i.e., lap-sized) dogs; larger dogs require a deposit of $20.

$–$$ Black Canyon Motel, 1605 E. Main, 970-249-3495 (800-348-3495; www.toski.com/black-canyon). The motel has select pet rooms, and there's a $5 fee per night. Dogs can usually be left unattended in the rooms for a short time. The motel also has a grassy dog-walking area where four-legged guests can do their thing off leash.

$–$$ Blue Fox Motel, 1150 N. Townsend, 970-249-4595. The motel has certain dog-specific rooms.

$–$$ Colorado Inn, 1417 E. Main, 970-249-4507. Dogs are permitted for $5 per night extra, and nondestructive ones can be left unattended in the room.

$–$$ Montrose Super 8 Motel, 1705 E. Main, 970-249-9294 (800-800-8000 [national number]). Dogs usually stay in smoking rooms only. A $20 deposit is required.

$$ Holiday Inn Express, 1391 S. Townsend, 970-240-1800 (800-550-9252)

$$ San Juan Inn, 1480 Highway 550, 970-249-6644 (888-681-4159; www.san juaninns.com). There's a $6 fee per night for dogs.

Paonia

$$ Bross Hotel Bed and Breakfast, 312 Onarga St., 970-527-6776 (www.paonia-inn.com). Well-behaved dogs who don't climb up on furniture can stay with their owners at this tastefully renovated B&B for $10 extra per night. Housed in a hotel built in 1906, each of the ten rooms has a private bath and is furnished with antiques and period reproductions as well as handmade quilts. There's also a hot tub on-site.

Somerset

$–$$$ Crystal Meadows Resort, 30682 County Rd. 12, 970-929-5656 (877-886-9678; www.crystalmeadowsresort.com). This nonworking ranch offers a variety of cabins and rooms that differ with regard to amenities like private baths and kitchen facilities, and additional accommodations are in the works. There's also a house, with full kitchen, that can sleep up to ten. Dogs can stay in any of them. You can leave your dog unattended inside but must keep him leashed when outside. RV and tent sites are available, too. Visit the resort's own restaurant for breakfast, lunch, and dinner. Open from Memorial Day to mid-November.

Campgrounds

Black Canyon of the Gunnison National Park, 15 miles east of Montrose via Highways 50 and 347. The monument has two campgrounds, one on the north rim, one on the south rim. There's also a small campground on East Portal Rd., in what is actually part of the Curecanti National Recreation Area.

State park campgrounds: Crawford State Park, 1 mile south of Crawford on Highway

92 (53 sites); Paonia State Park, 16 miles east of Paonia on Highway 133 (15 sites).

National forest campgrounds: McClure Campground, 12 miles north of Paonia Reservoir on Highway 133, at the top of McClure Pass (19 sites); Erickson Springs Campground, 6 miles down County Rd. 12 (turn off Highway 133, right before Paonia Reservoir; 18 sites).

Private campgrounds: Pleasant Valley Cabins and Campground in Cimarron; Bid-U-Well Guest Ranch near Crawford; Four Seasons River Inn and RV Park in Delta; Crystal Meadows Resort in Somerset (see "Creature Comforts").

DOGGIE DAYCARE
Crawford
Cottonwood Ranch and Kennel, 3994 G Dr., 970-921-7100. $15/day. Open 8 a.m.–5 p.m., Monday to Friday.

Delta
Deleff Kennels, 1951 B 50 Rd., 970-874-4058. $6–$8/day, depending on the size of dog. Open 7 a.m.–6 p.m., Monday to Saturday, or by appointment.

Montrose
Alta Vista Animal Hospital, 1845 E. Main, 970-249-8185. $8–$10/day, depending on the size of dog. Open 8 a.m.–5 p.m., Monday to Friday.

PET PROVISIONS
Delta
Sisson's Feed and Seed, 405 W. 5, 970-874-8376

Montrose
In the Jungle Pets, 16367 S. Townsend, 970-249-1797

CANINE ER
Montrose
Morningstar Veterinary Clinic (AAHA certified), 717 N. Cascade Ave., 970-249-8022.

Open 8 a.m.–5 p.m., Monday to Friday (until 5:30 p.m. on Wednesday); 8:30 a.m.–noon, second Saturday of every month.

RESOURCES
Bureau of Land Management, 2505 S. Townsend, Montrose, 970-240-5300

Delta Area Chamber of Commerce and Visitor Center, 301 Main St., Delta, 970-874-8616

Forest Supervisor's Office, Grand Mesa/Uncompahgre/Gunnison National Forests, 2250 Highway 50, Delta, 970-874-6600

Montrose Chamber of Commerce, 1519 E. Main, Montrose, 970-249-5000 (800-923-5515)

Montrose Visitor Information Center, 17253 Chipeta, Montrose, 970-249-1726

Ouray Ranger District, Uncompahgre National Forest, 2505 S. Townsend, Montrose, 970-240-5300

Paonia Ranger District, Gunnison National Forest, North Rio Grande Ave., Paonia, 970-527-4131

SIXTEEN

Gunnison, Crested Butte, and Lake City

THE BIG SCOOP

Dogs on the go will find attractions aplenty in the Gunnison area: forested hikes, rugged mountains to climb, and lots of water. Just be sure to keep an eye on your dog when you're both out enjoying the natural environment—wildlife and livestock harassment by otherwise well-meaning dogs is a perennial problem in the region.

Gunnison has the expected leash law within city limits. In Gunnison County, dogs can legally be under voice control.

For a generally dog-friendly, laid-back mountain town, Crested Butte has fairly strict dog regulations: There's a leash law within city limits, public tethering (i.e., tying up your dog outside a shop while you run in) is verboten, and dogs are not allowed in any of the five town parks. Nevertheless, dogs here seem to enjoy themselves as much as in any of the ski towns, and your dog won't be at a loss for encountering other butts to sniff. Mt. Crested Butte, which is the separate town at the ski area, allows dogs to be under voice control instead of on leash, and the no-public-tethering rule is confined to the ski resort's immediate base area.

Lake City, tucked in the mountains 55 miles south of Gunnison, requires dogs to be on leash in its downtown area, from 4th through 1st Sts.; they can be under voice control elsewhere in the town as well as on all Hinsdale County land. Unfortunately, dogs must refrain from setting paw in the town park.

TAIL-RATED TRAILS

There is limitless hiking in the Gunnison and Uncompahgre National Forests and BLM lands of which this region is largely composed. I've highlighted just a few of the most accessible trails. For more ideas, consult the "Aspen/Crested Butte/Gunnison Recreation Topo Map" put out by Latitude 40°. Keep in mind that many of the well-known hiking trails around Crested Butte are in wilderness areas, so your dog will have to stay on a leash. And because the town is a legendary mountain biking hub, choose non-wilderness trails carefully if you want to avoid dodging avid cyclists.

Crested Butte

 Green Lake. 7 miles round-trip. This hike to a gorgeous mountain lake begins right in Crested Butte, at the Nordic Center at 2nd and Whiterock. *Dogs can be off leash.*

Begin hiking up the dirt road that ascends from the left of the Nordic Center parking lot. At the top of the bench, go right on the dirt road (Wildcat Rd.). Just before the end of the road look for the trail on the left that's marked for Green Lake, which will take you up to a rocky jeep road known as Baby Head Hill. Eventually you'll come to a fork, at which you can only go right. Within less than 100 yards, the trail ends at a well-maintained dirt road (Trapper's Crossing Rd.). Go right at this road. The actual Green Lake Trail is about a half mile farther along Trapper's Crossing Rd.; look for the trail sign. (Unfortunately, you can't just drive to this point from town because the road leading to it is private.) From here, the trail is distinct all the way to the lake, as it winds through wildflower meadows and forest. Just before reaching the lake, pass by a trail that climbs steeply up to the right. The lake itself lives up to its name and is picturesquely situated at the base of an alpine cirque. Midsummer, the water temperature may even be warm enough for both you and your dog to enjoy a dip.

 Crested Butte Mountain. The ski area is open for hiking in the summer, though you won't be able to ride up the Silver Queen chairlift with your dog. Instead, follow the Yellow Brick Rd. (the summer service road) from the base area to the top of the Silver Queen, a distance of 4.75 miles. From there, trail signs will point you in the direction of the 1-mile (762 vertical feet) hike to the peak, where you'll top out at 12,162 feet, rewarded by a stunning panoramic view of the Elk Mountains and the backside of the Maroon Bells. *Dogs can be off leash.*

 Woods Walk to Peanut Lake. About 5 miles round-trip. Either walk or drive up Kebler Pass Rd. from Crested Butte. Just past Treasury Hill Rd. on the right, there's a place for one or two cars to park (before the dirt road designated private). There's also a pair of small parking pullouts a little farther up Kebler Pass Rd., on both sides of the road. *Dogs can be off leash.*

Head into the woods from the parking area after Treasury Hill Rd. You'll first pass a trail branch coming from the right. Then at the fork, stay right. The trail goes through a stand of aspen, then opens into a flower-filled meadow. Continue hiking west until you draw near a stylish house; turn left here. The trail then parallels Peanut Lake from above, with Crested Butte Mountain and Gothic Mountain dominating the view. Although your dog won't be within paw-dipping

access of the lake, you will cross a stream he can get wet in. The trail eventually ends at a fence and some abandoned-looking property and descends about fifty feet to Peanut Lake Rd. If you want to make a loop, walk back on the road along the lake; just before you reach pavement, take the small footpath up to the right. Stay on the straight, narrow path past a branch-off to the left, until you meet up with your original route by the house.

Another alternative is to continue on the **Lower Loop Trail**, which would add approximately 3 miles round-trip. After descending to Peanut Lake Rd., head left and cross the cattle guard. After about 200 yards, look for the sign for the Lower Loop Trail to the left. Eventually the trail splits into an upper and a lower tier; both tiers end at the road that goes up to Gunsight Pass. Take one route out and return on the other.

You can also access Peanut Lake Rd. from town by walking to the end of Butte Ave., four blocks north of Elk Ave. This will make for a shorter hike, but you'll forsake the lovely woods part of the hike described above.

Gunnison

Curecanti National Recreation Area. Curecanti, administered by the National Park Service, encompasses an area from about 5 miles west of Gunnison to the border of the Black Canyon of the Gunnison National Park. Its centerpiece is 20-mile-long Blue Mesa Reservoir, created by three dams constructed along the Gunnison River. There are also seven established hiking trails in the recreation area. The Elk Creek Visitor Center, off Highway 50 west, has a brochure that describes them. The 1.5-mile round-trip **Neversink Trail**, which provides good bird-watching opportunities, is the closest one to Gunnison, just off Highway 50, 5 miles from town. For a less frequented hike that's also near water, try the 4-mile round-trip **Curecanti Creek Trail,** accessed from Highway 92 north, 5.7 miles from the junction with Highway 50. Your dog will have to pass on the boat tours of Morrow Point Lake. *Dogs must be leashed throughout the recreation area, including all trails.*

Hartman Rocks. From Gunnison, head west on Highway 50 for approximately 1.5 miles to County Rd. 38 (Gold Basin Rd.). Turn left and drive for 2.4 miles to a parking area on the right, indicated by a small blue-and-white "Hartman Rocks" sign. *Dogs can be off leash.*

This 160-acre recreation area, which abuts BLM land, has a network of trails looping over and around hilly terrain, with sage, piñon, and juniper as the primary vegetation. There's no set destination—let your dog lead the way to wherever his nose takes him. Because the area is dry and hot, you'll want to avoid bringing Fido here midday during the summer. Actually, the best times to come are when motocross riding is not allowed on the front side of the trail: before 11 a.m. or after 6 p.m., Monday through Saturday, and all day Sunday. Bring plenty of water for the both of you, though your dog might be lucky enough to come across one of the water-filled stock tanks on the back side of the hill.

Signal Peak. Up to approximately 8 miles round-trip. From Main St. (Highway 135) in Gunnison, head east on Georgia Ave. Follow the road as it bends to the left, becoming Escalante Dr., and partially circumnavigate the Western State College campus. Turn into a parking lot on the right, just after the water storage tanks on the right and just before the athletic field. *Dogs can be off leash.*

The route to Signal Peak is actually a spur of the Colorado Trail. Although the

hike is not necessarily rewarding enough to merit covering the entire distance (unless you're on a bike), it's nice to have an option so close to town where your dog can hike with you leash-free. Just be sure to access it as described above, even though you may spot another access point along a four-wheel-drive road before the water towers; apparently this latter route crosses private property, and a "no dogs" sign has been posted by the owner to avoid canine-livestock conflict. (I've made an educated guess as to the origins of the sign; neither Gunnison Animal Control nor the BLM was aware of it.) And bring lots of water.

The trail you want begins through the fence at the edge of the parking area. Either take the straight shot up to the first radio tower or, for a more gradual ascent, hike left along the dirt road and follow the "Parcours" markers. Once on top of the hill, hike along the ridge toward the second radio tower. The trail follows a dirt road through the sagebrush and affords a nice panorama of the Gunnison Valley and the surrounding mountain ranges. Signal Peak is the cone-shaped feature to the northeast. Your dog might also just be interested in exploring the network of dirt roads and singletrack that winds around the radio tower hills.

CYCLING FOR CANINES

Any mountain-biking dog worth his snuff will want to say he's been to the Butte to bike, and several trails fit the bill for canine cycling companionship. The **Woods Walk** (see "Tail-Rated Trails") is a nice, gentle ride, as is biking on **Peanut Lake Rd.** The **Lower Loop Trail** (described briefly in the Woods Walk entry) is a popular ride to do with dogs. For something more technical, try **Snodgrass Mountain** as an out-and-back ride of a few miles, driving to the trailhead past Mt. Crested Butte—the loop that bikers usually do involves riding on trafficked roads. Or drive up Brush Creek Rd.

south of town and tackle the 5.5-mile **Farris Creek Loop.**

In Gunnison, **Signal Peak** and **Hartman Rocks** (see "Tail-Rated Trails") are both suitable for taking your dog along on a ride. Dogs visiting Lake City may especially enjoy the 7.6-mile round-trip ride to **Waterdog Lake,** which begins just outside of town a quarter mile up the road from the sewage treatment plant.

POWDERHOUNDS

Two great places to ski or snowshoe with your dog in Crested Butte are **Slate River and Washington Gulch Rds.** Both are unplowed after a certain point and provide wide-open touring in breathtakingly scenic surroundings. See *Snowshoeing Colorado,* by Claire Walter, for details on these and other options. In the Lake City area, the Lake City Nordic Association discourages dogs from the groomed Williams Creek and Slumgullion Pass trail systems; however, a couple of ungroomed areas make for suitable dog destinations. The **East Lakeshore** area, by Lake San Cristobal, includes an unplowed public road. The **Danny Carl** area, between Slumgullion and Spring Creek Passes on Highway 149 south, features a meadow as well as forested terrain. Note that dogs are not allowed at any of the yurts along the Hindsdale Haute Route system outside of Lake City.

CREATURE COMFORTS

Unless otherwise stated, dogs should not be left unattended in the room or cabin.

Almont

About 10 miles north of Gunnison on the way to Crested Butte, this small town is home to several cabin resorts. A few of the resorts listed here are closer to Taylor Reservoir, about a half-hour drive northeast of Almont.

$–$$ Holt's Guest Ranch, 1711 County Rd. 55 (2 miles from Taylor Reservoir), 970-641-2733. The ranch has sixteen fully equipped cabins that sleep anywhere from two to ten people, and dogs may stay for a $5 fee per night. "We don't particularly like dogs," admits the owner, "but we've been accepting them for so long that we'll continue to do so." You must keep your dog leashed when he's outside. Open mid-May to mid-October.

$–$$ Three Rivers Resort and Outfitting, 130 County Rd. 742, 970-641-1303 (888-761-3474; www.3riversresort.com). Situated at the confluence of the Taylor, East, and Gunnison Rivers (hence the name), the resort has thirty-five fully outfitted cabins, from studio to four bedroom, some along the Taylor River. Dogs must put down a $15 deposit. You can leave your dog unattended inside; he must be leashed when outside on the resort's property. The resort also offers guided rafting, kayaking, and fly-fishing trips (for humans only). Open beginning of May to November.

$$ Almont Resort, 10209 Highway 135, 970-641-4009 (www.almontresort.com). The resort advertises its accommodations as "rustic cabins with modern conveniences." However, about half of the twenty cabins don't have kitchen facilities, something to keep in mind if you're planning a cooking vacation. There's a $5 one-time pet fee. Dogs can be left unattended inside the cabins; the resort advises that you keep your dog leashed when outside because of the proximity to busy Highway 135.

Crested Butte dogs who are feeling a little hot under the collar like to go to easily accessible Long Lake to cool off—it's directly off Washington Gulch Rd.

$$ Silent Spring Resort, 905 County Rd. 744 (8 miles from Almont), 970-641-0583 (www.coloradodirectory.com/silentspring). You and your dog can relax here in one of the four secluded, extremely well-equipped log cabins. "We're big dog people," says the owner, "and we welcome anybody with pets." Two of the cabins were built within the past several years; the other two are older but restored, and one cabin has a fireplace, the other a wood-burning stove. There's a two-night minimum stay; many guests rent the cabins for a week at a time—and book well in advance. You can leave your dog unattended inside if he's in a travel crate; keep him on a leash outside the cabins. Open May 15 to September 15.

$$ Taylor Park Trading Post, located at Taylor Reservoir, 970-641-2555. Thirty-three cabins, fully furnished, can be shared with your dog. They range in size from studio to two bedrooms, and some have additional sleeping lofts. Closed November 4 to December 24.

$$$–$$$$ Harmel's Ranch Resort, 6748 County Rd. 742, 970-641-1740 (800-235-3402; www.harmels.com). This guest ranch offers a variety of accommodation options, from one- to three-bedroom cottages and suites (some with kitchens) and one-bedroom cabins to lodge rooms, duplexes, and a fourplex. What's most important is that your dog can accompany you in any of them, with either a $10 per night fee or $65 for the week. The ranch is on 150 acres surrounded by the Gunnison National Forest, and your dog can hike off leash on the property with you. Horseback riding, rafting, fishing, and children's activities are also available. Three lodging plans are available: room and breakfast plus two cookouts per week; room and three meals a day; room, three meals a day, and most ranch activities. There's a three-night minimum stay. Open late May to September 30.

Crested Butte

$$–$$$ The Claim Jumper, 704 Whiterock, 970-349-6471 (www.visit crestedbutte.com/claimjumper). To call this B&B unique, as it advertises, may be an understatement. Each of the six rooms is packed with memorabilia relating to a specific theme; the sports fan room, for example, is filled to the gills with athletic equipment, baseball hats, autographed pictures, pennants, souvenirs, and so on. And in the midst of all this, your dog is extremely welcome. "Dogs make great guests," emphasizes owner Jerry Bigelow. "I've never had a dog smoke in a room or take a towel." There's a $7 one-time fee, and large dogs are preferred over small noisy ones. You can even leave your dog unattended in the room, where he certainly won't run out of things to look at until you return. And Otis, the resident Newfoundland and canine concierge, can give your pooch the insider's view of Crested Butte. In fact, he'd be more than happy to go hiking with you and Rover.

$$–$$$$ Sheraton Crested Butte Resort, 6 Emmons Rd., 970-349-8000 (800-544-8448 [goes to the Crested Butte ski resort line, which books the Sheraton]; www.crestedbutteresort.com). This fairly new hotel near the ski area base now allows dogs year-round (it used to be from June through October only). However, dogs can stay in first-floor rooms only, all of which are smoking, and there's a $35 fee per night. Check with the front desk about leaving your dog unattended in the room.

$$$–$$$$ San Moritz Condominiums, 18 Hunter Hill Rd., 970-349-5150 (800-443-7459; www.sanmoritzcondos.com). Dog-friendly condos are a rare find at a ski area. "We love pets," says the manager of these ski-in/ski-out condos. You can leave your dog unattended inside (preferably in a travel kennel) as long as he doesn't bark the day away (though the

A hiking dog is a happy dog. (photo by Cindy Hirschfeld)

housekeepers will leave clean linens and towels outside your door when Fido guards the condo). A credit-card imprint is requested as a deposit, and there's a four-night minimum stay during the summer; four to five nights during the winter.

Gunnison

$ Gunnison KOA Kampground, 105 County Rd. 50, 970-641-1358 (800-562-1248). Canines are allowed in the camping cabins (you'll have to bring your own bedding and cooking gear). Open April 15 to November 1.

$ Long's Holiday Motel, 1198 W. Highway 50, 970-641-0536. Large dogs are assessed a $5 one-time fee to stay in one of the motel's five designated pet rooms.

$–$$ ABC Motel, 212 E. Tomichi, 970-641-2400 (800-315-2378 [national number]). The motel has some pet-designated rooms for $5 extra per night.

$–$$ Days Inn, 701 W. Highway 50, 970-641-0608 (888-641-0608). During the summer, the motel charges $10 per

night, per dog; in winter the fee goes down to $4 per night, per dog.

$–$$ Ferro's Blue Mesa Trading Post, 3200 Soap Creek Rd., 970-641-4671 (www.coloradodirectory.com/ferros). The trading post is actually located west of Gunnison, on the northwest side of Blue Mesa Lake and within spitting distance of the Curecanti National Recreation Area. You and your dog will have your choice of two fully outfitted log cabins, two RVs, one mobile home, or one cabin with everything but running water. Dogs should be leashed on the post's 40 acres when horses are around; Ferro's offers horseback rides, and guests can also bring their own horse along. The friendly owner put in a plug for his cats, saying that they're entertained by visiting dogs and vice versa. Open beginning of May to end of November.

$–$$ Hylander Inn, 412 E. Tomichi, 970-641-0700. Dogs are charged $5 per night extra, and they'll stay with you in one of several designated pet rooms that face Legion Park, across the street.

$–$$ Island Acres Motel, 38339 W. Highway 50, 970-641-1442. The motel takes "chihuahuas and toy poodles" (or similar-sized pooches) in smoking rooms only. Some rooms have kitchenettes.

$–$$ Shady Island Resort, 2776 N. Highway 135, 970-641-0416. The resort has ten cabins, including a three-bedroom house, and dogs can stay in any for a $5 fee per night, per dog. The cabins are located on 10 acres along the Gunnison River, and your dog needs to be leashed when outside. Open May 1 to November 15.

$–$$ Swiss Inn Motel, 312 E. Tomichi, 970-641-9962. Small dogs (poodle-sized) get the nod here.

$–$$ Western Motel, 403 E. Tomichi Ave., 970-641-1722. There's a $3 fee per night, per dog. Legion Park, across the street, provides ample dog-walking opportunities.

$$ Lake Fork Resort, 940 Cove Rd. (25 miles west of Gunnison), 970-641-3564 (800-368-9421; www.montrose.net/lake fork). Just a hop, skip, and a jump from Blue Mesa Lake, this resort has six fully equipped one-bedroom cabins, with additional two-bedroom cabins slated to be built. Dogs are permitted with a $15 one-time fee per dog. You must keep your dog leashed on the surrounding 36 acres.

$$ Lost Canyon Resort, 8264 Highway 135, 970-641-0181 (www.coloradodirectory.com/lostcanyonresort). The resort's seventeen studio to two-bedroom log cabins are scenically situated on 10 acres along the Gunnison River. About half of the fully equipped cabins also have fireplaces or woodstoves. Your dog can explore the property off leash as long as you're there to supervise him.

$$ Ranch House Bed and Breakfast, 233 County Rd. 48, 970-642-0210 (www.ranch housebnb.com). About a five-minute drive north of Gunnison, the B&B is in a historic ranch house built in 1875 and then owned by the governor of Colorado in the 1940s. "We're oriented toward people traveling with dogs or children," says owner Steve Shelafo. Of the three guest rooms, two have private baths and all are individually decorated. There's also a hot tub. As far as your dog goes, he'll enjoy the fenced dog-kennel area in back of the house, with separate dog runs and a common play area. Yukon, the B&B's black lab, is game for playing with visiting dogs.

$$ Rockey River Resort, 4359 County Rd. 10, 970-641-0174 (www.coloradodirectory.com/rockeyriverresort). For $5 per night, per dog, your pooch(es) can join you in one of these fourteen fully furnished cabins, ranging from studio to three bedrooms, on 7 acres along the Gunnison River. Dogs must be leashed when outside.

$$ Tomahawk Guest Ranch, 2943 County Rd. 27 (halfway between Gunnison and Lake City), 970-641-2104 (www.tomahawkguestranch.com). The ranch offers nine fully outfitted cabins with one to three bedrooms. You can leave your dog unattended inside, though he'd probably rather be out exploring the 40 acres of property leash-free with you. The ranch abuts BLM land. Open from May to mid-November.

$$$ Rockin 3AR Cabin, 14255 County Rd. 730, 970-641-2394 (www.coloradodirectory.com/rockin3ar). This small, picturesque log cabin in the Ohio Creek Valley, about 17 miles northwest of Gunnison, sleeps up to six people, with one bedroom, a living room, and full kitchen. Your dog can join you for a $25 one-time fee, and he can be left unattended inside (you can bring your horse too). The cabin is adjacent to proprietors Walter and Bunny Kelley's own house on 3.5 acres, and they'll provide meals (at additional cost) if you desire. In winter, particularly heavy snow might require a half-mile ski or snowmobile to reach the cabin.

Lake City

$–$$ Castle Lakes Cabins and Campground Resort, Cinnamon Pass Rd. (County Rd. 30), 970-944-2622. Dogs are accepted on a case-by-case basis; if they pass inspection they can have their pick of furnished one- or two-bedroom cabins, mobile homes, or RV trailers to stay in. The setting is gorgeous, on 45 acres above Lake San Cristobal and near 14,000-foot-plus Redcloud and Sunshine Peaks. It's also along the Alpine Loop Scenic Byway. Open May 15 to October 1.

$–$$ G & M Cabins, 331 Gunnison Ave., 970-944-2282 (www.colorado

Maryclare Scerbo and Clover investigate the ruins of a mining cabin in the Elk Mountains. (photo by Cindy Hirschfeld)

Open year-round except during April and November.

$$ Alpine Village, 631 N. Silver, 970-944-2266 (800-484-9074 [type in access code of 2101]). These eleven one- and two-bedroom, fully equipped log cabins are located in town. Dogs can be left inside unattended but for a short time only. Open June 1 to September 30.

$$ Lake City Resort, 307 S. Gunnison Ave., 970-944-2866 (www.coloradodi rectory.com/lakecityresort). The eight cabins range from studios to two bedrooms and come with all the necessities. There's a $5 fee per night, per dog. Although the cabins are in town, there's a grassy area around them where you can exercise your dog on leash. Open May 15 to October 1.

directory.com/gmcabins). For $10 extra per dog for the first night, $5 each night thereafter, you can bring your dog along to these ten in-town, fully furnished cabins, which range in size from studios to two bedrooms. During the winter only four cabins are available, with a three-night minimum stay.

$–$$ Town Square Cabins, 231 Gunnison Ave., 970-944-2236. All eight fully equipped cabins (studios and two bedrooms) are dog friendly, with a $10 one-time fee per dog. When exercising your pooch, note that dogs are not allowed in the town park, across the street. A convenience store and laundromat are located on site.

$–$$$ Crystal Lodge, Highway 149 (2 miles from Lake City), 970-944-2201 (877-GO-LODGE; www.crystallodge.net). Dogs are allowed in the lodge suites, which sleep from two to eight, or in the four two-bedroom cabins, but not in the upstairs lodge rooms. There's a $25 deposit per pet, and dogs should be kept leashed on the lodge's property. There's also a restaurant with a reputation for great homemade meals on the premises.

$$ Lakeview Resort, Lake San Cristobal, 970-944-2401 (800-456-0170; www.lake view-inc.com). Enjoy a stay with your dog at Colorado's second-largest natural lake, just outside Lake City. The resort offers lodge rooms, one-bedroom lodge suites, and one- to three-bedroom cabins with wood-burning stoves or fireplaces. There's a $6 fee per night, per dog, with a one-dog limit. The resort also has guided horseback rides and fishing trips. You must keep your dog leashed when outside. Open mid-May to October 1.

$$ Matterhorn Mountain Lodge, 409 N. Bluff, 970-944-2210. The Matterhorn has motel rooms, some with kitchenettes, as well as two fully outfitted cabins. Dogs are welcome for $10 extra per night, per dog, and they can be left unattended inside, preferably in a travel crate.

$$ Quiet Moose Lodge (formerly Western Belle), 1221 Highway 149, 970-944-2415 (800-650-1221; www.quiet moose.com). Dogs are welcome in any of the motel's rooms for $5 extra per night. They can be left unattended inside.

$$ **Wagon Wheel Resort, 249 Highway 149, 970-944-2264.** The resort, on the south edge of town, has cabins ranging from efficiencies to two bedrooms, all fully equipped. Dogs are welcome and can be left unattended in the cabins for a short time "as long as they don't raise heck." Open mid-May through mid-November.

$$ **Westwood Resort, 413 Gunnison Ave., 970-944-2205.** "We love animals," says the owner. One dog per cabin (there are eight, all fully equipped) is the policy here, along with a $10 one-time fee. There's a three-night minimum stay during July and August. Open from the beginning of May to mid-October.

$$–$$$ **Old Carson Inn Bed and Breakfast, 8401 County Rd. 30, 970-944-2511 (800-294-0608; www.oldcarsoninn.com).** The well-behaved dog who wants more upscale accommodations in Lake City may be able to stay at this B&B, which on occasion allows dogs in one of its rooms. The inn is in a modern log and frame house, and the potential dog-stay room has a queen-size bed, antique furnishings, and a private entrance for discreet dog walking. From mid-December through March, there's a two-night and three-room minimum.

$$–$$$ **Vickers Ranch, Highway 149 (1 mile south of Lake City), 970-944-2249.** Located on 2,000 acres just south of Lake City, the ranch has twenty-two log cabins, ranging in size from two to four bedrooms, all with kitchens and fireplaces. There's a $10 per night pet fee, with a limit of one dog per cabin. Your dog will want to do some sniffing around on this vast expanse of land—the Lake Fork of the Gunnison River runs on the property—but you'll have to keep him

leashed because of the cattle and horses. The ranch has guided horseback trips and rents jeeps. Open May 1 to mid-November (a winter stay can be arranged in advance, but there's a five-night minimum).

$$–$$$$ **Ryan's Roost, 9501 Highway 149, 970-944-2339.** Your dog will likely clamor to stay here when you tell him there are 95 acres that he can explore with you leash-free. Though the Ryans no longer rent out B&B rooms, they offer three fully equipped cabins, which sleep from five to eight people. You can leave your dog unattended in them. If you have a horse, you can bring it along, too, for a true family outing. Open June to October.

Ohio City
$ **Sportsmans Resort, County Rd. 771, 970-641-0172.** The resort, in a town of about fifty people, has nine fully furnished cabins, and you can leave your dog unattended inside. Open from the end of May to mid-November.

Parlin
$ **7-11 Ranch, County Rd. 76 (5 miles north of Parlin), 970-641-0666.** This working cattle ranch on 600 acres will let your dog be a guest as long as he doesn't chase the cattle. There are six fully furnished cabins that share a central bathhouse. (There's also a lodge with ten beds available for rental, but dogs are not allowed.) When outside on the property, your dog doesn't have to be on a leash as long as you can keep him under your voice control. The ranch offers guided horseback rides, including multi-day trips that your dog can accompany you on (check with the ranch for details on the dog regulations for these). Open mid-March to just before Christmas.

$$ **Q T Corner, 1 Earl Ave., 970-641-0485.** The Q and T in the name stands for the Quartz and Tomichi Rivers, two

excellent fishing venues that meet on the property of this small resort. The five fully equipped riverside cabins include four studios with separate kitchen areas, as well as a larger "family" cabin with two bedrooms and two baths. You can leave your dog unattended inside, though the resort's owners have now added small fenced areas behind each cabin for dog guests. Open May 1 to end of November.

Pitkin

$ Pitkin Hotel, 329 Main St., 970-641-2757 (www.pitkincolorado.com). To get away from it all, your dog might enjoy a stay at this historic, quaint hotel, which dates back to 1904. There are six private rooms, all with shared baths, as well as three bunkrooms (sleeping eighteen, six, and three, respectively). The teeny town of Pitkin, about 30 miles northeast of Gunnison, has one restaurant that hasn't been in operation recently, so you'll have to fend for yourself, though you're welcome to bring your own food and use the hotel kitchen to whip up a meal. Rather than leave your dog unattended in the room, the owner prefers that you attach him to one of the dog chains provided on the front porch or in back of the hotel, or put him in the fenced-in yard, and she'll keep an eye on him.

$–$$ Quartz Creek Lodge, 102 2nd St., 970-641-6174 (www.pitkincolorado.com). Despite the name, the seven attached cabin units that make up the lodge are actually located on Armstrong Creek in Pitkin. They vary in size, from one room to a living area with separate bedrooms, and all have full kitchens and outside porches. You can have your dog under voice control on the lodge's property. From mid-November to the beginning of June (approximately), there's a three-night minimum stay.

Campgrounds

Curecanti National Recreation Area, west of Gunnison along Highway 50, has major developed campgrounds at Stevens Creek, Elk Creek, Lake Fork, and Cimarron; smaller campgrounds around Blue Mesa Reservoir are at Dry Gulch, Red Creek, Ponderosa, and Gateview.

National forest campgrounds: **Cement Creek Campground,** 4 miles up Cement Creek Rd. outside of Crested Butte (13 sites); **Lake Irwin Campground,** at Irwin Lake, west of Crested Butte on Kebler Pass Rd. (32 sites); **Cold Spring, Lodgepole, Lottis Creek, North Bank, One Mile, and Rosy Lane Campgrounds** are all along the Taylor Canyon Rd. between Almont and Taylor Reservoir; **Lakeview Campground,** overlooking Taylor Reservoir (46 sites); **Williams Creek Campground,** on County Rd. 30 past Lake San Cristobal, outside Lake City (23 sites); **Slumgullion Campground,** off Highway 149 south of Lake City (21 sites).

Private campgrounds: **Gunnison KOA** (see "Creature Comforts").

WORTH A PAWS

Mountain Tails, 303 Elk Ave., Crested Butte, 970-349-5606. This pet store deserves special mention as a great place to visit. There's an enticing array of items for dogs (and cats too), including specialty collars and leashes, backpacks, booties, toys galore, and gourmet treats. You'll also find pet-themed items such as picture frames, mugs, cards, and jewelry. It's hard to say who will have more fun shopping—you or Fido.

DOGGIE DAYCARE

Gunnison

Critter Sitters and Outfitters (part of Gunnison Veterinary Clinic), 98 County Rd. 17, 970-641-0460. $10/day. Open 8:30 a.m.–5:30 p.m., Monday to Friday; 8:30 a.m.–noon and 5–7 p.m., Saturday; 8:30–9:30 a.m. and 5–7 p.m., Sunday.

Taylor Pet Care Center, 106 S. 11th St., 970-641-2460. $10/day. Open 8 a.m.–

5:30 p.m., Monday to Friday (Thursday until 7 p.m.).

Town & Country Animal Hospital, 1525 Highway 135, 970-641-2215. $13/day. Open 8 a.m.–5:30 p.m., Monday to Friday; 8 a.m.–1 p.m., Saturday.

PET PROVISIONS
Crested Butte
Mountain Tails, 303 Elk Ave., 970-349-5606

Gunnison
Critter Sitters and Outfitters, 98 County Rd. 17, 970-641-0460

J&B Fish and Supplies, 618 W. Tomichi, 970-641-2110

CANINE ER
Crested Butte
Animal Hospital of Crested Butte, 418 Belleview Ave., 970-349-1700. Open 9 a.m.–5 p.m., Monday to Friday.

Gunnison
Town & Country Animal Hospital (AAHA certified), 1525 Highway 135, 970-641-2215. Open 8 a.m.–5:30 p.m., Monday to Friday; 8 a.m.–1 p.m., Saturday.

RESOURCES
The Alpineer, 419 Sixth St., in Crested Butte, 970-349-5210 (www.alpineer.com)—maps, guidebooks, and friendly, knowledgeable advice about area trails

Bureau of Land Management, Gunnison Resource Area, 216 N. Colorado, Gunnison, 970-641-0471

Crested Butte/Mt. Crested Butte Chamber of Commerce, 601 Elk Ave., Crested Butte, 970-349-6438 (800-545-4505; www.crestedbuttechamber.com)

Gunnison County Chamber of Commerce, 500 E. Tomichi Ave. (Highway 50), Gunnison, 970-641-1501 (800-323-2453; www.gunnisoncounty.com)

Lake City Chamber of Commerce, 800 N. Gunnison Ave., 970-944-2527 (800-569-1874; www.lakecityco.com)

Taylor River/Cebolla Ranger District, Gunnison National Forest, 216 N. Colorado, Gunnison, 970-641-0471

Telluride, Ouray, and Silverton

THE BIG SCOOP

All three of these mountain towns are dog-friendly havens, with Telluride earning top honors. "Telluride has more dogs than people," claimed the guy behind the counter at the local pet supply store. While this may or may not be true, any town that sets aside designated "puppy parking" areas in its business district is definitely in step with the canine set. And pet pickup bags are amply provided throughout town.

Telluride's leash laws match its laid-back atmosphere: Dogs can be under voice control almost anywhere. The exceptions—where dogs must be leashed—are Colorado Ave. and anyplace within a block of it, and Town Park. (Note that during Telluride's many weekend summer festivals, dogs are not allowed at all in the park.) You can bring your dog to the Mountain Village—on a leash or under voice control—though a common misconception exists that dogs are out-and-out banned (and the actual ordinance regarding dogs has some contradictions within it). The only place in Telluride that truly bans dogs is the Lawson Hill subdivision (by Society Turn). Regulations have been revised to allow dogs to ride the gondola connecting Telluride proper and the Mountain Village: Now leashed dogs can ride in a designated pet cabin. There are only a few such cabins, so be prepared for a potential wait.

Ouray, ringed by mountains on three sides, provides a spectacular setting. Your dog, however, will probably prefer to spend most of his time exploring the nearby trails rather than dodging kids

and RVs on the town's busy main street. There is a leash law within city limits.

With only one paved road, Silverton would seem to be the kind of town where dogs roam the streets; in fact, we did see a couple of dogs on the loose during our visit. Nevertheless, there's a leash law within city limits (though not in surrounding San Juan County).

TAIL-RATED TRAILS

The area around Telluride, Ouray, and Silverton is filled with spectacular mountain hikes, many of them steeped in mining history. Some of the most accessible are described here. For more options, check out *Telluride Hiking Guide*, by Susan Kees; *Ouray Hiking Guide*, by Kelvin B. Kent; and, for Silverton, *Hiking Trails of Southwest Colorado*, by Paul Pixler. "Hiking Trails of Ouray County," a brochure and map put out by an association called The Trail Group, Inc., is another helpful resource.

Ouray

 Bear Creek National Recreation Trail. About 6 miles round-trip to the first creek crossing. Drive south out of Ouray on U.S. Highway 550. At about 2 miles from the signed turnoff for Box Canyon Falls, you'll pass through a tunnel; a parking area is immediately after it on the left. The trailhead is across the road, on the south side of the tunnel (which you'll actually hike on top of). *Dogs can be off leash.*

The most taxing part of this trail is the beginning section, which switchbacks dramatically up and up the side of the canyon. You'll encounter loose slate and quartzite along the first half of the trail; Clover didn't have a problem with it, and neither did Bruno, a ten-year-old shepherd mix we met on the trail (who had a bandaged paw, no less). But if your dog's a tenderfoot, keep an eye on him. At the top of the switchbacks, you'll be rewarded with a picture-perfect view of Red Mountain as well as a peek down the precipitous drop into Bear Creek Gorge. The narrow trail, built by miners in the late 1800s, has been carved out of the canyon's sides—if your dog has a fear of exposure you might want to keep him leashed. At 2.5 miles, pass the ramshackle remains of the Grizzly Bear Mine. About half a mile beyond, the trail descends to the creek, traveling through grasses and fir, with some good resting spots for you and your dog. Eventually the trail crosses a side creek. This was our turnaround spot, but you can continue another mile or so farther to the ruins of the Yellow Jacket Mine, and even beyond.

Weehawken Trail. 6.2 miles round-trip. Take Highway 550 south from Ouray. At the first switchback, turn right at the national forest access sign for Camp Bird Mine and Box Canyon Falls, then stay left at the fork. Follow the Camp Bird road for 2.6 miles to a small parking area at the trailhead, on the right. *Dogs can be off leash.*

This would be a particularly nice hike in the fall, when the aspens change. Begin by switchbacking up a wooded hillside on a narrow trail. Ascend first through an open meadow, then through aspens, all to the symphonic rumbling of Canyon Creek. Past the junction where a trail to the Alpine Mine heads off to the right (another good hike, which ends at a breathtaking overlook of Ouray), the trail snakes around a hillside, heading up the Weehawken Valley. Imposing volcanic

cliffs rise across the ravine. After crossing an avalanche basin, hike along a narrow shelf in the forest to the trail's eventual end at Weehawken Creek, where your dog can take a dip before the return hike out.

Ridgway

Ridgway State Park. The park is just off Highway 550 a couple miles north of Ridgway and is divided into three distinct sites: Pa-Co-Chu-Puk (try saying that one ten times in a row!), Dutch Charlie, and Dallas Creek. *Dogs must be leashed.*

Seventeen miles of trail, both paved and gravel, meander through the park. For a complete listing, pick up the trails guide at the visitor center. A few your dog may particularly enjoy: The **Dallas Creek Trail**, a 1-mile loop, begins at the Confluence Nature Area in the Dallas Creek site, following the creek and then ascending a small hill to provide a nice vista of the nearby San Juan Mountains. The **Piñon Park Trail**, in the Dutch Charlie site, runs about a mile from the visitor center to the marina. And the 3.5-mile (one way) **Enchanted Mesa Trail** skirts the edge of the mesa from Dutch Charlie to Pa-Co-Chu-Puk, with views of both the reservoir and the mountains. Be sure to bring water on this hike, as the terrain is dry. And, as in all Colorado state parks, dogs are not allowed on the swim beach at Ridgway.

Telluride

Jud Wiebe Trail. A 2.7-mile loop. From Colorado Ave. in town, walk three blocks north on Aspen St. to where the road dead-ends. The trailhead is here. (You can also access the Sneffels Highline trail from here, an 8.5-mile loop; because the trail enters a designated wilderness area; however, remind your dog to leash up.) *Dogs can be off leash.*

Immediately past the trailhead, go left

Ridgway
Ridgway Animal Hospital, 121 Sherman, 970-626-5001. Open 8:30 a.m.–4 p.m., Monday to Friday (closed Wednesday afternoon).

Telluride
Telluride Veterinary Clinic, 547½ W. Pacific Ave., 970-728-4461. Open 9 a.m.–5 p.m., Monday through Friday; until 8 p.m. on Thursday.

RESOURCES
Between the Cover Books, at 224 W. Colorado Ave., Telluride (970-728-4504), and Ouray Mountain Sports, at 772 Main, Ouray (970-325-4284), carry good selections of guidebooks and maps.

Norwood Ranger District, Uncompahgre National Forest, 1150 Forest, Norwood, 970-327-4261

Ouray Chamber Resort Association, 1222 Main (in front of the Hot Springs pool), 970-325-4746 (800-228-1876; www.ouraycolorado.com)

Silverton Visitor Center, 414 Greene St., 970-387-5654 (800-752-4494; www.silverton.org)

Telluride Visitor Services, 666 W. Colorado Ave., 970-728-3041 (800-525-3455; www.gotelluride.org)

EIGHTEEN

Mesa Verde and Vicinity

THE BIG SCOOP

Your four-legged companion won't be able to join you in viewing this area's main attraction—Mesa Verde National Park—but you'll still be able to explore much of the fascinating history and natural beauty of the area surrounding the "Green Table." And if your dog really wants to have something to tell his stay-at-home friends about, drive him 38 miles southwest from Cortez to the Four Corners National Monument, where he can put one paw in each state.

In November 2000, 164,000 acres of Bureau of Land Management lands were designated as the Canyon of the Ancients National Monument. The monument primarily encompasses the region west of Highway 666 and north of County Rd. G, including Lowry Pueblo and Sand Canyon. Though a more obvious "official" presence will be noticeable on the land in question, there won't be specific entrance gates or fees. The designation was made chiefly to protect the thousand of archaelogical sites in the area. A long-range management plan is in the works; as of spring 2001, how this may affect dog regulations has not been decided. Check at the Anasazi Heritage Center near Dolores (see "Worth a Paws") for the most up-to-date information.

Activity in the area surrounding Mesa Verde is centered in the small towns of Cortez, Dolores, and Mancos, which form a triangle. In Dolores, dogs can be off leash as long as they are under voice control. Cortez and Mancos both have leash laws. Cortez Centennial Park, located behind the Colorado Welcome Center in Cortez, provides a nice expanse of green for the dog who's feeling carbound. And in the Lizard Head Wilderness Area, about halfway between Cortez and Telluride off Highway 145, your dog can hike under voice command in the shadow of the reptilian-shaped monolith for which the area is named.

TAIL-RATED TRAILS

Trails in the region range from hot, sandy desert hikes to routes through the heart of the forest. The Visitor Information Bureau in Cortez puts out a great brochure with detailed descriptions called "Guide to Scenic Hiking Trails in Mesa Verde Country." All the trails are on national forest (nonwilderness) or BLM land, meaning lots of leash-free jaunts on which to take your dog. A few other options are described here.

 Mancos State Park/ Chicken Creek Trail. Up to 16 miles round-trip. From Mancos, head north on Highway 184 for a quarter mile, then east (right) on County Rd. 42. Go 4 miles to County Rd. N and turn left, which leads to the park entrance. To reach the trailhead, drive over the dam and around to the north side of the lake, where you'll

Yes, there was a canine component to Anasazi culture; the "ancient ones" kept dogs for work and companionship.

see a parking area and trailhead sign on the left. *Dogs must be leashed on the portion of trail that begins in the state park; they can be off leash on national forest land.*

This trail would be a good one for a dog during the day in summer—there's access to water as well as the pleasant shade of spruce and ponderosa pine once you reach the creek. Begin by hiking through a meadow. After about a quarter of a mile, when the trail bends to the right, it forks in the grass; stay to the left. Continue walking through tall grasses and, in summer, colorful wildflowers. Hike across and down a small clearing, after which you'll pass through a fence; this is the park boundary. The trail heads down a wide, gradual pitch to Chicken Creek. From here, it runs alongside the creek, crisscrossing the water several times and allowing your dog to cool his paws. Because this is an out-and-back hike, follow the creek bed for as long as you like. One note of caution: Because the trail receives a lot of horse use, the first mile may be heavily "cratered" when the dirt dries after a rainstorm.

Sand Canyon Trail. 12 miles round-trip. From Cortez, drive south on U.S. Highway 160/666. Make a right onto McElmo Rd. (across from the M&M Cafe). Go 12.5 miles to a trailhead parking area on the right. Alternate access is from the north, at Sand Canyon Pueblo: Drive north from Cortez on Highway 666 for 5.3 miles; make a left

If your dog tends to wander off trails, it's a good idea to keep him leashed in the desert so that he doesn't damage the fragile cryptogamic soil, which can take up to 100 years to form.

on Road P. Go 4.5 miles, then left on Road 18 at the T-intersection. After half a mile, follow the road as it makes a sharp curve to the right, turning into Road T. Turn left on Road 17 (1.4 miles); drive for a little over 3 more miles (follow the road as it bears right, becoming Road N). Look for a small parking area and BLM signage for Sand Canyon Pueblo on the left. *Dogs can be off leash (though note that since Sand Canyon is now part of the new Canyon of the Ancients National Monument, this policy could change).*

This is true desert hiking, best to do in the spring or fall. Be sure to bring a lot of water. As the "Sleeping Ute" mountain formation snoozes to the south, head north from the parking area at the southern trailhead, traveling across slickrock before picking up the red dirt trail. Your dog will have the chance to sniff out piñon, juniper, yucca, and prickly pear cactus. The level trail, which is easy to follow, is also marked with the occasional rock cairn. Along the way, the dog with an archaeological bent will enjoy viewing several Anasazi cliff dwellings, the first of which is in a large dome about half a mile from the trailhead. Other trail highlights include intriguing rock formations and sculpted canyons.

If you begin hiking from the north, the trail starts out somewhat rootier and rockier as it descends into the canyon. You may want to walk around the Sand Canyon Pueblo, which is in the process of being excavated, near the trailhead. The lack of interpretive material, however, may have you and your dog guessing at what you're supposed to be looking at.

Dolores Walking Trail. Runs for about half a mile along the Dolores River in the town of Dolores. Access is at either the 4th St. Bridge (take 4th St. south from Highway 145 through Dolores) or behind Joe Rowell Park, off

Highway 145 north just before entering downtown Dolores. *Dogs can be off leash.*

This wide gravel trail is great for a short stop or, if you're staying in Dolores, a morning or evening walk with Fido. Hot and thirsty canine travelers will appreciate the easy river access.

Dominguez and Escalante Ruins Hike. 1 mile round-trip. The hike starts at the Anasazi Heritage Center, 27501 Highway 184, in Dolores. *Dogs must be leashed.*

A paved trail winds up a gradual ascent to the Escalante Ruins, which were first documented by Spanish Franciscan friars in the eighteenth century but not excavated until 1976. Several shaded picnic tables are available along the trail for dining al fresco with your dog. At the top, take in the panoramic view of the surrounding area, including McPhee Reservoir and Mesa Verde. The Dominguez ruins are located right next to the museum building.

Mesa Verde National Park. As with all national parks, dogs are not allowed on any of the trails here. Their presence in the park is limited to parking lots and campgrounds (always on leash) and the Far View Lodge.

Ute Mountain Tribal Park, Towaoc (970-565-3751, ext. 282, or 800-847-5485). The park, which embraces about 125,000 acres, is a primitive area containing hundreds of Anasazi ruins, and admission is only with a Ute guide, by prior reservation. Dogs are discouraged as visitors, mainly because of the archaeological work in progress. The staff member I spoke with relayed an incident in which a dog had run off, only to come back carrying a vertebra in its mouth. To prevent similar scenarios, consider day-boarding Fido in Cortez if you want to visit the

park. The Cortez Animal Bed and Breakfast is the closest facility (see "Doggie Daycare").

CYCLING FOR CANINES

Sand Canyon (see "Tail-Rated Trails") is a scenic cycling option, best to do with your dog when temperatures are moderate. Biking from south to north gives you better riding terrain, and turning around before the trail gets too rocky will keep the round-trip distance under 10 miles (check at the Anasazi Heritage Center in Dolores—see "Worth a Paws"—before you go to find out if the off-leash policy has changed, since Sand Canyon is now part of the Canyons of the Ancients National Monument).

Or try the 10-mile round-trip **Cannonball Mesa** ride, which begins off McElmo Canyon Rd. about 8 miles past the Sand Canyon trailhead. For a detailed route description, pick up the brochure "Mountain and Road Bike Routes" that's put out by the Visitor Information Bureau in Cortez.

POWDERHOUNDS

Note that though the groomed trails in the Chicken Creek area near Mancos are on national forest land, the volunteers who maintain the ski trails ask that you leave Fido at home in winter. To access

Checking out the Anasazi ruins in Sand Canyon. (photo by Cindy Hirschfeld)

stay in any of the six full-service cabins or at the RV sites, but not in the lodge rooms. The complex is on 30 acres bordering the Dolores River, which your dog is welcome to explore on a leash. Open May 1 to October 31.

$$–$$$ **Lebanon Schoolhouse Bed and Breakfast**, 24925 Road T, 970-882-4461 (www.lebanonschoolhouse.com). This is probably the only chance your dog could have to stay overnight in a schoolhouse, and, to be expected, he should be on his best behavior. Dating from 1907, the converted building features an intriguing mix of architecture, with two separate living room/kitchen areas and five antique-furnished bedrooms, including a master suite and the bell-tower room. Although you won't be able to leave your dog unattended here, there's a nice fenced-in area outside where he can relax while you go out to dinner. And the "schoolyard" features colorful gardens and a picnic area. The three resident dogs may teach your dog some new-school tricks.

$$$ **The Red Elk Lodge**, 27060 Highway 145, 970-562-3849. The lodge has two fully outfitted cabins that sleep from six to eight people, each with one bedroom and a loft. Dogs are $10 extra per night.

Dove Creek
$ **Country Inn Motel**, 442 W. Highway 666, 970-677-2234 (www.fone.net/~countryn). The motel allows one dog per room for a $5 fee per visit.

Mancos
$ **A&A Mesa Verde Camper Cabins and RV Resort**, 34979 Highway 160 (directly across from the entrance to Mesa Verde), 970-565-3517 (800-972-6620). In addition to tent and RV sites, the canine-friendly A&A has three camping cabins where you can stay with your dog (you'll have to bring your own bedding, and there are no cooking facilities, though the

cabins do have heaters in winter). You can leave your dog unattended in the cabin for a short time. As an added bonus, pet-sitting is available for $7.50 per day, a handy option if you want to tour the national park.

$ **Mesa Verde Motel**, 191 Railroad Ave., 970-533-7741 (800-825-MESA). Only small dogs are allowed, with a $25 one-time fee.

$ **The Old Mancos Inn**, 200 Grand, 970-533-9019. The inn, located in a building dating from 1894, is a work in progress. Currently there are three downstairs rooms with private baths and antique furnishings. The upstairs rooms are hostel style, with shared bath, though plans are in the works to eventually convert some to rooms with private baths. But no matter what, "we'll always be pet friendly," promises owner Greg Raff (who's also the mayor of Mancos). Quiet dogs can be left unattended in the rooms. Or guest dogs might like to socialize with the two resident dogs at the inn. An antique shop, art gallery, and the Dusty Rose Cafe round out the premises.

$$ **Country West Motel**, 40700 Highway 160, 970-533-7073

$$ **Echo Basin Dude Ranch**, 43747 County Rd. M, 970-533-7000 (800-426-1890; www.echobasin.com). Dogs can stay in the A-frame cabins or tent and RV sites on this 600-acre former working ranch, though you may experience rather abrupt service when calling to inquire. A $100 deposit is required for a canine cabin stay. You can leave your four-legged dude unattended in the cabin for a couple of hours; be sure to keep him leashed when exploring the ranch's vast property. Closed from January to March.

$$ **Ponderosa Cabins**, 14068 Road 37, 970-882-7396 (www.coloradodirectory.

com/ponderosacabins). The two fully out-fitted cabins here are "pet friendly," says owner Jack Muller. One sleeps up to four people, and the other sleeps up to seven. There's a $10 one-time pet fee if your dog is a long-haired shedder. You can leave your dog unattended in your cabin for short periods as well as let him romp leash-free with you on the surrounding 8 acres, which are next to Summit Reservoir. Open April to end of November.

$$–$$$ Sundance Bear Lodge, 38890 Highway 184 (4 miles north of Mancos), 970-533-1504 (www.sundancebear.com). You and your dog will find a welcoming retreat at the lodge, tucked away on 80 acres close to national forest land. Accommodations consist of two rooms in the main house, a pondside log cabin, and a guesthouse duplex. Canine visitors are usually permitted only in the cabin (unless you rent out both sides of the guesthouse). The diminutive one-bedroom-plus-loft log cabin is the real thing and has a kitchenette and gas fireplace. You can rent it either B&B-style or with housekeeping included. Your dog can be left unattended inside and can explore the lodge's property with you off leash "if everybody's happy when their dog meets our dog," says owner Susan Scott. She adds that Chester, an Australian shepherd/Border collie mix, "mostly gets along with everybody." Three cats and two horses round out the animal welcoming committee.

Rico
$–$$ Rico Hotel, 124 S. Glasgow Ave. (Highway 145), 970-976-3000 (www.rico hotel.com). Your dog will certainly soak up some atmosphere at the hotel, built in 1925 as a boardinghouse for the Argentine Mine Company. Six of the 26 updated rooms have private baths; the others share facilities. Breakfast at the Argentine Grille next door is included. Dogs are discouraged from staying in the rooms on their own, but if you're really

in a bind, owner Jack Snow might be willing to keep an eye on your dog for a few hours. An outside kennel is also in the works. And at the end of the day, when you and Fido are exhausted from exploring the stunning peaks that sur-round the town, the vaulted-ceiling lobby with large stone fireplace is an inviting place to recoup your energy.

$$ Rico Motel, 24 S. Silver St., 970-967-2444. You may be able to leave your dog unattended in the room, depending on how well behaved he is.

Stoner
$$ Stoner Bed and Breakfast, 26085 Highway 145, 970-882-0110 (www.col orado-bnb.com/stoner). This small, rural B&B is located 16 miles northeast of Dolores in the tiny outpost of Stoner (yes, even dogs have been known to snicker at the name). One of the two guest rooms sleeps four and is located above the garage; it has cooking facilities and a deck. The other room, in the main house, has a double bed. Both have private baths. A resident Border collie mix is on hand to greet visiting dogs.

Campgrounds
Mesa Verde National Park. Off Highway 160, about 10 miles east of Cortez. The park's Morefield Campground has 490 sites.

Mancos State Park. See "Tail-Rated Trails" for directions (33 sites).

Forest Service campgrounds: McPhee Campground, at McPhee Reservoir near Dolores (73 sites); House Creek Camp-ground, also on the reservoir, reached via Forest Rds. 526 and 528 from Dolores (55 sites); Transfer Campground, north of Mancos on Forest Rd. 561 (12 sites); Mavreeso Campground (14 sites), West Dolores Campground (13 sites), and Burro Bridge Campground (15 sites) are located on Forest Rd. 535, 12.5 miles from Dolores on Highway 145 east. Private campgrounds: **Dolores River Cabins & RV Park** in Dolores; **A&A Mesa Verde Camper Cabins & RV Resort** and **Echo Basin Dude Ranch** in Mancos (see "Creature Comforts").

WORTH A PAWS

Anasazi Heritage Center, 27501 Highway 184, Dolores, 970-882-4811. Though your dog can't accompany you inside the museum to view the exhibits on Anasazi culture and artifacts on display, you're welcome to secure him to one of the benches outside while you wander through. The dog-friendly management can sometimes supply water dishes, and you can always fill up your dog's own dish from the "icy-cold water fountain," in the words of one museum staffer. Your dog can join you on the short hike up to the Dominguez and Escalante ruins; see "Tail-Rated Trails" for more information. The Heritage Center is open year-round except on Thanksgiving, Christ-mas, and New Year's Day. Hours are 9 a.m.– 5 p.m. during the summer; 9 a.m.–4 p.m. in winter. There's a $3 admission fee to the museum.

Lowry Pueblo. Excavated in 1928, the pueblo dates from A.D. 1090. It reflects styles of both the Chaco Anasazi (from the south) and the Northern Anasazi. You and your dog can take a self-guided tour of the pueblo and the adjoining Great Kiva as long as your dog remains on his leash. To reach the ruins, head north from Cortez on Highway 666 to Pleasant View (about 28 miles); turn left on County Rd. CC and drive 9 miles to the parking area.

Hovenweep National Monument. The monument, established in 1923, lies about 43 miles west of Cortez, straddling the Colorado/Utah border. The Square Tower Ruins, in Utah, are accessible by car; the other five ancestral Puebloan sites require short hikes. Your leashed dog is welcome to accompany you on this walk back through time (circa A.D. 1200). Bring lots of water. Expect to pay $3 per person, or $6 per vehicle, at the entrance. For more information, call 970-562-4282.

K & T Animal Board & Bath, Inc., 25628 Road L, Cortez, 970-564-8020. Wash that desert dirt from Rover's fur at this self-service dog wash. For $7 per dog, you'll get everything you need: shampoo, towels, grooming tools, and a dryer. (It's $1 extra to use a heavy-duty skunk shampoo.) Full-service grooming is also available.

DOGGIE DAYCARE
Cortez

Cedarwood Animal Clinic, 1819 E. Main, 970-565-6531. $9.50–$12/day, depending on the size of dog. Open 8 a.m.– 5 p.m., Monday to Friday; 9 a.m.–noon, Saturday.

Cortez Adobe Animal Hospital, 11314 Highway 145, 970-565-4458. Call for rates. Open 8 a.m.–5 p.m., Monday to Friday; 9 a.m.–noon, Saturday.

Cortez Animal Bed and Breakfast, 6815 Highway 160, 970-564-1385. $8–$10/ day, depending on the size of dog. Your dog will have plush accommodations in the indoor/outdoor heated kennels as well as four yards to play in with his fellow boarders. Hours are 8 a.m.–5 p.m., Monday to Friday; 8–10 a.m., Saturday. Late Saturday pickups and Sunday day-boarding can be arranged in advance.

K & T Animal Board & Bath, Inc., 25628 Road L, 970-564-8020. $7–$9/day, depending on the size of dog. Open 8 a.m.–5 p.m., Monday to Friday; 9 a.m.–2 p.m., Saturday. Earlier dropoffs and later pickups can be arranged in advance. There's also a self-service dog wash (see "Worth a Paws").

PET PROVISIONS
Cortez
Cortez Animal B&B, 6815 Highway 160, 970-564-1385

CANINE ER
Cortez
Cedarwood Animal Clinic, 1819 E. Main, 970-565-6531. Open 8 a.m.–5 p.m., Monday to Friday; 9 a.m.–noon, Saturday.

Cortez Adobe Animal Hospital, 11314 Highway 145, 970-565-4458. Open 8 a.m.–5 p.m., Monday to Friday; 9 a.m.–noon, Saturday.

Montezuma Veterinary Clinic, 10411 Highway 666, 970-565-7567. Open 8 a.m.–5 p.m., Monday to Friday; 8 a.m.–noon, Saturday.

RESOURCES
Colorado Welcome Center, 928 E. Main St., Cortez, 800-253-1616 (www.swcolo.org)

Dolores Visitor Center, 201 Railroad Ave., Dolores, 970-882-4018 (800-807-4712)

Mancos Visitor Center, 171 Railroad Ave., Mancos, 970-533-7434 (800-873-3310; www.mancos.org)

Mancos–Dolores Ranger District/Bureau of Land Management, San Juan/Rio Grande National Forest, 100 N. 6th St., Dolores, 970-882-7296

NINETEEN

Durango and Vicinity

THE BIG SCOOP

Dogs will find plenty to do in Durango, from sniffing out good hikes near town to wagging their tails at the world-class mountain bikers who frequent many of the trails. This is definitely a town geared toward outdoor activities. In addition, the resort area of Vallecito Lake, some 20 miles northeast of Durango, contains numerous dog-friendly accommodations (most along the order of cabins and campgrounds) and is surrounded by national forest land and hiking trails. It's also permissible for dogs to be under voice control in the Weminuche and South San Juan Wilderness Areas, both within the San Juan National Forest. And Pagosa Springs, an hour east of Durango, boasts the "world's largest hot springs" (for people only) in addition to nearby national forest trails (for dogs and people).

Note that in addition to the expected leash and dog-waste cleanup laws, Durango City Code prohibits tied-up dogs being left unattended on any public property. In other words, if you want to leave your dog outside while you dash in for a bagel and coffee, don't. (For your dog's safety, find a friendly passerby who's willing to dog-sit for a few minutes rather than leave your pet in the car on a warm day.) Within surrounding La Plata County, dogs can legally be off leash as long as they are under voice control and within your sight. In Pagosa Springs, dogs must be restrained, whether by leash or voice control. The Animal Control officer emphasizes, however, that you should be extravigilant if you choose to have your dog under voice

control to ensure against any wildlife-chasing escapades.

TAIL-RATED TRAILS

With the nearby San Juan National Forest as well as several trails in town, Durango is somewhat of a hiking mecca for dogs. The pamphlet "Hiking In and Around Durango," available at the Durango Area Chamber Resort Association, and Paul Pixler's *Hiking Trails of Southwest Colorado* describe many fine options in addition to those given here.

Durango

Colorado Trail/Junction Creek. 8 miles round-trip. From Main Ave. in town, turn west on 25th St. After 3.4 miles, turn left into the gravel parking area, just after the cattle guard. *Dogs can be off leash.*

This hike begins at the southwest terminus of the 469-mile Colorado Trail, completed in 1988. This portion of the trail offers excellent hiking, biking, and horseback riding, so be prepared to meet lots of other outdoor enthusiasts. Climb a fairly gentle grade for the first 2.5 miles. As it ascends, the trail clings to the side of a steep, walled ravine, providing breathtaking views (and challenging cycling if you're on a bike—you'd take a heckuva long tumble if your pooch got tangled up in your spokes). At 2.5 miles, cross a bridge and begin climbing a series of switchbacks for the next 1.5 miles to Gudy's Rest. The spectacular overlook is named for Gudy Gaskill, the driving force behind the construction of the

Colorado Trail. Stay for a while and let your dog savor the view before heading back the way you came.

 Red Creek. 6 miles round-trip. From Main Ave. in town, turn east on 32nd St. (by the City Market). Make a right on County Rd. 250 (toward Lemon Lake and Vallecito Lake), then go left at the next stop sign (Rd. 240). After a little over 7 miles, turn left on County Rd. 246 (at the sign marked "Colvic Silver"). Stay on this road for 1.2 miles, where you'll come to a gate; you may have to open (and close) it. After driving 0.3 mile farther, you'll see a small clearing on the right and another road leading up from it; you may want to park here, as the road gets a little rough after this point. If your car has four-wheel drive, continue straight through to the trailhead at road's end. *Dogs can be off leash.*

The trail follows Red Creek for most of the way, crisscrossing it several times, until about the last half mile, when it veers away to switchback steeply to the top of Missionary Ridge. This is a good hike for the active dog; you and he can enjoy a peaceful route through aspen, pine, and spruce accompanied by the symphony of the rushing creek. If you're feeling more ambitious, it's possible to make a slightly longer loop hike: Take a right on Missionary Ridge where the Red Creek Trail intersects the Missionary Ridge Trail (it's not signed). Look for the next distinct trail to the right after a short, steep climb. Descend down the ridge between Red Creek and the west fork of Shearer Creek; you'll end up back at the road to the Red Creek trailhead.

 Animas Mountain. 6 miles round-trip. From Main Ave. in town, turn west on 32nd St. At the T-intersection with W. 4th Ave., make a right. The road ends in a small parking lot at the trailhead. *Dogs must be leashed.*

Check out the sign at the trailhead to see the various loops available on this hike. In order to minimize hiker/biker conflict, a suggested hiking-only route is delineated by white arrows, and a suggested biking-only route is shown with blue arrows. Signs with white or blue arrows mark the routes along the way. The trail is dry, so bring water for you and your pooch.

Begin by climbing a series of gradual switchbacks; as you climb, the scenic Animas River Valley unfolds below. And you may hear the distinctive whistle of the Durango & Silverton Narrow Gauge train as it leaves town. Follow the route marked with the white arrows; it ascends through piñon, juniper, and stands of ponderosa pine. You'll eventually come to a series of vista points where you and your dog can enjoy views of the La Plata Mountains to the west and the Animas River as it snakes its way from the north through verdant flatlands. You can then either turn around once you've had your fill of views or continue up the trail, which loops back to the trailhead by way of the bike route. When you come to an unmarked juncture near the bottom of the mountain, stay left and head down the switchbacks to return to the parking area.

Animas River Trail. Enjoy an easy stroll along this approximately 6-mile paved trail that follows the Animas River through Durango. An easy place to access the trail is behind the Durango visitor center in Gateway Park, where parking is available. The trail runs close enough to the river that your dog can dip his toes in. And several parks along the way offer opportunities for a "green break." *Dogs must be leashed.*

Durango Mountain Park. From Main Ave. in town, turn west on 22nd St., which turns into Montview

DeChelly takes a rock-chewing break in Durango. (photo by Cindy Hirschfeld)

Pkwy. Drive until the road ends; several parking spots are available along the street. *Dogs must be leashed.*

This area, popular with mountain bikers (it's also known as the Test Tracks), consists of a network of crisscrossing trails. There are actually several access points, in addition to the one described above, from any of the streets that back up to the park. Don't expect to find any named or signed trails; this is a place to explore. You'll encounter two starting options from the Montview access: Go left on the trail at the road's end. A couple hundred feet later, another trail comes in from the north, which ascends up along a ridge. Or, stay on the lower trail and hike in the shade. You may have to do some puddle jumping in the spring. During the summer, the area is quite dry. Let your dog decide the route since there's no particular destination for these hikes.

Pagosa Springs

In addition to the trail described below, **Town Park** and the adjoining short, paved **River Trail** along the San Juan are pleasant respites for a dog. During our visit to town, we enjoyed watching an

agile black lab jumping in and out of the river to retrieve a stick while kayakers played in the current nearby.

Reservoir Hill. 6 miles of trail on 117 acres. From Hot Springs Blvd. off U.S. High-way 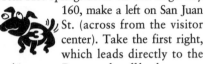 160, make a left on San Juan St. (across from the visitor center). Take the first right, which leads directly to the parking area. *Dogs can be off leash.*

You can make an infinite number of short loop hikes within the network of trails here. All the routes are clearly marked with blazes on the trees. You can ascend to various overlooks, including ones of the town, the hot springs, Wolf Creek Pass, and Pagosa Peak. A hike up to the San Juan overlook is a relatively quick way to view a nice panorama; your dog will discover lots of ponderosa pine and gambel oak to sniff through at the top as well as what could only be Paul Bunyan's picnic table.

There's no water along the trails, but you can fill up a water bottle at pumps at the main trailhead and at the water tower overlook.

CYCLING FOR CANINES

Because Durango offers such a bonanza of biking opportunities, picking up tips on suggested rides from locals is easy to do. Some areas to consider for short rides with Rover include the **Colorado Trail/Junction Creek** (see "Tail-Rated Trails"); the **Log Chute,** a short loop in the vicinity of the Colorado Trail that's not as heavily used; **Horse Gulch,** accessible from E. 8th Ave. and 3rd St. in Durango (your dog might enjoy the 4-mile **Meadow Loop**—go right at the first intersection you'll come to); **Lime Creek Rd.** (Forest Rd. 591), off Highway 550, a couple miles north of Purgatory (ride this old stagecoach route out and back for as long as you want); or the **Tuckerville Trail,** which starts at mile marker 11 off Middle Mountain Rd. near

Vallecito Lake and follows an old jeep road to a former mining site. Stop by **Hassle Free Sports, 2615 Main Ave., Durango, 970-259-3874 (800-835-3800)**, for maps and more specifics. In Pagosa Springs, the **Reservoir Hill** trail network (see "Tail-Rated Trails") is a great place to take along your dog for a short spin.

POWDERHOUNDS

Chimney Rock Archaeological Area. Although dogs are not allowed here during the summer, the Forest Service says that you're welcome to bring yours along as a ski or snowshoe partner in the winter. The 3.5-mile road up to the archaeological area is unplowed from about November to March, providing for an easy winter workout. To reach the area, drive 17 miles west from Pagosa Springs on Highway 160. At the Route 151 turnoff (by Lake Capote), turn south and continue for about 3 miles to the Chimney Rock entrance.

Pine River Valley Nordic Ski Club Trail System. A local Nordic club maintains a 10-kilometer network of groomed trails located on the southeast side of Vallecito Lake that wind along an unplowed road as well as through campgrounds and surrounding area. Your dog can accompany you, and because this is Forest Service land, he can be off leash. Call 970-884-7302 (Rick Callies) for more information.

CREATURE COMFORTS

Unless otherwise stated, dogs should not be left unattended in the room or cabin.

Bayfield

$$ Horseman's Lodge, 7100 County Rd. 501, 970-884-9733. Located halfway between Bayfield and Vallecito Lake, the motel allows dogs in any of its nine units, some with kitchenettes.

$$ Mountain Trails Inn and Cafe, 399 N. Mountain View Dr., 970-884-2780.

In what may be a disappointment to the erudite canine, dogs are not allowed anywhere on the Fort Lewis College Campus, located on the eastern end of town.

Dogs are allowed to stay in some of the motel's rooms for a $5 fee per night. There is a dog-walking area behind the motel (dogs should be kept leashed).

Durango

$ Country View Lodge, 28295 Highway 160 East, 970-247-5701. Dogs are allowed in smoking rooms only.

$ Durango East KOA & Kamping Kabins, 30090 Highway 160, 970-247-0783 (800-KOA-0793). Dogs are allowed in the cabins (you'll need to supply your own sleeping and cooking gear). There's a dog walk along a creek where you can bring your leashed companion. Open April 15 to October 15.

$ Lightner Creek Camper Cabins & Campground, 1567 County Rd. 207, 970-247-5406 (www.coloradovacation. com/camp/lightner). Dogs are allowed in the cabins as well as in the campground. The cabins are bare bones—you must bring sleeping bags and cooking equipment, and they have lighting but no electricity. Be sure to keep your dog leashed when outside. Open from the beginning of May to mid-September.

$–$$ Alpine Motel, 3515 N. Main Ave., 970-247-4042 (800-818-4042). The motel accepts dogs in some of its rooms, but as service can be terse, you and your dog may want to look elsewhere.

$–$$ Budget Inn, 3077 Main Ave., 970-247-5222 (800-257-5222). Dogs pay $10 extra per night plus a $10 deposit.

970-264-6814 (www.website.pagosa.net/ beourguest). The invitation extends to dogs, too, at this super-friendly B&B, which is also home to two dogs and a cat. Due to some unfortunate dog (or, more accurately, owner) experiences, however, the proprietors have had to reevaluate their pet policy, so make sure Fido is on his best behavior so that other dogs won't get the kibosh. You can pick from a variety of accommodations: five private rooms (three with their own baths), a lower-level area that sleeps sixteen, and an open sleeping loft in which you can rent a bed, hostel-style. Expect a $10 fee the first night for a dog, $5 per night thereafter. There's a lot next door where dogs can play while on leash.

$–$$ Bruce Spruce Ranch, 231 West Fork Rd. (16 miles northeast of Pagosa Spgs.), 970-264-5374 (www.bruce sprucer ranch.com). Dogs are welcome in all of the ranch's fully equipped cabins as well as in the RV and tent sites, on 40 acres bordered by national forest land. The large group facility known as the Faris House Lodge, however, does not allow pets; There's a $2.50 fee per night, per pet for the cabins. Dogs must be kept leashed when outside. The cabins are open May to October (the group facility stays open year-round).

$–$$ Piedra River Resort, Highway 160 and Piedra River (20 miles west of Pagosa Spgs.), 970-731-4630 (800-898-2006; www.horsebackriding.com). Dogs are allowed to stay in any of the one- and two-bedroom fully equipped cabins here., The owners request a credit-card imprint as a deposit against any damages. Keep your dog leashed (and picked up after) on the resort's 7 acres. As the website address implies, the resort also offers horseback riding. Open May to mid-November.

$–$$ Pinewood Inn, 157 Pagosa St. (Highway 160), 970-264-5715 (888-655- 7463; www.pinewoodinn.com). Dogs are allowed in select rooms, most of which are smoking, for $10 per night. One two-room cabin with kitchen is also available, and some of the motel rooms have kitchenettes.

$–$$ Skyview Motel, 1300 Highway 160 West, 970-264-5803 (888-633-7047). Dogs are welcome for a $5 fee per night. If you're paying with cash, a deposit might be required.

$–$$ Sportsman's Supply & Campground, 2095 Taylor Ln. (18 miles north of Pagosa Spgs.), 970-731-2300 (www.colorado vacation.com/camp/sportsman). The campground has six cabins that dogs can stay in. The owners prefer that you not leave your dog unattended in a cabin and require that you keep your dog leashed and clean up after him when exploring the campground's 10 acres. Open May 15 to November 15.

$$ Best Western Oak Ridge Lodge, 158 Hot Springs Blvd., 970-264-4173. Dogs can stay for $12 extra per visit.

$$ Indian Head Lodge, 631 Williams Creek Rd. (F.S. Rd. 640; 24 miles north of Pagosa Spgs.), 970-731-2282 (www.pag osa.com). For a $35 one-time fee, dogs (but no great big ones or wolf types, according to the proprietor) are allowed in the four cabins here, two of which come with kitchen facilities. Open end of May to mid-November.

$$ Pagosa Springs Inn, 3565 W. Highway 160, 970-731-4141 (888-221-8088). The hotel has some designated pet rooms.

$$ The Spa at Pagosa Springs, 317 Hot Springs Blvd., 970-264-5910 (800-832-5523; www.thespaatpagosasprings.com). The motel has its own hot springs (open to the public) as well as an on-site spa offering massage and other treatments. Your dog can join you for a $15 fee per night, per pet. Some rooms have kitchenettes or full kitchens.

$$ Super 8 Motel, corner of Piedra Rd. and Highway 160, 970-731-4005 (800-800-8000 [national number]). Dogs can stay here for $5 per night and a $20 deposit, though not in the motel's slightly more luxurious suites.

$$–$$$ Spring Inn, 165 Hot Springs Blvd., 970-264-4168 (800-225-0934; www.pagosasprings.net/springinn). Dogs are only allowed in smoking rooms.

$$$ Fireside Inn, 1600 E. Highway 160, 970-264-9204 (888-264-9204; www.firesidecabins.com). As far as dogs go, "just bring them and make sure they behave," say the operators of these one- and two-bedroom cabins. There's a $5 per night fee, per dog. Just a quarter mile outside of Pagosa Springs, the cabins are situated on 7 acres bordering the San Juan River.

$$$ Pagosa Realty Rentals, 40 Piedra Rd., 970-731-5515 (800-367-2140), has some dog-friendly homes available for short-term stays, with a $50 deposit.

$$$ Sunetha Management, 56 Talisman Dr., 970-731-4344 (800-365-3149), has a few short-term condo and home rentals available that will allow dogs with a $250 deposit.

Purgatory/Durango Mountain Resort

$$–$$$ Best Western Lodge at Purgatory, 49617 Highway 550 North, 970-247-9669 (800-637-7727; www.purgatorylodge.com). For $6 per pet, per night, your dog can stay with you at the base of Purgatory/Durango Mountain Resort ski area. Some units are condo style with full kitchens, ranging from studios to two bedrooms; others are standard hotel rooms.

$$–$$$$ The Nugget Cabin, 48721 Highway 550 (half mile south of Purgatory), 970-749-4742 or 970-385-4742 (www.nuggetcabin.com). Owner Dale Butt, who rents out this two-bedroom, 900-square-foot log cabin with outdoor hot tub, says dogs are "absolutely no problem" to have as guests. All you'll have to do is give a credit-card imprint as a deposit. As he puts no restrictions on four-legged occupants, you can leave yours unattended in the cabin (and go skiing, perhaps).

$$–$$$$ Sheraton Tamarron Resort, 40292 Highway 500 North (8 miles south of Purgatory/Durango Mountain Resort), 970-259-2000 (800-678-1000). Small to midsized dogs (those 50 pounds and under) get the nod here. There's a $15 per night fee, with a cap of $50 per stay. Check with the front desk about leaving your dog unattended in the room; a travel kennel is helpful for this. And housekeeping won't enter during that time. Amenities at the resort include indoor and outdoor pools, spa facilities, and two restaurants.

Vallecito Lake

$$ Circle S Lodge, 18022 County Rd. 501, 970-884-2473 (www.coloradovacation.com/lodges/circles). You can bring along your dog to stay in the one- to four-bedroom cabins for a $10 per night fee. One way to get Fido to be on his best behavior is to tell him that Virginia's Steakhouse is connected with the lodge and you might bring him some leftovers if he's lucky.

$$ DLR Lakefront Units, 14518 County Rd. 501, 970-884-4161. Dogs are welcome in any of the two- or three-bedroom cabins, which overlook the lake, and can be left unattended inside for short periods of time. Open May to September.

$$ Durango Resort on Vallecito Lake, 14452 County Rd. 501, 970-884-2517 (www.durangoresortonlake.com).

Formerly the Lake Haven, the resort allows dogs in about two-thirds of its lakeside cabins. They range from studio size to one that can sleep up to seventeen people, and all have full kitchens. There's a $10 fee per night, per pet. The lakefront location makes this an ideal base for water-loving hounds. Open May 1 to mid-October.

$$ Eagle's Nest, 18849 County Rd. 501, 970-884-2866 (www.coloradovacation. com/cabins/eagle). The Eagle's Nest complex, a mile from the lake's north end, permits dogs in any of its four cabins, all of which have three bedrooms and a kitchen. The owners also manage ten vacation homes (with three to four bedrooms) in the area, about half of which allow dogs. These rentals are available April through Christmas.

$$ Lone Wolf Lodge, 18001 County Rd. 501, 970-884-0414 (www.lonewolf lodge.com). For an extra $10 per night, dogs can stay in any of the four fully outfitted cabins here, which are a bit north of the lake. Keep your dog leashed when outside.

$$ Valley of Spruce Chalet, 19007 County Rd. 501, 970-884-2623. The friendly folks here welcome dogs in any of their six two- and three-bedroom cabins, situated on 9 acres along the Vallecito River. You can leave your nonbarking dog unattended in the cabin, and he can even run leash-free on the property as long as he "behaves and doesn't bite anyone." Open May to October.

$$–$$$ Bear Paw Lodge, 18011 County Rd. 501, 970-884-2508 (877-884-2508; www.coloradodirectory.com/bearpaw lodge). Dogs are permitted to stay in any of the lodge's one- to three-bedroom cabins, which have fireplaces or woodstoves, for a $10 fee per night. They must be kept leashed when exploring the wooded

property. The lodge is about a mile from the lake.

$$–$$$ Sawmill Point Lodge, 14737 County Rd. 501, 970-884-2669 (www.col oradovacation.com/lodges/sawmill). The lodge, across the road from the lake, has motel rooms with kitchenettes as well as two two-bedroom apartments. Dogs are allowed for $5 per night, per dog, and can be left unattended inside only in a travel kennel.

$$$ Croll Cabins, 4557 County Rd. 501A, 970-884-2083 (505-881-7235 in winter). There's a $10 fee per night for dogs to stay at these six lakeside two- to four-bedroom cabins. They must be kept leashed on the cabin property. Open from May to November.

Campgrounds

National forest campgrounds: Three campgrounds (**Florida, Miller Creek,** and **Transfer Park**) are at Lemon Reservoir, 17 miles northeast of Durango, via County Rds. 240 and 243; Vallecito Lake has seven campgrounds, including the 80-site **Vallecito Campground; Junction Creek Campground,** just west of Durango on 25th St. (38 sites), **East Fork Campground** (26 sites), **Wolf Creek Campground** (26 sites), and **West Fork Campground** (28 sites) are all reached via Highway 160 east from Pagosa Springs, heading up Wolf Creek Pass.

Private campgrounds: **Durango East KOA** and **Lightner Creek Campground** in Durango; **Bruce Spruce Ranch, Pagosa Riverside Campground,** and **Sportman's Supply and Campground** in Pagosa Springs (see "Creature Comforts" for all).

WORTH A PAWS

Pet Fair and Show. The La Plata County Humane Society hosts this fund-raising event each May at Durango's high school. Your dog can compete in judged categories such as "funniest looking," "most resemblance to owner," "best tail wagging," and "worst behaved." Call 970-259-2847 for information.

Pet Pride Day. Held in Pagosa Springs the second or third weekend of July in Town Park, this owner/dog event includes the 1-mile Paws Walk, with dogs in costume; competitions in categories such as best trick, best costume, and "longest" dog; information and pet products booths; and the K-9 9-K race, which you can run with or without a four-legged partner. The "pet blessing," done by a different denomination each year, opens the festivities. Proceeds from the day benefit the Upper San Juan Humane Society (970-731-4771).

Pack Rack (Humane Society thrift store), 269 Pagosa St., Pagosa Springs, 970-264-6424. As long as your dog is a well-behaved housebroken shopper, you can bring him along to explore the goods here, where sales fund the Upper San Juan Humane Society.

 Chimney Rock Archaeological Area. Only guided tours are available at the site of this one-time Anasazi community, located between Durango and Pagosa Springs, and dogs are not allowed to participate. A couple of kennels are available at the visitor center, where your dog can wait for you, but given the limited number, it's best to call ahead (970-883-5359). Dogs are welcome in wintertime (see "Powderhounds").

DOGGIE DAYCARE
Durango
Durango Animal Hospital, 2461 Main Ave., 970-247-3174. $21/day. Open 8 a.m.– 6 p.m., Monday to Saturday. Day boarding on Sunday can be arranged in advance for an additional charge.

Puppy Love, 130 County Rd. 234, 970-259-3043 (800-521-3843). $10/day. For an extra fee, the kennel will allow Durango & Silverton Narrow Gauge Railroad passengers to drop a dog off early, pick him up late, or bring him in on a Sunday. Regular hours are 7 a.m.–5 p.m., Monday to Saturday.

Willow Tree Kennels, 6510 County Rd. 203, 970-259-0018. $8.50–$10/day, depending on the size of dog, for regular day boarding; $20/day for dogs whose owners are taking the Durango & Silverton train, which involves an earlier dropoff and later pickup. Regular hours are 8 a.m.–5 p.m., Monday to Saturday.

Pagosa Springs
Pagosa Veterinary Clinic, 101 Cemetery Rd., 970-264-2148. $5/day. Open 8:30 a.m.–5 p.m., Monday to Friday; 9 a.m.–noon, Saturday.

PET PROVISIONS
Durango
Creature Comforts, 305 S. Camino del Rio (in the Centennial Shopping Center), 970-247-2748

Pagosa Springs
Creature Comforts, 135 Country Center Dr., Unit E, 970-731-9556
Pagosa Pet Parlor & Palace, 457 S. Highway 84, 970-264-5923

One attraction that dogs will have to skip is the Durango & Silverton Narrow Gauge Rail-road. If you opt to take the full-day trip on this historic coal-fired steam train, your dog can wait in comfort at one of several boarding kennels in Durango (see "Doggie Daycare").

CANINE ER

Durango

Durango Animal Hospital (AAHA certified), 2461 Main Ave., 970-247-3174. Open 8 a.m.–6 p.m., Monday to Saturday.

Pagosa Springs

Pagosa Veterinary Clinic, 101 Cemetery Rd., 970-264-2148. Open 8:30 a.m.– 5 p.m., Monday to Friday; 9 a.m.–noon, Saturday.

San Juan Veterinary Services, 102 Pike Dr., 970-264-2629. Open 9 a.m.–5 p.m., Monday to Friday.

RESOURCES

Bureau of Land Management, 15 Burnett Ct., Durango, 970-247-4082

Columbine Ranger District East, San Juan National Forest, 367 S. Pearl St., Bayfield, 970-884-2512

Durango Area Chamber Resort Association, 111 S. Camino del Rio, Durango, 970-247-0312 (800-525-8855;www.durango.org)

Pagosa Ranger District, San Juan National Forest, 180 Pagosa St., Pagosa Springs, 970-264-2268

Pagosa Springs Area Chamber of Commerce, 402 San Juan St., Pagosa Springs, 970-264-2360 (800-252-2204; www.pagosa-springs.com)

San Juan Public Lands Center, 15 Burnett Ct., Durango, 970-247-4082

Vallecito Lake Chamber of Commerce, 970-247-1573

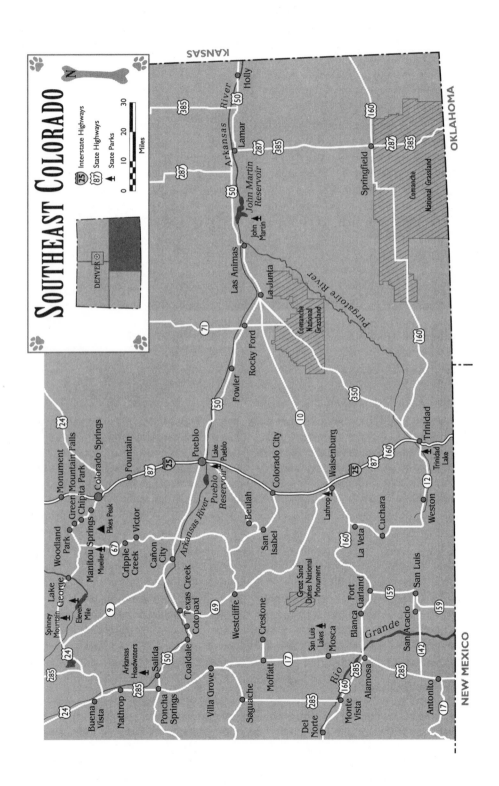

SOUTHEAST COLORADO

N

25 Interstate Highways
87 State Highways
▲ State Parks

Miles
0   10   20   30

DENVER ⊕

KANSAS

OKLAHOMA

NEW MEXICO

Holly
Arkansas River
50
385
287
Lamar
385
287
50
John Martin Reservoir
John Martin ▲
Springfield
160
287
385
Comanche National Grassland
Las Animas
La Junta
Purgatoire River
Comanche National Grassland
160
71
Rocky Ford
Fowler
350
50
Trinidad
10
Colorado City
Walsenburg
Trinidad Lake ▲
25
87
160
12
Weston
Pueblo
Lake Pueblo ▲
Pueblo Reservoir
Cuchara
Lathrop ▲
160
La Veta
25
87
Beulah
San Isabel
Fort Garland
Blanca
159
San Luis
159
San Acacio
142
Monument
24
Green Mountain Falls
Chipita Park
Colorado Springs
Fountain
87
Woodland Park
Manitou Springs
Mueller ▲
Pikes Peak
Victor
67
Cripple Creek
Cañon City
Arkansas River
Texas Creek
69
Cotopaxi
Westcliffe
Crestone
Great Sand Dunes National Monument
San Luis Lakes ▲
Mosca
117
Rio Grande
Lake George
Spinney Mountain ▲
Eleven Mile ▲
9
Arkansas Headwaters
Salida
50
Coaldale
Villa Grove
Saguache
Moffatt
285
Monte Vista
Alamosa
160
285
Antonito
17
24
285
Buena Vista
Nathrop
Poncha Springs
Del Norte

San Luis Valley and Vicinity

THE BIG SCOOP

The San Luis Valley encompasses a large portion of south-central Colorado. Though towns are few, small, and far between, your dog will exult in the thousands of acres of Rio Grande National Forest that stretch across the area. Leashed dogs are even allowed on the nature trail (4 miles round-trip) at the Alamosa National Wildlife Refuge, an 11,000-plus-acre preserve for thousands of birds on the Rio Grande River just southeast of Alamosa. You'll be pleased that a wide variety of accommodations welcomes dogs, from remote cabin resorts to luxury inns. There's even a motel in Monte Vista from which you and your dog can watch movies at the drive-in theater next door. Note that dogs will have to pass up a ride on the Cumbres and Toltec Scenic Railroad, one of the area's few "organized" attractions, which runs between Antonito and Chama, New Mexico.

TAIL-RATED TRAILS

 Great Sand Dunes National Monument. Located 38 miles northeast of Alamosa via U.S. Highway 160 east and Highway 150 north. *Dogs must be leashed.*

In 2000, federal legislation was passed to reclassify the monument as a national park. The official designation, however, is contingent on the purchase of Baca Ranch, a private inholding within the soon-to-be national park boundaries. As of spring 2001, the purchase was still pending. There are currently no plans to restrict access to dogs even when the national park designation takes effect, but it would be wise to call for an update (719-378-2312) before bringing your dog all the way here.

The sand dunes are the closest thing to the beach that your dog can experience in Colorado—minus all the water. At heights of nearly 700 feet (higher than many midwestern ski areas), the dunes are the tallest in North America. Though your dog might not quite appreciate the stunning contrast between snowcapped peaks in the background and 39 square miles of sculpted sand, he'll certainly enjoy burrowing his nose in something new and different. There are no set trails across the dunes, so you're free to explore, as long as Fido stays leashed. In June, July, and August, the temperature of the sand can get as high as 140°—which will burn paw pads—so stick to hiking during the early morning or evening if you visit during those months. The only water you'll find is that of Medano Creek, which borders the dunes on the east, so bring plenty along. For a change of pace from the sand, head east on the **Mosca Pass Trail**, which borders Mosca Creek and is on Forest Service land; your dog can hike here off leash.

San Luis Lakes State Park. 4 miles of trails. From Alamosa, head east on Highway 160 and turn north onto Highway 150. After 13.5 miles (a few miles before you reach the Sand Dunes), turn left onto Six Mile Lane; the park entrance is 8 miles farther on the right. *Dogs must be leashed.*

These hiking buddies eagerly anticipate their next adventure. (Photo by Cindy Hirshfeld)

Although the park does not contain the actual sand dunes of its well-known neighbor, the arid environment is desert-like, with only a few hardy plant species and a couple of shallow lakes. From the park, you and your dog are treated to a vista of extremes—the snowcapped four-teeners of the Sangre de Cristo Mountains fronted by the golden hues of the nearby Great Sand Dunes. (Stay until sunset and you and your four-legged friend may catch a stunner!)

There are two lakes at the park: the larger San Luis Lake, popular for water recreation, and the much smaller Head Lake, in the park's wildlife area. A connected series of wide gravel trails meanders along the eastern half of San Luis Lake, past a wetlands area, and about three-quarters of the way around Head Lake. Note that dogs are not allowed at the swim beach at San Luis Lake. The northern part of the park—the wildlife area—is closed to visitors (except by special advance arrangement) from February 15 to July 15.

CREATURE COMFORTS

Unless otherwise stated, dogs should not be left unattended in the room or cabin.

Alamosa

$ Alamosa KOA and Kamping Kabins, 6900 Juniper Ln., 719-589-9757 (800-

KOA-9157). Dogs are allowed in the three camper cabins here (you'll need to provide your own sleeping and cooking gear). Open May 1 to October 1.

$–$$ Rio Grande Motel, 2051 Main, 719-589-9095. Dogs are usually placed in smoking rooms here, though they can stay in nonsmoking rooms on request. There's an $4 fee per night.

$–$$ Sky-Vue Motel, 250 Broadway, 719-589-4945 (800-805-9164). The motel has eight pet rooms, one of which is nonsmoking. There's a $5 nightly fee per pet.

$$ Best Western Alamosa Inn, 1919 Main, 719-589-2567 (800-528-1234 [national number]). Dogs can stay at the motel for $6 extra per night.

$$ Holiday Inn of Alamosa, 333 Santa Fe Ave., 719-589-5833 (800-HOLIDAY [national number]). You need to put down a $25 deposit for your dog, and you can leave him unattended in the room for a short time. You'll also be asked to notify the front desk half an hour before you check out so that they can inspect your room and, hopefully, refund your deposit.

$$–$$$ Cottonwood Inn Bed and Breakfast, 123 San Juan Ave., 719-589-3882 (800-955-2623; www.cottonwood inn.com). "Well-behaved dog owners"—and their dogs—are welcome in the inn's suites, adjacent to the main building, with a $50 deposit. Two suites, one with modern, "Pottery Barn–style" decor, the other furnished with 1920s-era antiques, are open to dogs. All suites have a living room area, bedroom, bath, and kitchen. Quiet, nondestructive dogs may be left unattended in the rooms, as can all crated canines.

Antonito

$ Josey's Mogote Meadow, 34127

Highway 17 (5 miles west of Antonito), 719-376-5774 (800-877-2133; www.col oradodirectory.com/joseysmogotemead ow). Two cabins and two mobile homes (as well as an RV park) on 7 grassy acres are available to you and your dog. Open May 1 to mid-October.

$–$$ Narrow Gauge Railroad Inn, 5200 Highway 285, 719-376-5441 (800-323-9469; www.coloradodirectory.com/rrinn motel). Dogs are accepted with a $5 one-time fee. There's also an RV park here.

$–$$ Ponderosa Campground and Cabins, 19600 Highway 17 (16 miles west of Antonito), 719-376-5857 (www.col oradodirectory.com/ponderosacampcab ins). The campground also has five furnished cabins available, three equipped with a refrigerator and a hot plate for cooking and two with kitchenettes and private baths. Dogs are welcome as long as they're kept leashed when outside. Open Memorial Day to October 1.

$–$$$ Skyline Lodge, Forest Rd. 250 (about 49 miles from Antonito), 719-376-2226 (850-927-3337 in winter; www.col oradovacation.com/coloradoadven tureguides). The lodge, near Platoro Reservoir, wins the prize for remoteness of all the accommodations listed for Antonito. Luckily, a restaurant and a general store are on site (as well as stables). You could have an idyllic stay here with your dog in either a lodge room or one of sixteen fully outfitted cabins that sleep at least six. You'll be asked to put down a $25 deposit per pet. Dogs can be left unattended inside; they must stay on leash with their owners on the property, which is next to the Conejos River. Open from Memorial Day to the end of October.

$$ Conejos Cabins, Forest Rd. 250 (about 43 miles west of Antonito), 719-376-2547 (417-842-3279 or 877-827-9640 in winter, which is a good time to

book in advance, according to the proprietor; www.conejoscabins.com). Near the Continental Divide and well into the Rio Grande National Forest west of Antonito, these cabins on the banks of the Conejos River afford you and your dog relative solitude. The eleven one- and two-bedroom cabins are fully equipped, and some have fireplaces. There's a limit of one dog per cabin, with a $10 fee per night. Open Memorial Day to mid-October.

$$ Cottonwood Meadows Cabins, 34591 Highway 17 (5 miles west of Antonito), 719-376-5660. Dogs are permitted in these four one- and two-bedroom, fully equipped cabins with a $5 nightly fee. The owners also rent out a separate two-bedroom log cabin 15 miles west of Antonito on the Conejos River.

$$ Twin Rivers Guest Ranch and RV Park, 34044 Highway 17 (5 miles west of Antonito), 719-376-5710 (www.twn rvrs.com). There's a two-dog limit in the eight fully equipped cabins, which are on 15 acres by the Conejos River. Keep your dog on a leash on the property. If you happen to be traveling with your horse, he's welcome here too. Open May 15 to November 15.

$$–$$$ Conejos River Guest Ranch, 25390 Highway 17 (14 miles west of Antonito), 719-376-2464 (www.cone josranch.com). Choose from among the eight lodge rooms or six fully equipped one- to three-bedroom cabins. Part of the ranch's main building is 104 years old. There's a $10 one-time fee for dogs, who will probably be eager to explore the ranch's 12 acres within the Rio Grande National Forest—which they can do leash-free—or play along the mile of Conejos River frontage. If you do need to leave Fido behind for any length of time (say, to ride the Cumbres and Toltec Scenic Railroad), Shorty, the woman in charge, is willing

to dog-sit; two resident dogs may keep your dog company. A restaurant is on the premises, and horseback rides are available. Open May through November.

$$–$$$$ River's Inn and Swiss Cottage Bed and Breakfast, 317 River St., 719-376-6029 (www.coloradodirectory.com/swisscottagebb). Dogs are considered on a case-by-case basis at this B&B in downtown Antonito. Those that pass muster can stay in one of the four guest rooms, each with private bath, hardwood floors, and antique furnishings, for $10 extra per night. The house itself dates from 1917, and the rooms vary in size and decor, which accounts for the wide range of rates. You can leave your dog unattended inside only if he's in a travel crate; other options would be to contain him in the inn's fenced yard or see if owner Ursula Armijo might be able to keep an eye on him. The Swiss Cottage is a separate guesthouse behind the main house that is currently under renovation and will eventually be available for nightly rentals.

Blanca
$$ Mt. Blanca Game Bird and Trout, County Rd. CC, 719-379-3825 (www.mtblanca.com). Your dog can stay with you at this eight-room hunting lodge, within sight of 14,345-foot Blanca Peak, but the owners prefer you bring along a travel kennel for him. All rooms have private baths. Quiet dogs can be left unattended in the room (with or without kennel). About 75 acres surround the lodge, on which your dog can run and sniff leash-free (6,000 acres total comprise the available hunting preserve). And the three lakes within steps of the house are perfect for a quick doggie paddle, as long as guided fishing outings aren't taking place.

Creede
$–$$ Snowshoe Lodge, Highway 149 and 8th St., 719-658-2315 (www.creede-

co. com/snowshoe). The motel allows dogs for $5 extra per night, per dog.

$$ Broken Arrow Ranch, 32738 Highway 149 (12 miles southwest of Creede), 719-658-2484 (www.landoffice.net). For a $10 one-time fee, well-mannered dogs are allowed in the ten one- or two-bedroom rustic cabins, which are fully furnished and have wood cookstoves (as well as propane). Your dog can walk the 60 acres of property (bounded by national forest) off leash with you. Open Memorial Day to September 15.

$$ RC Guest Ranch, Highway 149 (17 miles southwest of Creede), 719-658-2253 (www.coloradodirectory.com/rrunningbarc). The ranch accepts dogs in its nine fully equipped cabins, which range from one to three bedrooms; you might be asked to put down a $25 deposit. You'll need to keep your dog leashed on the surrounding 40 acres. An on-site restaurant serves country-style dinners starting June 1; the ranch also offers horseback trail rides and pack trips as well as hunting trips. Open May 15 to November 1.

Crestone
$$ White Eagle Village, 67485 County Rd. T (4 miles west of Crestone), 719-256-4865 (800-613-2270; www.toski.com/white-eagle). This nonsmoking hotel offers a few designated pet rooms for $10 extra per night, and dogs can be left unattended inside. A restaurant, fitness room, sauna, conference center, and even an art gallery are located within the complex.

$$–$$$ Alder Terrace Inn, Alder St., 719-256-4975 (888-609-6407; www.crestonebaca.com). The inn offers one- and two-bedroom suites with kitchens. One dog at a time can stay in just one of the one-bedroom units, for $10 extra per night. In really special cases, you may be able to arrange a stay in a two-bedroom

suite with your dog, "but you'd really have to talk me into it—and I don't just mean catching me when I'm in a good mood," states Katy, the owner. In July 2001, the Alder Crest Hotel, under the same ownership, is slated to open, and Katy promises upscale accommodations that will also be pet-friendly.

Del Norte

$ Del Norte Motel, 1050 Grand Ave., 719-657-3581 (800-372-2331). The motel has a cafe that comes in handy if you or your dog need a snack.

Fort Garland

$ The Lodge, Highway 160 West at Gilpin, 719-379-3434. The owners of the motel say they're used to having dog guests, especially when field trials are being held in nearby Blanca. Most of the rooms are pet friendly, and a $5 one-time fee per dog is charged. All rooms have microwaves and refrigerators.

Moffatt

$$ Willow Spring Bed and Breakfast, 223 Moffatt Way, 719-256-4116 (www.willow-spring.com). Dogs with responsible owners are welcome to stay at this nine-room B&B, housed in a hotel built in 1910, with a $50 deposit. In keeping with the historic theme, the rooms, all of which share baths, are furnished with antiques, and Oriental rugs warm up the communal living room and parlor on the first floor. Check with the owners about letting your dog stay unattended in the room for short periods of time.

Monte Vista

$ Whispering Pines Motel, 401 Ulysses Blvd., 719-852-5952. Check at the front desk about the possibility of leaving your dog unattended in the room.

$–$$ Rio Grande Motel, 25 N. Broadway, 719-852-3516 (800-998-7129). There's a $5 fee per pet, per night.

$$ Best Western Movie Manor, 2830 W. Highway 160, 719-852-5921 (800-771-9468; www.coloradovacation.com/motel/movie). Unique in its own right, your stay here can be enhanced by the company of your dog. True to its name, the Movie Manor provides big-screen entertainment (from May to September) via the drive-in theater next door. Your room is equipped with speakers, so you can just lie on the bed and watch away. Dogs are restricted to smoking rooms only, however, and there's a $5 fee per night, per dog.

$$ Comfort Inn, 1519 Grand Ave., 719-852-3584 (800-221-2222 [national number])

Mosca

$–$$ Great Sand Dunes Oasis and Camper Cabins, 5400 Highway 150 North (at the entrance to the national monument), 719-378-2222. "We love pets," say the owners of the Oasis. Dogs are allowed in the four camping cabins (bring your own bedding) and at the teepee sites as well as in the two motel rooms, though the owners prefer that dogs be kept in travel kennels in the latter. Make sure your dog is on leash when outside. Open May 1 to October 31.

$$ Great Sand Dunes Lodge, 7900 Highway 50 North (at the entrance to the national monument), 719-378-2900. The motel allows dogs with a $10 one-time fee. Open April 1 to October 31.

Saguache

$ Hillside Motel, 440 Gunnison Ave. (Highway 285), 719-655-2524

$–$$ Saguache Creek Lodge, 21495 Highway 285, 719-655-2264. There's a $5 fee per dog, per night.

San Acacio

$$ Casa de Salazar, 603 Main, 719-672-

3608 (www.casadesalazar.com). Under new ownership as of June 2000, the Casa, housed in a Queen Anne Victorian, allows dogs in any of its four newly remodeled rooms for a $10 one-time fee. All rooms have private baths and are furnished in styles ranging from Art Deco to country. A stay here includes evening snacks as well as a full breakfast.

San Luis

$$ San Luis Inn, 138 Main St., 719-672-3399 (877-672-3331). Dogs are allowed in one room at the motel (and it's a smoking room) for $10 per night.

South Fork

Because Wolf Creek ski area is so close to South Fork, all cabin resorts, in addition to the motels, stay open year-round.

$–$$ Budget Host Ute Bluff Lodge, 27680 Highway 160 West, 719-873-5595 (800-473-0595; www.uteblufflodge.com). The lodge offers furnished cabins (from studio to two bedrooms) and motel rooms, and dogs are welcome in either for a $5 one-time fee. If you'll be staying in one of the cabins for three or more nights, there's a $25 one-time dog charge. Extra bedspreads are available for your dog's sleeping comfort.

$–$$ Grandview Cabins and RV Park, 613 Highway 149 West, 719-873-5541 (www.grandview.com). Most of the ten fully furnished cabins (some have fireplaces) are dog compatible. There's a $10 fee per night, per pet.

$–$$ The Inn Motel, 30362 Highway 160 West, 719-873-5514 (800-233-9723; www.coloradodirectory.com/innmotel cabins). It's $5 per night, per dog, for canine guests. Three two-bedroom cabins are also available for rent. You can leave your dog unattended inside if he's in a travel kennel.

$–$$ Spruce Lodge, 29431 Highway 160 West, 719-873-5605 (800-228-5605; www.thesprucelodge.com). The lodge, a log structure built in 1924, offers motel rooms and B&B rooms as well as two cabins with two bedrooms and a kitchen (the only difference between the motel and B&B rooms is that the motel rooms have private baths). There's a $10 nightly fee for dogs. The lodge is under relatively new ownership (which means that the previous owners are no longer available for dog sitting), but an outdoor kennel where dogs can be left unattended is being considered.

$–$$ Wolf Creek Ranch Ski Lodge, Highway 160 (9 miles west of South Fork), 719-873-5371 (800-522-9653; www.wolfcreekco.com/ranch). Your dog can join you in any of six fully equipped riverside cabins (one is actually a four-bedroom house) or eight motel rooms with kitchenettes.

$–$$ Wolf Creek Ski Lodge and Motel, 31042 Highway 160, 719-873-5547 (800-874-0416; www.southforkco.com/wclodge). Some of the motel rooms are also available with kitchenettes.

$–$$$ Chinook Lodge and Smokehouse, 29666 Highway 160 West, 719-873-9993 (888-890-9110; www.bbhost.com/chinooklodge). Your dog will probably start salivating as soon as you tell him that the lodge's eleven cabins, on 8.5 acres, are next to a smokehouse. All kinds of smoked meats are for sale year-round; in the summer, smoked trout and salmon join the menu. As for the cabins, they were built in the late 1800s and have been used for guest lodging since 1908. They range in size from one to two bedrooms, and most have kitchens and rock fireplaces. Dogs pay a $5 nightly fee.

$$ Comfort Inn, 0182 E. Frontage Rd., 719-873-5600 (800-285-6590). Dogs can stay in a few of the motel's rooms for a $10 fee per visit.

$$ Cottonwood Cove Lodge and Cabins, HC 33 Highway 149 West (13 miles from South Fork), 719-658-2242 (www.coloradodirectory.com/cotton woodcovelodge). Dogs are welcome in the resort's cabins, though not in the lodge, for a $10 one-time fee. All but three of the thirty fully outfitted cabins are pet friendly. They range from studio-size to three bedrooms, and you can leave your dog unattended inside. There's also a restaurant on the premises. Although the resort is open year-round, only six of the cabins are winterized.

$$ Goodnight's Lonesome Dove Cabins, 18065 Highway 160 West (6 miles west of South Fork), 719-873-1072 (800-551-3683; www.southfork.org/goodnights). In one of those happy coincidences of name and profession, the owners of this small lodging complex are actually the Goodnights. Dogs are permitted in the seven fully outfitted cabins, ranging from one to three bedrooms, for a $5 one-time fee per pet. They must stay on leash when outside the cabins.

$$ Lazy Bear Cabins, 29257 Highway 160 West, 719-873-1443 (877-873-1443; www.lazybearcabins.com). Dogs are welcome in any of the eight two-bedroom, fully outfitted cabins and can be left unattended inside as long as they're in a travel kennel. They can sniff around the surrounding 2.5 acres under voice control with their owners.

$$ South Fork Lodge and RV Park, 0364 Highway 149, 719-873-5303 (877-354-2345; www.coloradodirectory.com/southforklodge). Dogs can stay in six of the twelve fully furnished cabins for a $10 one-time fee, per dog, with smaller dogs more likely to get the nod. The owners ask that you be extradiligent

about not letting Fido on the bed. You can leave your dog unattended in the cabin if he's in a travel crate, and you must keep him on a leash when outside.

$$–$$$ Riverbend Resort, 33846 Highway 160 West, 719-873-5344 (800-621-6512; www.riverbend-resort.com). For a $10 one-time fee Rover can stay with you in one of the twelve fully equipped studio to four-bedroom cabins with fireplace at this resort that once did double service as a movie set for *National Lampoon's Vacation.* Although you should keep your dog leashed when walking around the property, he can play down by the river (South Fork of the Rio Grande) under voice control.

$$–$$$ Rocky Mountain Associates, 719-873-5688. This rental operation has units ranging from one bedroom, one bath to a four-bedroom, two-bath house. The units include two single-family homes, with three bedrooms and two baths, known as the Moore Cabins. Dogs are permitted on a case-by-case basis, with a deposit possible; you can leave your dog unattended inside.

Villa Grove
$ Inn at Villa Grove, 34094 Highway 285, 719-655-2203. This small motel has three rooms and accepts dogs with a $25 deposit. You can leave your dog unattended in the room. Also on site is the Villa Grove Trade, a convenience/general store with a deli.

Campgrounds
Great Sand Dunes National Monument, 38 miles northeast of Alamosa via Highways 160 and 150. The **Pinyon Flats** campground is open year-round.

San Luis Lakes State Park, about 25 miles northeast of Alamosa via Highway 17 and Six Mile Lane (51 sites).

TWENTY-ONE

Arkansas River Valley and Vicinity

THE BIG SCOOP

The San Isabel National Forest figures prominently in the area described in this chapter, which includes the Arkansas River towns of Buena Vista, Salida, and Cañon City as well as Monarch Pass to the west and the Wet Mountains to the south. This translates into a wide range of dog-friendly hikes, many with no leash requirements. The buff dog might want to hike up one of the eleven 14,000-foot-plus peaks that dot the Sawatch Range in the area west of U.S. Highway 285. You can also bring Fido to several more traditional tourist attractions. However, he will have to sit out the raft trips that draw crowds to the area during the summer.

All the major towns in this vicinity have leash laws in effect. In Fremont County (home to Cañon City), dogs can be under voice control as long as they remain within ten feet of their owner. And, unfortunately, all town parks in Salida are closed to canines.

TAIL-RATED TRAILS

The Forest Service offices in Salida and Cañon City and the BLM office in Cañon City can provide details on the hundreds of trails in the area. One easily accessible option is given below if you want to escape the Royal Gorge–focused bustle of Cañon City. In addition, the Cañon City visitor center has a brochure with nine local trail descriptions. And the visitor center in Salida sells *Back Country Trails in the Heart of the Rockies,* by Jim Stotler. (See "Resources" for the locations of the visitor centers.)

Waterdog Lakes. 3.4 miles round-trip. Although we haven't actually hiked this trail, the name itself may cause your dog's ears to prick up with interest. The trail leads to a pair of lakes scenically situated at the base of the Continental Divide near the top of Monarch Pass. Take U.S. Highway 50 west from Salida to the Monarch Park turnoff past Garfield. Parking is at the side of the highway. *Dogs can be off leash.*

Arkansas Riverwalk. About 2.5 miles of trail along the Arkansas River plus 1.2 miles around John Griffin Regional Park. There are a few different access points, but this one is the most central: From Highway 50 in Cañon City, head south on Raynolds Ave. (the second traffic light in town if coming from the east). After crossing the Arkansas (in less than a mile), look for a trailhead sign and a large parking area on the left. *Dogs must be leashed.*

Although just a short distance from busy Highway 50, the wide gravel riverfront trail seems miles away. It's just you and your dog, the rushing of the water, and the rustle of cottonwood leaves in this verdant setting. Benches are strategically placed in shady spots along the route. If you're looking for a good jogging path for you and the pooch, this is the place. Head west (under the bridge) from the parking area, and you'll get a nice view of the jagged Sangre de Cristo Mountains rising to the west. This direction will bring you to the loop around

John Griffin Regional Park, an 80-acre nature park that also has some unmaintained paths leading through it.

CYCLING FOR CANINES

Mountain-biking options abound in this area, but keep in mind that many of the ones you'll see mentioned in guides involve riding on dirt roads with vehicle traffic. When you want to take your dog along, try a section of the **Rainbow Trail,** which runs for 100 miles from southwest of Salida to Music Pass south of Westcliffe. One of the best parts to try is the one known as **Silver Creek,** which runs for 13 miles from the west end of the Rainbow Trail to Highway 285. Motorized vehicles (e.g., dirt bikes) are prohibited from a portion of the route. Reach the trail by driving 5 miles south of Poncha Springs on Highway 285. You can access a 5.5-mile (one-way) section of singletrack on the **Old Midland Railroad Grade** by going 5 miles east of Johnson Village on Highway 285/24, then heading north on Forest Rd. 315. The **South Fooses Creek Trail,** which includes 3 miles of jeep road and 3 miles of singletrack, is another good ride. Take Highway 50 about 4 miles west of Maysville to County Rd. 225 south.

POWDERHOUNDS

Dogs in search of snow have lots of great trails to sniff out in the area. One to try is the **South Fooses Creek Trail** (see "Cycling for Canines").

The **Browns Creek Trail** is an 11-mile round-trip ski or snowshoe to picturesque Browns Lake. Take Highway 285 about 11 miles north of Salida to County Rd. 270. Drive 1.5 miles to County Rd. 272; drive on this for 2 miles to an intersection, where you'll turn left. The trailhead is 1.5 miles farther.

North Cottonwood Creek Rd. runs into the heart of the Collegiate Range, near the base of the Continental Divide. From the stoplight in Buena Vista, drive north to County Rd. 350. Take a left, then a right at the intersection with County Rd. 361. A sharp left will bring you onto County Rd. 365 and to a plowed parking area, from where you'll commence skiing.

CREATURE COMFORTS

Unless otherwise stated, dogs should not be left unattended in the room or cabin.

Buena Vista

$–$$ **Alpine Lodge Resort, 12845 Highways 24 & 285 (Johnson Village), 719-395-2415 (888-322-4224).** The motel permits lap-sized dogs in two of its smoking rooms. There's a $35 deposit as well as a $5 fee per night. You can leave your dog unattended in the room as long as he's in a travel kennel.

$–$$ **Collegiate Peaks Family Inn and RV Park, 516 Highway 24 North, 719-395-2251 (888-PEAK-INN).** It's nice to know that "family" includes the dog at this Christian-run motel. There's a $5 fee per night.

$–$$ **Great Western Sumac Lodge, 428 Highway 24, 719-395-8111 (888-SUMAC-90).** Dogs are allowed in designated rooms with a $20 deposit and a $5 nightly fee.

$–$$ **Lakeside Motel, 112 Lake St., 719-395-2994 (800-248-7684).** Extremely well-behaved dogs and their responsible owners are welcome at the motel, with a potential $10 fee per dog, per night. There are only two rooms in which dogs of all sizes are allowed, though lap-sized dogs are also permitted in the other rooms. The motel is near one of the town parks where Cottonwood Creek widens, hence the "lake" in the name.

$–$$ **Piñon Court Motel, 227 Highway 24 North, 719-395-2433.** The motel rents out studio and one-bedroom apartment-style

Shanda, the mayor of Guffey. (photo courtesy of Bruce Buffington)

Perhaps the coolest town government in Colorado belongs to the hamlet of Guffey, northwest of Cañon City off Highway 9. The mayor, Shanda, is a golden retriever. She took office in 1993, when her feline predecessor, Whiffy Legone, retired from politics. Shanda presides over the town from her home at the Guffey General Store and Bootlegger Spirits, where you can visit her year-round. And Shanda's mayoral platform? "Her only platform is the front porch of the general store," says owner Bruce Buffington.

cabins that are fully equipped. You can leave your dog unattended inside, though your room won't get cleaned during that time. There's a park across the street where your leashed dog can stretch his legs.

$–$$ Thunder Lodge, 207 Brookdale Ave., 719-395-2245 (800-330-9194; www.thunderlodge.com). The lodge, on Cottonwood Creek in downtown Buena Vista, offers seven fully furnished log cabins that sleep from two to six, plus dog.

$–$$ Topaz Lodge, 115 Highway 24 North, 719-395-2427 (800-731-5906). The motel, across from a town park, accepts dogs for $5 extra per night.

$$ Arkansas Valley Adventures (AVA) Rafting and Cabins, 40671 Highway 24 (13 miles north of Buena Vista), 719-395-2338 (800-370-0581; www.coloradorafting.net). Dogs are allowed in any of the five cabins here with a $5 per night fee (the same as for an extra person). All cabins are one room, with two double beds; three have kitchens. Keep your dog leashed on the property, where there's plenty of room to run with him. The cabin operators also offer raft trips. Open mid-May to the end of September.

$$ Potter's House Bed and Breakfast, 28490 County Rd. 313, 719-395-6458. You and your dog can stay riverside in a log cabin on the Arkansas, with Mexican-style decor, hardwood floors, and a deck from which you can almost cast your fishing line. "Dogs love it here, especially if they like the water," says the owner. Your dog must promise, however, to be a good canine guest and not jump on any of the beds. There are resident dogs as well. Open May 1 to the end of September.

$$ Sagewood Cabins, 38951-B Highway 24 (11.5 miles north of Buena Vista), 719-395-2582. You and your dog can enjoy a quiet, relaxing stay in these fully furnished log cabins, decorated in a country style with some antiques. A few of the cabins have fireplaces. There's a $1.50 fee per dog, per night. You'll need to keep your dog leashed on the property, but the San Isabel National Forest is right next door. Open from April to the end of October (exact dates depend on the weather).

$$ Vista Court Cabins and Lodge, 1004 W. Main, 719-395-6557 (www.vtinet. com/vistacourt). Though dogs are not usually allowed in the lodge rooms, smaller ones (i.e., less than 40 pounds) can stay in any of the eight log cabins, which are fully equipped, for $5 extra per night during the winter, $10 per night in the summer. Large dogs can most likely be accommodated in winter but not during the motel's busy summer season. You'll need to keep your dog leashed on the 3 acres surrounding the cabins.

$$ Vista Inn, 733 Highway 24 North, 719-395-8009 (800-809-3495; www.vtinet. com/vistainn). Dogs are allowed in four designated pet rooms (two nonsmoking, two smoking) in this newer motel with a $50 deposit and a $7 nightly fee. There's a nice outdoor hot tub complex, and ample open space behind the motel where you can walk your dog. Continental breakfast is served daily—you can leave your dog unattended in your room for a short time in the morning while you eat, though not at other times.

$$–$$$ Woodland Brook Cabins, 226 S. San Juan, 719-395-2922 (www.wood landbrookcabins.com). Your dog will find a haven at Woodland Brook, where canines are actively welcomed (and he's sure to give a paws-up to the printed commentary on dog guests at the front desk). Fifteen fully equipped log cabins, ranging from studio to two bedrooms, are situated on 5 acres within walking distance of town. Built in 1910, they're clean and comfortable while retaining a rustic mountain cabin charm. Most have fireplaces. Appealing touches include colorful quilts and curtains, and dried flower arrangements. "We love animals," says owner Riaan van Niekerk, who has three of his own dogs as proof. Visiting dogs can explore the grounds off leash as long as they are under voice control and can perhaps pick up a few Frisbee-catch-

ing pointers from the resident dogs. You'll receive a supply of biscuits and poop pick-up bags for Fido on check-in—make extrasure you use the latter!

Cañon City

$ Fort Gorge Camper Cabins, Campground, and RV Park, 45044 Highway 50, 719-275-5111. Dogs are allowed in two of the three camper cabins at this complex located close to the Royal Gorge Bridge. Though you'll have to bring your own bedding and cooking gear, the cabins do come equipped with a small fridge. You can't leave your pooch unattended in the cabin, but there's a small fenced area with some hay and a doghouse where he can hang out if you need to leave him temporarily behind. Open May 1 to October 15.

$ Royal View Camper Cabins and Campground, 43590 W. Highway 50, 719-275-1900. There are three camper cabins (bring your own bedding) at the Royal View, which is 10 miles west of Cañon City, near Royal Gorge. Leashed dogs are allowed, although they can't be brought into the service building (which houses a grocery, game room, etc.).

$–$$ Best Western Royal Gorge Motel, 1925 Fremont Dr., 719-275-3377 (800-231-7317). Small to medium-sized dogs are permitted in smoking rooms only for a $15 one-time fee. You can leave your dog unattended in the room.

$–$$ The Historic St. Cloud Hotel, 631 Main St., 719-276-2000 (800-405-9666; www.stcloudhotel.com). The St. Cloud is one of the oldest hotels in Colorado that your dog has the opportunity to stay in. Built in 1879 in the nearby town of Silver Cliff, the hotel was dismantled and rebuilt in Cañon City, reopening in 1886. Today, each of the characteristically high-ceilinged twenty-five rooms is individually decorated, with some period furnishings.

One four-legged guest is allowed per room.

$–$$ **Holiday Motel, Highway 50 and 15th St., 719-275-3317.** With a $25 deposit (if you're paying with cash) and a $5 standard nightly fee, dogs are allowed in some of the motel's rooms. You can leave Fido unattended in the room.

$–$$ **Knotty Pine Motel, 2990 E. Main, 719-275-0461 (www.coloradovacation. com/motel/knotty).** There's a $5 one-time fee for small dogs, $10 for larger dogs. Although you can't leave your dog unattended in the room, you can leave him for a short time in the kennel behind the motel as long as he won't constantly bark.

$–$$ **Parkview Motel, Highway 50 and 3rd St., 719-275-0624.** Dogs are allowed in a few rooms for $5 to $10 extra per night.

$$ **Cañon Inn, 3075 E. Highway 50, 719-275-8676 (800-525-7727).** The motel has three (out of 152) designated pet rooms, each of which has sliding glass doors that open to the outside. A $50 deposit is required.

$$ **Comfort Inn, 311 Royal Gorge Blvd. 719-276-6900.** Dogs under 25 pounds

Climbing a fourteener provides a perfect photo opportunity. (photo by Stacy Gardner)

are permitted in designated pet rooms for a $10 one-time fee.

Coaldale
$ **Big Horn Park Resort, 16373 Highway 50, 719-942-4274 (877-942-4274; www.big hornpark.com).** The resort has a combination of motel rooms, camper cabins, and fully equipped log cabins. Dogs are allowed in a few of the motel rooms, one of the log cabins, and all of the camper cabins, with a $25 deposit. You can leave your dog unattended inside as long as you let the housekeeping staff know. Keep him leashed outside (where there's a half mile of frontage on the Arkansas River). Open April 1 to October 31.

$ **Hidden Valley Camper Cabins and Campground, 340 City Rd. 40, 719-942-4171.** Dogs are permitted in the five camper cabins (bring your own sleeping and cooking gear). They must be kept leashed on the property, which includes several ponds.

Cotopaxi
$–$$ **Arkansas River KOA and Loma Linda Motel, 21435 Highway 50, 719-275-9308 (800-562-2686; www.col oradodirectory.com/arkansasriverkoa).** This KOA offers you and your dog a whole slate of options for $5 extra per night: camping cabins (bring your own sleeping bag), furnished cabins without kitchens, motel rooms, and fully equipped cabins with kitchenettes. And there's access to the river for when your dog wants to cool off. Dogs must be kept on a six-foot leash when outside; there's to be "no barking, no biting, no fighting"; and all poop must be picked up. Open April 1 to October 31.

Monarch Pass Area
$$ **Monarch Mountain Lodge, Highway 50, near the top of Monarch Pass, 719-539-2581 (800-332-3668).** In its third decade of operation, the 100-room lodge,

across from Monarch ski area, allows dogs in smoking rooms only for $15 per night, per pet. Because you can't leave your dog in the room unattended, you'll need to find other lodging if you're bringing Fido along on a ski trip. But during the summer, you'll both be in the heart of the outdoor action.

$$ Ski Town Condominiums, Highway 50, next to the Monarch Mountain Lodge, 719-539-7360 (800-539-7380). Enjoy a stay with your dog in these two-bedroom condos near the top of Monarch Pass and the Continental Divide.

$$ Wagon Wheel Guest Ranch, 16760 County Rd. 220, 719-539-6063. This small, well-established guest ranch in Maysville, about halfway up Monarch Pass, has six cozy one-room cabins, all fully furnished and with extra touches such as handmade quilts and curtains. Dogs can recreate on leash with their owners on the surrounding 2.5 acres. Open Memorial Day to Labor Day.

Nathrop
$$–$$$ Love Ranch/Cabins at Chalk Creek, 18670 County Rd. 162, 719-395-2366 (www.coloradodirectory.com/loveranch). The guest ranch, on three acres in Chalk Creek Canyon, has three cabins, which dogs can stay in for a $10 one-time fee. The two larger, modern cabins have private baths; the one-room "rustic" cabin has its own private outhouse. All cabins have cooking facilities. From Memorial Day to Labor Day, the cabins are rented by the week only, from Saturday to Saturday; otherwise, there's a two-night minimum. Keep your dog leashed on the property. Open May to October.

Poncha Springs
$–$$ Poncha Lodge, 10520 Highways 50 & 285, 719-539-6085 (800-315-3952). Small nonshedding dogs get the okay here; three rooms (one nonsmoking) are

pet designated. Rooms have knotty-pine interiors.

$–$$ Rocky Mountain Lodge and Cabins, 446 E. Highway 50, 719-539-6008 (866-539-6008). Dogs are permitted in smoking rooms at the motel and in both of the one-room cabins (with kitchens) for a $10 fee per night.

Salida
$ Motel Westerner, 7335 W. Highway 50, 719-539-2618. You can leave your dog unattended in your room at this small motel.

$–$$ American Classic, 7545 Highway 50, 719-539-6655 (800-682-8513). Dogs are permitted with a $5 one-time fee. You'll also be asked to sign a pet release form taking responsibility for any damage done and agreeing that you won't leave Fido unattended in the room.

$–$$ Aspen Leaf Lodge, 7350 W. Highway 50, 719-539-6733 (800-759-0338). The motel has six designated pet rooms, three of which are nonsmoking. Dogs up to 50 pounds are allowed with a $6 nightly fee. There's also a pond on the property, and dogs can be off leash as long as they're under voice control.

$–$$ Circle R Motel, 304 E. Highway 50, 719-539-6296 (800-755-6296; www.salida.com/circlermotel). Dogs 30 pounds and under are accepted (with some size exceptions made) for $5 extra per night in summer, $3 per night in winter. One unit with a kitchenette is available, and there's a hot tub outside the motel.

$–$$ Econo Lodge, 1310 E. Highway 50, 719-539-2895 (800-55-ECONO). Dogs up to 40 pounds can stay in one of the motel's four pet rooms—two nonsmoking—for $5 extra per dog, per night. There's a gravel alley in back of the motel where you can walk your dog off leash if he's well behaved.

$–$$ Mountain Motel, 1425 E. Highway 50, 719-539-4420. The motel has five newer rooms and three cabins (two with kitchenettes); dogs are permitted in all with a $50 deposit.

$–$$ Rainbow Inn, 105 E. Highway 50, 719-539-4444 (800-539-4447). Lots of open space and picnic areas surround the motel, which your dog can enjoy as long as he is leashed. There's a $3 nightly fee for pets.

$–$$ Silver Ridge Lodge, 545 W. Highway 50, 719-539-2553 (877-268-3320). There's a $5 one-time fee for a dog.

$–$$ Travelodge, 7310 W. Highway 50, 719-539-2528 (800-234-1077). Dogs are allowed for $5 per dog, per night. Some rooms have Jacuzzi tubs.

$–$$ Woodland Motel, 903 W. 1st St., 719-539-4980 (800-488-0456). You've got to love a place like the Woodland, which has its priorities straight: The motel's listing of amenities is preceded by the word "pets." Canine guests are greeted with their own quilted dog cushion and biscuits on check-in. Their owners will appreciate the motel's simple but well-kept efficiency units and two-bedroom suites with full kitchens. There's an alley behind the motel for convenient dog walking.

$$ Flamuzzi Bed and Breakfast, 16140 Highway 50 (10 miles west of Salida), 719-539-9334 (www.flamuzzi.com). The B&B is actually a two-bedroom, one-bath house on the way to the Monarch ski area that you can rent out. (The unusual name is taken from the combination of flames, via a fireplace in one of the two living rooms, and the Jacuzzi outside.) As for the breakfast part, the owner will provide you with provisions, but it's up to you to actually prepare it. The house can sleep up to eight, and the decor is "rustic cozy." You can leave your dog unattended inside, or, if he gets along with dog-loving owner Troy Teske's Aussie shepherd mix and Irish Wolfhound mix, he can share their nearby dog run. As of now there's no extra deposit for dogs, but one may be implemented in the future.

$$–$$$ Beddin' Down Bed and Breakfast, 10401 County Rd. 160 (4 miles from Salida), 719-539-1815 (800-470-1888; www.beddindown.com). If your dog enjoys communing with farm animals, he'll enjoy visiting this 24-acre working ranch—"you name it, we've got it," says the owner, mentioning cows, horses, chickens, dogs, and cats as some of the residents. Dogs are allowed inside the rooms for $5 for one night, $10 (one-time fee) if you're staying more than one night, as long as they stay in a travel crate; if your dog doesn't have his own crate, you can borrow one from the owners. There are also some dog runs behind the house where your dog can stay if he's used to overnighting outdoors. The five rooms in the modern log main house all have private bath, TV, and VCR and feature varied decor, including the Pueblo sunrise room, which is "all John Wayne," another with aspen-log beds and furniture, and one that's "real frilly." The largest room sleeps eight to ten. A hot tub, snacks in the afternoon, and full breakfast round out the amenities.

$$$ Cedar Ridge Ranch, 12500 County Rd. 258 (between Salida and Buena Vista), 719-539-6639. Dogs will love Cedar Ridge, as they'll have lots and lots of property (1,100 acres) to explore leash-free. A two-bedroom guesthouse sleeps up to twenty people, while the bunkhouse cabin accommodates four. Both have kitchens, and the guesthouse also has an indoor sauna and hot tub. You can leave your dog unattended inside at your discretion. During the summer, the ranch offers horseback riding.

San Isabel
$$ The Lodge at San Isabel, Highway 165 (10 miles north of Rye), 719-489-2280. This family-style resort in the Wet Mountains includes cabins situated on the shores of Lake Isabel (although some have kitchens, you'll have to bring your own cooking and serving dishes). There's a $15 one-time fee for a dog, and he can be left unattended in the cabin. Open mid-May through October.

$$ Pine Lodge, 18488 Highway 165, 719-489-268 (www.pinelodge.accu link.net). Located within a couple hundred yards of Lake Isabel, these six rustic one-room cabins are dog-friendly. Four have full kitchen facilities; the other two have a microwave, refrigerator, and sink. You can let your dog sniff outside under voice control.

Westcliffe
$ Antlers Motel, 102 S. 6th St., 719-783-2426. If your dog gets a hankering for beer and chips, Antlers Liquor and General Store is conveniently located next door.

$–$$ Westcliffe Inn, Highway 69 and Hermit Rd., 719-783-9275 (800-284-0850). Dogs are allowed to stay in the motel's older rooms.

Campgrounds
Arkansas Headwaters Recreation Area. Part of the state parks system, the recreation area consists of 148 miles of the Arkansas River and the area immediately surrounding it. Several campgrounds along the way are accessible by vehicle, including Ruby Mountain (22 sites) and Hecla Junction (21 sites), off Highway 285 south between Buena Vista and Salida; and

Rincon (15 sites) and Five Points (21 sites), off Highway 50 east of Salida.

National forest campgrounds: Cottonwood Lake Campground, south on County Rd. 344 from Cottonwood Pass Rd. (28 sites); Collegiate Peaks Campground, west of Buena Vista on Cottonwood Pass Rd. (56 sites); Cascade Campground, 9 miles west from Nathrop on Chalk Creek Rd. (23 sites); Monarch Park Campground, Highway 50, near the top of Monarch Pass (38 sites); Oak Creek Campground, south of Cañon City on 4th St. to County Rd. 143 (15 sites); and Alvarado Campground, southwest of Westcliffe—take Highway 69 south to Schoolfield Rd. west (47 sites).

Private campgrounds: Arkansas River KOA in Cotopaxi, Hidden Valley Campground in Coaldale, Royal View and Fort Gorge Campgrounds in Cañon City (see "Creature Comforts" for all).

WORTH A PAWS
Royal Gorge Bridge. Your dog won't want to miss one of Colorado's most popular tourist attractions. The gorge boasts the world's highest suspension bridge, which spans the Arkansas River at 1,053 feet. Dogs are not allowed on the incline railway or the aerial tram, but you can take your leashed pooch on a walk across the bridge. The Royal Gorge Park encompasses 5,000 acres with lots of scenic overlooks that you and your dog can enjoy together. The park and bridge are located 8 miles west of Cañon City, via Highway 50, and are open year-round. There is an entrance fee. For more information, call 719-275-7507.

Buckskin Joe Park and Railway. Let your dog experience the Wild West during a visit to Buckskin Joe's (and he won't have to run behind a covered wagon to get there). A re-created Western town, the park allows leashed dogs to join you in touring the "historic" buildings, watching staged gunfights, and, of course, stocking up on souvenirs. Or maybe your dog would like to try his paw at panning for gold. Buckskin Joe's also operates the Royal Gorge Scenic Railway, which will take you and Fido on a thirty-minute round-trip ride to the rim of the gorge. The park is open May 1 to October 1. From Memorial Day to Labor Day, hours are 9 a.m.–6 p.m.; hours are shorter during the rest of May and September. The railway stays open from March to November 15; hours are 8 a.m.–8 p.m., Memorial Day to Labor Day, with shorter hours before and after those dates. Located 8 miles west of Cañon City, at Royal Gorge. For more information and ticket prices, call the park at 719-275-5149 or the railway at 719-275-5485.

Monarch Scenic Tram. The gondola whisks you and your leashed dog from the top of Monarch Pass to 12,000 feet in a matter of minutes, giving you a bird's-eye view of the neighboring peaks. There's a glass-enclosed observatory at the top for your viewing comfort, though you're free to wander around outside as well. This is a good option for the dog who doesn't want to work too hard for a panoramic vista. The gondola runs continuously throughout the day from May through early November. Call 719-539-4091 for current ticket prices or more information.

Bishop Castle. Your dog is welcome to tour this massive stone and iron work-in-progress with you as long as you keep him under control. Since 1969, Jim Bishop has worked on creating the castle-like structure, which is intended for public use, completely on his own. There's no admission charge, and the castle is open year-round. To reach it, drive 6 miles north from Lake San Isabel on Highway 165. You'll see a sign on the right side of the road; park alongside the roadway and cross it to get to the castle.

Arf Walk. Held annually the last Saturday of September, the walk benefits the Ark Valley Humane Society. Leashed and fully vaccinated dogs and their owners meet at Riverside Park in Salida (the only time dogs can sniff out this usually off-limits site) and go on a 2.25-mile stroll through downtown. After the walk, participants can browse the dog-related exhibits or enter contests for closest dog/owner look-alike, waggiest tail, and biggest and smallest dogs. Funds are raised through the registration fees, and all humans get a T-shirt. Water stations are set up along the walk route; owners should bring plastic bags to pick up after their pets. For more information, contact the Ark Valley Humane Society at 719-395-2737 (www.ark-valley.org).

Royal Gorge Route Rail-road. Unfortunately, dogs are not able to accompany their owners on this two-hour train ride along the Arkansas River through Royal Gorge. However, the railroad operators will help you find pet-sitting options for your four-legged traveler. The train operates year-round. Call 888-724-5748 (303-569-2403 if you're calling from the Denver metro area) for more information.

If your dog is hankering for some road snacks, stop by Bongo Billy's in Buena Vista (713 S. Highway 24) or Salida (300 W. Sackett) and pick up treats baked by the Colorado Barkery out of Salida. Flavors include Cheesy Bonz and Peanut Butter Delights. You'll find a yummy array of coffee drinks, baked goods, and sandwiches to choose from.

DOGGIE DAYCARE
Cañon City
Kenline Veterinary Clinic, 1426 S. 9th St., 719-275-2081. $8–$14/day, depending on the size of dog. Open 8 a.m.–6 p.m., Monday to Friday; 8 a.m.–5:30 p.m., Saturday.

Nathrop
Double J Cross Kennel, 17605 Highway 285, 719-539-4080. $15/day. Open 7 a.m.–6 p.m., Monday to Friday; weekends by appointment.

Salida
Mountain Shadows Animal Hospital, 9171 W. Highway 50, 719-539-2533. $6/day. Open 8 a.m.–noon and 1:30–5:30 p.m., Monday to Friday; 8 a.m.–noon, Saturday; 6–7 p.m., Sunday (for pickups).

PET PROVISIONS
Buena Vista
Martin Feed, 15415 County Rd. 306, 719-395-4044

Salida
Quality Farm and Country, 210 E. Rainbow Blvd., 719-539-8689

Westcliffe
Feed Barn, 61199 Highway 69, 719-783-9398

CANINE ER
Buena Vista
Buena Vista Veterinary Clinic, 30400 Highway 24 North, 719-395-8239; after hours: 719-395-6408. Open 8:30 a.m.–noon and 1:30–5 p.m., Monday to Friday; 9 a.m.–noon, Saturday.

Cañon City
Kenline Veterinary Clinic (AAHA certified), 1426 S. 9th St., 719-275-2081. Open 8 a.m.–6 p.m., Monday to Friday; 8 a.m.–5:30 p.m., Saturday.

Salida
Mountain Shadows Animal Hospital, 9171 W. Highway 50, 719-539-2533. Open 8 a.m.–noon and 1:30–5:30 p.m., Monday to Friday; 8 a.m.–noon, Saturday.

RESOURCES
Cañon City Chamber of Commerce, 403 Royal Gorge Blvd., 719-275-2331 (800-876-7922; www.canoncitychamber.com)

Custer County Chamber of Commerce, 2 Bassick Pl., Westcliffe, 719-783-9163

Greater Buena Vista Area Chamber of Commerce, 343 Highway 24 South, Buena Vista, 719-395-6612 (www.buenavistacolorado.org)

Heart of the Rockies Chamber of Commerce, 406 W. Highway 50, Salida, 719-539-2068 (877-772-5432; www.salidachamber.org)

Salida Ranger District, Pike/San Isabel National Forests, 325 W. Rainbow Blvd. (Highway 50), Salida, 719-539-3591

San Carlos Ranger District, Pike/San Isabel National Forests, and Bureau of Land Management, 3170 E. Main St., Cañon City, 719-269-8500

TWENTY-TWO

Pueblo and Points Southeast

THE BIG SCOOP

This chapter covers an area from the southeast plains of Colorado to Trinidad, about 20 miles north of the New Mexico border, up through the Cuchara Valley, and north to Pueblo, the metropolis of the region. It's a lot of territory for your dog to sniff, but the attractions he'll most want to explore tend to be spread out. Pueblo and the eastern plains, especially, can be ovenlike during the summer, so for your dog's sake, plan excursions to areas near water (see "Tail-Rated Trails," below, for some ideas). The dry Comanche National Grasslands area is best suited for a spring or fall visit.

In Pueblo, dogs must be leashed within city limits; on county land, they can be under voice control. Because the extensive River Trail system is overseen by the city, dogs must be kept leashed on all of the trails.

TAIL-RATED TRAILS

 Vogel Canyon (Comanche National Grasslands). 2.25 miles round-trip. The route to Vogel Canyon feels something like driving down an airport runway, so flat and open is the landscape. From La Junta, take Highway 109 south for 13 miles. Look for a sign to Vogel Canyon on the right. After 1 mile, turn left (at the sign) and proceed 2 miles to the parking lot. *Dogs are requested, but not required, to be on leash.*

Hiking Vogel Canyon is a bit like a step back in time to the frontier days of the prairie. You and your dog will likely be the only ones there. Four trails begin at the trailhead; a pleasant loop com-
bines portions of three of them. Start on the **Canyon Trail,** making your way through a cattle guard just past the parking area. The trail is marked by large stone cairns as it makes a gradual descent among large stands of juniper. It soon heads through the namesake grasslands, which also feature flowers and cacti. Eventually you'll reach some standing pools of water—actually a spring—where your dog may want to cool off, as the canyon is otherwise hot and dry. You'll see a three-way fork here, as well as a cairn; turn right to take the **Mesa Trail.** After crossing a dry streambed, go left, then through the fence opening, and follow the diagonal tracks in the grass. The trail is fairly clear, with some cairns along it.

Keep hiking below a series of rock outcroppings, ignoring any cairns you may spot above, until you come to a rectangular foundation. These are the remains of a stagecoach stop that operated in the 1870s. Just beyond them are three cairns in front of a rocky area. Scramble east up through the rocks, keeping to the left. At the top, look to the northeast for another cairn. Once you reach this cairn, you should be able to spot another to the east. The rest of the Mesa Trail follows a series of cairns. Shortly after climbing over a stile, your route intersects with the **Overlook Trail,** a wide gravel path. A left brings you back to the trailhead.

Lake Pueblo State Park. From Pueblo, take U.S. Highway 50 west to Pueblo Boulevard. Turn left (south) and drive about 4 miles to Thatcher

The Cuerno Verde Rest Area at the Colorado City exit off I-25 (Exit 74) has a large dog-walking area for pups on a leash.

Ave.; turn left (west), and drive 6 miles to the park entrance. (You can also access the park from the north, farther west on Highway 50, via McCulloch Boulevard.) *Dogs must be leashed.*

The park boasts 16.5 miles of paved trail, known as the **Dam Trail,** which runs along the north side of the lake and connects with the **Pueblo River Trail** system. The most scenic portion of the trail runs east from the Juniper Breaks Campground to the Rock Canyon area. There's also a short (1.5 miles round-trip) interpretive trail on the south side of the park, which begins at the Arkansas Point Campground and leads up a bluff.

Note that dogs are not allowed at the Rock Canyon swim beach area.

Lathrop State Park. From Walsenburg, head west on Highway 160 for a little more than 3 miles to the park entrance on the right. *Dogs must be leashed.*

The **Hogback Trail,** an easy 2-mile loop, winds through large stands of piñon and juniper as it ascends, via a series of moderate switchbacks, the Hogback Ridge. From the top, you'll have a nice view of the twin Spanish Peaks to the south and the Wet Mountains to the north—and, on a clear day, Pikes Peak. Pamphlets for a self-guided nature tour are available at the trail-head, which is on the north side of Martin Lake. Bring enough water for you and your dog, as the trail is dry.

Unfortunately, the park no longer has an off-leash animal exercise area; a group picnic facility has been constructed on the site. And note that dogs are not allowed on Martin Beach.

For picnicking with your dog in a less-frequented area of the park, try the North Martin Inlet.

 Pueblo River Trails. A paved trail system runs for about 21 miles through Pueblo, east–west along the Arkansas River and north–south along Fountain Creek. The Arkansas River Trail connects with the paved trails in Lake Pueblo State Park. *Dogs must be leashed.*

Although there are numerous trail access points in Pueblo, by far the nicest place to pick up the trail is at the Greenway and Nature Center just west of downtown. The most straightforward way to get there is to take Highway 50 west from town to Pueblo Boulevard. Turn left (south) and travel about 2.5 miles to Nature Center Rd. on the right (it's W. 11th St. on the other side of Pueblo Blvd.). Take the road to its end, where there's lots of parking at the Nature Center complex.

From here, either head east toward town (after about 2 miles, the trail gets a little sketchy and is not as scenic, however) or head west, where 3.5 miles of trail bring you to the state park. Hiking near the Nature Center is especially serene. The mighty Arkansas just purrs along at this point, and abundant cottonwood drape over the river. A small network of gravel paths begins behind the Nature Center and goes by the river, allowing your dog to dip his paws in. The Nature Center includes a large picnic area as well as a full-service restaurant, the Cafe del Rio, with outdoor seating—perfect for enjoying a beverage by the river with your dog.

If you're looking for a short walk closer to the center of town, the **Runyon Lake Trail** travels 1.2 miles around its namesake lake. Parking is available at the end of Juniper, by Runyon Field.

Trinidad Lake State Park. From Exit 14A off I-25 at Trinidad, follow the signs for Route 12; the park is about 3 miles west on Route 12, on the left. *Dogs must be leashed.*

The park has several hiking trails, the busiest of which is the 1-mile **Levsa Canyon** self-guided nature trail. For more secluded hiking with your dog— though you'll need to keep an eye out for mountain bikers—try the 4-mile (one way) **Reilly Canyon Trail** starting from its west end. To reach the trailhead, drive about 3 miles past the main park entrance and take a left at the Cokedale turnoff to access the Reilly Canyon entrance. Cross over two cattle guards; the trailhead is about 200 yards past the second one, on the left. The trail is hot and dry, so early morning—as well as spring and fall—are the best times to hike here with your dog. Bring lots of water. The trail meanders, with moderate ups and downs, through piñon and juniper woodlands along a mesa above the lake. You and your dog can enjoy photo-worthy views of the lake as well as of square-topped Fisher's Peak, which looms above Trinidad.

You can also reach this trail from the east via the first quarter mile of the Levsa Canyon Trail, which begins at the Carpios Ridge Campground at the main park entrance. The Reilly Canyon Trail, clearly marked, branches off to the west. Hiking from east to west, you'll encounter a fairly steep descent into Levsa Canyon.

To allow your panting pooch access to the lake, continue on the road to Reilly Canyon (see above), past the trailhead. Once the road turns east, it dead-ends shortly afterward close to the lake. Also at this junction, **Old Highway 12**, now unmaintained, heads west. Park your car along the shoulder and take your dog for a solitary walk near the Purgatoire River. The road ends about 2 miles later, at the park's western boundary.

The 2.5-mile **South Shore Trail**, while providing scenic views of the lake, follows a rather overgrown roadbed next to railroad tracks. Skip it.

CREATURE COMFORTS
Unless otherwise stated, dogs should not be left unattended in the room or cabin.

Beulah
$$$–$$$$ **Beulah House**, 8733 Pine Dr., 719-485-3201 (888-304-7831; www.pueblo online.com/beulah). "Good" dogs are welcome to stay with their owners in any of this B&B's four rooms, including a Spanish hacienda–style suite. Keep Fido leashed on the B&B's six acres because of abundant wildlife (the two resident German shepherds are under the same restriction). The owners also rent out several houses in the Wet Mountains where you can stay with your dog.

Colorado City
$ **Pueblo South/Colorado City KOA & Kamping Kabins**, 9040 I-25 South, 719-676-3376 (800-KOA-8646). Small dogs (poodle sized) are allowed in the cabins here for $2.50 per night extra, with a maximum total fee of $5. You'll have to supply your own bedding and cooking gear.

$$ **Greenhorn Inn**, I-25 at Exit 74, 719-676-3315. The motel has six designated rooms at the back of the motel for dogs—closest to where you should take Fido to do his thing. There's a $10 nightly fee. The motel also has an outdoor kennel where dogs can spend the night at no extra charge.

Cuchara
$$–$$$ **River's Edge Bed and Breakfast**, 90 E. Cuchara Ave., 719-742-5169 (www.ruralwideweb.com/rebb.htm). "We allow well-behaved dogs and extremely well-behaved children—and we prefer the dogs," quips owner Mike Moore. The B&B, on the Cuchara River

in town, has five guest rooms, some with private baths, all furnished with newer log furniture. Eight more rooms are available in the newly renovated Dodgeton Creek Inn next door. You can leave your dog unattended in your room at your own discretion, but he'll probably be more eager to explore the adjacent national forest land, about thirty yards away. In addition to breakfast, human guests can enjoy complimentary wine in the evening.

Fowler

$–$$ Blue Spruce Inn, 2nd and Highway 50, 719-263-4271. Dogs are considered on a case-by-case basis, with no more than two dogs allowed per room.

Holly

$ Gateway Motel, 1016 W. Colorado, 719-537-6805. You can leave your dog unattended in the room, but if he does any damage, "you're buying it," warns the motel operator. A recent guest ended up paying for a bathroom door and some carpeting in addition to his room fee.

La Junta

$ La Junta Travel Inn, 110 E. 1st St., 719-384-2504. Dogs pay $4 extra per night and are generally put in smoking rooms. You can leave your dog unattended in the room only if he's in a travel kennel.

$ Mid-Town Motel, 215 E. 3rd St., 719-384-7741. Pascal the bichon enjoys greeting dog visitors at this friendly place. You can leave your dog unattended in the room if he's in a travel kennel.

$ Stagecoach Motor Inn, 905 W. 3rd St., 719-384-5476. The motel takes small dogs (those under 40 pounds) only.

$ Westerner Motel, 1502 E. 3rd St., 719-384-2591. Small dogs (say, poodle sized and under) are allowed in smoking rooms only.

$$ Holiday Inn Express, 27994 Highway

Don't leave us behind! (photo by Cindy Hirschfeld)

50, 719-384-2900 (800-HOLIDAY [national number]). There's a $10 one-time pet fee.

$$ Quality Inn, 1325 E. 3rd St., 719-384-2571 (800-LA-JUNTA). Dogs are allowed only in smoking rooms in the motel's older wing.

Lamar

$ Blue Spruce Motel, 1801 S. Main, 719-336-7454. There's a $2 fee per night, per dog.

$ Golden Arrow Motel, 611 E. Olive St., 719-336-8725 (800-600-8091). Small dogs are allowed in smoking rooms only, with a $5 fee per night, per pet.

$ Lamar Super 8, 1202 N. Main, 719-336-3427 (800-800-8000 [national number]). Large dogs will have to pay a $5 one-time fee.

$ Passport Inn, 113 N. Main, 719-336-7746 (888-596-3100). There's a $5 fee per night, per dog.

$ Travelodge, 1201 N. Main, 719-336-7471. Dogs need to put down a $5 nightly fee.

$$ Best Western Cow Palace Inn, 1301 N. Main, 719-336-7753 (800-678-0344).

You can leave your dog unattended in the room, though if he barks excessively (till the cows come home?), the motel management will call Animal Control.

Las Animas

$ Colonial Inn, 638 Bent Ave., 719-456-0303. The motel operator emphasizes that a dog can't be left alone in the room.

$$ Best Western Bent's Fort Inn, 10950 E. Highway 50, 719-456-0011 (800-528-1234 [national number]). You can leave your dog unattended in the room "as long as he's not a barker."

La Veta

$$ Circle the Wagons Motel, 124 N. Main, 719-742-3233. Dogs can circle the wagons for a $5 one-time fee.

Pueblo

$ Country Bunk Inn, 3369 I-25 South (Exit 91), 719-564-1840. The motel has had "the whole gamut of critters" as guests, according to the owner, including horses, mules, goats, cats, ferrets, and, of course, dogs. You can leave your dog unattended in the room as long as you let the front desk know.

$ Motel 6 I-25, 4103 N. Elizabeth, 719-543-6221 (800-4-MOTEL6 [national number]). If you stay in one of the motel's "studio" rooms, which have kitchenettes, there's a $25 deposit for your dog; otherwise, there's no deposit. You can leave your dog unattended in the room as long as he's in a travel kennel.

$ Pueblo KOA & Kamping Kabins, 4131 I-25 North, 719-542-2273 (800-KOA-7453). You'll need to bring your own bedding and cooking supplies for the cabins.

$–$$ Microtel Inn, 3343 Gateway Dr., 719 (Exit 94), 719-242-2020 (888-771-7171 [national number]). Dogs are welcome with a $50 deposit, and nonbarkers

can be left unattended in the room. A continental breakfast (bagels, muffins, cereal, etc.) is included in the rate.

$–$$ Motel 6 West, 960 Highway 50 West, 719-543-8900 (800-4-MOTEL6 [national number]). You can leave your dog unattended in the room as long as he's in a travel kennel.

$–$$ Piñon Inn, 4803 N. I-25, 719-545-3900. There's a $10 fee per night, per pet, and you can leave your dog unattended in the room at this motel and truck stop.

$–$$ USA Motel, 414 W. 29th St., 719-542-3268. You can leave your dog unattended in the room as long as you let the folks at the front desk know.

$$ Best Western Townhouse Motel, 730 N. Sante Fe, 719-543-6530. Dogs get the nod for one of the several pet rooms.

$$ Hampton Inn, 4703 N. Freeway, 719-544-4700 (800-972-0165). Only dogs under 25 pounds are allowed, and they generally have to stay in a smoking room, for a $25 one-time fee.

$$ Holiday Inn of Pueblo, 4001 N. Elizabeth, 719-543-8050 (800-465-4329 [national number]). Dogs can stay in smoking rooms only.

$$ Ramada Inn, 2001 N. Hudson, 719-542-3750. Dogs are accepted with a $75 deposit. You can leave yours unattended in the room if he's in a traveling kennel.

$$ Villager Lodge, 800 Highway 50 West, 719-543-6820 (800-328-7829 [national number]). Small to medium-sized dogs are accepted with a $100 deposit.

Rocky Ford

$ Melon Valley Inn, 1319 Elm Ave., 719-254-3306 (800-367-5991). Dogs are welcome with a $10 deposit.

Springfield

$ J's Motel, 265 Main, 719-523-6257. Dogs can stay for $4 extra per night.

$ The Stage Stop, 1033 Main, 719-523-4737. This older hotel (the building dates from 1906) has two downstairs rooms, with private baths, where dogs are usually put. However, if you'd prefer an upstairs room with shared bath for you and your dog, it can probably be arranged.

$ Starlite Motel, 681 Main, 719-523-6236. There's a $5 fee per night for a dog.

Trinidad

$ Frontier Motel, 815 Goddard Ave., 719-846-2261

$ Trail's End Motel, 616 E. Main, 719-846-4425. There's a $5 one-time pet fee, and the motel has recently updated its rooms.

$–$$ Budget Host Trinidad, 10301 Santa Fe Trail Dr., 719-846-3307 (800-BUD-HOST). It's $5 extra per night for a dog.

$–$$ Budget Summit Inn, 9800 Santa Fe Trail Dr., 719-846-2251. Dogs are welcome in outside-facing rooms for a $10 one-time fee.

$–$$ Downtown Motel, 516 E. Main, 719-846-3341. Small dogs only, please, with a $5 one-time fee. The motel is, indeed, in downtown Trinidad.

$–$$ Super 8 Motel, 1924 Freedom Rd. (Exit 15 off I-25), 719-846-8280 (800-800-8000 [national number]). Dogs pay a $10 one-time fee at this newer Super 8.

$$ Best Western Trinidad Inn, 900 W. Adams, 719-846-2215 (800-955-2215). Dogs 25 pounds and under get the okay here. They can be left unattended if they have a travel kennel in which to stay.

$$ Days Inn, 702 W. Main, 719-846-2271 (800-DAYS-INN [national number]). There are four designated pet rooms, and the fee for your dog is $6 per night.

$$ Stone Mansion, 212 2nd St. 719-845-1625 (877-264-4279; www.bbdirectory. com/inn/stone-mansion). Well-behaved dogs are accepted at this B&B on a case-by-case basis. The mansion, built in 1904 of handcut sandstone, has three antique-furnished guest rooms, two with private baths. A unique feature is the early-twentieth-century showers, which have side sprays as well as the usual overhead fixtures. You'll get a gourmet breakfast and will be just two blocks from downtown Trinidad.

$$–$$$ Chicosa Canyon Bed and Breakfast, 32391 County Rd. 40 (12 miles from Trinidad), 719-846-6199. This B&B on a century-old ranch has a cozy cabin that sleeps up to four people plus your dog (he can't stay in the main guest rooms). He'll have plenty to explore on the ranch's 64 acres, where he can hike off leash with you. Two bird dogs are permanent residents at the inn; they might be able to show your dog a trick or two.

$$–$$$ Holiday Inn, 9995 County Rd. 69.1 (Exit 11 off I-25), 719-846-4491 (800-HOLIDAY [national number])

Walsenburg

$ Rio Cucharas Inn, 77 Taylor Rd., 719-738-1282. This motel near the Cuchara Ski Valley is under new ownership, and it doesn't appear to be as super dog-friendly as it was previously. Nonetheless, dog guests are still allowed. In addition to motel-style rooms, the inn has three more expensive suites, each with fireplace.

$ Western Inn Motel, 521 North Walsen Ave., 719-738-3362

$–$$ Country Budget Host, 553 Highway 85/87, 719-738-3800 (800-BUD-HOST).

Dogs are allowed in smoking rooms only. Note that the motel is not open for business on Sundays.

$$ Best Western Rambler Motel, Highway 85/87, Exit 52 (off I-25), 719-738-1121. It's smoking rooms only for dogs.

Campgrounds

Lake Pueblo State Park. See "Tail-Rated Trails" for directions (401 sites).

Lathrop State Park. See "Tail-Rated Trails" for directions (96 sites).

Trinidad Lake State Park. See "Tail-Rated Trails" for directions (62 sites).

National forest campgrounds: Camping is allowed in the parking area at Vogel Canyon (see "Tail-Rated Trails" for directions).

Private campgrounds: Pueblo KOA and Pueblo South/Colorado City KOA (see "Creature Comforts").

WORTH A PAWS

Bent's Old Fort National Historic Site. 8 miles east of La Junta and 15 miles west of Las Animas, on Highway 194. An influential frontier trading post on the Arkansas River, Bent's Fort was in operation from 1833 to 1849. Today a reconstruction operated by the National Park Service allows visitors to experience the fort's heyday through tours and interpretive activities. Your dog is welcome to accompany you throughout your visit as long as you keep him on a leash and with you at all times. Open 8 a.m.–5:30 p.m. daily, Memorial Day to Labor Day; 9 a.m.–4 p.m. the rest of the year. There is an entrance fee. Call 719-383-5010.

Feet and Fur. If you and Fido are in the Pueblo area near the end of September, sign yourselves up for this annual fundraising 5K walk. The course begins and ends at Pueblo's City Park, off of Pueblo Blvd. and Goodnight Ave. The walk is followed by contests, including pet/owner look-alike, best dog costume, and best kisser (dogs, that is!). You and your dog can also get pet care information and various freebies at booths set up in the park, view demonstrations by local 4-H groups and police K-9 units, or check out the dog agility course. Money raised through registration fees and pledges benefits the Pueblo City/County Animal Shelter, the Southern Colorado Spay/Neuter Association, the Pueblo Humane Society, and the Animal Welfare Society. You can register in advance at the shelter, 1595 Stockyard Rd. in Pueblo (719-542-3474), or at the park on event day.

Four Paw Spa, 3853 Goodnight Ave., Pueblo, 719-561-1382. Is your lovable pooch starting to smell up the backseat after rolling in that suspicious-looking stuff out at the reservoir? Bring him here for a quick spruce-up. For $8 you can clean your dog in one of the special wash bays—shampoo, towels, and blow dryer are provided. You'll need to call for an appointment; walk-ins are not accepted. Appointments are readily available days, evenings, and weekends, including Sundays. Grooming is also available if you'd rather leave the washing to someone else.

DOGGIE DAYCARE
La Junta
Colorado Veterinary Clinic, 30488 Highway 50, 719-384-8111. $4.50–$5.50/day, depending on the size of dog. Open 8 a.m.–noon and 1–5:30 p.m., Monday to Friday, 8 a.m.–noon, 1–3 p.m., Saturday.

The town of Cuchara is a popular dog spot. The Boardwalk Saloon, on the town's main street, has become unofficially known as the Dog Bar because so many dogs hang out in front of it (and sometimes inside).

Krugman Small Animal Clinic, 502 E. 1st, 719-384-5050. $5/day. Open 8 a.m.–noon, 1–5:30 p.m., Monday, Tuesday, Wednesday, Friday; 8 a.m.–noon, Thursday and Saturday.

Lamar

Eaton Veterinary Clinic, 1004 E. Maple, 719-336-5068. $5/day. Open 8 a.m.–5 p.m., Monday to Friday; 8 a.m.–noon, Saturday.

Lamar Veterinary Clinic, 1209 E. Olive, 719-336-8484. $5.50/day. Open 8 a.m.–noon and 1–5 p.m., Monday to Friday; 8 a.m.–noon, Saturday.

Pueblo

Four Paw Spa, 3853 Goodnight Ave., 719-561-1382. $15/day. Open 6 a.m.–6 p.m., daily.

Kamp-4-Paws, 1412 32nd Ln., 719-545-PAWS. $5/day. Open 8 a.m.–6 p.m., Monday to Friday, 8 a.m.–2 p.m., Saturday.

Pets & Friends Animal Hospital, 3625 Baltimore Ave., 719-542-2022. $7–$8/day, depending on the size of dog. Open 8 a.m.–5:30 p.m., Monday to Friday; 8 a.m.–noon, Saturday.

Pueblo Small Animal Clinic, 1400 Highway 50 East, 719-545-4350. $6–$8/day, depending on the size of dog. Open 8 a.m.–12:30 p.m. and 1–5:30 p.m., Monday to Friday; 8 a.m.–noon, Saturday.

Pueblo West Boarding Kennels, 776 E. Paseo Dorado Dr., 719-547-3815. $7/day. Open 9 a.m.–5:30 p.m., Monday to Saturday. Day boarding during other times can be arranged in advance.

Trinidad

Fisher's Peak Veterinary Clinic, 1617 Santa Fe Trail, 719-846-3211. $6.50–$11/day, depending on the size of dog.

Open 8 a.m.–5 p.m., Monday to Friday; 8 a.m.–noon, Saturday.

Trinidad Animal Clinic, 1701 E. Main, 719-846-3212. $5–$7/day, depending on the size of dog. Open 8 a.m.–5 p.m., Monday to Friday; 8 a.m.–noon, Saturday.

Walsenburg

Rio Cucharas Veterinary Clinic, 22540 Highway 160, 719-738-1427. $8–$12/day, depending on the size of dog. Open 8 a.m.–4 p.m., Monday to Friday; 8–11 a.m., Saturday.

PET PROVISIONS
Pueblo

Animal Kingdom, 339 S. Santa Fe Dr., 719-544-4510

Pet Paradise, 1501 Moore, 719-564-6191

PetsMart, 4230 N. Freeway, 719-595-9000

Pueblo Feed & Supply, 1811 Santa Fe Dr., 719-542-6787

Sweeny Feed Mill of Southern Colorado, Inc., 403 E. 4th, 719-544-1041

Trinidad

Marty Feeds, 326 N. Commercial, 719-846-3376

Walsenburg

Storleder Feeds, 217 E. 4th, 719-738-1920

CANINE ER
La Junta

Colorado Veterinary Clinic, 30488 Highway 50, 719-384-8111. Open 8 a.m.–noon, 1–5:30 p.m., Monday to Friday; 8 a.m.–noon, 1–3 p.m., Saturday.

Krugman Small Animal Clinic, 502 E. 1st, 719-384-5050. Open 8 a.m.–noon,

1–5:30 p.m., Monday, Tuesday, Wednesday, Friday; 8 a.m.–noon, Thursday and Saturday.

Lamar
Eaton Veterinary Clinic, 1004 E. Maple, 719-336-5068. Open 8 a.m.–5 p.m., Monday to Friday; 8 a.m.–noon, Saturday.

Lamar Veterinary Clinic, 1209 E. Olive, 719-336-8484. Open 8 a.m.–noon, 1–5 p.m., Monday to Friday; 8 a.m.–noon, Saturday.

Pueblo
Pets & Friends Animal Hospital (AAHA certified), 3625 Baltimore Ave., 719-542-2022. Open 8 a.m.–5:30 p.m., Monday to Friday; 8 a.m.–noon, Saturday.

Pueblo Small Animal Clinic (AAHA certified), 1400 Highway 50 East, 719-545-4850. Open 8 a.m.–12:30 p.m., 1–5:30 p.m., Monday to Friday; 8 a.m.–noon, Saturday.

Trinidad
Fisher's Peak Veterinary Clinic, 1617 Santa Fe Trail, 719-846-3211. Open 8 a.m.–5 p.m., Monday to Friday; 8 a.m.–noon, Saturday.

Trinidad Animal Clinic, 1701 E. Main, 719-846-3212. Open 8 a.m.–5 p.m., Monday to Friday; 8 a.m.–noon, Saturday.

Walsenburg
Rio Cucharas Veterinary Clinic, 22540 Highway 160, 719-738-1427. Open 8 a.m.–4 p.m., Monday to Friday; 8–11 a.m., Saturday.

RESOURCES
Carrizo Unit, Comanche National Grasslands, 27162 Highway 287, Springfield, 719-523-6591

Colorado Welcome Centers, 109 E. Beech, Lamar, 719-336-3483; 309 Nevada Ave. (Exit 14A off I-25), Trinidad, 719-846-9512

Forest Supervisor's Office, Pike/San Isabel National Forests, 1920 Valley Dr., Pueblo, 719-545-8737

Greater Pueblo Chamber of Commerce, 302 N. Santa Fe Ave., 719-542-1704 (800-233-3446; www.pueblochamber.org)

Timpas Unit, Comanche National Grasslands, 1420 E. 3rd St., La Junta, 719-384-2181

Colorado Springs and Vicinity

THE BIG SCOOP

Despite being Colorado's second-largest urban center, Colorado Springs, picturesquely situated near the base of massive Pikes Peak, is an exceedingly good place to bring your dog for a vacation. National forest hiking trails are within a twenty-minute drive of downtown, and some forward-looking folks have established several off-leash areas in city and county parks. (There are leash laws within city limits as well as in many areas of El Paso County.) Many area lodging places allow pets. And you can even bring Rover along to some of the many locales to which tourists in the Springs traditionally flock (see "Worth a Paws").

If your dog has a special interest in old mining towns, ghosts, or, perhaps, gambling, pay a visit to nearby Victor and Cripple Creek (though he will have to sit out any casino forays). Whatever activities you choose, your dog is likely to find something to catch his interest in or around Colorado Springs.

TAIL-RATED TRAILS

Of the state parks in the area, two—Eleven Mile and Spinney Mountain—don't have hiking trails, and the one that does—Mueller—doesn't allow dogs on them. But there are plenty of hiking opportunities in city and county parks as well as in the Pike National Forest that you can enjoy with your dog. To research options in addition to the ones described here, stop by the Pikes Peak Ranger District office in Colorado Springs (see "Resources").

Seven Bridges Trail. About 4.5 miles round-trip. From downtown Colorado Springs, take Tejon Ave. south; follow the road as it bends to the right and turns into Cheyenne Blvd. After 2.5 miles you'll come to a fork with signs pointing left for Seven Falls and right for North Cheyenne Cañon Park; stay right. Follow the road through the park. At Helen Hunt Falls, the road begins to switchback. Shortly after, you'll reach a fork where Gold Camp Rd. goes off to the right, and High Dr. is straight ahead. Park in the dirt lot on the left here. *Dogs can be off leash.*

Begin your hike by walking past the wooden gate at the west side of the parking area. The first half mile, which leads to the actual trail, takes you and your dog along a closed section of Gold Camp Rd. The road, which was a rail line at the turn of the century, stretches all the way to Cripple Creek; because of a tunnel cave-in that's never been repaired, an approximately 8-mile section is closed to vehicle traffic. Just before you would cross North Cheyenne Creek, take an unmarked trail that heads uphill on the right side of the road; stay straight rather than continuing uphill at the first switchback, and you'll be on the Seven Bridges Trail. (An alternate access point is off Gold Camp Rd. on the other side of the creek: There's a rusted metal sign indicating the North Cheyenne Creek Trail, the name by which this hike used to be known. However, you'll merely recross the creek on a couple of planks and wind up intersecting the first trail.) You'll hike along the north side of the creek for just a short while before reaching the first bridge. The trail then follows the twists and turns of the creek, ascending up the scenic drainage via a moderate grade. In addition to the plentiful water, your dog will appreciate the shade of ponderosa pine and Douglas fir. Altogether, you'll cross six bridges, despite the trail's name (there's been some bridge reconstruction and relocation due to flooding). After the sixth bridge, the trail climbs more steeply, away from the creek. Tell your dog to take care when crossing the section of exposed, sandy slope.

The Seven Bridges Trail officially ends when it intersects the Pipeline Trail, 1.5 miles from its start off Gold Camp Rd. However, when we hiked this trail, that intersection wasn't clear. We continued along the trail as it paralleled a smaller creek, ultimately reaching a plateau and a large stand of aspen, which made a good turnaround point. On the way back, you'll get a good down-canyon vista of the eastern plains. Shoes with good traction come in handy on the return trip, as some of the downhills are a bit slippery. Your dog, with his grippy paws, should have no problem.

Bear Creek Regional Park. This 1,235-acre park has 10 miles of trails, with several access points. The section your dog will be most interested in is the *voice command area, where dogs can be off leash.* The trailhead is in the parking area west of 21st St. at the intersection with W. Rio Grande Ave. *Dogs must be leashed in the rest of the park, and they are not allowed on the Nature Center trails in the western portion of the park.*

The off-leash area includes a wide trail that makes a 0.75-mile loop. It's a great spot for an after-work hike for local dogs or a close-to-town break for travelers. Look for the red "voice command area" sign at the west side of the parking lot. Though you'll never get far from the noise of traffic on 21st St., your dog will be too excited at having an area set aside for him and his friends to notice. And he can even splash in nearby Bear Creek. You can also reach the trail that leads into the park's western section from the 21st St. parking area; just remember that your dog will have to leash up.

Garden of the Gods. From downtown Colorado Springs, drive north to Fillmore St. and make a left to head west (it turns into Fontmore once you cross Mesa Rd.). At 30th St., turn right to reach the park's visitor center. If you're coming from Highway 24, head north on Ridge Rd. near Old Colorado City to arrive at the park. There is no entrance fee from either access. *Dogs can be off leash in the dog run area; they must be leashed elsewhere.*

On its own, the Garden of the Gods would only rate about one-and-a-half tail wags. However, the dog who's done his homework will know to sniff out the **off-leash dog run area,** which covers about eighteen acres on the east side of the Foothills Trail, near Rock Ledge Ranch. To access this area, park at the visitor center and walk through the tunnel from the parking lot, which comes out at the section of the Foothills Trail south of Gateway Road. Head south on the trail for about an eighth of a mile; you'll see signs that demarcate the dog run area, which encompasses a section of open field adjacent to the trail. Alternate access is from the Rock Ledge Ranch parking area; look for the signs from 30th St., just south of the Garden of the Gods visitor center. The dog run area begins near the parking lot. (Note that dogs are not allowed at Rock Ledge Ranch, which is a living history site.)

The main attraction of Garden of the Gods itself, a city park, is the vivid red sandstone formations that are clustered in the area. Several short trails, some natural surface, some paved, wind around the rocks. The longest, at 2.25 miles, encircles part of the park. Though you'll likely marvel at the landscape, your dog may find the Garden less than heavenly: There are no water sources for him, and the trails can be crowded. During the summer, try to visit early in the day or late in the afternoon for cooler temperatures and less company.

 Palmer Park. For the dog park, in the southeast corner of the park, enter at the intersection of Academy Blvd. and Maizeland Rd. To reach the central part of the park from downtown Colorado Springs, head north on N. Nevada Ave.; turn right onto Fillmore St. and right onto Union Blvd. Turn left at the next intersection (Paseo Rd.) and drive into the park. *Dogs can be off leash in the dog park and in the voice-command area; they must be leashed in the rest of the park.*

In a *Field of Dreams*–like scenario ("if you build it, they will come") the city parks department converted a former baseball field into the Springs' first official **dog park** in the fall of 2000, and local canines have been visiting in scores ever since. The one-plus-acre grassy site is contained within a chainlink fence and includes human and dog drinking fountains as well as picnic tables and benches. It's still a work in progress; for example, some old playground equipment is scheduled to be installed sometime in 2001, providing dogs with an obstacle/agility course to play in. As for the rules and regulations, dogs must be licensed and have updated shots, females in heat are not allowed, aggressive dogs should stay at home, and owners must pick up after their pets (poop bags are supplied).

Snow can be a dog's best friend. (photo by Cindy Hirschfeld)

The rest of Palmer Park contains lots of unnamed trails that meander throughout; just look for the dirt roads and parking pullouts to access them. However, your dog will first want to head to the **Yucca Area,** where there are 27.5 acres on which he can run off leash (as long as he stays under voice control). To reach the dog run, turn left off Paseo Rd. at the Lazy Land/Ute Crest sign, then follow signs to the Yucca Area/Ute Crest parking section. The voice-command area encompasses a gravel road, which runs across the mesa top, and the land on either side of it, providing great views of Pikes Peak to the west. Just keep an eye out for the signs to make sure your dog stays within the parameters of the dog run. If you visit during June, you'll catch the beauty of flowering yucca.

North Cheyenne Cañon Park. From downtown Colorado Springs, take Tejon Ave. south; follow the road as it bends to the right and turns into Cheyenne Blvd. After 2.5 miles you'll come to a fork with signs pointing left for Seven Falls, right for North Cheyenne Cañon Park; stay right. *Dogs must be leashed.*

This city park, with scenic North Cheyenne Cañon at its center, has several hiking trails for dogs to sniff out. The park's western end borders national forest land, where even more trails await discovery (see the Seven Bridges Trail description, for one example). You might begin with a stop at the well-stocked visitor center at the Starsmore Discovery Center located at the park's entrance. The Columbine Springs Trail runs for 3 miles through the park; you can access it from the lower trailhead behind Starsmore, from a midpoint trailhead off the park road, and from the upper trailhead across from Helen Hunt Falls. The 2-mile round-trip Mount Cutler Trail begins to the left of the park road, 1.4 miles from the park entrance. It makes a gradual ascent up the flanks of Mount Cutler, providing panoramic views of Colorado Springs, including the renowned Broadmoor Hotel and grounds. Near the top, you'll also be able to see the Seven Falls in South Cheyenne Cañon. And you might hear the hourly chiming of the Will Rogers Shrine on nearby Cheyenne Mountain. Although there's no water along the trail itself, North Cheyenne Creek is across from the trailhead. Driving farther west up the canyon brings you to Helen Hunt Falls, where your dog can enjoy the cool spray. A short trail leads past these falls up to Silver Cascade Falls.

Fountain Creek Regional Park. Located south of Colorado Springs between Widefield and Fountain. Take I-25 south to Highway 160 (Exit 132); turn left and drive about half a mile, where you'll come to the exit for south U.S. Highway 85/87. Take this exit and make an immediate right onto Willow Springs Rd. Turn left before the parking lot onto the dirt road, then left again to reach the parking area and trail access. *Dogs must be leashed.*

The **Fountain Creek Trail** runs for a level 2.5 miles through the park, allowing your dog ample sniffing opportunities among the creek's riparian habitat. The wide, flat dirt trail also makes a good jogging venue. Though you'll never really get away from the drone of highway noise in the background, the park provides a welcome refuge from the surrounding development. If you head north on the trail, you'll come to the Willow Springs Fishing Ponds and the 0.75-mile "Fishing Is Fun" loop trail, where your dog can learn all about fishing from interpretive signs (though the ponds themselves have been closed to fishing due to PCE concentration in the water). Past the ponds you can also access the **Fountain Creek Regional Trail,** which extends for 6.5 miles from the northern end of the park to Circle Dr. in Colorado Springs. Heading south on the Fountain Creek Trail brings you to two wildlife observation pavilions, where your dog can gaze out on a ten-acre pond and the resident waterfowl. (Note that dogs are not allowed on the nature center trails in the Cattail Marsh Wildlife Area, which lies east of the Fountain Creek Trail.) The trail continues through two open meadow areas before ending near the Hanson Nature Park in Fountain.

Monument Valley Park Trail. Runs for 2.2 miles along Monument Creek through Monument Valley Park. From the downtown business district on Tejon St., head east on Bijou St. for two blocks to the park. If you're driving, park on West View Pl. This brings you to the southern terminus of the trail. *Dogs must be leashed.*

Monument Valley Park is where your dog can come to sniff and be sniffed by the dogs who call the Springs home. The trail makes for a nice urban stroll as it follows the creek. In the park's southern end, you may want to detour to get a

Jasmine finds the perfect cool-down spot.
(photo by Helmut Tingstad)

closer look at the various ponds, fountains, and the Horticultural Art Society demonstration gardens. For the first 1.3 miles, the trail runs along both sides of the creek (with a slight detour at Uintah St.), providing a loop option. Another loop (0.7 mile), in the park's northern end, makes up the **Monument Valley Fitness Trail,** good to know if your dog is really interested in getting a workout.

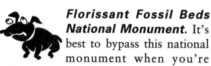 **Florissant Fossil Beds National Monument.** It's best to bypass this national monument when you're with your dog: Not only are dogs not allowed on any trails, they're also discouraged from being in the picnic areas. In case Fido wonders what this place is all about anyway, you can let him know that 35 million years ago, a 15-mile-long lake dominated the landscape of the present-day monument site. Over the next 700,000 years, repeated eruptions from a nearby volcano eventually buried the lake's entire ecosystem, and over the ensuing millions of years, the plant and animal remains became fossilized. Today, the monument's visitor center presents fossil displays, and hiking trails lead visitors to petrified tree stumps. The monument is about 30 miles west of Colorado Springs off U.S. Highway 24.

 Mueller State Park. The park, located off Highway 67 on the way to Cripple Creek, offers more than 85 miles of hiking trails, and your dog is not allowed on any of them. Dogs are allowed in the park's camping and picnic sites.

CYCLING FOR CANINES

The 7-mile **Waldo Canyon Trail** is one of the most popular hiking and biking routes near Colorado Springs. It begins right off the north side of Highway 24, about 2 miles west of Manitou Springs. The upper part of the trail is actually a 3-mile loop. The 5.5-mile **Lovell Gulch Trail** starts at County Rd. 22, north of Woodland Park, and features great views of Pikes Peak.

Close to downtown Colorado Springs, the 4-mile **Captain Jack's Frontside Loop** begins at the closed section of Gold Camp Rd.; follow the Seven Bridges Trail (see "Tail-Rated Trails") but continue on the switchbacks up the trail as it leaves Gold Camp Rd. Take a right at the intersection with the Jones Park Trail, then another right on High Dr. to return to the parking area. It's best to do this ride between October 31 and May 1, when High Dr. is closed to vehicle traffic.

You can also bring your bike and your dog to Rampart Reservoir outside of Woodland Park (there's a $3 day-use fee for the area). The **Rampart Reservoir Trail** extends around the lake for 11.6 miles. Begin from the Dikeside Boat Ramp and ride counterclockwise; that way your dog will be ready to turn around before you ever reach the campgrounds, where he'd be treading close to leash-required territory.

POWDERHOUNDS

The 3-mile round-trip **Crags Trail** is one of the closest places to Colorado Springs with consistent snow coverage for skiing and snowshoeing. To access the trail, take Highway 24 west to Highway 67 south. Just past the entrance to Mueller State Park, look for Forest Rd. 383 on the left; follow it to the Crags Campground and the trailhead. Some unmarked spur trails lead off the main trail providing more opportunities for snow travel.

The **Horsethief Park** trail system starts from Highway 67 a few miles south of the Crags Trail turnoff. It's about a 3-mile round-trip to Horsethief Park and back, a little over 2 miles round-trip to Horsethief Falls, and about 5 miles round-trip via the Pancake Rocks Trail.

After a storm or during a good snow, the trail around **Rampart Reservoir** is skiable/snowshoeable. Forest Rd. 306, which goes directly to the reservoir, is closed during the winter, so you'll need to access the Rampart Reservoir Trail via the 1.4-mile Rainbow Gulch Trail, off Forest Rd. 300.

CREATURE COMFORTS

Unless otherwise stated, dogs should not be left unattended in the room or cabin.

Chipita Park

$$$ **Chipita Lodge B&B Inn,** 9090 Chipita Park Rd., 719-684-8454 (877-CHIPITA; www.chipitalodge.com). Although the B&B does not permit dogs in the historic main lodge, two nicely furnished cabins on the premises welcome dog guests with a $50 deposit. Each cabin has two bedrooms, one bath, and a full kitchen, and one has laundry facilities too. You can leave Rover unattended inside at your discretion, though each cabin also has a small fenced yard where he might prefer to stay. And there's a prime outdoor hot tub with a view.

Colorado Springs

$–$$ **Beverly Hills Motel,** 6 El Paso Blvd., 719-632-0386. The motel accepts

"mature dogs and mature adults." You can leave your dog in the room unattended.

$–$$ **Buffalo Lodge,** 2 El Paso Blvd., 719-634-2851 (800-235-7416). This historic lodge, which is practically in Manitou Springs, dates from the early 1900s, and the exterior has that classic 1950s vacation-spot look. The rooms are large, modern, and comfortably furnished. Dogs are permitted in three of the rooms, all of which have wood floors, for $10 per night. You must keep your dog leashed on the four-acre property.

$–$$ **Motel 6 Colorado Springs,** 3228 N. Chestnut, 719-520-5400 (800-4-MOTEL6 [national number])

$–$$ **Sunflower Motel,** 3703 W. Colorado Ave., 719-520-1864 (877-850-9005). Dogs are allowed in designated rooms with a $25 deposit.

$–$$$ **Best Western Palmer House,** 3010 Chestnut St., 719-636-5201 (800-223-9127). There's a $25 deposit for a dog plus a $10 fee per night.

$–$$$ **Econo Lodge,** 430 W. Garden of the Gods Rd., 719-532-1010 (800-55-ECONO; www.econolodge.com). The motel accepts "dogs that aren't yappers" in certain pet designated rooms with a $20 deposit.

$–$$$ **Red Roof Inn,** 8280 Highway 83, 719-598-6700 (800-RED-ROOF [national number]). You can leave your dog unattended in the room as long as he's in a travel kennel. The motel is across from the Air Force Academy south gate.

$–$$$ **Villager Premiere,** 8th and Cimarron Sts., 719-473-5530 (800-328-STAY [national number]). Formerly a Holiday Inn Express, the Villager has standard rooms as well as apartment-style suites, with two bedrooms, living room, dining room, and full kitchen.

$$ Best Western Airport Inn, 1780 Aeroplaza Dr., 719-574-7707. The motel allows dogs for $10 extra per night.

$$ Drury Inn, 8155 N. Academy Blvd., 719-598-2500 (800-DRURY-INN [national number]). You might be able to leave your dog unattended in the room for short periods of time; inquire at the desk.

$$ Fireside Executive Suites, 620 N. Murray Blvd., 719-597-6207 (800-597-6202). Dogs can stay in the fully equipped one- and two-bedroom suites here for $10 extra per night, per dog. It's okay to leave a dog unattended in the room.

$$ Maple Lodge, 9 El Paso Blvd., 719-685-9230. The motel accepts dogs for nightly stays in most of its rooms from May to the end of September. There's a $7 fee per night, per pet.

$$ Ramada Inn North, 3125 Sinton Rd., 719-633-5541 (800-272-6232 [national number]). There's a $25 one-time fee for a dog. You can leave your dog unattended in the room, but housekeeping won't enter during that time.

$$ Ramada Limited, 520 N. Murray, 719-596-7660 (800-272-6232 [national number]). There's a $25 one-time pet fee, and you can leave your dog unattended in the room but housekeeping won't come in to clean while he's there.

$$ Rodeway Inn, 2409 E. Pikes Peak Ave., 719-471-0990 (800-228-2000 [national number]). A $40 deposit is required for a dog. You can leave your dog unattended in the room as long as you put out the "do not disturb" sign to alert the housekeepers.

$$ Sleep Inn, 1075 Kelly Johnson Blvd., 719-260-6969 (888-875-3374). Dogs are

put in smoking rooms only with a $50 deposit. The motel is in the process of reworking its policy, so call for an update.

$$ Travelodge, 2625 Ore Mill Rd., 719-632-4600 (800-929-5478). Dogs are generally allowed only in smoking rooms for $20 extra per visit. They can be left unattended in the room, preferably in a travel kennel, but housekeeping won't enter during that time.

$$–$$$ Apollo Park Executive Suites, 805 S. Circle, 719-634-0286 (800-666-1955). This place rents out one- and two-bedroom units with kitchens on a nightly, weekly, or monthly basis. Dogs under 35 pounds are allowed, but only in the lower-level units; it's $10 extra per night or a $100 one-time fee if you're staying for a month. You can leave your dog unattended inside.

$$–$$$ Comfort Suites of Colorado Springs, 1055 Kelly Johnson Blvd., 719-536-0731 (888-515-3131). Most of the rooms here are large one-room suites with microwave and refrigerator ("executive suites" have a separate bedroom). The pet policy is being reevaluated as to whether a fee or a deposit will be required, so call to see what's been decided.

$$–$$$ Days Inn, 2850 S. Circle Dr., 719-527-0800. Dogs are allowed with a $25 deposit.

$$–$$$ Hampton Inn South, 1410 Harrison Rd., 719-579-6900 (800-HAMPTON [national number]). The hotel has suites and minisuites available in addition to standard rooms. There's a $15 one-time pet fee with a limit of two dogs per room. You can leave your dog unattended inside as long as you put the inn's "pet in room" sign on your door and let the front desk know. You'll also be asked to sign a pet agreement form and refrain from bringing Fido into the lobby because food is served there. Rates include continental breakfast.

$$–$$$ Holiday Inn Garden of the Gods, 505 Popes Bluff Trail, 719-598-7656 (800-962-5470 [national number]). Dogs 25 pounds and under are permitted in some of the hotel's rooms. If you're paying with cash, a $50 deposit is required. You can leave your dog unattended in the room as long as you inform the front desk.

$$–$$$ La Quinta Inn, 4385 Sinton Rd., 719-528-5060 (800-531-5900 [national number])

$$–$$$ Naturenest Cabin Rentals, 2502 W. Colorado Ave., #208, 719-636-3637 (www.naturenest.com). This property management company rents out a variety of cabins and mountain homes in the vicinity of the Springs, including the Ute Pass area and Cripple Creek. For the cabins that allow dogs, you'll be asked to put down a higher security deposit in addition to $10 extra per night for one dog, $15 nightly for two dogs. Your dog should be at least a year old, and the company prefers that you keep him in a travel kennel if you need to leave him unattended inside.

$$–$$$ Quality Inn and Suites, 1440 Harrison Rd., 719-576-2371 (800-228-5151 [national number]; www.quality inn.com). This recently renovated hotel (it used to be the Budget Inn) allows dogs in smoking rooms only, with a $50 deposit and a $5 per night, per pet, fee. You can leave your dog unattended in your room, and if you can walk him while the room is being cleaned, the housekeepers will be extra appreciative.

$$–$$$ Quality Inn Garden of the Gods, 555 W. Garden of the Gods Rd., 719-593-9119 (800-828-4347). A $50 deposit is required for a dog.

$$–$$$$ Doubletree World Arena, 1775 E. Cheyenne Mountain Blvd., 719-576-8900 (800-222-8733 [national number]).

Now that the Antlers Hotel downtown has changed from a Doubletree to an Adams Mark and no longer accepts pets, this is the only dog-friendly Doubletree in town (southwest of downtown, actually). Dogs are welcome for $10 extra per night. On-site amenities include a restaurant and bar (with room service), a workout area, hot tub, and indoor pool.

$$–$$$$ Radisson Inn North, 8110 N. Academy Blvd., 719-598-5770 (800-333-3333 [national number]). The hotel offers standard rooms, minisuites, and larger suites with a Jacuzzi. Your dog is welcome if he's 25 pounds or under, with a $50 deposit, and he can be left unattended in the room as long as he's in a travel kennel.

$$–$$$$ Residence Inn North by Marriott, 3880 N. Academy Blvd., 719-574-0370 (800-331-3131 [national number]). Dogs are allowed at this apartment-style hotel for $15 extra per night, with a maximum total of $150 (if your stay extends past ten nights). You can leave your dog unattended inside, preferably in a travel kennel.

$$–$$$$ Residence Inn South by Marriott, 2765 Geyser Dr., 719-576-0101 (800-331-3131 [national number]). This Residence Inn charges a $50 one-time fee for a dog. You can leave Rover unattended inside your room, and the staffers at the front desk may even be willing to do some dog walking if you ask nicely.

$$–$$$$ Wyndham Colorado Springs, 5580 Tech Center Dr., 719-260-1800 (800-962-6982 [national number]). This former Marriott has morphed into the Wyndham, but it's still dog friendly. There's a $250 deposit, so you'll want to make sure Fido behaves; you can leave him unattended in the room. The full-service hotel features a restaurant (and room service), pool, sauna, hot tub, fitness center, and such amenities as bathrobes in the rooms.

$$$ Radisson Suites Airport, 1645 N. Newport Rd., 719-597-7000 (800-333-3333 [national number]). Dogs 50 pounds and under can stay, with a $100 deposit. You can leave your dog unattended in the room for a short time if you're on the hotel premises, say, at the restaurant. Rates include a breakfast buffet.

$$$ Towneplace Suites by Marriott, 4760 Centennial Blvd., 719-594-4447 (800-257-3000 [national number]). These studio to two-bedroom suites with full kitchens are very similar to the Marriott's Residence Inn, except that housekeeping does not come in daily. The fee for a dog is $150 per visit, whether you're staying a night or a month, so unless you'll be at the hotel long-term, it's certainly not an economical option. You can leave your dog unattended inside your room.

Cripple Creek

$$ Cozy Cabins, 232 Thurlow, 719-689-3351 (www.cripple-creek.co.us/cozy.html). Dogs are accepted on a case-by-case basis. There are two cozy cabins, the actual Cozy Cabin and the Cowboy Cabin. The one-bedroom Cozy was built in 1930 and features a fireplace and some antique furnishings. The modern Cowboy, next door, has two bedrooms and a boatload of cowboy decor; in fact, the cabin is dedicated to Roy Rogers and Dale Evans. The refrigerators in both cabins are stocked with breakfast goodies and snacks for your enjoyment. You might be able to leave your dog unattended inside, preferably in a travel kennel, at the cabin owner's discretion.

$$ Greyhound Ranch Bed and Breakfast, 401 S. 2nd, 719-689-2599 (www.greyhoundranch.com). Living up to its name, this homey B&B does take dogs, of any variety. It's named in honor of the owners' three miniature greyhounds (under 10 pounds each). Three guest rooms with shared bath are available, and the breakfast is hearty. The house was built in 1895 during the time of the Cripple Creek gold rush and is furnished with antiques and vintage photos. There's plenty of open space nearby in which to walk Fido, and you can leave him unattended in the room or in the adjacent fenced yard for short periods of time (e.g., while you are eating dinner).

$$ Little Burro Inn and Lost Burro Campground, 4023 Teller Rd. 1, 719-689-2345 (www.lostburro.com). The "inn" is actually a two-bedroom mobile home adjacent to the campground and equipped with kitchen and washer/dryer. The 15-acre wooded property with stream is about 4 miles from Cripple Creek. You can leave your dog unattended inside only if he's in a travel crate; there's an outdoor kennel, too, for stay-behind dogs that would prefer to be outside.

$$–$$$ The Victorian Lady Bed and Breakfast, 127 W. Carr, 719-689-2143. Dogs are allowed on a case-by-case basis, depending on size and temperament. If your dog makes the grade, you'll need to pay $10 extra per night for him. If the owner decides that your dog is too big to stay in the room or if you're heading off to the casinos, your dog can hang out in the yard—just make sure you have a way to restrain him, as the fence is not supersecure. Open Memorial Day to Labor Day.

$$–$$$$ Double Eagle Hotel and Casino, 442 E. Bennett, 719-689-5000 (800-711-7234; www.decasino.com). Your dog is welcome to accompany you here on a gambling vacation if you put down a $100 deposit. You can leave Fido in the room unattended while you try your luck in the adjoining casino as long as he doesn't make a nuisance of himself.

Fountain
$ Colorado Springs South KOA and Kamping Kabins, 8100 S. Bandley Dr., 719-382-7575 (800-KOA-8609). Small dogs (those under 20 pounds) are allowed in the one- and two-room cabins for a $3 fee per dog, per night (there's no extra charge to have them at the campsites). You'll have to bring bedding and cooking supplies. There are two large fields on site, as well as Fountain Creek, where you can exercise him on a leash.

Green Mountain Falls
$–$$ Falls Motel, 6990 Lake St., 719-684-9745

$$ Rocky Top Motel and Campground, 10090 W. Highway 24, 719-684-9044. Very small dogs (from 10 to 15 pounds) are allowed for $5 per night. Some rooms have kitchenettes.

Lake George
$$ Lake George Cabins and RV Park, 8966 County Rd. 90, 719-748-3822. Dogs are allowed in the log cabins as well as in the RV and tent sites. There are ten adjoining one-room cabins, nine with kitchens. You'll need to keep your dog leashed on the property, but plenty of hiking trails in Pike National Forest are nearby.

Manitou Springs
$–$$ Park Row Lodge, 54 Manitou Ave., 719-685-5216 (800-818-PARK). The motel charges a $5 one-time fee for all dogs, along with a $25 deposit for larger dogs. Some of the rooms have kitchenettes.

$$–$$$ Dream Gables, 105 Washington Ave., 719-685-4636 (www.manitou springs.com/dreambb.html). This location in downtown Manitou Springs offers two options: a four-bedroom house that dates from the late 1880s and a one-bedroom cabin (with kitchenette) that was constructed in the early 1900s. Both have what the owner calls "cottage style" decor. You can leave your dog unattended inside, though if he causes any problems, that privilege would, of course, be modified. Ingredients for a continental breakfast are provided in the house or cabin for a small extra charge.

Monument
$$ Falcon Inn, 1865 Woodmoor Dr., 719-481-3000 (800-779-3008). Dogs are allowed with a $50 deposit. You can leave yours unattended in the room, but he'll have to be in a travel crate if you want housekeeping to come in during that time.

Tarryall
$$ Ute Trail River Ranch, 21446 County Rd. 77 (21 miles from Lake George), 719-748-3015 (www.coloradodirectory. com/utetrailriverranch). This rustic fishing camp on Tarryall Creek features turn-of-the-century log cabins outfitted with wood or gas stoves and Western decor. For $10 extra per night, dogs are allowed to stay in five of the seven cabins (there's a central showerhouse). The owners ask that you keep your dog leashed on the property's thirty-five acres, but the ranch is surrounded by Pike National Forest land, where you and Fido can hike leash-free (note that you will need to leash him back up if you venture into the nearby Lost Creek Wilderness). Open from mid-May to mid-October (though the cabins that don't permit dogs are available year-round).

Victor
$–$$ Victor Hotel, 4th St. and Victor Ave., 719-689-3553 (800-748-0870). Originally a bank, this century-plus-old property, which is on the National Register of Historic Places, now houses the Victor Hotel. The cozy, modern rooms have exposed brick walls and nice woodwork. There's a $10 one-time fee for a dog, and you can leave yours unattended inside. The hotel reputedly has a resident

ghost, Ed, so if your dog starts barking at seemingly nothing in the hallway, don't tell him he's just being silly.

Woodland Park

$-$$ Coachlight Motel and RV Park, 19253 Highway 24, 719-687-8732 (www.coachlight.net). Dogs are permitted in most of the motel's rooms with a $50 deposit (though especially big, long-haired dogs may be discouraged from staying). Five new one-room cabins with microwaves and refrigerators, and weekly RV rentals are also available.

$$-$$$ Triple B Ranch, 27460 N. Highway 67 (3.5 miles north of Woodland Park), 719-687-8899 (877-687-8899; www.triplebranch.com). This working horse ranch is on eighty acres and backs to the Pike National Forest, so you and your dog certainly won't be at a loss for things to do here. In addition to horseback riding, there's a full slate of activities (volleyball, archery, and games, to name a few), hay rides (and sleigh rides in winter), a petting zoo, and an indoor pool and a hot tub—plus an eighteen-hole golf course is just across the road. The owners do ask that you keep your dog leashed on the property, so as not to interfere with the working dogs on the ranch. Fifteen cabins of various sizes are available for rent—some with full kitchens, some with kitchenettes, some with fireplaces—as well as the four-bedroom original homestead house (built in the 1950s). There's also a restaurant on site. You'll be asked to put down a $50 deposit for your dog, and it is okay to leave him unattended inside.

$$-$$$$ Eagle Fire Lodge and Conference Center, 777 E. Highway 24, 719-687-5700 (eaglefirelodge.com). The lodge offers a range of recently remodeled accommodations, including standard and large-size hotel rooms, and two-bedroom suites that are in separate little log cabins.

Some units have fireplaces and kitchens; all come with a microwave and refrigerator. You can leave your dog unattended inside if he stays in a travel kennel.

Campgrounds

Eleven Mile State Park. About 11 miles from Lake George via County Rd. 92 (350 sites).

Mueller State Park. About 3.5 miles south of Divide on Highway 67 (132 sites).

National forest campgrounds: **Meadow Ridge Campground** (19 sites) and **Thunder Ridge Campground** (21 sites) are both at Rampart Reservoir, 4.2 miles east of Woodland Park via County Rd. 22 and Forest Rd. 300; **South Meadows Campground** (64 sites), **Colorado Campground** (81 sites), and **Painted Rocks Campground** (18 sites) are north of Woodland Park off Highway 67; **The Crags Campground,** at the end of Forest Rd. 383 off Highway 67, is south of Divide (17 sites).

Private campgrounds: **Colorado Springs South KOA and Kamping Kabins** in Fountain, **Lake George Cabins and RV Park** in Lake George, **Rocky Top Motel and Campground** in Green Mountain Falls, **Lost Burro Campground** (under Little Burro Inn entry) in Cripple Creek.

WORTH A PAWS

U.S. Air Force Academy. Your leashed dog is welcome to tour the grounds of the Air Force Academy with you, but he won't be able to go in any of the buildings. The **Falcon Trail** makes a 12-mile loop around and through the academy; pick up the "Visitors Map and Guide" at the academy visitor center to see the trail's route and access points. The **New Santa Fe Regional Trail** begins at Ice Lake and skirts the academy's eastern side, running north for about 14 miles to Palmer Lake. Eventually this gravel trail will extend south to connect with other trails in Colorado Springs. If you're doing the driving tour of the Academy and want to let your dog stretch his gams, stop at the Environmental Overlook off Academy Drive just south of the turnoff for the visitor center. A short trail begins at the northeast end of the parking lot (look for the signs). For a quick out-and-back, stick to the wide gravel trail that goes to the overlook. There's also a nice loop option through ponderosa pine and gambel oak: Take the path leading to the right from the overlook, then stay right at the small trail intersection to return to the parking lot. You can reach the academy from Exits 156B or 150B off I-25.

Cripple Creek Narrow Gauge Railroad. Small to medium-sized dogs (this includes retrievers) can accompany their owners on the 4-mile round-trip ride that goes from Cripple Creek halfway to Victor and back. The narrated tour passes by historic mines and ghost towns. Trains leave every 45 minutes from the station at Bennett Avenue in Cripple Creek from mid-May to mid-October. Call 719-689-2640 for more information and rates.

Pikes Peak Highway. Second only to the road up Mount Evans as the quickest

Buck wonders where his next treat will come from. (photo by Cindy Hirschfeld)

way to bring your dog to the top of a Colorado fourteener, the Pikes Peak Highway snakes 19 miles to the 14,110-foot summit of legendary Pikes Peak. Once at the top, your dog can feel his fur ripple in the breeze and enjoy a breathtaking view of the eastern plains, up and down the Front Range, and the Sawatch and Mosquito ranges to the west. The road, a combination of pavement and gravel, is open year-round (Wednesday to Sunday from December to March). Access is from Highway 24 just outside of Cascade, and you will have to pay a toll fee. For more information, call 719-684-9383 or 800-DO-VISIT.

Manitou Cliff Dwellings Museum. Leashed dogs are welcome to tour the outdoor areas of this reconstructed example of Anasazi architecture and culture built in 1906. Genuine Anasazi artifacts are also on display. The Cliff Dwellings, located off Highway 24 just west of Colorado Springs, are open year-round, unless there's a lot of snow or ice. Call 719-685-5242 or 800-354-9971 for more information.

Seven Falls. You're welcome to bring Fido and his leash to this series of seven waterfalls that cascade 181 feet in South Cheyenne Cañon, on the southwestern side of Colorado Springs. An elevator brings you to the Eagle's Nest viewing platform, or you and your dog can tackle the 224 stairs along the falls, which lead to a 2-mile round-trip nature trail that ends at an overlook of Colorado Springs and the plains beyond. Open year-round, the falls are illuminated at night by multicolored lights from mid-May to Labor Day. Admission is charged. Call 719-632-0765 for recorded information.

Gigi's, 728 Manitou Ave., Manitou Springs, 719-685-4772. Billed as the "animal lovers' giftshop," Gigi's is more than your typical pet supply store. You'll find all manner of unique collars, leashes, and other pet accessories as well as dog-themed items for humans, including Christmas ornaments and windchimes covering all the breeds. Your dog, who is welcome to browse along with you, will want to sniff out the array of treats and toys.

Dog Washes. Mike's Natural Pet Market, 3539 N. Carefree Cir., Colorado Springs, 719-570-1488, offers a self-service dog wash. The $10 price includes your dog's choice of organic shampoo and conditioner, towels, dryer, and grooming tools. Mike's also carries a selection of super-healthy dog foods and herbal supplements. Petco (three locations; see "Pet Provisions") charges $9 for its self-service dog wash, which includes shampoo, towels, and dryer.

American Heart Walk. Heart-healthy dogs on leash are welcome to join their owners in this annual pledge walk sponsored by the American Heart Association each June. A 3-mile course wends it way along the road past Seven Falls in South Cheyenne Cañon in southwest Colorado Springs. Participants can register either as individuals or as teams, and there are incentive prizes for raising various levels of pledges. Food, family-friendly activities, and some vendors at the start of the course, at the El Pomar Center, round out the event. Call the Pikes Peak Division of the American Heart Association at 719-635-7688 for more information.

Bark in the Park. Has your dog ever attended a minor-league baseball game (or even a major-league game, for that matter)? Bring Fido to howl on the Colorado Springs Sky Sox—the Colorado Rockies' AAA farm team. What started as an annual event became a regular occurrence in 2000, and now every Wednesday home game is "dog night." The stadium has large, grassy picnic areas along the first- and third-base lines

where dogs and their owners can sit during the game (bring a blanket). You might want to engage in a vigorous play session with your dog before arriving; that way, he won't be as tempted to chase down baseballs during the main event, though both dogs and kids have been seen scurrying after foul balls. One dollar of every ticket sold goes to the Humane Society of the Pikes Peak Region. There's a canine-themed pregame show each time, with dog-related demos, as well as "Puppie Palooza," an expo of dog-product and service booths on the stadium's main concourse. As if that's not enough, the best-dressed dog at each game wins prizes from the Sox and Big Dog sportswear, and specials on hot dogs mean that you and Fido can share one of baseball's most time-honored food traditions. Finally, according to marketing director Rai Henniger, the usual postgame fireworks show is not held on Wednesday nights "in deference to our canine friends." The Sky Sox Stadium is at 4385 Tutt Blvd. (corner of Powers Blvd. and Barnes Rd.). For more information, call the Sky Sox ticket line at 719-597-SOXX.

Canine 5K Pet Fest/Strut Your Mutt. Held in one of the Colorado Springs parks on the third Saturday in September, this annual 5K run/walk and one-mile stroll is for dogs and their owners. After the race, your dog can amble among the booths of pet products and information; compete in contests such as best pet tricks, doggie musical chairs, dog/owner look-alike; or check out canine demonstrations. Your registration fee (as well as pledges that you raise for the event) nets a T-shirt, a gift for your dog, breakfast snacks, and a goodie bag for both you and Fido. All proceeds benefit the Humane Society of the Pikes Peak Region (719-473-1741; www.k95kpet fest.org). Register at the Humane Society (610 Abbott Ln. in Colorado Springs) or on the day of the event.

Colorado Springs Canine Frisbee Championships. During the last Saturday in May or the first one in June, Frisbee-toting dogs gather in Cottonwood Creek Park in the Springs to show off their leaping and catching prowess. The competition, put on by the Colorado Disc Dogs, features two events: the minidistance, in which dogs receive points for catching distance and a bonus for midair catches in sixty-second rounds; and the free flight, in which they demonstrate their best freestyle tricks in ninety seconds. There's no entrance fee, and anyone and their dog is welcome, regardless of your dog's previous competitive experience. You can also just bring your dog to watch; maybe he'll get inspired to compete the next year. For more information, contact Rick Brydum at 303-759-8785 (frflyers@aol.com) or log on to the Colorado Disc Dogs website, www.varinet. com/~eyebum/nocodido.html.

Cave of the Winds. Dogs are not allowed on the cave tours of this mile-long cavern or at the nighttime laser show.

Cheyenne Mountain Zoo and Will Rogers Shrine of the Sun. It's probably no surprise that dogs aren't allowed in the zoo, but you should be aware that they're also not allowed at the Will Rogers Shrine (Rover can ride up in the car with you, but he's not supposed to set paw outside). The zoo does have one kennel where a poodle-sized dog can stay, at no charge; it's available on a first-come, first-served basis. For more information, call 719-633-9925.

Ghost Town Wild West Museum. Dogs are discouraged from visiting this reconstructed frontier town in Colorado Springs.

North Pole and Santa's Workshop. Your dog won't be able to visit Santa at his mid-May through Christmas Eve residence west of Colorado Springs.

Pikes Peak Cog Railway. You won't be able to bring your dog on the Swiss-made cog train that climbs to the summit of Pikes Peak. If you're considering bringing Fido to doggie daycare, know that the round-trip ride takes just over three hours, and trains operate from late April to late October, leaving from the depot on Ruxton Ave. in Manitou Springs. Call 719-685-5401 for reservations and fee information.

DOGGIE DAYCARE
Black Forest
Canine Care Center, 7580 Ponca Rd., 719-495-4209. $8.50–$9.75/day, depending on the size of dog. Open 8 a.m.–6 p.m., Monday to Friday; 8 a.m.–3 p.m., Saturday; 5–6 p.m. (summer), 4–5 p.m. (winter), Sunday (pickups only).

Dogs' Best Friend Bed and Breakfast, 7305 Maine Ln., 719-495-2983. $8/day. Open 8–11 a.m., 2–6 p.m., Monday, Thursday, and Friday; 8–11 a.m., Tuesday, Wednesday, and Saturday; 5–8 p.m., Sunday (pickups only).

Colorado Springs
Airway Boarding Kennels, 5280 E. Edison, 719-574-1886. About $5/day. The owner stresses that proof of an internasal bordatella vaccination received every six months is required, and all vaccinations must be vet-administered. Open 8 a.m.–5:30 p.m., Monday to Friday; 8 a.m.–4 p.m., Saturday.

Broadmoor Bluffs Kennel, 43 E. Old Broadmoor Rd., 719-636-3344. $8–$11/day, depending on the size of dog. Open 7 a.m.–5:30 p.m., Monday to

Friday; 8 a.m.–5:30 p.m., Saturday; closed for lunch 12:30–1:30 p.m., all days.

Clearview Animal Lodge, 3928 S. Hancock Expressway, 719-393-8075. $1–$1.50/hour, depending on the size of dog, up to $12/day. Open 8 a.m.–5:30 p.m., Monday to Friday; 8 a.m.–4 p.m., Saturday and Sunday.

Countryside Kennel, 7945 Maverick Rd., 719-495-3678. $9/day, with a 15-minute nature walk available for an extra $5. Open 7 a.m.–5:30 p.m., Monday to Saturday.

Rampart Kennels, 5977 Templeton Gap Rd., 719-591-0066. $1/hour. Open 7 a.m.– 6 p.m., Monday to Friday. Daycare is available only during warmer months.

Sunrise Kennels, 6580 Vincent Dr., 719-598-8220. $7/day. Open 7:30 a.m.– 5:30 p.m., Monday to Friday; 7:30 a.m.– 3:30 p.m., Saturday.

Top Dog Daycare, 3116 Karen Pl., 719-448-9600. $15/day. Open 6 a.m.–6 p.m., Monday to Friday; 8 a.m.–6 p.m., Saturday; 7–9 a.m. and 4–6 p.m., Sunday.

Woodmen Kennels, 6440 Vincent Dr., 719-598-4154. $7/day. Open 7:30 a.m.– 5:30 p.m., Monday to Friday; 7:30 a.m.– 3:30 p.m., Saturday.

Falcon
Fox and Hounds, 5335 JD Johnson Rd., 719-683-5544 (888-K9SCHOOL). Call for rates and hours.

Grand Paws Kennel, 13750 Canter Rd., 719-683-3852. $5–$10/day, depending on the size of dog. Open 9 a.m.–5 p.m., Monday to Saturday; earlier pickups and later dropoffs can be arranged by appointment, as can day boarding on Sundays for $25 extra (unless you drop off your dog on Saturday night).

Fountain
Land of Ahs Kennels, 12599 Jordan Rd., 719-382-1126. $10–$15/day, depending on the size of dog. Open 7 a.m.–5 p.m., Monday to Friday; 7 a.m.–noon, Saturday.

Woodland Park
Doggie Day Care with Cats on the Side, 719-641-9193. $15/day. Call for details on this at-home daycare service.

PET PROVISIONS
Colorado Springs
Brookhart's Farm and Ranch Store, I-25 and Baptist Rd., 719-488-1300

Circle F Ranch Supply, 115 E. Garden of the Gods Rd., 719-599-5100; 711 N. Union Blvd., 719-578-0666

Colorado Agri-Feed, 4625 Park Vista Blvd., 719-599-5961

ENOB Feed and Pet Supply, 6480 N. Academy Blvd., 719-522-9208

Mike's Natural Pet Market, 3539 N. Carefree Cir., 719-570-1488 (see "Worth a Paws")

Petco, 1820 W. Uintah, 719-578-1123; 5720 N. Academy Blvd., 719-536-0160; 1650 E. Cheyenne Blvd., 719-540-8090

PetsMart, 571 N. Academy Blvd., 719-570-1313; 2160 Southgate Rd., 719-447-0624; 7680 N. Academy Blvd., 719-531-7870

Pikes Peak Animal Supply, 5286 E. Edison, 719-591-1448

Fountain
Dawn Meadows Feed Tack and Horsetel, 8250 S. Highways 85 and 87, 719-382-7069

Manitou Springs
Gigi's, 728 Manitou Ave., 719-685-4772 (see "Worth a Paws")

CANINE ER
Colorado Springs
Animal Emergency Care, 5752 N. Academy Blvd., 719-260-7141. Open 6 p.m.– 8 a.m., Monday to Friday; 24 hours on weekends and holidays.

Animal Emergency Center of Colorado Springs P.C. (AAHA certified), 2812 E. Pikes Peak Ave., 719-578-9300. Open 6 p.m.–8 a.m. Monday to Friday; 24 hours on weekends and holidays.

RESOURCES
Colorado Springs Convention and Visitors Bureau, 104 S. Cascade, Suite 104, Colorado Springs, 719-635-7506 (800-DO-VISIT; www.coloradosprings travel.com)

Cripple Creek Welcome Center, 5th and Bennett Ave., Cripple Creek, 719-689-3315 (877-858-GOLD; www.cripple-creek.co.us)

Manitou Springs Chamber of Commerce, 354 Manitou Ave., Manitou Springs, 719-685-5089 (800-642-2567; www.mani tousprings.org)

Pikes Peak Ranger District, Pike National Forest, 601 S. Weber St., Colorado Springs, 719-636-1602

Fourteener Dogs

Climbing "fourteeners," or peaks with elevations 14,000 feet or above, has become an increasingly popular summertime (and occasionally wintertime) activity in Colorado. It's also somewhat controversial, as many believe that the large numbers of hikers tromping up and down the trails is causing irreparable damage to the alpine environment. You can easily deduce that many people are even less thrilled about dogs on fourteeners.

If you and your dog share most hiking outings, however, chances are you're not going to be easily dissuaded from bringing him along for the really spectacular stuff. With this in mind, I've compiled the following listing of fourteeners, grouped according to dog suitability. After turning back about half a mile from the summit of Snowmass Mountain because Clover and another dog couldn't handle the knife-edge ridge, I realized that some advance knowledge would have saved us the frustration of an "incomplete" trek.

Athletic dogs can successfully summit many fourteeners. Be sure to bring plenty of water. Dog booties (see the "Gearhound" appendix) are also an excellent accessory to take along, as tender paws can easily get worn ragged on talus or scree slopes, or other rough terrain. And if you're out to tackle peaks that require heavy-duty rock scrambling or knife-edge ridges, do both of yourselves a favor and leave Rover at home.

The categories that follow assume you'll ascend via the easiest routes. Nearly all fourteeners have alternate ascents that may or may not be suitable for dogs. For more specifics on routes, refer to *Colorado's Fourteeners: From Hikes to Climbs,* by Gerry Roach; *A Climbing Guide to Colorado's Fourteeners,* by Walter R. Borneman and Lyndon J. Lampert; and *Dawson's Guide to Colorado's Fourteeners,* volumes 1 and 2, by Louis Dawson.

"I CAN DO THIS!"

Mount Antero
Mount Belford
Mount Bierstadt
Mount Bross
Mount Columbia
Culebra Peak
Mount Democrat
Mount Elbert
Mount Evans
Grays Peak
Handies Peak
Mount Harvard
Humboldt Peak
Huron Peak
La Plata Peak
Mount Lincoln
Mount Massive
Missouri Mountain
Mount Oxford
Pikes Peak
Mount Princeton
Quandary Peak
Redcloud Peak
San Luis Peak
Mount Shavano
Mount Sherman
Sunshine Peak
Tabeguache Peak
Torreys Peak
Uncompahgre Peak
Mount Yale

"GIVE ME A BOOST UP THAT ROCK, WILL YA?"

Blanca Peak
Castle Peak
Challenger Point
Ellingwood Point
Mount of the Holy Cross
Mount Lindsey
Windom Peak

"PLEASE LEAVE ME BEHIND"

Capitol Peak
Crestone Needle
Crestone Peak
El Diente Peak
Mount Eolus
Kit Carson Peak
Little Bear Peak
Maroon Peak
North Maroon Peak
Pyramid Peak
Mount Sneffels
Snowmass Mountain
Sunlight Peak
Wetterhorn Peak
Mount Wilson
Wilson Peak

"I COULDN'T IF I WANTED TO"

Longs Peak—it's in Rocky Mountain National Park, where dogs are prohibited from all trails.

Dogs want to see the view from the top too. (photo by Alyssa Pumphrey)

# Gearhound

These days, as much thought is going into dog gear as into people gear; you can find an array of canine accessories that will make your dog's travels and hikes easier and more enjoyable. The well-equipped dog will want to have at least some of the following items in his travel bag. Phone numbers and websites are provided for each manufacturer; call to find out which stores near you carry the items that your dog can't wait to get his paws on.

DOG PACKS

Backpacks for dogs are a great invention: they allow Rover to schlep his own food, water, treats, or poop bags on long day hikes or multiday outings (assuming you don't overburden him, of course). And at the end of a backpacking trip, you can make your dog carry out the trash! Just as with packs for people, your dog should come in for a fitting before purchase to make sure the pack carries comfortably on his back. With the variety of packs available, your dog should be able to find at least one that suits him. Mountaineering or high-end pet specialty stores are your best bets for pack shopping. A few of the sturdier packs we've found are listed here.

Rocky Mountain K-9 Accessories, in Boulder, has developed a unique modular pack system that can be customized for you and your dog's outings. The basic K-9 Trailblazer pack includes the harness, a Cordura pack that sits on top of the dog's back, a collapsible water bowl, a nylon emergency leash, two insulated water-bottle holders with 28-ounce bottles, and

even a small pouch that hooks on the pack's outside for holding poop pick-up bags. Two accessory packs can replace the Trailblazer, which zips off the harness: The Oasis contains two additional water bottles, and the Adventurer includes a twenty-two-piece dog/human first-aid kit. Both accessory packs come with the poop bag and extra leash. 303-448-1942; www.rockymountaink9.com.

Mountainsmith, a Colorado company well known for its human packs, offers three sizes of dog packs, with carrying capacity keyed to the dog's weight. The packs have been revised for 2001, with a more streamlined shape, fleece-lined straps and buckles, reflective trim, mesh fabric on the harness for venting, and adjustable shoulder, hip, and chest straps. All packs still feature Cordura panniers, compression straps, and a double-layer construction. A D-ring on the harness makes for easy leash attachment. 800-426-4075; www.mountainsmith.com.

Wolf Packs, out of southern Oregon, makes three styles of dog packs in four sizes. All packs are made out of water-repellent, urethane-coated Cordura nylon; the side-release buckles are padded with Polartec 300 fleece for Fido's comfort. The top-of-the-line Banzai Explorer pack has ballistic nylon side guards, compression straps, and reflective trim. The Trekker Reflector pack features reflective material for safety. The one-size-fits-all Saddle Bag is lightweight and streamlined, designed for short day hikes (and for use by assistance dogs, who may need to maneuver in tight spaces). The Wolf Packs website has helpful information on fitting your dog's pack and training him to hike with it. 541-482-7669; www.wolf packs.com.

Granite Gear, a northern Minnesota company that also produces people packs and canoe gear, manufactures the Ruff Rider dog pack. With a Cordura exterior and a Polartec 200 fleece underside, the packs comes in three sizes and three colors. Nifty features include an adjustable harness, reflective trim, tubular nylon webbing that won't chafe, and detachable saddle bags, useful for when your dog is crossing streams or maneuvering through tight spaces. There's also a D-ring on the pack so you can connect the leash directly to it. If your dog is incredibly hard on his packs, get him the totally bomber Expedition dog pack, which was designed for Will Steger's Ellsmere Island dog-sled trip. 800-222-8032; www.granitegear.com.

Ruffwear, in Bend, Oregon, has a three-model line of canine-specific packs, available in two colors. The premier Palisades Pack, in three sizes, has lots of bells and whistles, including removable saddle bags (handy for stream crossings), an integrated hydration system (à la Camelbak) so you can empty water directly into your dog's bowl, a webbing handle you can grasp to lift your dog over obstacles on the trail, compression straps, fabric reinforcement at wear points, and two leash attachment points. The more basic Approach Pack, also in three sizes, has a suspension-system harness and includes the webbing grab handle. Both packs have fleece-padded buckles and straps as well as reflective trim.

The newer Day Tripper (one size only) is appropriate for day hikes and other short outings where you want Fido to carry some of the load. The flat saddle bags extend right out of the mesh yoke for a streamlined fit. The pack also has a webbing handle on the harness, a gear cord for stashing oversized items, and reflective trim. 888-783-3932; www.ruff wear.com.

Caribou, out of Alice, Texas, produces the value-priced Woofer dog pack. Made out of nylon pack cloth and Cordura, the pack comes in two sizes. Quick-release buckles make for easy attachment, and a mesh yoke keeps your dog's back cool. 800-824-4153; www.caribou.com.

Walkies Outdoor Dog Gear, based in Davis, California, has two pack styles. The Dog Pack has a unique Y-shaped, fleece-padded harness (with leash attachment point at the rear), based on the design of dog-sledding harnesses, which makes the pack less likely to slide from side to side. Constructed of 1,000-denier Cordura Plus, the pack comes in five sizes and three colors. All straps are fully adjustable, and fleece-encased webbing keeps Fido comfy. The super-sleek Urban Dog Pack, also available in five sizes, is designed for short day outings, with flat saddle bags that have diagonal zips, a leash attachment point, and reflective trim. 888-211-6692.

DOG BOOTIES

The cutest thing next to infant socks may be dog booties, sturdy little "shoes" that slip on your dog's paws to protect them from snow and ice balls, hot desert rock, or sharp-edged talus. Clover always gets lots of compliments when she's sporting her set. The key is to find booties that will stay on. Allow your dog to get accustomed to his booties by letting him wear them around the house a few times before your first outing. And on snowy days, he'll get the snuggest fit if you put his booties on before he gets out of the car.

Ruffwear makes Bark 'N Boots in five sizes. The booties, made of 500-denier Cordura with flexible recycled-tire-rubber soles, have a band that wraps around the dog's leg at the top of the bootie and secures with a D-ring and Velcro closure. 888-783-3932; www.ruffwear.com.

Duke's Dog Fashions, in Beaverton, Oregon, produces fashionable two-tone booties out of 1,000-denier Cordura or fleece, with double-soled construction. The booties stay on by means of a Velcro strap that snugs around the top. Duke, the company's namesake, was a Lab from Crested Butte. 800-880-8969; www.dukesdog.com.

Expedition Outfitters has taken over the distribution of the booties that Wolf Packs used to sell: Summer Pad Protectors, with a double sole of ballistic nylon and a Cordura upper, and Winter Pad Protectors, made of Polartec 300. Both styles of booties close with a Velcro strap. 408-257-1754; www.expedition outfittersonline.com.

Cool Paw Productions, in Tempe, Arizona, offers three styles of booties in six sizes: Polar Paws, designed for winter use, are made of heavy fleece and Cordura, with a nonskid Tough-Tek sole and a Velcro strap closure. They also have a water-resistant stretchy sock top to keep snow from getting into the bootie. Tuff Paws, intended for hiking, are constructed of ballistic nylon lined with fleece and have double-layer soles and a double Velcro strap closure. Innovative Cool Paws protect paws from scorching surfaces by means of special insulating granules in the sole that activate to form a cool, gel-like layer when water is added. The booties are made of heavy-duty nylon with Velcro straps. 800-650-PAWS.

Walkies Outdoor Dog Gear makes booties, available in five sizes, made of 1,000-denier Cordura Plus with long-wearing Dupont Hypalon soles. The tall height and the two Velcro-strap closures

on each bootie mean hyperactive dogs are less likely to shed one en route. Each set of booties comes with a convenient mesh storage sack. 888-211-6692.

TRAVEL BOWLS

A collapsible food/water bowl is an invaluable travel aid. It's lightweight and can easily be stashed in a backpack or fanny pack so your dog has something to drink out of on the trail.

The sturdiest we've found so far are made by **Ruffwear** and feature the tag line "for dogs on the go." Two models of the bowls—the Quencher and the Go Between—come in 1- and 2.5-quart sizes and are made of polyester pack cloth with a waterproof, ripstop nylon liner. The lighter Trail Runner model has a 24-ounce capacity. The Quencher and Go Between feature an optional cinchable top, so you can leave some food in it without worrying about spillage. 888-783-3932; www.ruffwear.com.

Cool Paw Productions makes similar bowls, with Cordura and pack cloth outers and ripstop nylon interiors, in 1- and 2-quart sizes. 800-650-PAWS.

Granite Gear has two circular packable bowls: the Grrrub Bowl, for food, has a drawstring closure; the Slurpin Bowl, for water, is open topped. Both come in three sizes. 800-222-8032; www.gran-itegear.com.

Walkies Outdoor Dog Gear offers two folding waterproof travel bowls that compact down to pocket size when not in use; you can attach them to a pack via a Velcro strap. The bowls are available in 1- and 2-liter sizes, and one has a nylon top with locking drawstring closure to keep leftover food inside. 888-211-6692.

LEASHES

In some cases, a leash is more than just a leash. For example, the Absorber Leash from **Granite Gear** has a stretchy base covered with accordion-pleated nylon. When Rover tugs at it, you're less likely to get your arm wrenched out of its socket, as the leash absorbs some of that force. 800-222-8032; www.granitegear.com.

The **Ruffwear** Knot-a-Leash is made of 10-millimeter climbing-style rope with a mini-carabiner at one end that clips to your dog's collar. It also has a grip-friendly tubular webbing handle and is slightly stretchy (there's a companion Knot-a-Collar). 888-783-3932; www.ruffwear.com.

OTHER COOL STUFF

People have PowerBars for quick energy pick-me-ups during outings; now active dogs have **Zuke's Power Bones.** Made by A Guy and His Dog Company in Durango, the nutritious treats include beef, high-fructose corn syrup, durum wheat flour, dried beet molasses, brewer's yeast, apple, carrot, fish meal, dried cheese, canola and flax-seed oils, and a complement of vitamins and minerals. Yum! Bite-size Power Bones are also available. New Trek 'N Treats have less fat and fewer carbo-hydrates than Power Bones for the trail dog who's not expending as much energy. 888-364-7693; www.powerbone.com.

The **Doggies Sleeping Bag** from Rocky Mountain K-9 Accessories has a padded-foam bottom, thick fleece lining, and water-repellant nylon outer. It can be used as a blanket or sleeping-bag style, thanks to Velcro closures. The bag, avail-able in two sizes, comes with a nylon stuff sack. 303-448-1942; www.rocky mountaink9.com.

Air Major Pet Products, in Cave Creek, Arizona, produces the **Travel Duffel** out of ballistic nylon for all of your dog's gear. The bag includes a waterproof com-partment for storing dry food, a mesh side pocket for water bottles, two addi-tional side pockets, and an adjustable shoulder strap and carrying handles that allow you to carry the duffel backpack-style. There's also a Food Duffel that car-ries up to 40 pounds of dry food; you can pour the food directly into Rover's bowl by partly opening the zip closure. 888-383-3357; www.airmajor.com.

Clover won't leave on a trip without her **Kibble Kaddie** from Ruffwear. This travel pouch holds 8 to 10 pounds of dry food, which can then be poured into your dog's bowl via the sealable "kibble chute" on the side. The top-loading clo-sure rolls down and secures with a quick-release buckle, similar to the way a pad-dling dry bag works. And a bungee-like gear cord on the front is a convenient place to stash Fido's travel bowl. 888-783-3932; www.ruffwear.com.

The **Mt. Bachelor Pad,** from Ruffwear, is a roll-up blanket that your dog can snooze on in the hotel and car. One side is fleece-lined; the other is made of water-resistant poly-cloth. Attached Velcro straps secure the roll, which weighs just over a pound, when Fido is on the go. 888-783-3932; www.ruffwear.com.

Cool Pooch, in Chicago, makes the **Cool Pooch Sport Water Bottle,** which you can safely share with your dog. The plastic bottle has a funnel-shaped cup that attaches at the top and an attached straw. You drink from the straw, then bend it over to pour water into the cup for Fido to slurp. 877-CLPOOCH; www.coolpooch.com.

Ruffwear offers two **canine/human first-aid kits:** the Hiker and the larger Traveler. In addition to a complete supply of med-ical aids for treating on-trail injuries—including cohesive tape that sticks to itself, allowing you to create a bandage over fur—the kits come with the "Pet First Aid Quick Guide to Animal Emergencies." 888-783-3932; www.ruffwear.com.

Index

About the Author

Photo by Tamra Hoppes

CINDY HIRSCHFELD is a freelance writer and editor, specializing in outdoor activities and travel, for publications including *Skiing* magazine, *Back Country* magazine, and *The Denver Post*. She and her golden retriever, Clover, live in Aspen, Colorado, where they hike, run, bike, ski, and climb together. Clover's special passion is her continual quest for the biggest stick she can carry. Blue, a black tabby cat, allows Cindy and Clover to share an apartment with him; he has made his feelings about *Canine Colorado* known by chewing large chunks out of the cover of the first edition.